NEXUS TOEFL® iBT
Listening

3 Level

성공적인 학습을 위한 단계별 전략!
Development & Progress for Completion
NEXUS TOEFL *i*BT Listening Level 3

지은이 넥서스영어교육연구소, 박종현, Jacob Cho,
　　　Jeffrey S. Zeter, JoAnn Woods, Virginia Hanslien,
　　　Mary French, Yvonne Raub
펴낸이 안용백
펴낸곳 (주)도서출판 넥서스

출판신고 1992년 4월 3일 제311-2002-2호 ①
121-840 서울시 마포구 서교동 394-2
Tel (02)330-5500 Fax (02)330-5555

ISBN 978-89-6000-628-7 54740

저자와 출판사의 허락없이 내용의 일부를 인용하거나
발췌하는 것을 금합니다.

가격은 뒤표지에 있습니다.
잘못 만들어진 책은 구입처에서 바꾸어 드립니다.

www.nexusEDU.kr
NEXUS Edu는 (주)도서출판 넥서스의 초·중·고 학습물 전문 브랜드입니다.

성공적인 학습을 위한 단계별 전략!
Development & Progress for Completion

NEXUS TOEFL® iBT

Listening

3

Level

NEXUS Edu

머리말

영어를 배우는 데 있어서, 네 가지 언어 영역을 균형 있게 학습해야 할 필요성은 오랫동안 인지되어 왔다. 하지만 국내 영어 학습 현실 속에서 그런 학습을 진행하기에는 현실적 여건이 따라 주질 못했다. 먼저 말하기나 쓰기 부분의 공인된 평가가 많지 않았던 탓도 있겠지만, 현실적으로 수업시간에 활용할 수 있는 다양한 학습 모델이 많지 않았기 때문이기도 하다.

그러나 CBT 토플이 iBT로 바뀌어 speaking과 writing이 새롭게 추가되면서 여러 변화가 생겼다. 전반적인 문제 유형이 일차원적 문제 풀이 방식에서 벗어나 제공되는 정보를 잘 정리하여 이해하고, 이해한 내용을 다시 정리하여 표현할 수 있는 능력이 더 중요하게 되었다. 이런 능력 향상은 영어를 배울 때 암기와 반복에 의존하는 학습 방식보다는 절제된 문장 구조 속에서 "organized thoughts"를 할 수 있도록 유도하는 학습 방식을 통해 더 효과적으로 향상될 수 있다. 말하기나 쓰기의 통합적인 영역에서만 이런 능력이 필요한 것이 아니라, 독해 및 청취 영역에서도 마찬가지이다. 문제에 근거한 내용만을 맞히는 것이 아니라, 문단 간의 정보 관계를 전체적으로(global understanding) 훑을 수 있는 훈련이 되어야 한다. 따라서 토플을 단기간에 한 권으로 끝을 내려한다거나 한 학기의 강의 수업 방식으로 짧은 시간에 높은 성적을 올리기에 급급하기보다는 위와 같은 학습 방식에 초점을 맞춰 체계적인 계획을 가지고 접근하게 되면, 토플 성적 이외에도 전반적인 영어 실력을 키워갈 수 있으리라 생각된다.

넥서스 토플은 전반적으로 위와 같은 취지로 기획되었다. 다시 말해, 각 단원마다 주어진 스킬만 배우고 끝내는 것이 아니라 앞서 학습한 스킬을 다시 반복학습할 수 있게 하고, 지문을 통합적으로 활용하며, 짧은 시간 안에 정보의 구조를 파악하는 능력을 훈련할 수 있도록 구성하였다.

짧은 시간에 점수를 올리려는 전략적인 학습 방식을 선호하기보다는 체계적인 학습 계획과 그에 맞는 적절한 교재를 활용하여 토플 점수 향상 이외에도 영어로 생각하고 정리하는 표현 기술을 잘 연마할 수 있도록 학습하는 데 있어 이 교재가 많은 도움이 되기를 바란다.

| 넥서스영어교육연구소 |

이 책의 특징

1 단계별 기본 학습 훈련 장치 강조
- Second listening, note-taking practice를 통해 길어진 청취 지문을 효과적으로 들을 수 있게 도와 주는 기본 훈련 장치를 구성하였다.

2 다양한 테마의 강의와 대화 지문 구조의 체계적 분석
- 다양한 주제의 강의와 대화를 들려 주고, 그 구조를 체계적으로 분석할 수 있는 activity를 마련하였다.

3 체계적인 학습 스킬과 전략 구성
- 새롭게 바뀌는 *i*BT Listening Section에서 나오는 질문 유형을 철저히 분석하고, 질문 유형이 요구하는 기본적인 strategies를 바탕으로 listening skill을 체계적으로 습득할 수 있도록 구성하였다.

4 어휘력 확장의 학습
- 토플에 자주 쓰이는 테마와 관련된 기본 어휘 학습을 강조(동의어, 반의어, 영영 해석)하여, 어휘 능력 향상을 도모하였다.

5 *i*BT 실전에 맞춘 단계별 연습
- Mini-Exercise, Practice, Actual Test, Progress Test, Final Test로 이어지는 단계별 연습으로 *i*BT Listening을 완벽하게 대비할 수 있도록 구성하였다.

이 책의 구성

Overview

해당 Chapter에서 학습할 질문 유형을 미리 알아 두기 위하여 전체적인 개관, Question Types, 해결 전략 등을 소개했다.

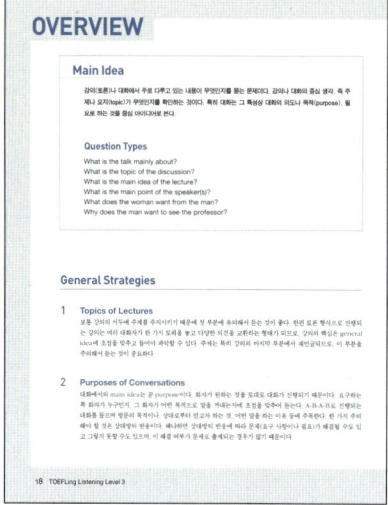

Pre Test

학습에 들어가기 전, 각 Chapter에서 다룰 문제 유형에 대한 우선 학습 테스트를 제시하였다.

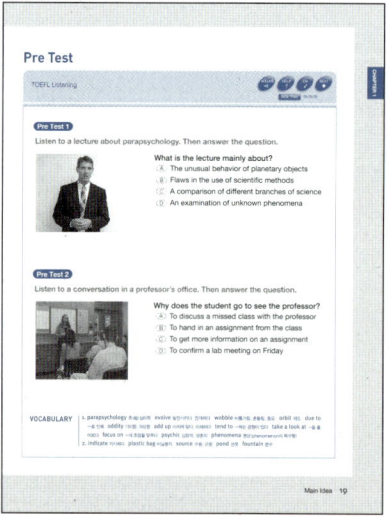

Mini-Exercise

Overview에서 정리한 전략을 바탕으로 구체적인 문제 유형에 맞는 Skill을 익히고, 다시 듣고 Dictation을 훈련할 수 있도록 구성하였다.

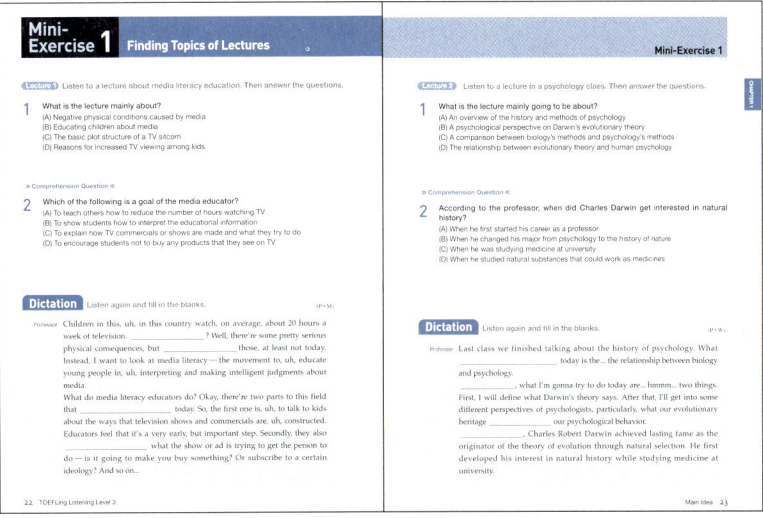

Vocabulary Preview

Mini-Exercise, Practice와 Actual Test에 들어가기 앞서 거기서 다룰 주요 어휘를 테스트 형식으로 제시하였다.

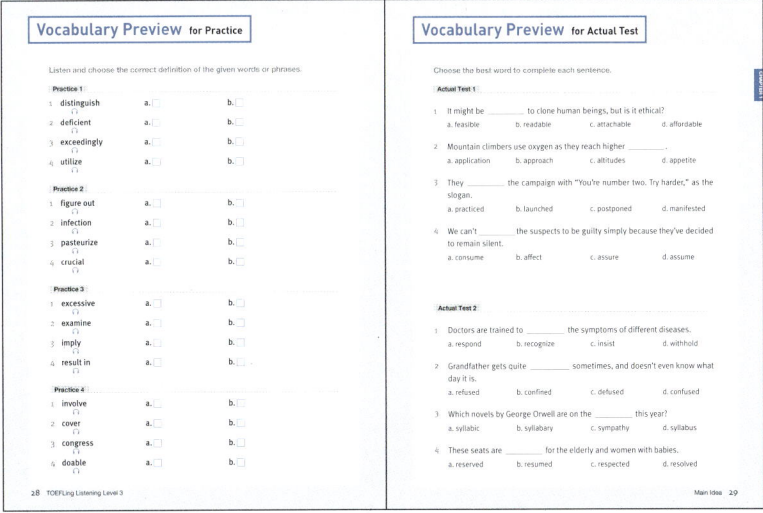

Practice

해당 Chapter에서 학습한 질문 유형을 중점적으로 물어 본다. Note-taking을 완성하도록 하는 훈련을 통해 긴 지문을 효과적으로 정리하는 습관을 갖도록 구성하였다.

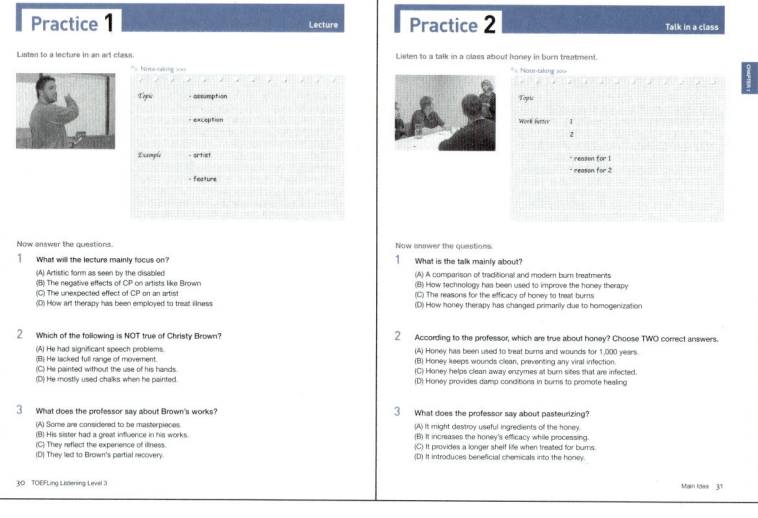

Actual Test

실전 감각을 높일 수 있도록 실제 테스트와 유사하게 구성하였다. Practice와 마찬가지로, Note-taking할 수 있는 공간을 마련하였다.

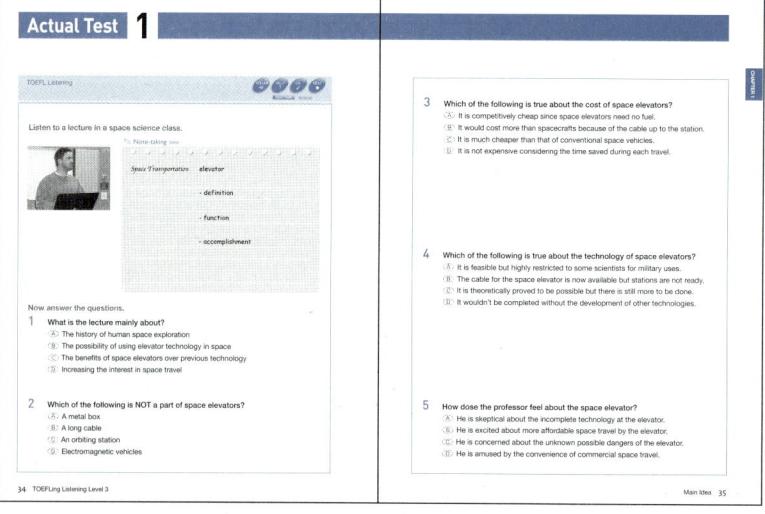

Progress Test

2개 Chapter가 끝날 때마다 앞에서 학습한 Skill들을 누적 출제하여 각각의 Skill들을 복습할 수 있도록 구성하였다.

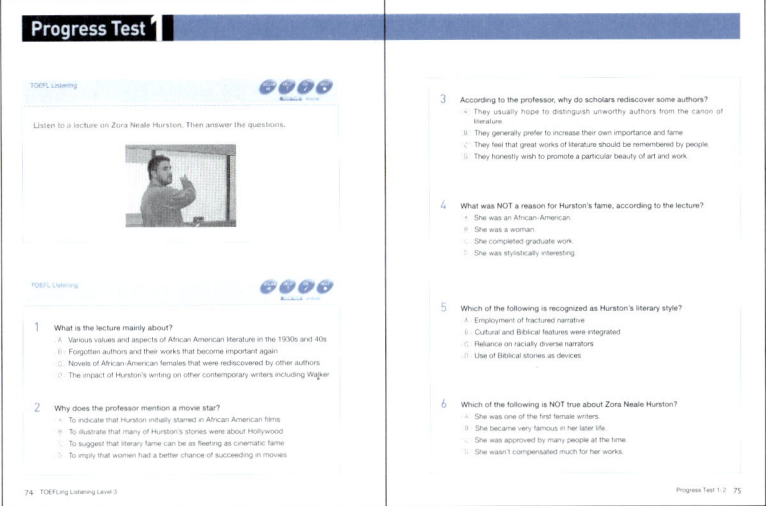

Dictation

Exercise와 Actual Test 및 Progress Test의 스크립트를 들으면서 Dictation 연습을 해 볼 수 있는 코너를 따로 마련해 두었다. 하단 부분에서는 지문 이해에 도움이 되도록 주요 구문을 정리하였다.

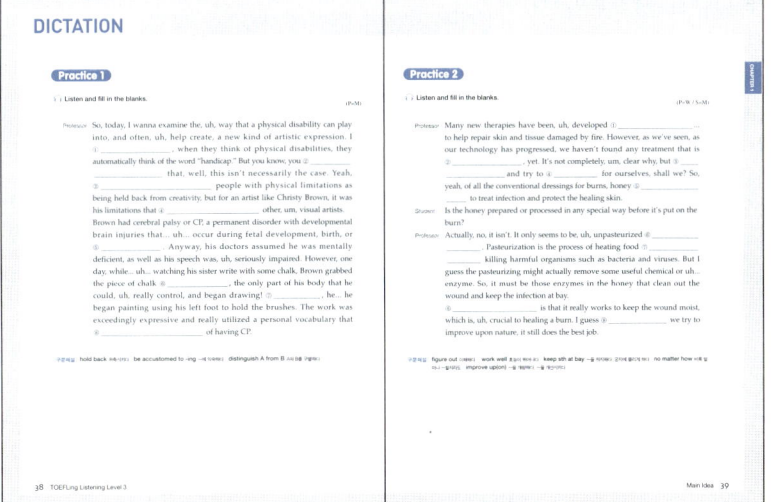

Vocabulary Review

앞에서 배운 단어들을 토대로, 어휘 학습을 반복할 수 있도록 구성하였다.

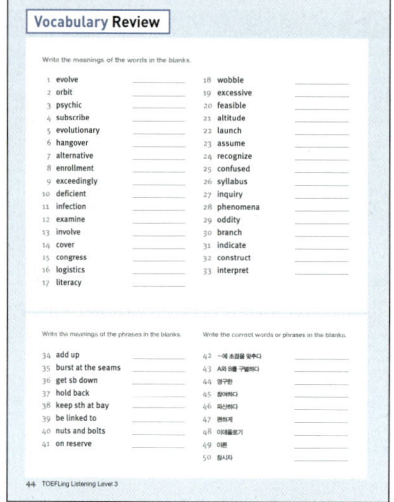

Final Test

Chapter 1~6를 아우르는 모든 Skill을 종합적으로 평가해 Skill을 마스터했는지 점검해 볼 수 있다.

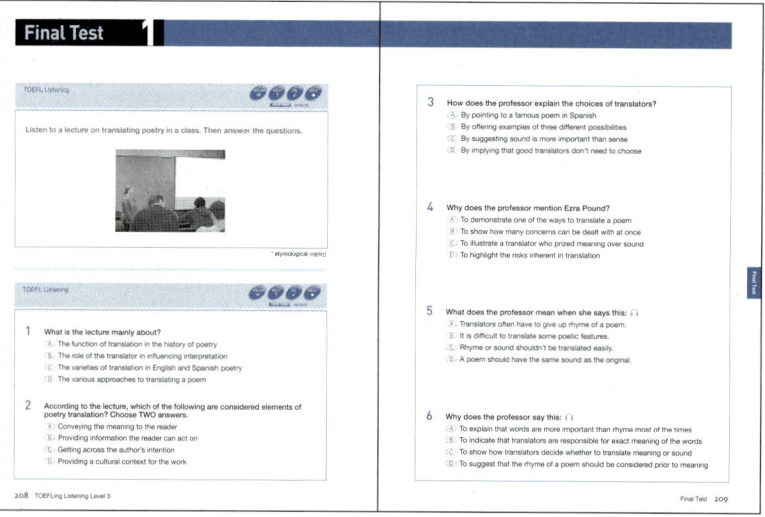

목차

■ **Introduction to *i*BT TOEFL**

CHAPTER 1 Main Idea
Finding Topics of Lectures & Finding Purposes of Conversations • 17

CHAPTER 2 Supporting Details
Important Information & True or False • 45

■ **Progress Test 1 · 2** • 73

CHAPTER 3 Process / Classification
Identifying Process & Classifying Information • 81

CHAPTER 4 Organization
*Organization of the Informaton Presented
& Organization-Rhetorical Connection* • 109

■ **Progress Test 3 · 4** • 137

CHAPTER 5 Stance / Inference
Stance & Inference • 145

CHAPTER 6 Function
Function-Purpose • 173

■ **Progress Test 5 · 6** • 199

■ **Final Test** • 207

Introduction to *i*BT TOEFL

*i*BT (Internet-based Test) TOEFL이란?

*i*BT는 Internet-based Test의 약자로 인터넷을 통해 시험을 치르게 하는 차세대 토플이다. 기존의 CBT가 미국으로 유학 오는 외국 학생들의 실제 영어구사능력을 제대로 측정하지 못한다는 비판에 대한 대안으로 새롭게 만들어졌으며 특히 말하기 능력에 대한 평가를 요구하는 미국 대학들의 요청에 따라 Speaking Section을 신설했다. 기존 CBT와는 달리 언어영역간의 통합을 접목시킨 것이 특징이며 학생들이 얼마나 빠르게, 제대로 미국 대학 생활에 적응해 갈 수 있을지에 대한 지표를 대학에 제공해 준다.

미국에서는 2005년 9월부터 시작되었고, 한국에서는 2006년 5월부터 실시되며, *i*BT가 실시되면 기존의 CBT 방식으로는 더 이상 시험이 치러지지 않는다.

CBT에서 *i*BT는 어떻게 달라졌나?

	CBT	*i*BT
Skills Test	Reading Listening Grammar * Writing은 별도	Reading Listening Writing Speaking
Test time	3.5 hours	4 hours
Reading	4~5 지문 (250~350 words) 각 지문당 11개 문제 (시간 70~90분)	3~5 지문 (700 words) 각 지문당 12~14개 문제 (시간 60~100 분)

Listening	1. 11~17개 대화
	   (각 지문당 1개의 질문)
	2. 2~3개 짧은 대화
	   (각 지문당 2~3개의 질문)
	3. 4~6개 미니 강의와 토론
	   (각각 3~6 개 문제)
	(시간 40~60분)
		1. 4~6개의 강의 및 교실토론
		   (각 지문당 5~6개의 질문)
		2. 2~3개의 대화
		   (각 5~6개의 질문)
		(시간 60~100분)

Speaking	없음	1. 2개의 independent tasks
		   일반 토픽에 대한 개인의 의견 발표
		2. 4개의 integrated tasks
		   읽고 들었던 것을 근거하여 말하기
		(시간 20분)

Writing	One independent task
	토픽에 대한 의견을 개진하기
	(시간 30분)
		1. 1개의 integrated task
		  읽고 들은 내용에 근거하여 쓰기 (20분)
		2. 1개의 independent task
		  토픽에 대한 의견을 개진하기 (30분)

Structure (Grammar)	20~25개의 문제 (시간 15~20분)	없음
전체 점수	300	120
피드백	점수만 제공	Section별 점수와 총점 제공

iBT 시험 유형 세부 분석

iBT의 전체 시험 구성과 문항 수, 제한 시간은 다음과 같다.

Section	지문종류	지문	새로 추가된 특징
Reading		3~5 지문 (각 지문 당 12~14문제)	- 전문용어를 설명하는 Glossary - Multiple focus 정보를 분류하거나 summary를 완성하는 문제 추가
Listening	Lecture	4~6 지문 (각 지문당 6문제)	- Replay 문제 추가 - Note-taking 허락
	Conversation	2~3 지문 (각 지문당 5문제)	
Break		10분	
Speaking	Speaking	2문제	경험 또는 의견 말하기
	Reading → Listening → Speaking	2문제	- 제시된 안건을 읽고 그 안건에 대한 강의를 듣고 정리해서 말하기 - 제시된 안건을 읽고 안건에 대한 대화를 듣고 정리해서 말하기
	Listening → Speaking	2문제	- 강의를 듣고 요약하여 말하기 - 대화를 듣고 요약해서 말하기
Writing	Writing on topic	1개의 토픽	제시된 안건에 대한 의견 쓰기
	Reading → Listening → Writing	1개의 토픽	읽고 들은 내용에 근거하여 요점을 정리하여 논리적으로 쓰기

*i*BT Total Score Range Comparisons

Internet-based Total	Computer-based Total	Percentile Rank
111 - 120	273 - 300	97.6 - 100
96 - 110	243 - 270	85.9 - 96.8
79 - 95	213 - 240	64.8 - 85.0
65 - 78	183 - 210	45.6 - 63.6
53 - 64	153 - 180	29.9 - 44.3
41 - 52	123 - 150	16.7 - 28.6
30 - 40	93 - 120	7.4 - 15.8
19 - 29	63 - 90	1.7 - 6.5
9 - 18	33 - 60	0.1 - 1.2
0 - 8	0 - 30	0.04

*i*BT Listening Section의 구성

· 문제 유형으로 본 Listening Section에서 요하는 Listening Skills

1. Listening for basic comprehension
- 요지와 중요한 내용들, 요지와 관련된 핵심적인 세부 사항을 이해하는 능력

2. Listening for pragmatic understanding
- 화자의 태도나 확실성 정도를 인식하는 능력
- 화자의 목적 또는 역할, 기능을 인식하는 능력

3. Connecting and synthesizing information
- 정보가 어떻게 조직되어 제시되는지를 인식할 수 있는 능력
- 제공되는 아이디어 사이의 관계를 이해하는 능력(signal words를 파악할 필요가 있음)
- 듣기 지문에 암시되어 있는 내용에 의해 결론을 도출하거나 올바른 추론을 하는 능력
- 강의나 대화 안의 정보를 연결할 수 있는 능력
- 강의나 대화 안에서 화제가 어떻게 바뀌는지, 예시나 여담, 대화나 강의를 벗어난 이야기 등을 인식할 수 있는 능력

· Listening Section의 형식

듣기 자료	문제 개수	시간
4~6 강의, 강의당 3~5분, 500~800 가량의 어휘로 구성	지문당 5~6	60~90분
2~3 대화, 대화당 약 3분 소요, 12~25번 정도의 대화의 교환이 이루어짐	지문당 5~6	

Academic Lectures
- "a monologue by professor"인 유형이 있고, 학생의 질의 · 응답이 포함된 "talk in a class" 유형, 교수를 포함하는 학생들 사이의 "discussion", 세 가지 유형이 있다.

Conversations in an Academic Setting
- iBT에서 대화는 교수 또는 조교와의 면담 상황에서 벌어지는 경우가 많다. 또는 행정 직원이나 사서, 서점 직원 등과의 대화도 나온다.

· Listening Section의 특징

1. 강의나 대화나 기본적으로 길어졌기 때문에 Note-taking이 허용된다.
2. 'well, uh, hmmm...'과 같이 실제로 말하듯이 자연스럽게 언어가 사용된다.
3. 북미식 발음 이외의 엑센트가 나타날 수 있다.
4. 기존 CBT의 Short Conversation이 사라졌다.
5. 새로운 형태의 문제가 출제된다. 대화 및 강의의 일부를 다시 듣고 화자의 태도나 의도, 확실성 정도를 가늠하는 문제 형태로, 화자의 tone 또는 다른 힌트를 통해 화자가 논의되고 있는 화제나 주제에 대해 어떤 입장을 취하고 있는지 파악해야 한다.

Chapter 01
MAIN IDEA

OVERVIEW

Main Idea

강의(토론)나 대화에서 주로 다루고 있는 내용이 무엇인지를 묻는 문제이다. 강의나 대화의 중심 생각, 즉 주제나 요지(topic)가 무엇인지를 확인하는 것이다. 특히 대화는 그 특성상 대화의 의도나 목적(purpose), 필요로 하는 것을 중심 아이디어로 본다.

Question Types

What is the talk mainly about?
What is the topic of the discussion?
What is the main idea of the lecture?
What is the main point of the speaker(s)?
What does the woman want from the man?
Why does the man want to see the professor?

General Strategies

1 Topics of Lectures

보통 강의의 서두에 주제를 주지시키기 때문에 첫 부분에 유의해서 듣는 것이 좋다. 한편 토론 형식으로 진행되는 강의는 여러 대화자가 한 가지 토픽을 놓고 다양한 의견을 교환하는 형태가 되므로, 강의의 핵심은 general idea에 초점을 맞추고 들어야 파악할 수 있다. 주제는 특히 강의의 마지막 부분에서 재언급되므로, 이 부분을 주의해서 듣는 것이 중요하다.

2 Purposes of Conversations

대화에서의 main idea는 곧 purpose이다. 화자가 원하는 것을 토대로 대화가 진행되기 때문이다. 요구하는 쪽 화자가 누구인지, 그 화자가 어떤 목적으로 말을 꺼내는지에 초점을 맞추어 듣는다. A-B-A-B로 진행되는 대화를 들으며 방문의 목적이나, 상대로부터 얻고자 하는 것, 어떤 말을 하는 이유 등에 주목한다. 한 가지 주의해야 할 것은 상대방의 반응이다. 왜냐하면 상대방의 반응에 따라 문제(요구 사항이나 필요)가 해결될 수도 있고 그렇지 못할 수도 있으며, 이 해결 여부가 문제로 출제되는 경우가 많기 때문이다.

Pre Test

TOEFL Listening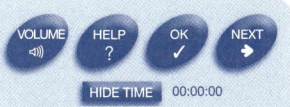

Pre Test 1

Listen to a lecture about parapsychology. Then answer the question.

What is the lecture mainly about?
- Ⓐ The unusual behavior of planetary objects
- Ⓑ Flaws in the use of scientific methods
- Ⓒ A comparison of different branches of science
- Ⓓ An examination of unknown phenomena

Pre Test 2

Listen to a conversation in a professor's office. Then answer the question.

Why does the student go to see the professor?
- Ⓐ To discuss a missed class with the professor
- Ⓑ To hand in an assignment from the class
- Ⓒ To get more information on an assignment
- Ⓓ To confirm a lab meeting on Friday

VOCABULARY

1. **parapsychology** 초(超)심리학 **evolve** 발전시키다, 전개하다 **wobble** 비틀거림, 흔들림, 동요 **orbit** 궤도 **due to** ~로 인해 **oddity** 기이함, 괴상함 **add up** 이치에 맞다, 이해되다 **tend to** ~하는 경향이 있다 **take a look at** ~을 훑어보다 **focus on** ~에 초점을 맞추다 **psychic** 심령의, 영혼의 **phenomena** 현상(phenomenon의 복수형)
2. **indicate** 지시하다 **plastic bag** 비닐봉지 **source** 수원, 근원 **pond** 연못 **fountain** 분수

Dictation Listen and fill in the blanks.

Pre Test 1
(P=M)

Professor As, uh, as we've looked at the way that scientific inquiries have evolved over the centuries, we've seen how, how, uh, a lot of questions have been answered. For example, the wobble of the moon's orbit... okay? Then again, a lot of explanations were rethought primarily due to oddities in the data. Yeah, so when something seems strange, _____, then scientists tend to _____ it. Actually there are many questions that are thought to be odd or strange... and for many of them, we don't have the answers. Okay, so uh, let's look at a completely different branch of science today — one that not everyone would even agree it's science — that primarily focuses on explaining oddities, _____, things we can't even see. This is parapsychology. Parapsychologists, uh, do two things: they, uh, investigate and try to find a scientific basis for things that most other scientists don't even believe in — psychic communication, telepathy, those kinds of things... and they _____ scientific methods to understanding these phenomena...

Pre Test 2
(S=M / P=W)

Student Hi, Professor. Could I talk to you about this assignment _____?

Professor Sure. What's the problem?

Student Well, um, you told us that we should bring a water sample into lab on Friday, but I _____ class last time and didn't hear the explanation about that.

Professor Oh. Well, uh, really it's pretty simple. You've _____ two things: get a small sample of water — you can even put it in a plastic bag. Secondly, it must be from any source on campus.

Student Even, like, the sink in my dorm?

Professor Sure, _____. Or the pond, or the fountain outside of this building. Then, uh, then just bring it to class and we'll examine it in lab.

Student Oh. Okay. Well, _____.

Vocabulary Preview for Mini-Exercise

Listen and choose the correct definition of the given words or phrases.

Mini-Exercise 1

1.
   1. consequence   a. ☐   b. ☐
   2. literacy   a. ☐   b. ☐
   3. subscribe to   a. ☐   b. ☐

2.
   1. perspective   a. ☐   b. ☐
   2. evolutionary   a. ☐   b. ☐
   3. heritage   a. ☐   b. ☐

3.
   1. hangover   a. ☐   b. ☐
   2. alternative   a. ☐   b. ☐
   3. immunity   a. ☐   b. ☐

Mini-Exercise 2

1.
   1. permanent   a. ☐   b. ☐
   2. enrollment   a. ☐   b. ☐
   3. burst at the seams   a. ☐   b. ☐

2.
   1. all of a sudden   a. ☐   b. ☐
   2. be broke   a. ☐   b. ☐
   3. get somebody down   a. ☐   b. ☐

3.
   1. participate   a. ☐   b. ☐
   2. semester   a. ☐   b. ☐
   3. at ease   a. ☐   b. ☐

Mini-Exercise 1 Finding Topics of Lectures

Lecture 1 Listen to a lecture about media literacy education. Then answer the questions.

1 What is the lecture mainly about?
(A) Negative physical conditions caused by media
(B) Educating children about media
(C) The basic plot structure of a TV sitcom
(D) Reasons for increased TV viewing among kids

» Comprehension Question «

2 Which of the following is a goal of the media educator?
(A) To teach others how to reduce the number of hours watching TV
(B) To show students how to interpret the educational information
(C) To explain how TV commercials or shows are made and what they try to do
(D) To encourage students not to buy any products that they see on TV

Dictation Listen again and fill in the blanks. (P=M)

Professor Children in this, uh, in this country watch, on average, about 20 hours a week of television. _____? Well, there're some pretty serious physical consequences, but _____ those, at least not today. Instead, I want to look at media literacy — the movement to, uh, educate young people in, uh, interpreting and making intelligent judgments about media.
What do media literacy educators do? Okay, there're two parts to this field that _____ today. So, the first one is, uh, to talk to kids about the ways that television shows and commercials are, uh, constructed. Educators feel that it's a very early, but important step. Secondly, they also _____ what the show or ad is trying to get the person to do — is it going to make you buy something? Or subscribe to a certain ideology? And so on...

Mini-Exercise 1

Lecture 2 Listen to a lecture in a psychology class. Then answer the questions.

1 What is the lecture mainly going to be about?
(A) An overview of the history and methods of psychology
(B) A psychological perspective on Darwin's evolutionary theory
(C) A comparison between biology's methods and psychology's methods
(D) The relationship between evolutionary theory and human psychology

≫ Comprehension Question ≪

2 According to the professor, when did Charles Darwin get interested in natural history?
(A) When he first started his career as a professor
(B) When he changed his major from psychology to the history of nature
(C) When he was studying medicine at university
(D) When he studied natural substances that could work as medicines

Dictation Listen again and fill in the blanks. (P=W)

Professor Last class we finished talking about the history of psychology. What _____ today is the... the relationship between biology and psychology.
_____, what I'm gonna try to do today are... hmmm... two things. First, I will define what Darwin's theory says. After that, I'll get into some different perspectives of psychologists, particularly, what our evolutionary heritage _____ our psychological behavior.
_____, Charles Robert Darwin achieved lasting fame as the originator of the theory of evolution through natural selection. He first developed his interest in natural history while studying medicine at university.

Main Idea 23

Mini-Exercise 1

Talk in a class 3 Listen to a talk in a class about homeopathic medicine. Then answer the questions.

1 What is the talk mainly going to be about?
(A) Homeopathy in the treatment of alcoholism
(B) The effectiveness of homeopathy in treating some diseases
(C) The reason why homeopathy may not really work
(D) The criticism on homeopathy and alternative medicine

≫ **Comprehension Question** ≪

2 In homeopathy, what is ingested?
(A) An antibiotic agent that kills the disease effectively
(B) A placebo that doesn't contain any drug
(C) A small portion of the virus that causes the disease
(D) Harmless and unknown substances

Dictation Listen again and fill in the blanks. (P=M / S=W)

Professor You've all heard of the saying, "the hair of the dog," right? This idiom _____ the belief that consuming a mixture involving the hair of the dog would effectively treat diseases such as rabies that the dog may have carried. Well, it is frequently used to refer to alcoholic beverages consumed with the intent of lessening the effects of a hangover which was of course caused by the alcohol. Okay, now I wanna talk about homeopathy which has a similar notion in alternative medicine, and, and _____ _____ certain illnesses, okay?

Student So, you _____ that causes a disease? Isn't it a vaccine?

Professor However, we know why a vaccine works—it creates an immunity in your body. Not like it can actually cure the disease. Well, some conventional physicians claim that _____, then it is the human mind that cures the disease.

* homeopathic 동종요법

Mini-Exercise 2: Finding Purposes of Conversations

Conversation 1 Listen to a conversation between two teaching assistants. Then answer the questions.

1 Why does the man want to talk to the woman?
(A) To discuss the English Department's structure
(B) To inform her there will be a TA's lounge
(C) To talk about an alternative place for the TA's lounge
(D) To find out if she agrees with the man's opinion

» Comprehension Question «

2 What will they probably do next?
(A) They will go to the office to request TA's lounge.
(B) They will wait until a suitable place for them to use.
(C) They will go to see if there is room for TA's lounge.
(D) They will talk to the professors about their needs.

Dictation
Listen again and fill in the blanks. (TA1=M / TA2=W)

TA1 Can I _____?

TA2 Sure, what is it?

TA1 Did you hear that they are closing down the TA's lounge? I mean permanently. I was just told they're turning it into office space for the new professors.

TA2 Well, I do see the need for more office space; enrollment is up, classes _____, so yeah, they need more space.

TA1 Don't you think we need the lounge to relax between classes? I think we should appeal to someone that we do need some place for this. Now _____ to relax.

TA2 I think you're right, but what if there really is no room or _____?

TA1 Hey, I just thought of something — the English Department is moving to a new building. There must be some space available there.

TA2 Oh, we'll have to go see to _____.

Mini-Exercise 2

Conversation 2 Listen to a conversation between two students. Then answer the questions.

1 Why does the man want to see the woman?
(A) To ask if there are any jobs he could do
(B) To find out how much he could get an hour
(C) To hear how she managed to work and study
(D) To learn about the working condition of cafeteria

» Comprehension Question «

2 How did the woman feel about working?
(A) She didn't like working on campus.
(B) She thought the job was complicated.
(C) She didn't have enough time to study.
(D) She felt it wasn't easy to study after work.

Dictation Listen again and fill in the blanks. (S1=W / S2=M)

Student 1 So, what did you want to see me for?
Student 2 Well, I wanted to ask you about the job you had at the cafeteria.
Student 1 Why, _____?
Student 2 You know, I never have any money. It seems like _____. And, it's really getting me down. The only thing I can do _____ more money. And I wanted to ask if it was okay... I mean, did you have enough time for the school work?
Student 1 What do you think? You work 4 to 5 hours a day and 4 days a week. And after work, you're so exhausted.
Student 2 But still, you've managed to have a good grade and money _____, right? How did you do that?
Student 1 Well, there are some things you _____ when you think about getting a job.

Mini-Exercise 2

Conversation 3 Listen to a conversation between a professor and a student. Then answer the questions.

1 Why does the student go to see the professor?
(A) To ask about methods for reducing the students' stress during a group discussion
(B) To inform the professor about the problems associated with small group discussions
(C) To discuss the pros and cons of working as a group for the project
(D) To get advice on improving student participation in the group discussion

» Comprehension Question «

2 Why does the professor suggest smaller groups?
(A) because students can have more time to talk
(B) because students can create their own guidelines
(C) because students will feel more relaxed
(D) because smaller groups will be more easily managed

Dictation Listen again and fill in the blanks.   (S=W / P=M)

Student   Hi, do you have a second? I want to talk about my group project.
Professor _____. So, what about it?
Student   Well, I'm a leader of this project and there are 5 other members in my group. The thing is... every time we have a discussion, _____ get them to talk!
Professor What do you mean?
Student   I really _____ other members to participate. I don't know how we could finish the project this semester.
Professor Umm, well, so, all together, it's 6 people in your group, right? Okay... why don't you just make them work in even smaller groups, like two or three of them to ask and answer uh... some questions. You know, I think, since it's beginning of a semester, students might be uncomfortable to talk, but this seems to _____. Then, they could return to the larger group and give a mini-presentation.

Main Idea

Vocabulary Preview for Practice

Listen and choose the correct definition of the given words or phrases.

Practice 1
1. distinguish   a. ☐   b. ☐
2. deficient   a. ☐   b. ☐
3. exceedingly   a. ☐   b. ☐
4. utilize   a. ☐   b. ☐

Practice 2
1. figure out   a. ☐   b. ☐
2. infection   a. ☐   b. ☐
3. pasteurize   a. ☐   b. ☐
4. crucial   a. ☐   b. ☐

Practice 3
1. excessive   a. ☐   b. ☐
2. examine   a. ☐   b. ☐
3. imply   a. ☐   b. ☐
4. result in   a. ☐   b. ☐

Practice 4
1. involve   a. ☐   b. ☐
2. cover   a. ☐   b. ☐
3. congress   a. ☐   b. ☐
4. doable   a. ☐   b. ☐

Vocabulary Preview for Actual Test

Choose the best word to complete each sentence.

Actual Test 1

1. It might be _____ to clone human beings, but is it ethical?
   a. feasible   b. readable   c. attachable   d. affordable

2. Mountain climbers use oxygen as they reach higher _____.
   a. application   b. approach   c. altitudes   d. appetite

3. They _____ the campaign with "You're number two. Try harder," as the slogan.
   a. practiced   b. launched   c. postponed   d. manifested

4. We can't _____ the suspects to be guilty simply because they've decided to remain silent.
   a. consume   b. affect   c. assure   d. assume

Actual Test 2

1. Doctors are trained to _____ the symptoms of different diseases.
   a. respond   b. recognize   c. insist   d. withhold

2. Grandfather gets quite _____ sometimes, and doesn't even know what day it is.
   a. refused   b. confined   c. defused   d. confused

3. Which novels by George Orwell are on the _____ this year?
   a. syllabic   b. syllabary   c. sympathy   d. syllabus

4. These seats are _____ for the elderly and women with babies.
   a. reserved   b. resumed   c. respected   d. resolved

Main Idea

Practice 1

Lecture

Listen to a lecture in an art class.

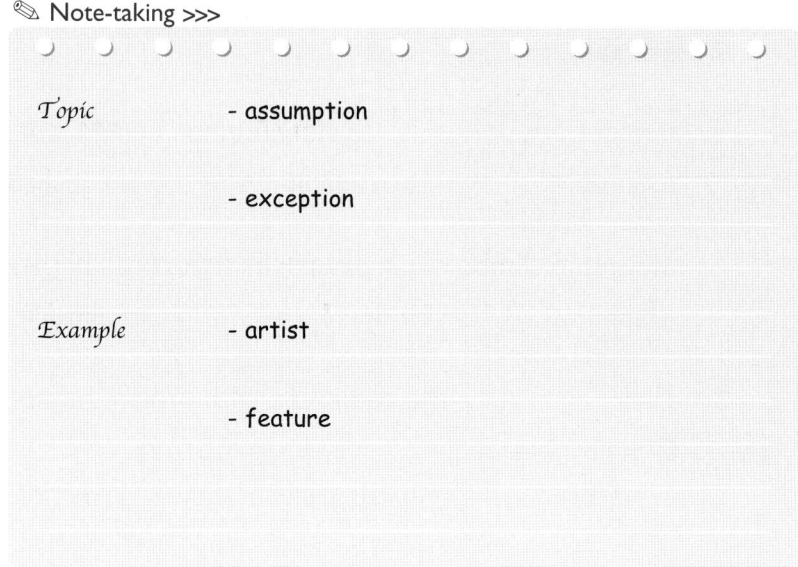

Note-taking >>>

Topic
- assumption

- exception

Example
- artist

- feature

Now answer the questions.

1. What will the lecture mainly focus on?

   (A) Artistic form as seen by the disabled
   (B) The negative effects of CP on artists like Brown
   (C) The unexpected effect of CP on an artist
   (D) How art therapy has been employed to treat illness

2. Which of the following is NOT true of Christy Brown?

   (A) He had significant speech problems.
   (B) He lacked full range of movement.
   (C) He painted without the use of his hands.
   (D) He mostly used chalks when he painted.

3. What does the professor say about Brown's works?

   (A) Some are considered to be masterpieces.
   (B) His sister had a great influence in his works.
   (C) They reflect the experience of illness.
   (D) They led to Brown's partial recovery.

Practice 2

Talk in a class

Listen to a talk in a class about honey in burn treatment.

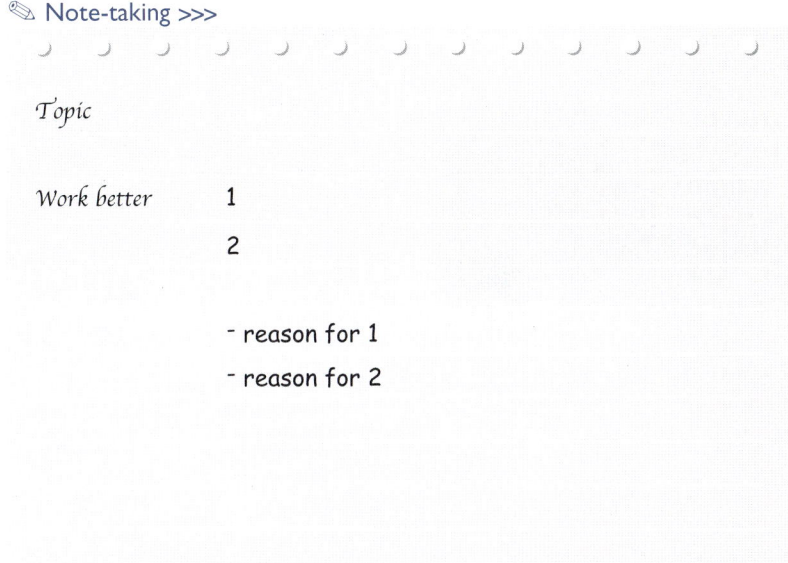

Now answer the questions.

1 What is the talk mainly about?

(A) A comparison of traditional and modern burn treatments
(B) How technology has been used to improve the honey therapy
(C) The reasons for the efficacy of honey to treat burns
(D) How honey therapy has changed primarily due to homogenization

2 According to the professor, which are true about honey? Choose TWO correct answers.

(A) Honey has been used to treat burns and wounds for 1,000 years.
(B) Honey keeps wounds clean, preventing any viral infection.
(C) Honey helps clean away enzymes at burn sites that are infected.
(D) Honey provides damp conditions in burns to promote healing

3 What does the professor say about pasteurizing?

(A) It might destroy useful ingredients of the honey.
(B) It increases the honey's efficacy while processing.
(C) It provides a longer shelf life when treated for burns.
(D) It introduces beneficial chemicals into the honey.

Practice 3

Talk in a class

Listen to a talk in a pathology class.

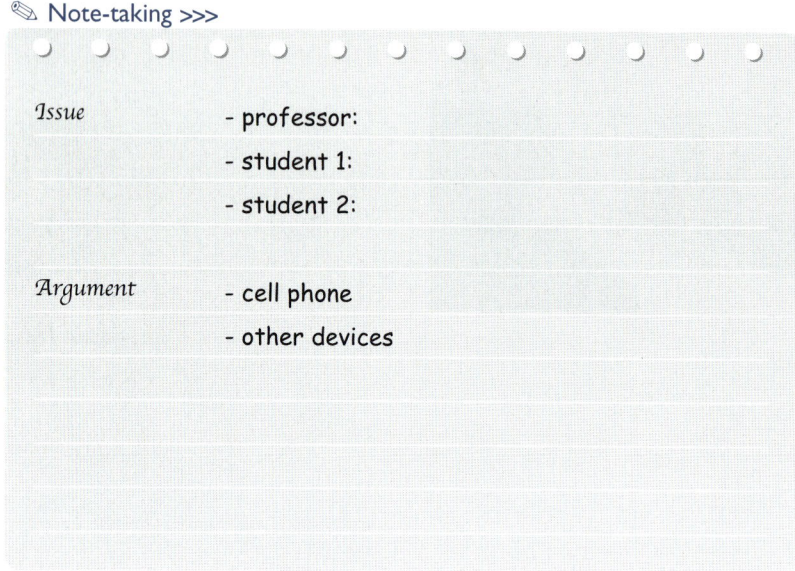

Note-taking >>>

Issue
 - professor:
 - student 1:
 - student 2:

Argument
 - cell phone
 - other devices

Now answer the questions.

1. What will the talk mainly be about?

   (A) The types of electromagnetic energy released by various devices
   (B) The need for more rules governing the use of cellular technology
   (C) Medical data showing the increased incidence cell-phone related tumors
   (D) The health problems claimed to be linked with cell phone usage

2. What can be inferred about the two students?

   (A) They don't agree with the professor's opinion.
   (B) They agree to the idea that the professor suggested.
   (C) The man doesn't agree with the professor's opinion.
   (D) The woman agrees that cancer and cell phone usage are related.

3. Which of the following statements is NOT true, according to the professor?

   (A) Cell phones do emit some energy that could be harmful to brain.
   (B) No one is certain whether cell phones cause brain cancer or not.
   (C) A cell phone emits a different energy type than others.
   (D) Some other devices send off the same type of energy as cell phones.

Practice 4

Conversation

Listen to a conversation at the campus newspaper office.

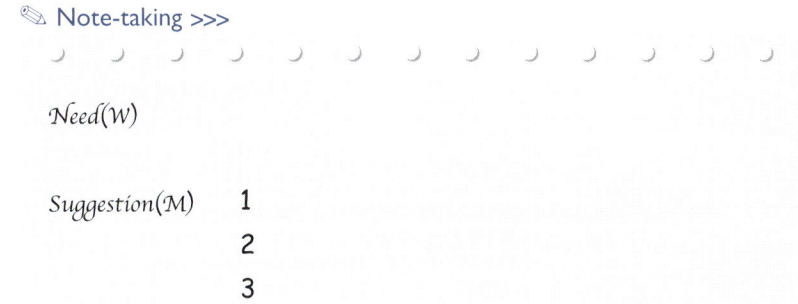

Note-taking >>>

Need(W)

Suggestion(M) 1
2
3

Now answer the questions.

1 Why does she want to talk to the man?

(A) To find out the topic of the assignment meeting
(B) To ask about the materials to prepare for the meeting
(C) To ask how she could join the campus paper as a writer
(D) To learn more about the writing for the campus paper

2 What does the man tell the woman to bring to the meeting?

(A) An interview with the newspaper's editor
(B) A sample of an article she has written
(C) A list of stories she might like to write
(D) A recommendation from her high school editor

3 Which of the following statements is true?

(A) The woman attended the assignment meeting for the paper.
(B) The woman scheduled an interview with the editor tonight.
(C) The woman is interested in reporting on student government.
(D) The woman met the man in high school when she was an editor.

Actual Test 1

TOEFL Listening

Listen to a lecture in a space science class.

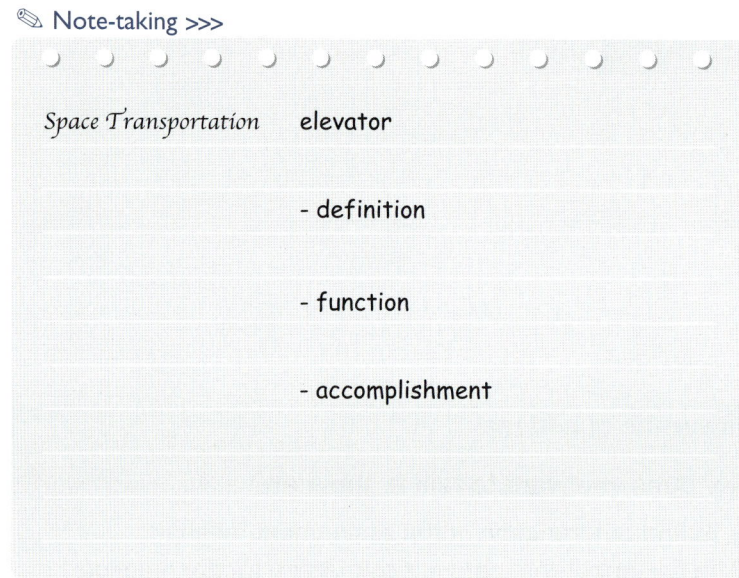

Note-taking >>>

Space Transportation   elevator

- definition

- function

- accomplishment

Now answer the questions.

1 What is the lecture mainly about?
- Ⓐ The history of human space exploration
- Ⓑ The possibility of using elevator technology in space
- Ⓒ The benefits of space elevators over previous technology
- Ⓓ Increasing the interest in space travel

2 Which of the following is NOT a part of space elevators?
- Ⓐ A metal box
- Ⓑ A long cable
- Ⓒ An orbiting station
- Ⓓ Electromagnetic vehicles

3 Which of the following is true about the cost of space elevators?
- Ⓐ It is competitively cheap since space elevators need no fuel.
- Ⓑ It would cost more than spacecrafts because of the cable up to the station.
- Ⓒ It is much cheaper than that of conventional space vehicles.
- Ⓓ It is not expensive considering the time saved during each travel.

4 Which of the following is true about the technology of space elevators?
- Ⓐ It is feasible but highly restricted to some scientists for military uses.
- Ⓑ The cable for the space elevator is now available but stations are not ready.
- Ⓒ It is theoretically proved to be possible but there is still more to be done.
- Ⓓ It wouldn't be completed without the development of other technologies.

5 How dose the professor feel about the space elevator?
- Ⓐ He is skeptical about the incomplete technology at the elevator.
- Ⓑ He is excited about more affordable space travel by the elevator.
- Ⓒ He is concerned about the unknown possible dangers of the elevator.
- Ⓓ He is amused by the convenience of commercial space travel.

Actual Test 2

TOEFL Listening

Listen to a conversation between two students.

Note-taking >>>

Man's problem

Woman's answer

Reserve   - meaning

                 - how to use

Now answer the questions.

1   Why does the man want to talk to the woman?
- Ⓐ To discuss the syllabus from their class in the library
- Ⓑ To find out the name of the textbook to look for in the library
- Ⓒ To ask where he could get the book assigned in the class
- Ⓓ To see if he is looking for the right textbook for the class

2   What does the woman say about the book?
- Ⓐ She didn't see it assigned on the syllabus.
- Ⓑ She doesn't think it's worth reading.
- Ⓒ It isn't mandatory for students to buy.
- Ⓓ It can be found in the library.

3 What is NOT true about reserve items?
- Ⓐ Reserve items can be checked out.
- Ⓑ Reserve items can be photocopied.
- Ⓒ Reserve items must be read in the library.
- Ⓓ Reserve items cannot leave the library.

4 What does Peter say about the reserve desk?
- Ⓐ He does not know where it is located.
- Ⓑ He has a friend who works there.
- Ⓒ He did not know what it was for.
- Ⓓ He finds the librarians unhelpful.

5 What does June say about the length of the article?
- Ⓐ It should take three hours to read.
- Ⓑ It will not take very long to read.
- Ⓒ It is almost as long as the book.
- Ⓓ It can be read in about 1/2 hour.

DICTATION

Practice 1

🎧 Listen and fill in the blanks.

(P=M)

Professor So, today, I wanna examine the, uh, way that a physical disability can play into, and often, uh, help create, a new kind of artistic expression. I ① _____, when they think of physical disabilities, they automatically think of the word "handicap." But you know, you ② _____ _____ that, well, this isn't necessarily the case. Yeah, ③ _____ people with physical limitations as being held back from creativity, but for an artist like Christy Brown, it was his limitations that ④ _____ other, um, visual artists. Brown had cerebral palsy or CP, a permanent disorder with developmental brain injuries that... uh... occur during fetal development, birth, or ⑤ _____. Anyway, his doctors assumed he was mentally deficient, as well as his speech was, uh, seriously impaired. However, one day, while... uh... watching his sister write with some chalk, Brown grabbed the piece of chalk ⑥ _____, the only part of his body that he could, uh, really control, and began drawing! ⑦ _____, he... he began painting using his left foot to hold the brushes. The work was exceedingly expressive and really utilized a personal vocabulary that ⑧ _____ of having CP.

|구문해설| **hold back** 위축시키다　**be accustomed to -ing** ~에 익숙하다　**distinguish A from B** A와 B를 구별하다

Practice 2

🎧 Listen and fill in the blanks.

(P=W / S=M)

Professor   Many new therapies have been, uh, developed ① _____ ... to help repair skin and tissue damaged by fire. However, as we've seen, as our technology has progressed, we haven't found any treatment that is ② _____ , yet. It's not completely, um, clear why, but ③ _____ and try to ④ _____ for ourselves, shall we? So, yeah, of all the conventional dressings for burns, honey ⑤ _____ to treat infection and protect the healing skin.

Student   Is the honey prepared or processed in any special way before it's put on the burn?

Professor   Actually, no, it isn't. It only seems to be, uh, unpasteurized ⑥ _____ . Pasteurization is the process of heating food ⑦ _____ killing harmful organisms such as bacteria and viruses. But I guess the pasteurizing might actually remove some useful chemical or uh... enzyme. So, it must be those enzymes in the honey that clean out the wound and keep the infection at bay. ⑧ _____ is that it really works to keep the wound moist, which is, uh, crucial to healing a burn. I guess ⑨ _____ we try to improve upon nature, it still does the best job.

|구문해설| **figure out** 이해하다   **work well** 효능이 뛰어나다   **keep sth at bay** ~을 저지하다, 궁지에 몰리게 하다   **no matter how** 비록 얼마나 ~할지라도   **improve up(on)** ~을 개량하다, ~을 개선시키다

DICTATION

Practice 3

🎧 Listen and fill in the blanks.

(P=M / S1=M / S2=W)

Professor: It's becoming the, uh, exception these days not to be able to pull out one's cell phone anywhere at anytime, right. And yet, ① _____ these useful devices may be, they also, uh, ② _____ potential dangers. There are some cases that show, uh, excessive cell phone uses ③ _____ ..., and well, have any of you thought about that?

Student 1: Well, why would a cell phone cause brain cancer but a regular phone wouldn't?

Student 2: Isn't it the radiation that cell phones emit right toward the brain? It's obvious that ④ _____ .

Professor: Well, I don't think that, uh, either side has made a conclusive case yet. We will examine various cases, today, that might ⑤ _____ this electromagnetic energy. All right? Now, it's true that cell phones do emit a low level of electromagnetic energy, excessive exposure to, uh, which ⑥ _____ brain tumors. But many devices use electromagnetic energy, yet there's not evidence that implicates them in negative health. So... ⑦ _____ .

|구문해설| **be linked to** ~와 관련된 **right toward** 곧바로 ~을 향하여 **either side** 양측 모두 **result in** ~한 결과를 낳다 **It's not cut and dried.** 그것이 결정적인 이야기는 아니다.

Practice 4

🎧 Listen and fill in the blanks.

(S1=W / S2=M)

Student 1 Hi. I was wondering ① _____ .
Student 2 I can try. Were you interested in writing for the campus paper?
Student 1 Yes. I was editor of my high school newspaper and I'd really ② _____ the campus paper, but I don't know ③ _____ .
Student 2 Well, your best bet ④ _____ the assignment meeting tonight. Our editor has a list of stories she wants to cover for this week's paper, and we can always use another writer.
Student 1 Okay… ⑤ _____ covering the student congress and stuff. I wrote a lot about school politics in high school.
Student 2 Well, ⑥ _____ . It might be a good idea to bring a clipping of something you've written to the meeting. To show her ⑦ _____ . Maybe come a little early to talk to the editor?
Student 1 Okay, I will. That's really helpful. Thanks. See you tonight.

|구문해설| **wonder if + 절** ~에 대해 궁금하다 **get involved with** ~와 관련되다, ~을 담당하다

DICTATION

Actual Test 1

🎧 Listen and fill in the blanks.

(P=M)

Professor Since we've been successfully launching people and objects into space, ① _____ that all the space transportation methods would involve some kind of spacecraft, right? Well, but one of the future of space transport could actually involve an elevator.

Now... first... ② _____ by an elevator before I get into the nuts and bolts of the thing, okay? Um, I'm not talking about some metal box that ③ _____ a skyscraper. What I'm talking about is a long cable that goes from the earth's surface out into space, and that has its center at an orbiting station that's about 20,000 miles ④ _____. And so what would happen would be that these electromagnetic vehicles, carrying anything from people to objects, could travel up and down this cable. Everyone got the picture?

Now, ⑤ _____ this space elevator as a possible transportation method while there are spacecrafts that ⑥ _____, launching so many times? What, uh, what would this accomplish? Well, it would cut down on the costs of launching individual vehicles. ⑦ _____ run up the side of a cable ⑧ _____. And so this would make commercial space travel — for both tourism and exploration, a lot more economically feasible. Now there's a lot ⑨ _____ on here, obviously. Lots of logistics to work out. But it's definitely within the realm of possibility.

|구문해설| **nuts and bolts** 기본, 실제적인 상세함 **get the picture** 뜻을 파악하다 **blast off** 이륙하다(=take off) **logistics** (업무의) 세부 계획

Actual Test 2

🎧 **Listen and fill in the blanks.**

(S1=M / S2=W)

Student 1   Hey, you're in my media studies class, aren't you?

Student 2   Yes, right. I recognize you, too. I'm June.

Student 1   Nice to meet you, June. I'm Peter. Well, listen, ① _____ something on the syllabus and I wonder ② _____ .

Student 2   Well, sure. What is it?

Student 1   Okay, so see here, where Professor Wilson tells us to read an article from *Listening to Media* for next Monday? But that's not one of the textbooks ③ _____ .

Student 2   Oh, yeah. No, that's on reserve in the library.

Student 1   Ah, I see... um... what does that mean? What's reserve?

Student 2   That's when the professor has the library ④ _____ for students to use. They can't ⑤ _____ , but you can read them in the library, or photocopy what you need to read and ⑥ _____ .

Student 1   Oh, okay! I've seen the reserve desk. I just didn't know ⑦ _____ !

Student 2   Right, just go up there and tell them your class and what book you want. I think you can use it for up to three hours at a time. But it should only ⑧ _____ read the article.

|구문해설| **confused about** ~에 대해 파악이 안 되는   **on reserve** 별도로 마련해 놓은   **check out** 대출하다

Vocabulary Review

Write the meanings of the words in the blanks.

1. evolve _____
2. orbit _____
3. psychic _____
4. subscribe _____
5. evolutionary _____
6. hangover _____
7. alternative _____
8. enrollment _____
9. exceedingly _____
10. deficient _____
11. infection _____
12. examine _____
13. involve _____
14. cover _____
15. congress _____
16. logistics _____
17. literacy _____

18. wobble _____
19. excessive _____
20. feasible _____
21. altitude _____
22. launch _____
23. assume _____
24. recognize _____
25. confused _____
26. syllabus _____
27. inquiry _____
28. phenomena _____
29. oddity _____
30. branch _____
31. indicate _____
32. construct _____
33. interpret _____

Write the meanings of the phrases in the blanks.

34. add up _____
35. burst at the seams _____
36. get sb down _____
37. hold back _____
38. keep sth at bay _____
39. be linked to _____
40. nuts and bolts _____
41. on reserve _____

Write the correct words or phrases in the blanks.

42. ~에 초점을 맞추다 _____
43. A와 B를 구별하다 _____
44. 영구한 _____
45. 참여하다 _____
46. 파산하다 _____
47. 편하게 _____
48. 이데올로기 _____
49. 이론 _____
50. 창시자 _____

Chapter 02

SUPPORTING DETAILS

OVERVIEW

Supporting Details

Detail 문제는 강의(토론)나 대화에서 언급한 구체적인 정보를 얼마나 잘 파악하고 있는지를 확인하는 유형이다. 말하는 사람이 '직접 언급한 사실'을 바탕으로 답을 찾아야 하므로 짐작되거나 개인적인 추론을 바탕으로 답해서는 안 된다. 중요하다고 생각되는 정보는 Note-taking하여 문제 풀이 시 참고하는 것이 좋다.

Question Types

What does the professor say about ~?
What is mentioned as the reason why ~?
What is the man's suggestion for ~?
What is the best definition about ~?
What evidence was given by the professor for ~?
According to the conversation, what does ~ mean?
Who / When / Where / Why / How ~?
What is NOT true about ~?
What is true about ~?

General Strategies

1 Important Information

강의의 지엽적인 부분보다는 요점과 직접적으로 관련된 중요 정보를 확인하는 문제 유형이다. 어떤 것에 대한 정의(Definition), 예(Example), 장점(Benefit), 이유(Reason), 원인(Cause), 결과(Result), 문제점(Problem), 증거(Evidence)로 제시하는 정보들이 이에 속한다. 새로운 정보가 등장할 때마다 그것이 어떤 역할(정의, 문제점, 증거 등)을 하는지를 파악하고 성격을 부여하면서 듣도록 한다.

2 True or False

강의나 대화에서 언급된 내용을 토대로 선택지의 내용이 사실인지 거짓인지를 파악하는 문제이다. 이 경우에는 보통 지문에서 언급한 내용을 조금씩 변경하여 오답으로 제시한다. 때문에 대개 오답은 partly right, but partly wrong인 내용이 해당한다.

Pre Test

TOEFL Listening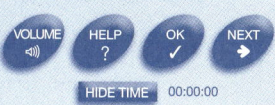

Pre Test 1

Listen to a talk in a class. Then answer the question.

According to the professor, what cast doubt on the timeline of humans coming after dinosaurs?

- Ⓐ The fact that some dinosaur fossils were found to have been faked
- Ⓑ A change in how paleontologists took measurements of fossil age
- Ⓒ The discovery of possible human footprints in a dinosaur fossil bed
- Ⓓ The finding of a human fossil that was much older than seemed possible

Pre Test 2

Listen to a conversation during a campus tour. Then answer the question.

What does the man tell the woman to do to get the library card?

- Ⓐ Attend the orientation later in the day
- Ⓑ Submit a scanned copy of student ID
- Ⓒ Have her ID registered at the library
- Ⓓ Fill out a library card request form

VOCABULARY

1. **fake** 날조하다 **extinct** 멸종하다 **mainstream** 주류를 이루는 **consensus** 여론 **track** (*pl.*) 발자국 **contradict** (설명·행동 따위가) ~에 모순되다 **footprint** 발자국 **irrefutable** 반박할 수 없는 **coexist** 공존하다 **erosion** 침식 **contemporary** 동시대의 **carving** 조각
2. **periodical** 정기 간행물 **president** (대학의) 총장, 학장 **renovate** 보수 공사하다, 개축하다 **orientation** 오리엔테이션 **scan** (데이터를) 훑다 **pretty** 꽤 **actually** 실제로

Dictation Listen and fill in the blanks.

Pre Test 1
(P=M / S=W)

Professor There are, uh, always people out there who doubt science... who think the earth is flat, who think the moon landing was faked... and those who suggest that dinosaurs and humans _____, closely together...

Student I thought it was common knowledge that humans _____ about... 60 million years after dinosaurs became extinct.

Professor Well, that's the mainstream scientific consensus. _____, the so-called Paluxy man tracks of Paluxy River seemed to contradict this. The river _____ numerous dinosaur footprints found in its bed near Glen Rose, Texas. Also... there were some other tracks that some claimed to be human, in the same fossil bed. This seemed irrefutable proof that man and dinosaur coexisted. However, close study has shown they were the result of numerous different phenomena — _____ dino tracks, erosion, and some contemporary carvings — not prehistoric man.

Pre Test 2
(S1=M / S2=W)

Student 1 This is the campus library. It's one of the oldest buildings at the school, _____ the 1850s. The library itself has one of the largest collections in the state — over 1.5 million books, periodicals, and recordings.

Student 2 Wow. _____ a mansion or something.

Student 1 Actually, the library used to be the college president's house in the 19th century. It's large, because during those days, people usually had large families. In fact, the last president to live there before the building was renovated had 8 kids!

Student 2 Um, so _____ to do to get a library card? _____ at orientation later today, or...?

Student 1 Actually, bring your student ID, which you should already have, and bring it to the front desk at the library. They'll scan your bar code into the computer and then you can use your ID as your library card. It's pretty easy, actually.

Vocabulary Preview for Mini-Exercise

Listen and choose the correct definition of the given words or phrases.

Mini-Exercise 1

1.
   1. eternal   a. ☐   b. ☐
   2. lofty   a. ☐   b. ☐
   3. successor   a. ☐   b. ☐

2.
   1. offspring   a. ☐   b. ☐
   2. reproductive   a. ☐   b. ☐
   3. participate   a. ☐   b. ☐

3.
   1. financial   a. ☐   b. ☐
   2. semester   a. ☐   b. ☐
   3. tuition   a. ☐   b. ☐

Mini-Exercise 2

1.
   1. remedial   a. ☐   b. ☐
   2. incur   a. ☐   b. ☐
   3. inability   a. ☐   b. ☐

2.
   1. theft   a. ☐   b. ☐
   2. notice   a. ☐   b. ☐
   3. character   a. ☐   b. ☐

3.
   1. notorious   a. ☐   b. ☐
   2. valid   a. ☐   b. ☐
   3. definitely   a. ☐   b. ☐

Mini-Exercise 1 Important Information

Lecture 1 Listen to a lecture on alchemy. Then answer the questions.

1. What reason does the professor give for alchemical experimentation? Choose TWO correct answers.
   (A) It could offer information about chemistry.
   (B) It could provide bottomless riches.
   (C) It could enable a person to escape death.
   (D) It could expand scientific knowledge.

≫ Comprehension Question ≪

2. According to the talk, what did the alchemists ultimately succeed in doing?
   (A) Learn how to alter the properties of various metals
   (B) Find new uses for previously known substances
   (C) Create the first established scientific methodology
   (D) Discover the physical characteristics of metals

Dictation Listen again and fill in the blanks. (P=M)

Professor Alchemy, the... ancient art of seeking to harness the power of and transform metals through chemistry, had _____ two goals. One was material: the alchemist wanted to turn a worthless metal into gold. The other was spiritual — if the philosopher's stone — the mysterious substance that would allow the alchemist to _____ — was discovered, then it could _____. Some pretty lofty goals, don't you think? The first records we have on alchemy are from the Greeks and Egyptians. While these early people like their successors, were unsuccessful at obtaining _____, what they did manage to do was _____ the properties of different metals, such as lead, mercury and all other kinds of things. In fact, though we would consider their goals highly unscientific today, these alchemists were really our first chemists.

Mini-Exercise 1

Lecture 2 Listen to a lecture about animals and cooperation. Then answer the questions.

1. According to the professor, which of the following is NOT a characteristic of a eusocial animal?
   (A) Producing all of a colony's offspring
   (B) Tending to the society's young
   (C) Sacrificing one's self for the society
   (D) Giving up reproductive capabilities

≫ Comprehension Question ≪

2. Among eusocial animals, what is the main producer's task?
   (A) To feed the offspring
   (B) To bear the young
   (C) To create the shelter
   (D) To make the food

Dictation Listen again and fill in the blanks. (P=W)

Professor We've been looking at various ways in which animal societies cooperate or don't cooperate and, um, some of the possible reasons for that. Today I want to hone in on eusocial animals, _____ what, uh, some researchers call "extreme cooperation." Okay, _____ what it means to be a eusocial animal. In this type of organization, the majority of members of the society give up their reproductive potential _____ _____ the offspring of a main producer. So, whether the animals _____ the main producer, they spend their entire life taking care of the young of the society. We see this in bees and ants and other such creatures. The fact that all sense of individual purpose is sacrificed to the society... well, you can see _____, can't you?

* eusocial 진사회성의

Mini-Exercise 1

Conversation 3 Listen to a conversation about financial aid. Then answer the questions.

1 What is the student worried about?
(A) Being short of money for the tuition
(B) Late tuition payment for the registration
(C) Eligibility to get the financial aid
(D) The complicated process of registering

»Comprehension Question«

2 According to the officer, why hasn't the student received her check?
(A) She was disenrolled from the school.
(B) She did not pay her taxes last year.
(C) She neglected to submit a form.
(D) She did not pay her tuition.

Dictation Listen again and fill in the blanks. (S=W / FAO=M)

Student	Hi, I was expecting my financial aid check, like, a week ago, and _____ _____ .
FAO	Hmmm... let's get to the bottom of this... actually, this shows that you haven't completed your paperwork for this semester. That's _____ _____ for you.
Student	Excuse me? But I... can you tell me _____ ?
FAO	Um... yes, we never received a tax form.
Student	Oh no... _____ . I can't pay my tuition without the check and I'm afraid I'll be disenrolled if I don't pay soon.
FAO	We can expedite the process and have the check to you in two weeks if you get the form to us today. And we can write a note to the registrar, explaining the circumstances, so you won't be disenrolled.
Student	Thanks so much. I _____ now.

Mini-Exercise 2　True or False

Lecture 1　Listen to a lecture in a technical writing class. Then answer the questions.

1　What does the professor say about poor writing skills?
(A) They create the need for more writers in the tax-funded workplace.
(B) They complicate communications between the government and taxpayers.
(C) They make it impossible for workers to advance beyond the remedial classes.
(D) They are usually not noticed by most people who are most affected by them.

»Comprehension Question«

2　What is a problem associated with bad writing itself?
(A) Decreased motivation of the taxpayers
(B) Increased needs for more writers
(C) Decreased federal funding for writing classes
(D) Increased wasteful time caused by it

Dictation　Listen again and fill in the blanks.　(P=M)

Professor　So listen to this: a recent report claims that states are having to spend _____ a billion — that's right, a billion — dollars a year on remedial writing classes for their employees. The inability of state workers to express themselves clearly _____ for state agencies, but also for the taxpayers who rely on these employees to get accurate, clear information.

And this doesn't include the cost that the actual bad writing itself is incurring. Okay, so you're asking yourselves how could bad writing itself cost money? Well, _____ — and time is money — caused by instructions that _____. The customer has to ask questions that should already be answered, the worker has to take time to answer the questions. Or the time it takes to redo the poor writing. It's not something we really think about much, but _____.
And it makes good writers to be in high demand in the workplace.

Mini-Exercise 2

Talk in a class 2 Listen to a talk in a film studies class. Then answer the questions.

1 What does the professor say about a MacGuffin?
(A) It is a seemingly minor plot detail that explains much.
(B) It is a minor part of a story used to capture attention.
(C) It is the main motivation for an actor or actress' behavior in a film.
(D) It is a term for when actors commit some kind of crime in a film's plot.

≫ Comprehension Question ≪

2 Why does the student mention the theft of money in a film?
(A) To give an example of the professor's point
(B) To show an example that might be an exception
(C) To highlight her knowledge of the use of MacGuffins
(D) To explain the need to capture the audience's attention

Dictation Listen again and fill in the blanks. (P=M / S=W)

Professor Something that we'll notice as we study these next few films by Alfred Hitchcock, is the use of a plot device that the director _____ the MacGuffin. Now then... uh — how can we define a MacGuffin? Well, _____, it's a detail in the plot that isn't nearly _____ _____ — it's just something that advances the story and holds the viewers' attention.

Student Oh, so for example, would Janet Leigh's character in *Psycho* stealing the money from her boss be considered a... a... _____ again?

Professor MacGuffin. Bingo. The theft of the money is just something Hitchcock does to get the woman to the Bates Motel, where the real story of the movie starts. It really isn't an important part of the film.

Mini-Exercise 2

Conversation 3 Listen to a conversation between two students. Then answer the questions.

1 What does the man say about the presentation?
(A) The time given to answer questions is short.
(B) Students are not allowed to ask questions after the presentation.
(C) There are some reminders for making a good presentation.
(D) The professor would ask a question if other students wouldn't.

≫ Comprehension Question ≪

2 Which of the following is NOT true about the man? Choose TWO correct answers.
(A) He is taking the same class that the woman took last semester.
(B) He has taken one of the professor's classes before.
(C) He didn't get a good grade on the presentation.
(D) He thought the professor's feedback was useful.

Dictation Listen again and fill in the blanks. (S1=W / S2=M)

Student 1 I'm pretty nervous. I have to give a presentation in class today.

Student 2 Oh, don't be nervous. I'm sure you'll do fine. Anyway, everyone in our class is really nice — they won't give you a hard time or anything.

Student 1 _____ the other students — I'm worried about the professor! He's notorious for being a really tough grader on presentations.

Student 2 Well, he definitely gives a lot of feedback, but I don't think it's _____ _____. I had him last semester, and I was super nervous, too, but every comment he made was valid and helpful.

Student 1 Well, _____ should I do to get a good grade?

Student 2 Just make sure to _____ the class, speak clearly and slowly, and be ready to answer questions. He'll definitely ask you a lot of questions.

Student 1 Hmmm... I would never _____ .

Vocabulary Preview for Practice

Listen and choose the correct definition of the given words or phrases.

Practice 1
1. infection   a. ☐   b. ☐
2. eliminate   a. ☐   b. ☐
3. withstand   a. ☐   b. ☐
4. evolve   a. ☐   b. ☐

Practice 2
1. violence   a. ☐   b. ☐
2. source   a. ☐   b. ☐
3. provoke   a. ☐   b. ☐
4. debate   a. ☐   b. ☐

Practice 3
1. behavior   a. ☐   b. ☐
2. infancy   a. ☐   b. ☐
3. integrate   a. ☐   b. ☐
4. crucial   a. ☐   b. ☐

Practice 4
1. variation   a. ☐   b. ☐
2. evaporate   a. ☐   b. ☐
3. likelihood   a. ☐   b. ☐
4. irrefutable   a. ☐   b. ☐

Vocabulary Preview for Actual Test

Choose the best word to complete each sentence.

Actual Test 1

1. Ancient Egypt has always _____ me.
   a. fastened   b. furthered   c. fascinated   d. formatted

2. This kingdom is filled with wonderful _____.
   a. credibility   b. creatures   c. creed   d. claim

3. He resisted _____ to cry out.
   a. a fondness   b. a superiority c. a favor   d. an impulse

4. They are _____ only through comprehensive testing.
   a. detectable   b. blissful   c. cheerful   d. surprised

Actual Test 2

1. Thirty miles is too far to _____ to work every day.
   a. commute   b. communicate   c. commit   d. conflict

2. How is the growth _____ in that market?
   a. ceaseless   b. potential   c. apparent   d. tranquil

3. Their marriage ended because they were simply not _____.
   a. spontaneous   b. inert   c. marvelous   d. compatible

4. I notice you've been eating a lot of fruit _____.
   a. potentially   b. recent   c. pessimistically d. lately

Supporting Details 57

Practice 1   Lecture

Listen to a lecture in a biology class.

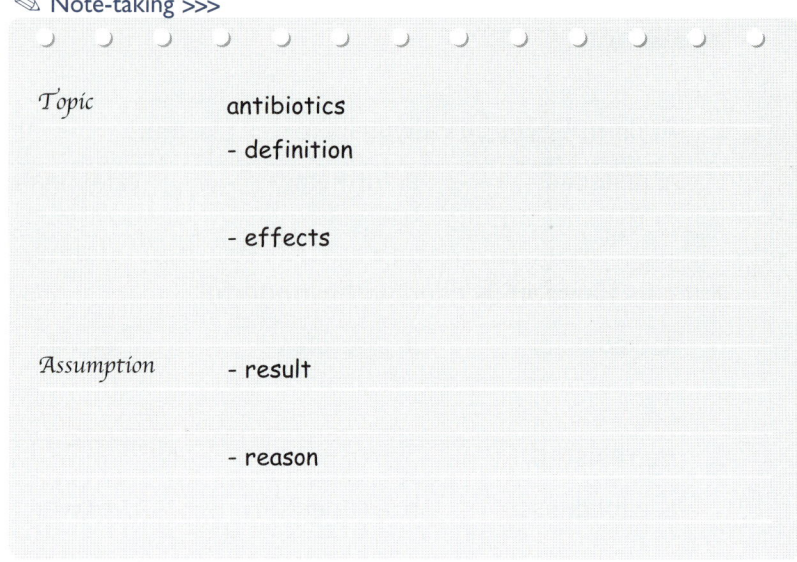

Now answer the questions.

1   How does the professor define antibiotics?

   (A) It is medicine that can slow down bacterial reproduction.
   (B) It is a treatment to kill bacteria that cause serious infections.
   (C) It is a disease prevention therapy that has lost its effectiveness.
   (D) It is a kind of medicine that few people use today.

2   According to the professor, what was the assumption of antibiotics in the 70s?

   (A) They had unexpected side effects.
   (B) They should only be used in the most serious cases.
   (C) They would get rid of infectious diseases.
   (D) They were responsible for a whole host of diseases.

3   What reason is given for people not responding to antibiotics?

   (A) Several new, untreatable diseases have recently evolved.
   (B) Bacteria have evolved to resist the effect of antibiotics.
   (C) People are no longer immune to certain infections.
   (D) Bacteria are no longer the primary cause of infection.

Practice 2

Talk in a class

Listen to a talk in a class about Futurism.

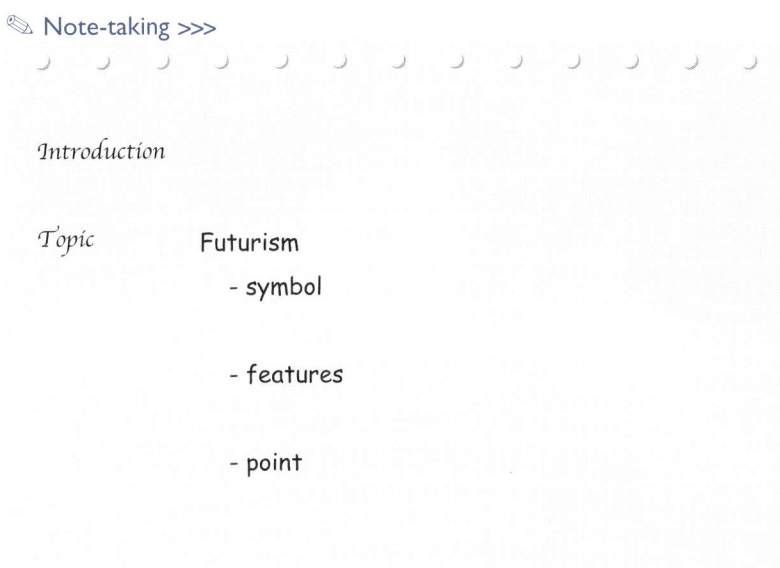

Note-taking >>>

Introduction

Topic   Futurism
- symbol
- features
- point

Now answer the questions.

1   Which of the following can be considered as a symbol of Futurism?

(A) Trees and plants
(B) Tall buildings
(C) Cars and trains
(D) Money and fame

2   Which of the following is NOT a characteristic of Futurism?

(A) Reverence for speed
(B) Mistrust of technology
(C) Glorification of war
(D) Love of machines

3   According to the professor, why did the Futurists want to provoke people?

(A) They thought that art needed to be more controversial.
(B) They didn't think people appreciated new technology.
(C) They wanted people to carefully ponder culture and its change.
(D) They were interested in attracting attention to their art.

Practice 3

Discussion

Listen to a discussion about socialization.

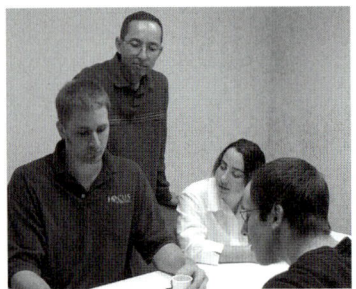

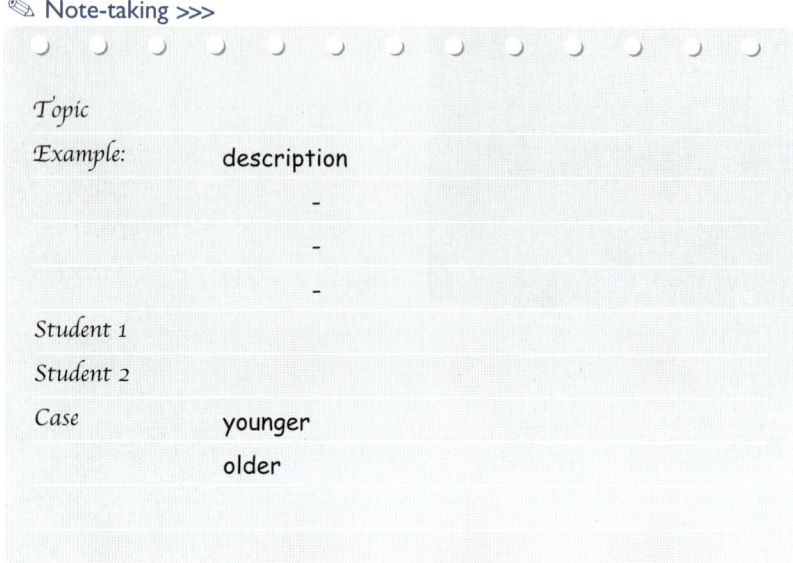

Topic
Example: description
                -
                -
                -
Student 1
Student 2
Case   younger
                older

Now answer the questions.

1 What reason is given for the difficulty of integrating the girls into society?

(A) The girls refused to live in houses.
(B) The man who found the girls was extremely cruel.
(C) Both girls acted as though they were wolves.
(D) People were afraid of the girls' strange behavior.

2 What does the man say about humans?

(A) Humans are intelligent, verbal animals who walk on two feet.
(B) Humans are capable of a wide range of speech.
(C) Humans are able to act in many different ways.
(D) Humans are animals who live in connected societies.

3 According to the professor, why would some consider the girls not human?

(A) They did not eat the same foods as others in their society.
(B) They were unable to connect to other human beings.
(C) They were unable to speak a single word.
(D) They did not want to live outside of their wolf pack.

Practice 4   Conversation

Listen to a conversation about space.

Note-taking >>>

Article   about

Meaning of water

Student 1

Student 2

Now answer the questions.

1 Why do astronomers think that the water is there year-round?

(A) The temperature do not allow for evaporation.
(B) They have taken images of it in all seasons.
(C) They are making assumptions based on Earth's conditions.
(D) The temperature variations are quite extreme.

2 According to the professor, what can the presence of water mean?

(A) Water is only one of several things needed to support life.
(B) Water is a common planetary feature, but does not prove there will be life.
(C) Water is a likely indicator that life may have existed on Mars.
(D) Life is more likely in places where there is water and carbon dioxide.

3 How do astronomers know that the ice is water and not carbon dioxide?

(A) There is no carbon dioxide on the Martian surface.
(B) Carbon dioxide would have already evaporated.
(C) The water ice looks different than carbon dioxide ice.
(D) Samples brought back from a space probe indicate it's water.

Supporting Details   61

Actual Test 1

TOEFL Listening

Listen to a lecture on body chemistry.

✎ Note-taking >>>

Today's Class   What is an emotion?

   - past explanations

   - modern scientist's thought
      eg. Darwin

* spleen 비장

Now answer the questions.

1 What is the talk mainly about?
　Ⓐ The attempt by science to influence emotional behavior
　Ⓑ The study of emotion in Darwin's *Origin of Species*
　Ⓒ The failed attempts of science to explain emotion
　Ⓓ The scientific explanation for human emotions

2 According to the lecture, what has NOT been an explanation for emotions?
　Ⓐ The influence of magical creatures
　Ⓑ The chemical activity of the body
　Ⓒ The electrical pulses in the brain
　Ⓓ The result of different organ functions

3   What does the professor say about Darwin?
  Ⓐ He was mostly interested in studying the emotions of animals.
  Ⓑ He saw similar physiology accompaniments to emotion among certain animals.
  Ⓒ He considered emotions to be a result of the human brain's structure.
  Ⓓ He thought emotions interfered in animals' abilities to survive.

4   According to the professor, how do emotions relate to survival?
  Ⓐ They help us to avoid danger or any harm.
  Ⓑ They ensure that we fall in love and get married.
  Ⓒ They enable us to respond empathetically to others.
  Ⓓ They draw us to dangerous pursuits and behaviors.

5   Which of the following is true about impulses? Choose TWO correct answers.
  Ⓐ These can change our experiences differently.
  Ⓑ These are caused with some physical changes in the body.
  Ⓒ These are not much related to the responses of the body.
  Ⓓ These can affect the nerves in the body.

Actual Test 2

TOEFL Listening

Listen to a conversation between two students.

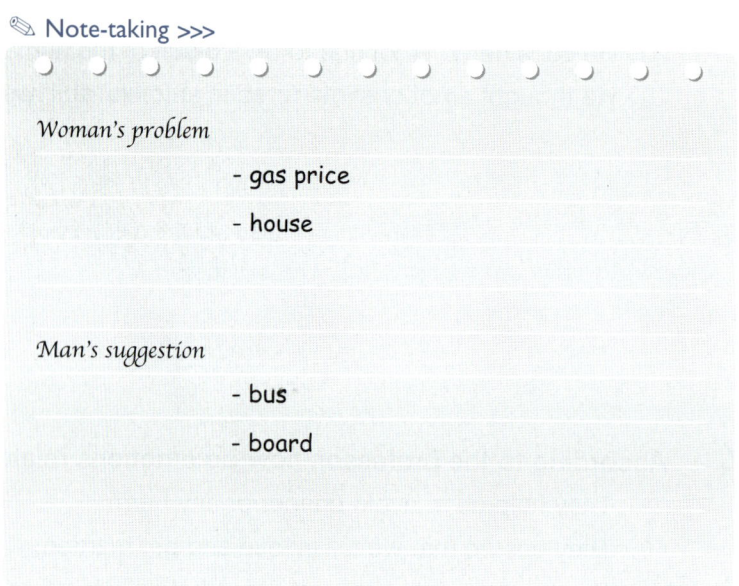

Note-taking >>>

Woman's problem
- gas price
- house

Man's suggestion
- bus
- board

Now answer the questions.

1. What does the woman want to find out?
   - Ⓐ Methods of cutting costs of car ownership
   - Ⓑ Problems with sharing housing
   - Ⓒ Moving out of one's current house
   - Ⓓ Ways to find an affordable housing near campus

2. What reason does the woman give for not taking the bus?
   - Ⓐ She is always behind schedule.
   - Ⓑ Her last class ends too late to take the bus.
   - Ⓒ She doesn't live near a bus stop.
   - Ⓓ The bus takes too long to get to campus.

3   What does the man say about the housing bulletin board?
    Ⓐ It contains recent information on housing.
    Ⓑ It is located in the housing center on campus.
    Ⓒ It is a good place to find properties for sale.
    Ⓓ Its information is better than the campus housing department's.

4   What is the woman concerned about in getting a roommate?
    Ⓐ The roommate might wake her up too early.
    Ⓑ The roommate might not let her store her bike.
    Ⓒ The roommate might make too much noise.
    Ⓓ The roommate might not clean the house.

5   How will the woman ensure that she finds a compatible roommate?
    Ⓐ She will ask friends for recommendations.
    Ⓑ She will answer an ad on the housing board.
    Ⓒ She will post her own ad on the housing board.
    Ⓓ She will move into the man's house.

DICTATION

Practice 1

🎧 **Listen and fill in the blanks.**

(P=W)

Professor We take antibiotics for granted today... in fact, we overuse them, according to some researchers. But ① _____ 75 years that we've consistently used antibiotics to battle infections of the body. Okay, so everyone knows what antibiotics are, right? — Medicines that kill the bacteria that cause infections. Now, when we first discovered these medicines in the 1930s, we were suddenly able to treat diseases that, until then, ② _____, like pneumonia, tuberculosis, ③ _____. Even a small infection could kill someone. But ④ _____, and we gained the upper hand over these bacteria. And so, by the 1970s ⑤ _____, wow, we're going to eliminate all infectious diseases from the earth! How great! However, what we've started to notice ⑥ _____ is not a reduction, or near elimination of these diseases, but an increase in people whose infections aren't responding to antibiotics. This occurs because of antibiotic resistance. Bacteria strains have evolved ⑦ _____ the effects of antibiotics and so are not slowed down by this medicine. In fact, these bacteria are able to reproduce, creating even stronger strains ⑧ _____ treatment.

|구문해설| **take ~ for granted** ~을 당연한 것으로 여기다 **gain[get, have] the upper hand** 우위를 차지하다, 제압하다 **because of +** 단어 또는 구 ~ 때문에(because +절) **even[much, still, far] +비교급 ~ than** ⋯ ⋯보다 훨씬 더 ~하다 (비교급 강조)

Practice 2

🎧 **Listen and fill in the blanks.**

(P=M / S=W)

Professor It's no secret that the 20th century was a time of rapid change in technology, transportation, communication and so on... we went from most people walking or using horses ① _____ at the beginning of the century, to ② _____ travel long distances at a faster speed, ③ _____ to the moon. Now, there are certainly some problems that have arisen because of these changes, but today I ④ _____ a group of artists from the early 20th century who really celebrated these developments — the Futurists. Can anybody tell me anything about them?

Student Well... they were ⑤ _____, the power of machines, right?

Professor Yes. The machine was a symbol... for their own energy and power. We can see speed ⑥ _____ interesting ways in their art. But they valued violence and conflict as well, as sources of energy and renewal. And these, of course, made some people angry — as violence is not a good thing. However, for the Futurists, provoking people into debating these issues was ⑦ _____. They wanted people to seriously think about culture and what made it move.

|구문해설| **not only A but (also) B** A뿐만 아니라 B도 (= B as well as A)　**look at** ~을 자세히 보다　**as well** 게다가, 또한　**more or less** 얼마간, 다소

Supporting Details 67

DICTATION

Practice 3

🎧 Listen and fill in the blanks.

(P=M / S1=W / S2=M)

Professor How important, really, is the first year of a child's life in its development? Well, ① _____ in India. Two girls, one about 2 years old and the other about 8, were found living with wolves in the wild. It was presumed the girls had been with the animals since infancy… the person who found them tried to integrate the girls into human society, but it was difficult, ② _____, and each acted ③ _____ than a human. For instance, walking on all fours.

Student 1 (*negatively*) Can we even really call them human?

Student 2 You ④ _____ speak to be human, though. And humans are capable of a wide range of strange behaviors — that doesn't make them less human.

Professor For many, ⑤ _____ is the most essential element of being human. And these girls really couldn't do that. The younger girl died within a year of ⑥ _____ the wolf pack — much as a wild animal would do. The older girl learned a few words and could walk on two legs but was never able to connect. So in body, she was human, ⑦ _____, perhaps more like a wolf. So it seems that, in some really crucial ways, we become a member of our species during that first year…

|구문해설| **take a look at** ~을 살펴보다 **one ~, the other …** 하나는 ~이고, 나머지 하나는 …이다 **be capable of +(동)명사** ~할 능력이 있다

Practice 4

🎧 Listen and fill in the blanks.

(S1=M / S2=W)

Student 1 Have you read this article? ① _____ what the professor was saying in astronomy class last week.

Student 2 What article are you talking about?

Student 1 It was in the paper this morning. It's all about how astronomers have confirmed the presence of frozen water in pretty big quantities on Mars. They are fairly certain that the water is there throughout the year 'cause there isn't enough variation in temperature on the planet ② _____ ...

Student 2 Okay... but what does ③ _____ class?

Student 1 Well... ④ _____ the relationship of water to the likelihood of finding evidence of life? Well, finding irrefutable evidence of water now makes it really just a matter of time before we find traces of living things...

Student 2 Well... maybe. I mean, ⑤ _____, like frozen carbon dioxide? There's plenty of that on Mars, too, and it looks like water ice. That wouldn't support any life we know...

Student 1 Actually, they thought of that. But the frozen CO_2 at the pole where they found the water ice is gone — it's a lot more susceptible to evaporation, you know. So they know ⑥ _____ there. Then... uh... Mars is a lot like Earth ⑦ _____ .

|구문해설| **what[how]** 주어 + 동사 ~하는 것[방법]   **enough** + 명사 + **to**부정사 ~하기에 충분한 …   **plenty of** 많은, 충분한   **look like** + 명사 ~처럼 보이다

Supporting Details 69

DICTATION

Actual Test 1

🎧 **Listen and fill in the blanks.**

(P=M)

Professor: Every day we experience different emotions, right? Happiness, sadness, even just boredom... but what exactly do they mean? I mean, what is an emotion? Well, this is a question that has ① _____ humans ever since they started to be conscious of their own consciousness. Past explanations have pointed to different organs, like the heart or the spleen, as being the source of emotion. Others have pointed to supernatural creatures like devils or angels ② _____.

So, what do modern scientists think about these impulses that ③ _____ how we experience and respond to the world? Well, something that we know is that ④ _____ _____ detectable changes in a person's nervous system and body chemistry. Darwin pointed out that many of the physiological accompaniments to emotion—adrenaline spikes, increased heartbeat, and so on—are ⑤ _____ among higher-order mammals, monkeys, dogs, humans. So for him, this meant that emotions were really practical measures taken by the body to ensure survival. Fear is very functional, in other words, in ⑥ _____ that might hurt us. Things that make us happy—family, good food, and so on—well, these are things we seek, and are good for us. So, many scientists see these impulses ⑦ _____, if at times mysterious, elements of the body.

|구문해설| **be conscious of** ~을 알다, 인지하다(=be aware of, be cognizant of) **have an impact on** ~에 영향을 미치다 **keep away (from + 명사)** (~에) 가까이 가지 않다

Actual Test 2

🎧 Listen and fill in the blanks.

(S1=W / S2=M)

Student 1 Man, gas prices are killing me lately. It's costing me a fortune to ① _____ campus…

Student 2 Why don't you take the bus? It's a lot cheaper, isn't it?

Student 1 That'd be nice, but the bus stops running at 8 and my last class doesn't end until 8:30! Well, so, I was thinking maybe I could ask you how you found your place. ② _____ move closer to campus.

Student 2 Well, have you checked out the housing board in the student center? It's got all these flyers for roommates posted on it. The board itself is continually updated. By the way, so the information is really fresh. That's how I found my place. And my rent is ③ _____ .

Student 1 Hmm… I didn't even know there was a housing board. It sure would save me a lot of time and aggravation if I could just bike to class. But ④ _____ is move into somebody's house that was always partying and making a lot of noise.

Student 2 Well, one thing you could do ⑤ _____ , saying that you're looking for a cheap, quiet room to rent. That way you could make sure that your conditions are clear.

Student 1 I guess I could interview any potential roommate, too, ⑥ _____ .

Student 2 Right. And frankly, it's nice to have a buddy to chat with at the end of the day.

Student 1 This is a pretty good idea. Wow, this could really ⑦ _____ .

|구문해설| **Why don't you + 동사 원형** ~ 하는 게 어때? **stop + 동명사** ~하는 것을 그만두다, 그만두다 (stop + to부정사: ~하기 위해 멈추다) **not A until B** B가 되어서야 비로소 A하다   **I wish + 주어 + 가정법과거 동사** ~하면 좋을 텐데, ~이기를 바란다   **If + 주어 + 과거동사 ~, 주어 would/should/could/might + 동사원형…** 만일 ~라면 …할 텐데(가정법과거)

Vocabulary Review

Write the meanings of the words in the blanks.

1. fake
2. extinct
3. contradict
4. erosion
5. scan
6. pretty
7. actually
8. harness
9. transform
10. alchemist
11. property
12. cooperate
13. potential
14. entire
15. sacrifice
16. extreme
17. financial
18. semester
19. registrar
20. inability
21. accurate
22. crucial
23. nervous
24. definitely
25. antibiotic
26. untreatable
27. eliminate
28. withstand
29. provoke
30. integrate
31. strange
32. confirm

Write the meanings of the words in the blanks.

33. participate in
34. give up
35. take care of
36. hand in
37. make sense
38. take a look at
39. can afford to
40. be capable of
41. take ~ for granted
42. get used to

Write the correct words or phrases in the blanks.

43. 정확한
44. 세부사항
45. 꾸준히
46. 변화, 변동
47. 가능성
48. 적게 하다
49. 의좋게 지낼 수 있는
50. 제적하다
51. 발표
52. 고쳐 쓰다

PROGRESS TEST

Listening Comprehension Section Directions

This section measures your ability to understand conversations and lectures in English. You will hear each conversation or lecture only one time. After each conversation or lecture, you will answer some questions about it. The questions typically ask about the main idea and supporting details. Some questions ask about a speaker's purpose or attitude. Answer the questions based on what is stated or implied by the speakers.

You may take notes while you listen. You may use your notes to help you answer the questions. Your notes will not be scored. If you need to change the volume while you listen, click on the **Volume** icon at the top of the screen. In some questions, you will see this icon: 🎧 This means that you will hear, but not see part of the question.

Some of the questions have special directions. These directions appear in a gray box on the screen. Most questions are worth one point. If a question is worth more than one point, it will have special directions that indicate how many points you can receive. You must answer each question. After you answer, click on **Next**. Then click on **OK** to confirm your answer and go on to the next question. After you click on **OK**, you cannot return to previous questions.

You will have 20 minutes to answer the questions in this section. A clock at the top of the screen will show you how much time is remaining. The clock will not count down while you are listening to test material.

Progress Test 1

TOEFL Listening

Listen to a lecture on Zora Neale Hurston. Then answer the questions.

TOEFL Listening

1 What is the lecture mainly about?
- Ⓐ Various values and aspects of African American literature in the 1930s and 40s
- Ⓑ Forgotten authors and their works that become important again
- Ⓒ Novels of African-American females that were rediscovered by other authors
- Ⓓ The impact of Hurston's writing on other contemporary writers including Walker

2 Why does the professor mention a movie star?
- Ⓐ To indicate that Hurston initially starred in African American films
- Ⓑ To illustrate that many of Hurston's stories were about Hollywood
- Ⓒ To suggest that literary fame can be as fleeting as cinematic fame
- Ⓓ To imply that women had a better chance of succeeding in movies

3 According to the professor, why do scholars rediscover some authors?
- Ⓐ They usually hope to distinguish unworthy authors from the canon of literature.
- Ⓑ They generally prefer to increase their own importance and fame
- Ⓒ They feel that great works of literature should be remembered by people.
- Ⓓ They honestly wish to promote a particular beauty of art and work.

4 What was NOT a reason for Hurston's fame, according to the lecture?
- Ⓐ She was an African-American.
- Ⓑ She was a woman.
- Ⓒ She completed graduate work.
- Ⓓ She was stylistically interesting.

5 Which of the following is recognized as Hurston's literary style?
- Ⓐ Employment of fractured narrative
- Ⓑ Cultural and Biblical features were integrated
- Ⓒ Reliance on racially diverse narrators
- Ⓓ Use of Biblical stories as devices

6 Which of the following is NOT true about Zora Neale Hurston?
- Ⓐ She was one of the first female writers.
- Ⓑ She became very famous in her later life.
- Ⓒ She was approved by many people at the time.
- Ⓓ She wasn't compensated much for her works.

Progress Test 2

TOEFL Listening

Listen to a conversation in a professor's office. Then answer the questions.

TOEFL Listening

1 Why does the student want to talk to the professor?
   (A) To complain about her grade on his last essay
   (B) To clarify and defend her main claim in the paper
   (C) To discuss the professor's comment on his essay
   (D) To disagree with the professor's comments

2 What does the man say about Jensen's theory?
   (A) It was not widely known by most scholars.
   (B) He only agreed with some of it.
   (C) He found extensive support for it.
   (D) It had some serious flaws in logic.

3 What does the professor say about the theory?
- Ⓐ It has been proved to be false in past years.
- Ⓑ It should not have been included in the essay.
- Ⓒ He thinks it is most likely the correct interpretation.
- Ⓓ It is not approved by most of scholars in the field.

4 What does the professor want the student to do?
- Ⓐ To provide more evidence to show Jensen is right
- Ⓑ To mention opinions that disagree with the theory
- Ⓒ To eliminate mention of the controversy from the paper
- Ⓓ To remove her opinion of the controversy from the paper

5 Why didn't he mention the controversy over the theory at all?
- Ⓐ Because he didn't know that he has to put it in the paper.
- Ⓑ Because he wan't sure whether the theory was widely accepted.
- Ⓒ Because he was concerned about not being clear on his point.
- Ⓓ Because he was aware of other opinions on the theory.

6 What reason does the professor give for his suggestion?
- Ⓐ It will add more length to her paper and improve her grade.
- Ⓑ It will simplify the claims that the woman is making.
- Ⓒ It will make the woman's argument more clear.
- Ⓓ It will increase the reader's trust of the writer.

DICTATION

Progress Test 1

🎧 Listen and fill in the blanks.

(P=M)

Professor An interesting phenomenon in the world of literature is that people can achieve some measure of, uh, fame... ① _____ ... and then disappear from the public's awareness almost completely. In this way it's, uh, ② _____ being a movie star or something... but sometimes, authors are "rediscovered" by scholars decades later, who feel that the author's contribution to literature ③ _____.
The scholar becomes a kind of, of a champion of the forgotten author, trying to restore his or her place in the, uh, canon, the "must-read" books in a culture.
So, this is certainly the case with Zora Neale Hurston, an African-American novelist who, uh, published a number of stories and novels... primarily in the 1930s and 40s. She achieved a fair bit of fame, not only because she was one of very few females, ④ _____ African-American females, publishing during that time, but also because she was a real stylistic innovator. She employed the, uh, rhythms, cadences, or intonation of African-American folk tales, ⑤ _____ that shaped her culture, to tell stories that had an impact on readers across racial and gender lines. At the peak of her career, she was awarded the prestigious Guggenheim fellowship, completed grad work at Columbia University, and published five books within ten years. And then, um, then her career ⑥ _____ altogether... yeah... ⑦ _____.
It wasn't really until the 1980s, when novelist Alice Walker stumbled upon Hurston's works and began to promote Hurston as an important American writer, that the contemporary literary establishment acknowledged her contribution. Since then, Hurston has been a, uh, key figure in discussions of both American and African-American literatures of the 20th century.

|구문해설| **not only A but also B** A뿐 아니라 B도   **have an impact on readers across racial and gender lines** 인종과 성별에 관계없이 독자들에게 영향을 주다   **at the peak of her career** 작가로서의 전성기에

Progress Test 2

Listen and fill in the blanks.

(S=M / P=W)

Student Good afternoon, professor, can I talk to you for a minute?

Professor Sure, come in...

Student Okay, I wanted to talk to you about the last essay.

Professor All right, go ahead...

Student Um, one thing you commented on was that Jensen's theory about the role of the miniature paintings in Indian royal life was not universally accepted, right? But I read at least three articles that talked about his theory and ① _____ .

Professor Yeah. There are many scholars out there who accept Jensen's idea that the paintings were a way to educate members of the royal court in Indian history and Hindu mythology as gospel... I didn't mean to imply that ② _____ .

Student But then are there scholars who disagree?

Professor Yes. The point that I'm trying to make, though, and this is what I don't think I was clear about, is not that I think you have to disagree with Jensen. He ③ _____ his claims, and you do too, as you defend him in your paper. But you don't mention the controversy ④ _____ .

Student Well, I thought that ⑤ _____ the strength of my claim. If I tell the reader not everyone agrees with him, maybe they won't trust me.

Professor Actually, by giving the whole picture to your reader, you're building even more trust. It shows that you respect the reader enough to ⑥ _____ . You give them the evidence for both sides, give your opinion, and let the readers decide. It's ⑦ _____ ignoring a part of the argument.

|구문해설| **cast any doubt on** ~에 대해 의심을 품다 **have some support for his claims** 그의 주장을 지지하다 **build even more trust** 더 큰 신뢰를 구축하다 **ignoring a part of the argument** 논쟁의 일부를 무시하는 것

Vocabulary Review for Progress Test

Choose the synonym of the underlined word in the sentence.

Progress Test 1

1. Oxford as a prestigious university lays claim to nine centuries of continuous existence.
   a. renowned   b. monotonous   c. benign   d. immoral

2. Some people are in favour of restoring capital punishment for murderers.
   a. reversing   b. reconvening   c. reconstituting   d. restating

3. All this month, the National Museum of European Art and Culture features works by ten important European modernists, reflecting the strength of contemporary art in Europe.
   a. contaminant   b. modern   c. stylish   d. alternate

4. Historians generally acknowledge her as a genius in her field.
   a. contain   b. admit   c. disdain   d. inspirit

Progress Test 2

1. The article should be submitted to the editor who was assigned to comment on it.
   a. remark   b. command   c. portray   d. translate

2. The Prime Minister was asked how he could defend a policy that increased unemployment.
   a. conjure   b. contemplate   c. plead   d. support

3. He is a person of integrity and is respected by everyone in his department.
   a. venerated   b. defied   c. provoked   d. subdued

4. Their marketing strategy for the product involves obtaining as much free publicity as possible.
   a. design   b. scheme   c. feud   d. reputation

Chapter 03
PROCESS / CLASSIFICATION

OVERVIEW

Process / Classification

Process는 강의나 대화에서 드러나는 단계, 절차, 시간상의 순서를, Classification은 전체 내용을 일정 기준에 따라 분류하는 것을 가리킨다. Speaker는 자신이 말하려고 하는 것을 쉽고 명확하게 설명하기 위해서 이런 방법들을 동원하게 되는데, 그렇기 때문에 이런 형식 자체가 전체 내용을 이끌어가는 중요 정보라고 볼 수 있다. 이 유형은 다음과 같은 형태로 질문한다.

Process를 물을 때

Which of the following are the steps of ~?
In what order, does the professor say about ~?
Indicate whether each of the following is a step in the process. Check the correct box for each phrase.

Classification을 물을 때

What's the difference between ~?
Which of the following can be an example of ~?
Classify the phrases below. Check the correct box for each phrase.
According to the conversation, how does A differ from B?
In the lecture, the professor is explaining two different types of ~. Fill in the table with the correct description for each item.

General Strategies

1 Process

강의나 주요 정보를 어떤 순서나 절차, 또는 연대순으로 나열한 것을 말한다. 언급할 내용을 한꺼번에 얘기한 다음 하나씩 풀어서 설명하는 경우도 있고, 하나의 절차나 순서를 언급하고 그것에 관한 구체적 설명까지 말한 다음 다시 다른 절차나 순서로 넘어가는 경우도 있다. Process는 강의나 대화의 주제와 밀접한 관련이 있다. 예를 들어 실험 과정이나 역사적 사건을 설명할 때, 또는 어떤 인물의 전기를 다룰 때 두드러진다. 절차나 순서를 따라가며 어려운 용어나 중요한 정보를 배열하고, 각각의 세부적인 설명을 메모하면서 듣도록 한다.

2 Classification

어떤 것의 특징을 특정한 기준에 따라 분류하여 비교·대조하는 것을 가리킨다. 예를 들어, 조기 유학의 좋은 점과 나쁜 점이라든가, 문학 사조의 구분 같은 것들이다. 비교의 기준(크기, 범위, 시기, 특징 등)이 무엇인지, 비교 대상(서로 다른 이론, 연구 방법, 연구 목적 등)이 무엇인지를 알고 공통점과 차이점을 파악한다. 비교하고 있는 대상에 대한 세부적인 설명을 메모하거나 비교하면서 예로 든 내용에 주목한다.

Pre Test

TOEFL Listening

Pre Test 1

Listen to a lecture on cave animals. Then answer the question.

Indicate whether each phrase below explains troglobites, troglophiles or trogloxenes. Check the correct box.

	Troglobites	Troglophiles	Trogloxenes
Can not leave the cave			
Live in the cave, but go out to feed			
Mostly at the top of the food chain			
Live either in the cave or elsewhere			

Pre Test 2

Listen to a conversation in the campus bookstore. Then answer the question.

Indicate whether each phrase below is a step in the process. Check the correct box.

	Yes	No
Place an order to the publisher		
Have the distributor to delivery the book		
Tell them how you want the book sent		
Tell them your bank account number		
Specify the book you want to order		

VOCABULARY

1. **inhabit** 거주하다　**categorize** 분류하다　**range from A to B** A에서 B까지 분포되어 있다　**classify** 분류하다　**feed on** ~을 먹고 살다　**pollen** 꽃가루
2. **out of stock** 재고가 없는　**place an order** 주문하다　**distributor** 배급업자　**take a while** 시간이 좀 걸리다

Dictation Listen and fill in the blanks.

Pre Test 1
(P=M)

Professor So... cave inhabiting animals can be categorized as troglobites, troglophiles, trogloxenes. _____, cave-inhabiting animals range from tiny microscopic organisms to huge mammals. However, not all these creatures are cave-limited species. Uh... these cave dwellers or cave limited species are called troglobites, all right? Okay... some cave animals are called troglophiles, umm, animals which _____..., but can also live outside, such as cockroaches and spiders... okay? And others are trogloxenes; they live in the caves, but _____. Bats and cave crickets are the examples. Well, people and elephants _____ cave visitors. Studies have found that the cave food chain is quite complex, but everything ultimately _____. Bats are the only creatures which regularly go outside caves to feed. They leave the cave at night to feed on insects, fruits and pollen.

Pre Test 2
(S=W / C=M)

Student Excuse me. I'm trying to find a copy of the Economics 210 textbook.
Clerk Okay, ... oh, actually, this book _____ right now.
Student Out of stock? But I need the book for class this week!
Clerk Well, this happens with popular classes sometimes... umm, well, what you can do is... contact the publisher directly.
Student Do I visit their website and _____?
Clerk Well, that's possible but it would take a few more days. If you just call them up, then, I think it can save a couple of days. Call the publisher's number, then ask for the distributor that is closest to your region, or you can leave your address and number for them to call back, but it will again _____ have the nearest distributor to call you for your order.
Student So I should just ask for the number...
Clerk Right, you call the distributor and _____ the textbooks. You will need the name of the author and the exact title of the book.
Student All right, I guess all I need to know is the number.
Clerk Oh, you will have to decide on the delivery options, either express or standard. For express, they _____.

Vocabulary Preview for Mini-Exercise

Listen and choose the correct definition of the given words or phrases.

Mini-Exercise 1

1.
   1. target   a. ☐   b. ☐
   2. publish   a. ☐   b. ☐
   3. broaden   a. ☐   b. ☐

2.
   1. abolish   a. ☐   b. ☐
   2. opponent   a. ☐   b. ☐
   3. desperate   a. ☐   b. ☐

3.
   1. reputed   a. ☐   b. ☐
   2. insanity   a. ☐   b. ☐
   3. severe   a. ☐   b. ☐

Mini-Exercise 2

1.
   1. relentless   a. ☐   b. ☐
   2. progression   a. ☐   b. ☐
   3. exclusively   a. ☐   b. ☐

2.
   1. testify   a. ☐   b. ☐
   2. identify   a. ☐   b. ☐
   3. attorney   a. ☐   b. ☐

3.
   1. astronomy   a. ☐   b. ☐
   2. massive   a. ☐   b. ☐
   3. asteroid   a. ☐   b. ☐

Mini-Exercise 1: Identifying Processes

Lecture 1 Listen to a lecture about women's magazines. Then answer the question.

Which of the following were the steps in the creation of the women's magazine industry? Check the correct box for each phrase.

	Yes	No
Women wrote to publishers demanding magazines		
More subjects that interested women were added		
A segmented women's magazine market was created		
The industry realized the market potential of ladies' journals		
More women desired highly differentiated information		

Dictation

Listen again and fill in the blanks. (P=M)

Professor Ok, everybody, so... uh, there has been a... a definite evolution of magazines targeting women, beginning with a very small number being aimed at women and arriving at the situation today, where 2 out of 3 magazines target women.

In the 18th century, at... uh... the beginning of the magazine publishing industry, there were about fifteen national publications. Had to start somewhere, right? Anyway, _____ men. However, by the end of the 18th century, the first publication aimed at women was launched. Called *the Lady's Magazine and Repository of Entertaining Knowledge*, this journal _____ _____ regarding housekeeping and other related subjects. First, women became aware that there could be magazines aimed specifically at their interests. The magazine _____ useful information and broadened subjects for a variety of women. Then they bought these magazines in droves. The magazine industry responded by creating more and more "ladies' journals" _____. Later, there appeared some magazines that provide very specialized information for women, such as fashion, cosmetics. _____ the nineteenth century, there were as many women's magazines as there were men's.

Mini-Exercise 1

Discussion 2 Listen to a discussion in an American history class. Then answer the question.

Which of the following is a step in the process of implementing Brown's raid on Harper's Ferry? Check the correct box.

	Yes	No
Made diplomatic attempts to persuade the government		
Examined other things available for fixing the situation		
Proved that he could be a good new leader of slavery		
Motivated followers in different regions to gather in one place		
Had tried to fix the situation using a system of rules of the government		

Dictation Listen again and fill in the blanks. (P=W/S=M)

Professor John Brown was an abolitionist, or an opponent of human slavery, who believed that violence was justified... _____ an absolutely horrifying situation. Thus, he _____ his infamous raid on Harper's Ferry, Virginia.

Student I thought most abolitionists believed that violence is wrong...

Professor John Brown probably _____ ... I mean he had looked for ways to resolve the situation using the law. But he _____ _____ in America and had gone on too long that change would not come soon enough. Basically, he felt the situation was too dire and desperate to work within the bounds of the law. Well, so... as the next step, he examined the options available for fixing the situation. Brown's options were: _____ ... or to use force to stop slavery now. Brown chose the latter option and planned a revolt. But how? I mean how could he verify that he could achieve his goal? Of course, he _____ , so he thought he had to motivate people, followers as a next step. So, he planned to increase the number of his followers by providing slaves with guns to overthrow their masters in Harper's Ferry, Virginia. After Harper's Ferry, other slave communities would hear the news and stage their own uprisings.

Process / Classification 87

Mini-Exercise 1

Discussion 3 Listen to a discussion about King George III. Then answer the question.

1 Which of the following is a step in the process? Check the correct box.

	Yes	No
Interpret the results based on the examination		
The body is taken out of the ground to harvest the needed DNA		
Send back the results to the lab for additional DNA testing		
Obtain possible parts of the body for samples of DNA from the dead		
Run laboratory tests to find the sample's makeup		

Dictation
Listen again and fill in the blanks.   (P=M / S=W)

Professor King George III of England _____ his reputed insanity. Yep... the guy acted like he was crazy. But what caused his madness? This has been a source of great interest to researchers.

Student Well, since he has long been dead, _____ _____, right?

Professor Posthumous DNA exams can often tell important information. The first step in determining what is wrong with a dead person is to access his or her DNA. For King George, they had to find something from his body to get a DNA sample from it. Fortunately, they found three strands of _____ _____. They sent the sample containing his DNA to a lab for testing. Researchers carefully removed King George's hairs from the wig and sent them for testing. The second step in determining _____ _____ a dead person is analyzing the results. For King George, when the tests came back, researchers found that his hair contained over 300 times the toxic level of arsenic! Finally, the researchers went through a diagnosis step to determine what was wrong with the dead person. After further investigation, the researchers discovered the powder _____ _____ wigs was triggering and making more severe a disease the king had called porphyria — the symptoms of which looked like insanity!

* porphyria 포르피린증(대사 이상 질환)

Mini-Exercise 2: Classifying Details

Lecture 1 Listen to a lecture about Pablo Picasso. Then answer the questions.

1 Indicate whether each phrase below explains Picasso's Blue Period or Rose Period. Check the correct box.

	Blue Period	Rose Period
A harlequin standing with an ape		
A portrait of a clown, his wife and child		
A skinny, pale old man hunched over a guitar		
A group of acrobatic performers		

» Comprehension Question «

2 Which of the following is true of the subjects in Picasso's Blue Period?
(A) They are often circus performers.
(B) They are often quite sad looking.
(C) They are usually wearing blue clothing.
(D) They are usually ugly and dirty.

Dictation
Listen again and fill in the blanks.   (P=W)

Professor Pablo Picasso remains one of the most influential painters of the 20th century. Part of his, uh, impact, I think, really stems from his relentless willingness to experiment and innovate, ... and so we have a number of different styles apparent in his work, each capturing a progression in his thinking about _____ , ... so for instance, _____ , when he was still in his late teens, and just out on his own in the world, we had _____ the "Blue Period." The subjects of these paintings are almost exclusively people, half-starved and depressed looking, with shades of blue highlighting the melancholy mood. His next move saw a kind of lightening up, _____ painting primarily subjects from the circus, using a warm, bright, pinkish color as the main tone. This _____ his "Rose Period."

Mini-Exercise 2

Lecture 2 Listen to a lecture in a criminal justice class. Then answer the questions.

1 Classify the phrases below. Check the correct box for each phrase.

	Simple Recognition	Evidential Identification
Footprints		
Ear shaped		
Blood splatter		
Eye glasses		

» **Comprehension Question** «

2 Which of the following would be the best identification source, according to the lecture?
(A) Eye color
(B) Hairstyle
(C) Thread from clothes
(D) Blood sample

Dictation Listen again and fill in the blanks. (P=M)

Professor There are two types of suspect identification _____ police investigations. The first type is called simple recognition. In simple recognition, a witness testifies that he or she can identify aspects of a suspect, _____. Of course, the more distinct and unchangeable the aspects are, the better. The second type of suspect identification is evidential identification. Evidential identification _____ _____ at the scene that is unique to them. Classically, this is the fingerprint, but other items such as hair or body fluids are also unique and good for identification purposes. _____, even a string off a sweater may be evidential identification. When going into court, prosecutors prefer that police have both types of identification. Evidence is sometimes rejected due to mishandling, while witnesses _____ _____ defense attorneys. Having both types of evidence makes an airtight case.

Mini-Exercise 2

Conversation 3 Listen to a conversation in an astronomy class. Then answer the questions.

1 Classify the phrases below. Check the correct box for each phrase.

	Stars	Planet
Burning gas in space		
Bounce off light		
Cold and dark		
Hot and emit heat		

» **Comprehension Question** «

2 Why are dark matter objects considered cold?
(A) Light from a star reflects off of them.
(B) They do not generate own light or significant heat.
(C) They seem larger than other heavenly bodies.
(D) They continually release nuclear reactions.

Dictation Listen again and fill in the blanks. (S1=M / S2=W)

Student 1 I don't seem to understand my astronomy class. You're a science major, can you help me?

Student 2 Sure, what's wrong?

Student 1 I need to identify some items for my homework as I find them in the sky, but _____ they are stars or "dark matter" objects.

Student 2 OK, _____ . Stars are any massive objects that have sustained a continual release of heat and light through nuclear reactions. The closest star to us, a small yellow star, is the sun. It just seems larger than the other stars _____ . Other stars are red giants and white dwarfs. _____ , dark matter objects do not generate their own light or significant heat. This is why they are called cold. Some dark matter objects include planets and asteroids. The only reason we see dark matter objects is because _____ them. Does that help?

Student 1 You bet! Thanks!

Vocabulary Preview for Practice

Listen and choose the correct definition of the given words or phrases.

Practice 1

1. trend　　　　　　a. ☐　　　b. ☐
2. obesity　　　　　a. ☐　　　b. ☐
3. responsibility　　a. ☐　　　b. ☐
4. mandate　　　　a. ☐　　　b. ☐

Practice 2

1. literary　　　　　a. ☐　　　b. ☐
2. characteristic　　a. ☐　　　b. ☐
3. preceding　　　　a. ☐　　　b. ☐
4. fragment　　　　a. ☐　　　b. ☐

Practice 3

1. class　　　　　　a. ☐　　　b. ☐
2. attribute　　　　a. ☐　　　b. ☐
3. supply　　　　　a. ☐　　　b. ☐
4. vibrate　　　　　a. ☐　　　b. ☐

Practice 4

1. undergraduate　 a. ☐　　　b. ☐
2. survey　　　　　a. ☐　　　b. ☐
3. candidate　　　 a. ☐　　　b. ☐
4. accomplish　　　a. ☐　　　b. ☐

Vocabulary Preview for Actual Test

Choose the best word to complete each sentence.

Actual Test 1

1. He tries to show what's going on outside the _____ of the mainstream art world.
   a. layer   b. class   c. boundary   d. bound

2. Print media makes it easy to _____ public opinion, and the film and radio can carry the process further.
   a. sever   b. manipulate   c. dispatch   d. transact

3. The review _____ widespread corruption in the police force.
   a. exposed   b. expired   c. exiled   d. excavated

4. As the popularity of Internet auction sites has increased, so has the number of reported cases of _____.
   a. fraud   b. drawback   c. accretion   d. advocation

Actual Test 2

1. Musicians _____ that digital technology allows music to be easily copied and sent over the Internet, robbing them of royalties.
   a. mute   b. signify   c. mourn   d. complain

2. The _____ is awarded to community programs that enhance legal education, improve legal services, or provide legal information to the public.
   a. grant   b. dogma   c. appliance   d. caption

3. I have _____ a book fair for twenty years, which makes me meet the requirement for this job.
   a. appeased   b. availed   c. organized   d. sojourned

4. Leaders from both countries had a meeting to discuss the _____ peace plan.
   a. conformed   b. proposed   c. alleged   d. bestowed

Process / Classification

Practice 1

Lecture

Listen to a lecture in a nutrition class.

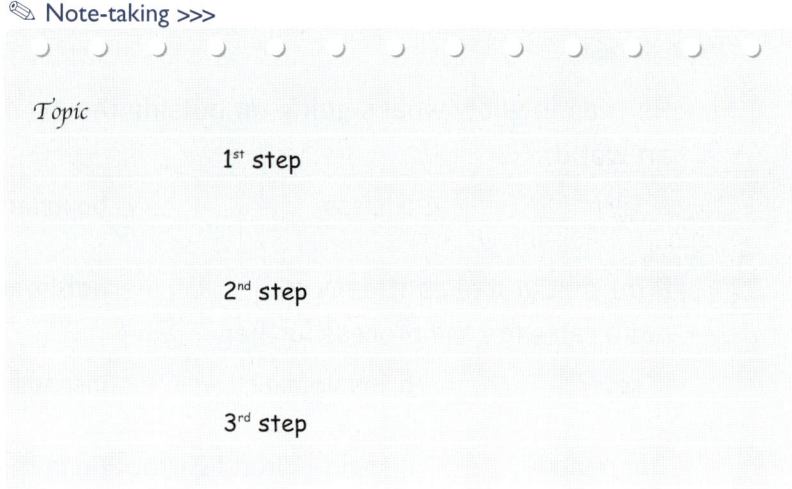

Note-taking >>>

Topic

1st step

2nd step

3rd step

Now answer the questions.

1 What is the lecture mainly about?

(A) Results of marketing strategies in the 1970s
(B) Noticeable effects of convenience and speed
(C) Steps to create a healthier country
(D) Importance of personal responsibility

2 According to the lecture, which of the following are true? Choose TWO correct answers.

(A) Americans weigh more now than 35 years ago.
(B) Healthier life choices make people healthier.
(C) Portion sizes increase as people grew used to them.
(D) People eat 3 times as much as they should, today.

3 Which of the following are steps in restoring America's health? Check the correct box.

	Yes	No
Have people exercise more, avoiding easiness and comfort		
Encourage people to be involved in a healthier life style		
Persuade people to visit a health care on a regular basis		
Promote national campaigns for healthier lives		
Change people's perspectives toward what they consume		

Practice 2

Talk in a class

Listen to a talk in a literature class.

Note-taking >>>

Topic

- modernism:

- postmodernism:

Now answer the questions.

1   What is the talk mainly about?

(A) The near indistinguishability of postmodernism from modernism
(B) The superiority of modernist writing to postmodernist writing
(C) A comparison between two major forms of 20th century writing
(D) An overview of writing styles from ancient to modern times

2   Which of the following is true about the two literary movements?

(A) They share many of the same characteristics.
(B) One is very traditional while the other breaks from tradition.
(C) The differences between them are not always obvious.
(D) Neither should properly be considered a 20th century movement.

3   Classify the phrases below. Check the correct box for each phrase.

	Modernism	Postmodernism
Search for universal truth		
Rejection of tradition		
Fragmentation of viewpoints		
Embracing multiple perspectives		

Process / Classification

Practice 3

Lecture

Listen to a lecture in a musicology class.

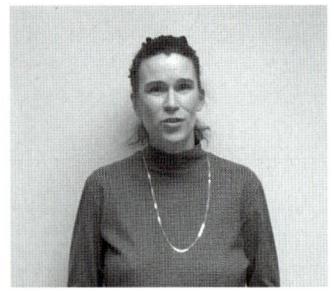

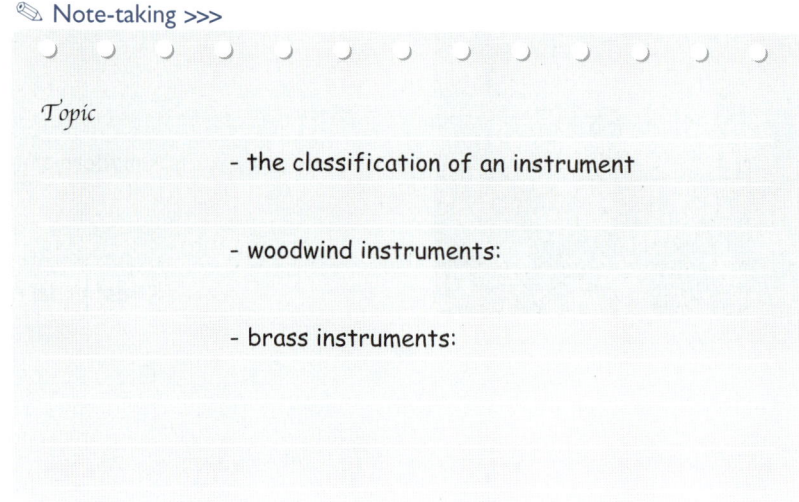

Note-taking >>>

Topic

- the classification of an instrument

- woodwind instruments:

- brass instruments:

* reed 리드(악기의 혀)

Now answer the questions.

1 Check the correct box.

	Woodwind	Brass
Players make vibration using their lips		
Players use reeds or the design to provide vibration		
A wood instrument that doesn't have a reed to make sound		
Usually made of a metal made from copper and zinc		

2 Which of the following is NOT true about woodwind instruments? Choose TWO correct answers.

(A) They were originally made from wood products.
(B) The reed is made from wood or similar products.
(C) They have a sound that reminds people of trees.
(D) Some of wood instruments are classified as brass.

3 Which of the following is NOT an explanation of brass instruments? Choose TWO correct answers.

(A) They should not be classified by how the sound is made.
(B) The sound come from the player buzzing their lips.
(C) Most of them are made of a yellow-coloured metal.
(D) A part of the instrument touching the mouth is a reed.

Practice 4

Conversation

Listen to a conversation between two students.

✎ Note-taking >>>

Topic

1st step:

2nd step:

3rd step:

Now answer the questions.

1 Why does the man go to see the woman?

(A) To complain about few hours of professors' lecture.
(B) To find out the way to run for student senate
(C) To ask the reason of being student senate
(D) To ask what student senate can do and have to do

2 Which of the following is a step in the process of running for student senate? Check the correct box.

	Yes	No
Have many people support the candidacy		
Ask what other people are most frustrated about		
Various promotional activities on campus		
Motivate students to vote for the candidate with the best idea		

3 Which of the following are true? Choose TWO correct answers.

(A) Running for office guarantees winning the election.
(B) Ads in the paper are useful in a campaign.
(C) The president always listens to senators.
(D) 200 or more signatures are needed to campaign.

Actual Test 1

Listen to a lecture in an art history class.

Note-taking >>>

Today's Class photography

- documentary
- artistic
- spiritual

Now answer the questions.

1. What is the lecture mainly about?
   - Ⓐ The artistic achievements of photographers
   - Ⓑ The methods used by nature photographers
   - Ⓒ Photo proof of the existence of ghosts
   - Ⓓ Different uses of photography in the 19th century

2. Why does the professor mention historical museums?
   - Ⓐ To indicate where most spirit photographs can be found
   - Ⓑ To tell the students why they should do more research
   - Ⓒ To give an example of documentary uses of photography
   - Ⓓ To compare them with photography used in other types of museums

3 Indicate whether each phrase below explains documentary, artistic and spirit photography. Check the correct box.

	Documentary	Artistic	Spiritual
Control film to create supernatural images			
Try to take photos to make creative images			
Leave the shutter open for more exposure time			
Take photos of images for preservation purpose			

4 What is NOT a way to create a spirit photograph, according to the lecture?
- Ⓐ Have the person in the photo move
- Ⓑ Allow light to enter the camera chamber
- Ⓒ Place one image on top of another while developing
- Ⓓ Take photos during the full moon

5 According to the professor, why was spirit photography so popular?
- Ⓐ People didn't understand photos could be manipulated.
- Ⓑ People wanted to believe in the existence of spirits.
- Ⓒ People thought cameras had magical powers.
- Ⓓ People considered the photos as a kind of art.

Actual Test 2

TOEFL Listening

Listen to a conversation between a professor and a student.

Note-taking >>>

Student's problem
- about the meeting

Professor's suggestion
- planning the meeting
- deciding the issues
- focusing

Now answer the questions.

1. Why does the man go to see the professor?
   A. To ask about issues to discuss in the meeting
   B. To get advice on the problem with his monthly meeting
   C. To express his appreciation for the comments
   D. To complain how wasteful the meeting is

2. Which of the following is true about the meeting?
   A. Most members are from the same department.
   B. The meeting is held on weekly basis on campus.
   C. Campus issues are discussed in the meeting.
   D. The meeting has been held for many years.

3 Which of the following is a step in the process? Check the correct box.

	Yes	No
Prepare issues that you want to discuss in the meeting		
Clearly understand and share what the problems are		
Decide the most serious problem out of many		
Focus only on defining the issue or the problem		

4 What does the student say about the meeting?
- Ⓐ There aren't many results after the meeting.
- Ⓑ The meeting takes more time than he thought.
- Ⓒ The meeting is held unnecessarily too often.
- Ⓓ The meeting requires much preparation time.

5 Why does she say this: 🎧
- Ⓐ To advise the issues that should be discussed.
- Ⓑ To ask what they are discussing in the meeting.
- Ⓒ To show how to decide on a topic for the meeting.
- Ⓓ To determine which issue the man wants to discuss.

DICTATION

Practice 1

🎧 Listen and fill in the blanks.

(P=M)

Professor Over the past thirty-five years, the average person in the United States ① _____ . Obesity is ② _____ . How can America correct the trend and become a healthier nation? It was claimed that the attitudes towards food, ③ _____ , should be changed. Back in the 1970s, a marketing strategy in the food industry convinced people that large portions are a good value. The new attitude that must be created is that healthier food in proper portions is a better value. Therefore, ④ _____ for a healthier nation is... to reorient people to fitness instead of convenience. Most U.S. citizens believe that convenience and speed are the keys to a better life, but in reality, such convenience often makes people not have much energy or enthusiasm and ⑤ _____ . After that, a third step in creating a healthier nation is to teach them by repeating the importance of personal responsibility ⑥ _____ . Instead of looking to the government, doctors or corporations to fix the trend, each individual American must look to their own life's issues. If each American starts ⑦ _____ , business and culture will respond to that trend. But if the government attempts to mandate health, the reactionary, negative choices of the people to the government's pressure can easily cause the U.S. ⑧ _____ it currently occupies, which leads its citizens toward ever increasing weight gains.

|구문해설| **a key to** ~에 대한 주요 요소 **be fixed in one's mind** 마음속에 각인시키다 **in a rut** 틀(판)에 박힌

102　TOEFLing Listening Level 3

Practice 2

🎧 Listen and fill in the blanks.

(P=W / S=M)

Professor Okay, so we're going to look at both modernist and postmodernist writing this term ① _____ understanding the two biggest literary movements of the 20th century.

Student They sound so similar — is there really a big difference between them?

Professor Well, lines ② _____. However, there are some characteristics that should signal to you what is modernist, and what is postmodernist. Modernist novels, modernism in general, ③ _____ _____ the handed down forms of the past. The modernists reject tradition, recent tradition anyway, and ④ _____ _____ of, say form and content. Some modernists turned to the ancient world or other cultures to find meaning. Others sought to look at contemporary culture ⑤ _____. The belief in a truth, though, is crucial here. This idea of truth, and hence the major point of the preceding literary movement, is something completely rejected by post-modernists. Thus, postmodernist novels are often fragmented, with many different perspectives and voices. The narrative ⑥ _____. This is because postmodernists think ⑦ _____ _____, and that our perspectives are often the result of our times, not any universal truth.

|구문해설| **tend to** ~하는 경향이 있다   **as a means of** + (동)명사 ~에 대한 수단으로서   **break down** ~을 파기하다

DICTATION

Practice 3

🎧 Listen and fill in the blanks.

(P=W)

Professor: As most of you know, there are hundreds of different musical instruments, ① _____. Each of these instruments is part of a class or family of instruments. With some simple examination, ② _____ the classification of an instrument.

Okay, woodwind instruments, well, ③ _____ many different types of materials, share the common attribute that a player must supply air movement through the instrument and the air movement causes the instrument to provide the vibration necessary for sound. Most woodwinds use reeds to provide vibration, but a few, such as flutes, ④ _____.

In contrast, brass instruments require the player to provide air movement and to provide the needed vibrations. In brass instruments, like trumpets, the vibrations ⑤ _____ into the mouthpiece of the instrument. Well, the view of most scholars is that the term brass instrument should be defined by the way the sound is made, ⑥ _____, and not by whether the instrument is actually made of brass. Thus, as exceptional cases one finds brass instruments made of wood, like the cornet, and woodwind instruments ⑦ _____, like the saxophone.

|구문해설| **rely on** ~에 의존하다   **in contrast** 이와는 대조적으로   **as exceptional case** 예외의 경우로

Practice 4

🎧 Listen and fill in the blanks.

(S1=M / S2=W)

Student 1 You know, ① _____ the way undergraduates are ignored at this university. Most of our classes are taught by grad students — professors make very little time to see us... I really wish I could change this. I heard you ran for student senate... I really want to know ② _____ ...

Student 2 Well, the university president attends meetings to get a sense of what's on students' minds. So, that might work... umm... I guess the first thing you should do ③ _____ . You know, if they are frustrated by the issue...

Student 1 Well, how do I do that?

Student 2 You can uh, do a survey, I guess. And if you're convinced that there are enough people who think there should be something done, then, the next step is ④ _____ . At our school you need to get two hundred signatures from current students supporting your candidacy and turn them in to the student senate office.

Student 1 Wow, ⑤ _____ .

Student 2 Yes, it is. Well, that's not the end of it. ⑥ _____ is to launch your campaign. You'll want to make posters, flyers, and maybe put an advertisement in the paper. You might want to participate in a couple of debates on campus, so people know ⑦ _____ and what you want to accomplish. If everything goes smoothly, then you may even be elected to the senate!

|구문해설| **be sick of** ~에 대해 질리다   **run for** ~에 출마하다   **get a sense of** ~에 대해 이해하다   **turn in** ~을 제출하다   **put an advertisement** 광고를 게재하다

Process / Classification 105

DICTATION

Actual Test 1

🎧 Listen and fill in the blanks.

(P=M)

Professor So, since 1836 when the first photographic image was taken, there have been ① _____ for photography. Some of it has been documentary — the preservation of images of people and places that ② _____. We see this type of photography often in history books, archives, or historical museums.

Another use of photography ③ _____. Artists like Man Ray or Alfred Steiglitz used the camera to create beautiful and unusual images, pushing the boundaries of the medium. And then, ④ _____ photography that I'll call "spirit photography." Essentially, because of the "real" nature of the camera and film, people would be convinced that a photographic image was showing them a picture of reality. Most people didn't realize, ⑤ _____, how easy it was to manipulate film and negatives. Double exposures, light leaks in the cameras, and having a subject move during the time the shutter was open to create a ghostly image were common methods of "capturing" the spirit on film. So, when the ghostly image of a person ⑥ _____ another image, people really believed they were seeing evidence of the spirit world! Though popular and convincing for many years, by the beginning of the 20th century, spirit photography ⑦ _____.

| 구문해설 | **how easy it was to manipulate film and negatives** 간접 의문문의 어순 (의문사+주어+동사)

Actual Test 2

🎧 Listen and fill in the blanks.

(S=M / P=W)

Student Oh, Dr. Smith. I wanted to say thank you for your kind comments on my last history paper. Well, also I came to ask you for another thing...

Professor Go ahead, what is the matter?

Student Nothing serious, actually, just, there is this meeting that students from all the different disciplines meet ① _____ different issues on campus. But the thing is that ② _____ something... and ③ _____ this meeting. I mean I just feel like we're wasting our time.

Professor Hmm... one of the possible reasons I can suspect is poor organization, or planning of the meeting. Many times you wouldn't know where you are going ④ _____ . The first thing you should do is to decide the issues that you guys want to discuss. That helps you to set your goal of the meeting. Are we here ⑤ _____ ? Or to discuss library policies? All right? Then, clearly define what the issue is, or the problem is, there could be several problems, but the more important thing is that you focus only on defining the issue or the problem. ⑥ _____ other issues or any details. Once you found out what the problem is, then, now you are ready to ⑦ _____ , which is proposing solutions. Now, it is important to have all the members add possible ideas. You might be thinking that ⑧ _____ , but don't worry, after several ideas added, you all know which of those are good or bad... you will see what I mean...

|구문해설| **end up** ~으로 끝나다, ~에 그치다   **feel like** ~같은 생각이 들다   **set one's goal** ~의 목표를 세우다   **move on the next step** 다음 단계로 넘어가다

Process / Classification 107

Vocabulary Test

Write the meanings of the words in the blanks.

1. target _____
2. broaden _____
3. opponent _____
4. desperate _____
5. progression _____
6. exclusively _____
7. uprising _____
8. insanity _____
9. investigation _____
10. melancholy _____
11. starve _____
12. suspect _____
13. testify _____
14. recognition _____
15. prosecutor _____
16. attorney _____
17. mishandle _____
18. evidential _____
19. astronomy _____
20. massive _____
21. sustain _____
22. dwarf _____
23. asteroid _____
24. mandate _____
25. literary _____
26. clear-cut _____
27. hence _____
28. narrative _____
29. determine _____
30. candidate _____
31. fraud _____
32. manipulate _____
33. genre _____

Write the meanings of the phrases in the blanks.

34. be fixed in one's mind _____
35. in a rut _____
36. get a sense of _____
37. as a means of _____
38. put an advertisement _____
39. run for _____
40. move on the next step _____
41. end up _____

Write the correct words or phrases in the blanks.

42. ~같은 생각이 들다 _____
43. 파기하다 _____
44. 목표를 세우다 _____
45. ~에 대한 주요 요소 _____
46. A에서 B까지 분포되어 있다 _____
47. ~을 담당하고 있는 _____
48. 재고가 없는 _____
49. 물질 _____
50. 폐지하다 _____
51. 가차 없는 _____

Chapter 04
ORGANIZATION

OVERVIEW

Organization

Speaker는 자신이 말하고자 하는 내용을 가장 효과적으로 전달하기 위한 방법으로 배경 설명, 비교, 예시, 이유 등을 제시하여 강의를 준비하게 되는데, 이를 Organization(강의나 이야기가 진행되는 구조)이라고 한다. 중심 주제와 그에 대한 설명이 어떤 관계로 어떻게 배열되고 있는지, Speaker가 그와 같은 구조를 사용하는 이유가 무엇인지를 파악하는 것이 목적이다.

Question Types

How does the professor explain ~?
How does the professor clarify his/her point about ~?
How does the man develop the topic?
Why does the woman say about ~?
Why does the professor mention ~?

General Strategies

1 Organization

이야기의 구조를 파악하기 위해서는 먼저 중심 주제를 인지하여야 한다. 그리고 Speaker가 그것을 뒷받침하기 위해 어떤 설명 구조를 사용하고 있는지를 살펴 본다. Speaker가 다음과 같은 방식으로 자신의 의견을 Supporting 한다.

- By giving examples
- By comparing & contrasting or classifying
- By showing sequence or process
- By showing cause & effect
- By providing evidence or possible explanation
- By defining or describing characteristics

2 Rhetorical Connection

Speaker가 어떤 정보를 주는 이유가 무엇인지를 염두에 두고 듣는다. 전체 내용과 어떤 식으로 연결되어 있는지는 다음 사항들을 인식함으로써 보다 쉽게 이해할 수 있다.

- To change the topic
- To give an example of ~
- To explain or describe
- To support the speaker's point
- To suggest
- To introduce or conclude

Pre Test

TOEFL Listening

Pre Test 1

Listen to a lecture in a genetics class. Then answer the question.

How does the professor emphasize the problem of decreased immunity?

- Ⓐ By explaining the relative ineffectiveness of the vaccines
- Ⓑ By giving background information on vaccine research
- Ⓒ By comparing the infection rates before and after 1963
- Ⓓ By providing an example of the complications caused by measles

Pre Test 2

Listen to a conversation in the campus health center. Then answer the question.

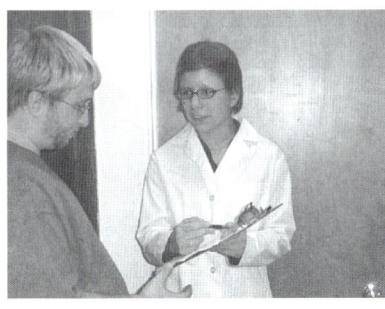

Why does the doctor tell the student the consequence of not getting much rest?

- Ⓐ To emphasize the importance of immediate rest
- Ⓑ To encourage the man to get some rest after school
- Ⓒ To compare the man's illness to a more familiar one
- Ⓓ To suggest to the man that he drop his classes

VOCABULARY
1. reduction 감소   measles 홍역   outbreak (전쟁, 유행병 등의) 발발, 창궐   at fist glance 처음에 언뜻 보기에   susceptible ~하기 쉬운   contract (병에) 걸리다   unimmunized 면역성을 받지 못한   administer (약을) 투여하다
2. vital sign 생명징후(맥박 수, 호흡, 혈압, 체온 등)   prescribe 처방하다   show up 출석하다   wind up in the hospital 병원에 입원하다   make up 보충하다

Organization 111

Dictation Listen and fill in the blanks.

Pre Test 1 (P=W)

Professor Over the past three decades, _____ in the number of measles outbreaks. Obviously this is primarily because of the modern widespread use of measles vaccines. "Good news" _____. Well, it, uh, it seems so at first glance. However, then we've got these recent studies that show something interesting about the inheritance and immunity of measles. We've discovered that the moms who, _____ this disease are more likely to have kids who are naturally susceptible to contracting measles. In other words, their natural immunity _____ _____. Based on the, uh, the study, what we've seen is that almost 33 percent of unimmunized babies born after 1963, when the vaccines were first regularly administered, were infected with measles. This figure stands _____ the only 12 percent of unimmunized babies born to older moms who hadn't been vaccinated. So this is a pretty interesting consequence of vaccination programs...

Pre Test 2 (S=M/ D=W)

Student I feel terrible, doctor. My head aches, my whole body is sore, and _____ _____. Is there something you can give me to make me feel better?

Doctor Well, by looking at your symptoms and taking your vital signs, it seems the reason for your feeling this way is _____. All I can tell you is that you should get a lot of rest, and make sure you drink a lot of liquids until you get well.

Student But I can't rest. I've got two exams this week and a presentation in my class. My professors _____!

Doctor Well, if you don't go home and get into bed for the next few days, you're going to _____. You'll wind up in the hospital. Your body needs a break, so it can get better. I'll write a note to your professors _____. And I'm sure, really, that they'll understand. After all, if you go to class, you'll get them sick!

Vocabulary Preview for Mini-Exercise

Listen and choose the correct definition of the given words or phrases.

Mini-Exercise 1

1.
   1. more or less a. ☐ b. ☐
   2. ground a. ☐ b. ☐
   3. conference a. ☐ b. ☐

2.
   1. linguistics a. ☐ b. ☐
   2. convince a. ☐ b. ☐
   3. thesis a. ☐ b. ☐

3.
   1. journey a. ☐ b. ☐
   2. resurrection a. ☐ b. ☐
   3. labyrinth a. ☐ b. ☐

Mini-Exercise 2

1.
   1. invasive a. ☐ b. ☐
   2. havoc a. ☐ b. ☐
   3. livelihood a. ☐ b. ☐

2.
   1. outlaw a. ☐ b. ☐
   2. hesitant a. ☐ b. ☐
   3. come up with a. ☐ b. ☐

3.
   1. exceptional a. ☐ b. ☐
   2. testimonial a. ☐ b. ☐
   3. average a. ☐ b. ☐

Mini-Exercise 1 Organization

Discussion 1 Listen to a discussion in a women's history class. Then answer the questions.

1 How does the professor explain the first ladies' public role?
(A) By giving brief biographical accounts of previous first ladies work in social issues
(B) By comparing Eleanor Roosevelt's interest in feminism to subsequent interests of others
(C) By indicating the first lady who initiated the public role that previous first ladies didn't
(D) By providing an example of Eleanor Roosevelt's work in civil rights for African Americans

» **Comprehension Question** «

2 Why did Eleanor Roosevelt open her press conferences to women only?
(A) To promote the cause of women's rights
(B) To highlight the role of women in journalism
(C) To show that women are adept at reporting
(D) To defy her husband's notion of the role of women

Dictation Listen again and fill in the blanks. (P=W / S=M)

Professor Okay, so let's think about _____. What is it that they do?

Student Well, it seems like the first lady always champions some kind of social issue... health care, literacy or something like that...

Professor Right. But this wasn't always the case. In fact, it was really Eleanor Roosevelt, Teddy Roosevelt's wife, who _____ presidents' wives to have a public role. Before that, first ladies were _____. She turned her focus onto a variety of different issues that affected the people of this country. One of her main interests was _____ in this country... What's an example of this? Well, how about the fact that she would hold weekly press conferences, _____? This resulted in many American newspapers hiring their initial female reporters, so that they _____ the White House.

Mini-Exercise 1

Conversation 2 Listen to a conversation between a student and a teaching assistant. Then answer the questions.

1 How does the woman advise the man to improve his application?
(A) By giving more personal information about his interests and accomplishments
(B) By providing examples of the points that will make the application better
(C) By including a comparison of his own work to that of his professors
(D) By showing him how to better organize the information he has included

» Comprehension Question «

2 What does the woman say about including the student's intention to study there?
(A) It is not something that should be included.
(B) It is okay that it is included in the application but not necessary.
(C) It is something that is required to include.
(D) It is one of the essential pieces of information to write about.

Dictation Listen again and fill in the blanks. (S=M / TA=W)

Student Hi, I'm trying to _____ to help me fund a linguistics research trip to Lithuania next fall... I'm just not really sure it's any good. I've written down what I intend to do, but I really _____.

TA Well, I think that kinda stuff is important to _____, but on the other hand, grants are competitive. _____. So have you talked about why your project, in particular, _____ another student's?

Student Um, not really, no... How do I convince the department of that?

TA Why not talk about how your project is different from anything any of the other students are doing, for example? Or how the research will really benefit, not just your thesis, but also _____ in the near future.

Mini-Exercise 1

Discussion 3 Listen to a discussion in a world history class. Then answer the questions.

1 How does the professor explain the labyrinth at Chartres?
(A) By providing the most common religious activity of people whenever they visit
(B) By comparing its complication of the structure to that of a labyrinth in Jerusalem
(C) By providing the basic definition, and the extended definition of its symbolic significance
(D) By showing the details of its construction as a reason for being a central belief in Christianity

» Comprehension Question «

2 What did the labyrinth symbolize to the early Christians? Choose TWO answers.
(A) The pilgrimage to Chartres
(B) The journey in life
(C) The resurrection of Jesus
(D) The notion of rebirth

Dictation Listen again and fill in the blanks. (P=W / S1=W / S2=M)

Professor What is a pilgrimage, anyway?
Student 1 It's a religious journey of some kind, isn't it?
Student 2 Yeah, like when pilgrims go to _____?
Professor Right. For European Christians during the Middle Ages, Jerusalem was _____, but most people couldn't go that far, so they'd go to closer places, like France's Chartres Cathedral. There was a labyrinth that _____ paths or passages, with a single path leading to the center. It was just 260 meters, but that's not the point. The pilgrims who came to Chartres _____ in two ways. Essentially for them, the labyrinth's path to the center was the path of our long, hard lives — from birth to death. As the pilgrim then _____, the journey symbolizes personal resurrection — you know, _____, so to speak, which is a central belief of the Christian religion.

* labyrinth 미로, 미궁

116 TOEFLing Listening Level 3

Mini-Exercise 2 Rhetorical Connection

Lecture 1 Listen to a lecture in an environmental studies class. Then answer the questions.

1 Why does the professor tell the students about the release of nutria in Louisiana?
(A) To describe the appearance and behavior of the animal
(B) To give background information on invasive species' native habitat
(C) To demonstrate how invasive species can cause problems
(D) To contrast the nutria to different types of invasive species

» Comprehension Question «

2 What does the professor say about the method used to reduce the population of nutria?
(A) It was used for the first time on invasive species.
(B) It is a short term solution that wouldn't work in the long term.
(C) It might not work for all invasive species.
(D) It is an ideal solution for all invasive species.

Dictation Listen again and fill in the blanks. (P=M)

Professor: Invasive species are a, uh, a major problem globally. Uh, what do I mean by invasive species, anyway? Plants and animals that wind up in a place where they aren't originally from, and then _____ the environment, throwing things out of balance...

You guys know what nutria is, right? Well, it's a furry rodent. And, in the 1930s, a bunch of these nutrias _____ the marshlands of Louisiana. Good for the nutria, maybe, but bad for the marshes. _____ a lot of the native plants as well as the surrounding sugar cane fields, so _____ as well as the livelihood of the farmers. However, by using nutria fur in coats and hats, people have been keeping the population down. But, _____ all invasive species problems.

* nutria (동물) (남미산) 누트리아

Mini-Exercise 2

Discussion 2 Listen to a discussion about puppetry in a political science class. Then answer the questions.

1 Why does the professor explain the times and places where free expression was prohibited?
(A) To provide background for the puppetry used to make a political statement
(B) To give a possible explanation for the creation of puppets
(C) To contrast the methods of criticism in the past to those of modern times
(D) To show how puppetry got popular in those times and places

≫ Comprehension Question ≪

2 According to the professor, what is Punch?
(A) A famous character in 17th century puppet shows
(B) A famous puppeteer
(C) A name of famous puppet show
(D) Another name for puppet

Dictation
Listen again and fill in the blanks. (P=M / S=W)

Professor In times and places where _____, people may be hesitant to speak freely because of fear of their government, or those in power. Well, so, people come up with some pretty creative ways of _____. Most common ways we can think of _____, cartoons, and so on. Now, one of the unique methods _____. You know what a puppet is, right? A doll that you can move, either by pulling strings... or by putting your hand inside its body and moving your fingers. Alright, the history of puppetry, in fact, is really _____.

Student Well, because it's a lot easier for a puppet to make a political statement than a person? It seems less dangerous to those in power, maybe?

Professor Exactly. Let's, uh, let's look at Punch, a puppet character who was the star of many puppet shows in both England and France starting in the 17th century.

Mini-Exercise 2

Lecture 3 Listen to a lecture in a marketing class. Then answer the questions.

1 How does the professor introduce her lecture on testimonials?
(A) By describing a recent ad campaign by a soap producer
(B) By giving an example of the first use of testimonials
(C) By providing a hypothetical scenario about a new product
(D) By indicating the students consult the case study in their books

≫Comprehension Question≪

2 Why does the professor say people might not like your new soap?
(A) Because they will assume that its quality is poor.
(B) Because they don't know anything about it.
(C) Because they would think it's too expensive.
(D) Because they might feel that it's unsafe to use.

Dictation Listen again and fill in the blanks. (P=W)

Professor Okay. You've got a product that _____, um, say this new soap. You know that it's exceptional soap. It's really gonna change people's perceptions about _____. But, uh, well nobody's heard of it. If they see it on the shelves at the store, and nobody's told them about it, chances are _____ their own soap. This is where advertising comes in—how to convince people to buy a certain product. A really effective way to do this is _____. A famous person people know and trust, or even just _____ that people can relate to. If you include these kinds of people talking about _____, your customers are going to be much more likely to trust the product and therefore, buy it.

Vocabulary Preview for Practice

Listen and choose the correct definition of the given words or phrases.

Practice 1

1. competition   a. ☐   b. ☐
2. benefit   a. ☐   b. ☐
3. bias   a. ☐   b. ☐
4. gender   a. ☐   b. ☐

Practice 2

1. conflict   a. ☐   b. ☐
2. tactic   a. ☐   b. ☐
3. impartial   a. ☐   b. ☐
4. consensus   a. ☐   b. ☐

Practice 3

1. frustrated   a. ☐   b. ☐
2. petition   a. ☐   b. ☐
3. signature   a. ☐   b. ☐
4. submit   a. ☐   b. ☐

Practice 4

1. represent   a. ☐   b. ☐
2. metabolism   a. ☐   b. ☐
3. measurement   a. ☐   b. ☐
4. restrict   a. ☐   b. ☐

Vocabulary Preview for Actual Test

Choose the best word to complete each sentence.

Actual Test 1

1. The major concerns of most teachers in education today is how to improve student _____.
   a. arrangement   b. discipline   c. differentiation   d. diffidence

2. The _____ value of this new method of analysis has still to be proven.
   a. privileged   b. preventive   c. precautious   d. predictive

3. Brad's _____ and easygoing demeanor make him an ideal candidate for the position.
   a. expectancy   b. expertise   c. explanation   d. expiration

4. When doctors treat patients, they have to explain a broad range of _____ facts, such as current symptoms, necessity of the operation or treatment, and expectations for recovery.
   a. diagnosis   b. diabetic   c. diagnostic   d. dexterous

Actual Test 2

1. The new law should allow more disabled people to enter the _____ of American life.
   a. mainstream   b. age   c. maintenance   d. attitude

2. They hope to _____ the Asian movie market within three years.
   a. denote   b. dedicate   c. contribute   d. dominate

3. He deserves the prize due to his constant _____.
   a. recovery   b. rehabilitation   c. activation   d. innovation

4. The actor remains confident and _____ untroubled by his recent problems.
   a. more often   b. seemingly   c. other than   d. permanently

Practice 1

Discussion

Listen to a discussion in an economics class.

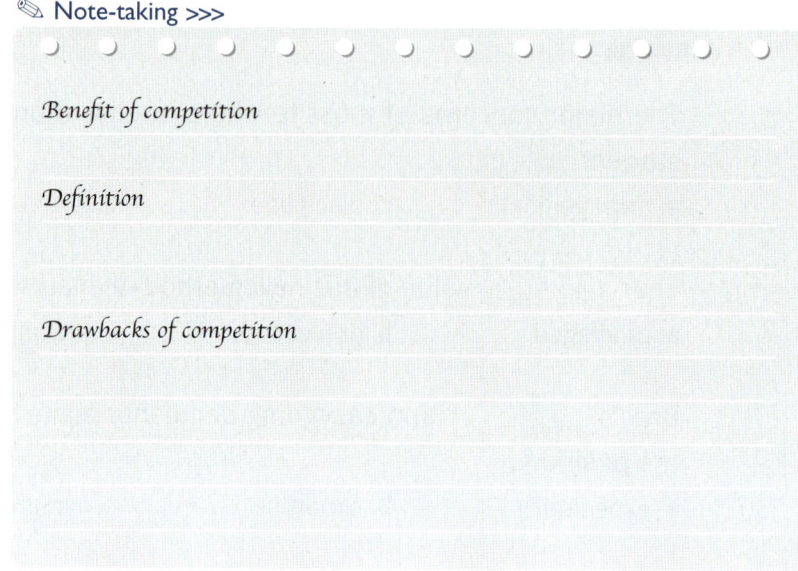

Note-taking >>>

Benefit of competition

Definition

Drawbacks of competition

Now answer the questions.

1. How does the professor introduce the discussion?

   (A) By referring to how competition was discussed in previous lectures
   (B) By giving an example of the disadvantages of competition
   (C) By describing Smith's theory of competition
   (D) By discussing why competition is ultimately a failure

2. How does the professor organize the talk?

   (A) By describing the process of market discrimination
   (B) By comparing two examples of market discrimination
   (C) By contrasting the benefits of the free market with its problems
   (D) By classifying the different kinds of problems in the market

3. Why does the professor mention a person's characteristics?

   (A) To show that all viewpoints are welcome in a free marketplace
   (B) To underscore the irrelevance of politics to employment practices
   (C) To illustrate something that might negatively affect employment
   (D) To show what employers usually consider them when they recruit people

Practice 2

Talk in a class

Listen to a talk in a resource management class.

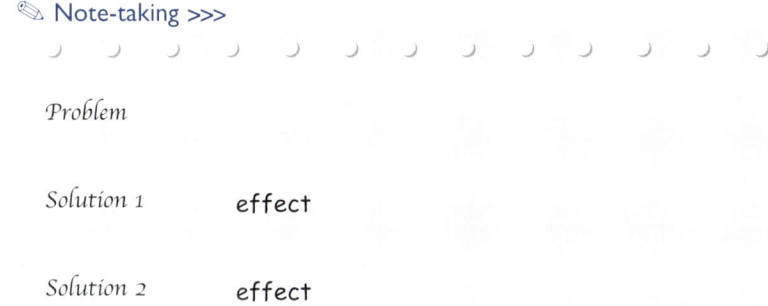

Note-taking >>>

Problem

Solution 1   effect

Solution 2   effect

Now answer the questions.

1 How does the professor introduce the talk?

(A) By providing background information on treaties and laws
(B) By offering an analysis from a resource expert
(C) By describing an example of a resource dispute
(D) By mentioning the purpose of preventative diplomacy

2 Why does the professor mention treaties?

(A) To propose that they be used to address resource disputes
(B) To imply that people have neglected to mention them
(C) To describe a case study on dispute resolution she has read
(D) To suggest the mechanisms are in place to possibly solve the problem

3 How does the professor explain preventative diplomacy?

(A) By explaining the importance of variety of effort
(B) By describing the steps of its mechanism
(C) By providing other views regarding the method
(D) By comparing the previous laws

Practice 3 — Conversation

Listen to a conversation between two students.

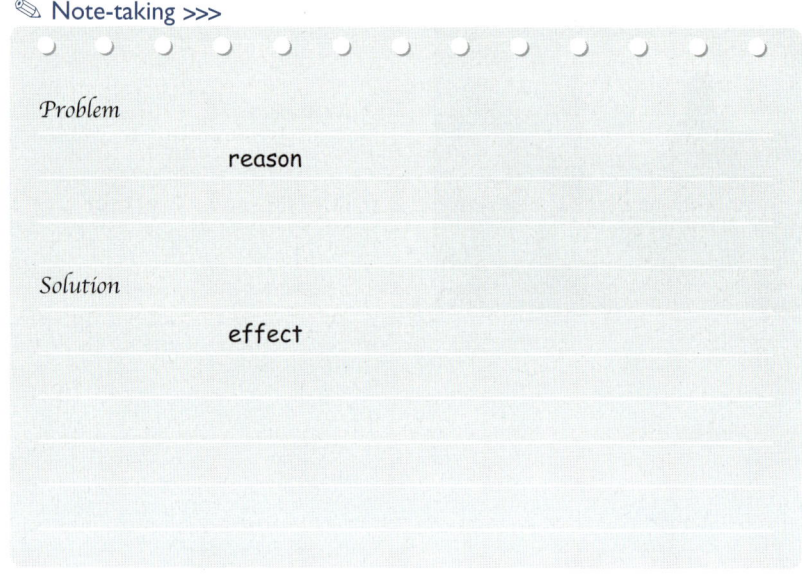

Note-taking >>>

Problem

    reason

Solution

    effect

Now answer the questions.

1 How does the woman offer her solution?

(A) By writing a letter to the college president
(B) By explaining a similar campaign at another college
(C) By suggesting breaking into the library with the man in protest
(D) By describing the process of making a proposal

2 According to the conversation, why doesn't the library stay open during finals?

(A) It is not a custom at most colleges.
(B) Most students don't want it to stay open.
(C) There aren't enough financial resources.
(D) The librarians have refused to work past midnight.

3 What does the woman say that she should do? Choose TWO answers.

(A) Have the students who agree with her sign the petition
(B) Appeal to the school to keep the library opened during the final weeks
(C) Discuss the issue with many other students and the president
(D) Ask the library to consider the extended hours with the president of the school

Practice 4

Lecture

Listen to a lecture in a biology class.

✎ Note-taking >>>

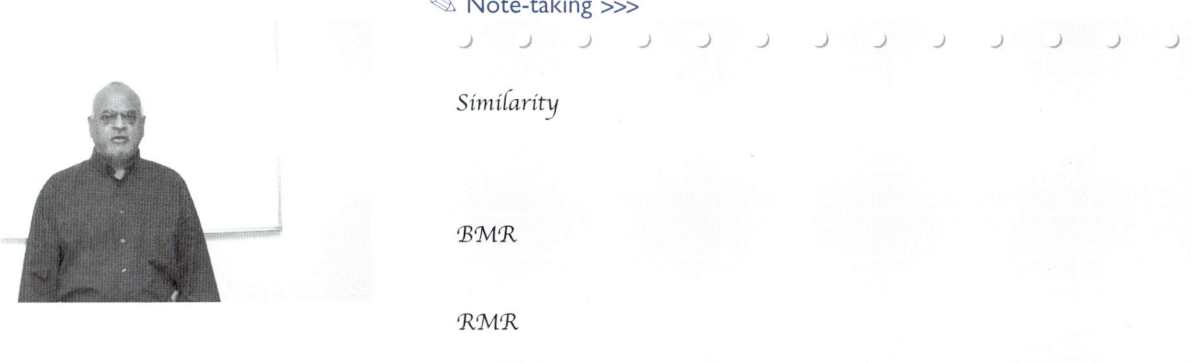

Similarity

BMR

RMR

Now answer the questions.

1. How does the professor introduce the two measurements?

   (A) By comparing the places where the measurements would be taken
   (B) By pointing out what can be learned from both measurements
   (C) By providing their major features that differentiate each other
   (D) By indicating the popularity of both measurements in medical uses

2. How does the professor explain BMR?

   (A) By comparing the results of different people in various ages
   (B) By contrasting the rule with previous methods of finding out metabolic rates
   (C) By describing the required condition to make the accurate measurement
   (D) By explaining the mathematical equation that describes it

3. According to the professor, which of the following is NOT true about BMR and RMR?

   (A) A person's height is less related to metabolic rates.
   (B) As people get older, they get lower metabolic rates.
   (C) Greater body mass will cause high metabolic rates.
   (D) Exercise can prevent getting low metabolic rates.

Actual Test 1

TOEFL Listening

Listen to a lecture on the Tree of life in a biology class.

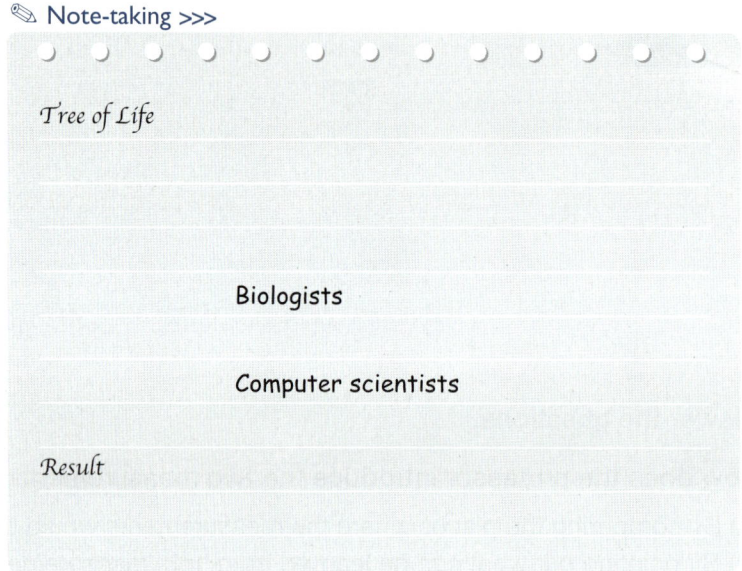

Now answer the questions.

1. What is the lecture mainly about?
   - Ⓐ A genealogical history of scientists around the world
   - Ⓑ A computer program that simplifies medical diagnosis
   - Ⓒ An ambitious project to trace the history of organisms
   - Ⓓ An effort by scientists to learn more computing skills

2. How does the professor introduce the Tree of Life?
   - Ⓐ By showing the students a model
   - Ⓑ By comparing it to a family tree
   - Ⓒ By contrasting it to the Genome Map
   - Ⓓ By describing the process of evolution

3 How does the professor describe the project Tree of Life?
- Ⓐ By providing specific definition of the project for both parties
- Ⓑ By suggesting roles that should be imposed to both scientists
- Ⓒ By listing the factors that should be considered to succeed
- Ⓓ By classifying the role of biologists and computer scientists

4 According to the professor, what is the role of the computer scientists in the project?
- Ⓐ They will distribute the information via computer.
- Ⓑ They will develop the needed technology.
- Ⓒ They will interpret the results of the Tree of Life.
- Ⓓ They will enter the necessary data.

5 Which of the following is a benefit that the completion of the project will bring? Choose TWO answers.
- Ⓐ A better perception of life evolution
- Ⓑ A better understanding of the planet
- Ⓒ More knowledge of our bodies
- Ⓓ A clearer picture of the unknown viruses

Actual Test 2

TOEFL Listening

Listen to a discussion in a film studies class.

Note-taking >>>

New Wave

Changes

Jean Luc Godard

Now answer the questions.

1   What is the discussion mainly about?
   - Ⓐ The definition and examples of art house film
   - Ⓑ French directors who succeeded in Hollywood
   - Ⓒ The features of that new kind of movie making
   - Ⓓ A history of French film in the late 1950s and early 1960s

2   What does the professor say about the New Wave's influence?
   - Ⓐ It has a great influence on how people enjoy movies.
   - Ⓑ Only film critics really care about New Wave films.
   - Ⓒ It has helped modern art house films to become popular.
   - Ⓓ Its influence can be seen in modern films.

128   TOEFLing Listening Level 3

3. How does the professor organize his explanation of New Wave?
   - (A) By describing the process of the revolution
   - (B) By categorizing its changes into two elements
   - (C) By contrasting American actors with French ones
   - (D) By using "Breathless" to illustrate the movement's main features

4. Why does the professor mention Jean Luc Godard?
   - (A) To demonstrate his stylistic innovation, which is representative of the New Wave
   - (B) To contrast his films with those of other New Wave directors
   - (C) To suggest that his camera work has influenced Hollywood
   - (D) To imply he is the best known New Wave director who led the movement

5. According to the professor, how were New Wave plots different?
   - (A) They shunned naturalistic acting techniques for avant garde ones.
   - (B) They refused to resolve all of the problems of the characters.
   - (C) They were not usually positive or easily understood.
   - (D) They relied on the audience's understanding of this film technique.

DICTATION

Practice 1

🎧 Listen and fill in the blanks.

(P=M / S=W)

Professor Okay, so we've been looking at the different ways in which competition ① _____, creating benefits for both workers and employers; in terms of wages, conditions, and so on. What I want to do today is ② _____, discussing a couple of issues that ③ _____; market and pre-market discrimination. Let's start with market discrimination. Anyone know what that means?

Student Well, I know that, at different time periods, different groups of people ④ _____, depending on the society's biases at the time.

Professor Right. So, we have the idea that ⑤ _____ characteristics, such as a person's race, ethnicity, gender, or even political views might cause prospective employers to not hire them. So, this kind of contradicts the free market promise that you can get a good wage by working hard... If you ⑥ _____ to compete, ⑦ _____, right? And since your job choices are severely limited, you wind up getting very little say about the conditions you work under. You ⑧ _____ another job if there really aren't any other jobs for you, right?

|구문해설| **in terms of** ~의 측면에서   **look at the flip-side** 숨은 측면을 살펴보다   **prevent ~ from ~ing** + 목적어 ~이 …하지 못하게 하다

Practice 2

🎧 Listen and fill in the blanks.

(P=W / S=M)

Professor　If we want to limit the occurrence of violent conflict in the future, we've got to ① _____ for groups to cooperate on resource distribution. Well, so, ② _____ for these conflicts… but… the problem with these is that they are often broken… and because these things ③ _____ — the government telling people, "hey this is how it is," these are ④ _____, which in the end doesn't cut down on conflict. But there is a more effective tactic known as "preventative diplomacy." How this works is that first, you bring together a variety of different people — experts on the resource as well as the people who are directly affected — and then create an impartial environment where ⑤ _____ cooperation and consensus.

Student　Yeah, but come on… people are emotional, especially when they perceive that ⑥ _____. How can we get past that?

Professor　Well, the idea is that at all times, you focus on the resource, not people's emotions. We want to come up with something that will, if not satisfy everyone, at least not cause anyone to feel that ⑦ _____, because that's where ⑧ _____.

|구문해설| **cut down on~** ~(의 수량)을 줄이다; ~을 삼가다, 절제하다　**A as well as B** B뿐 아니라 A도　**at all times** 언제나

DICTATION

Practice 3

🎧 Listen and fill in the blanks.

(S1=M / S2=W)

Student 1 I'm so frustrated... my dorm ① _____ to study in... Most people are finished with finals, so they're relaxing and having a good time, but I still have two exams left! I ② _____, but...

Student 2 Yeah, ③ _____ ... My dorm is really loud, too.

Student 1 So, actually I was gonna ask you if you want to go to the library to study.

Student 2 But the library ④ _____ 30 minutes. You didn't know they close at midnight?

Student 1 Are you sure?

Student 2 Yeah, I don't understand why the library closes so early... Most college libraries stay open 24 hours during final weeks.

Student 1 ⑤ _____? It would be so helpful to have a place to go to get some peace and quiet.

Student 2 Well, I guess because they don't have the money ⑥ _____ _____.

Student 1 It's only for two weeks each semester. It seems to me that they could find the money somewhere. It's really important to students. I know lots of people who feel like we do.

Student 2 Well, maybe we should do something about it...

Student 1 Like what? Break into the library?!

Student 2 No, but we could ⑦ _____. We could get a lot of signatures from students who want expanded hours, ⑧ _____ to the president. If we ⑨ _____, something might change.

Student 1 That could work. ⑩ _____ this semester, but maybe it'll make a difference

|구문해설| **blame A for B** B에 대해 A를 탓하다   **around the clock** 24시간 계속하여   **expanded hours** 연장 시간

Practice 4

🎧 Listen and fill in the blanks.

(P=M)

Professor   Okay... so both BMR and RMR are estimates of how many calories ① _____, _____ you were to do nothing but rest for 24 hours. They represent the minimum amount of energy ② _____, the body's normal metabolic activity including your heart beating, lungs' breathing and maintenance of body temperature, etc.
BMR stands for Basal Metabolic Rate, and ③ _____ Basal Energy Expenditure, or BEE. BMR measurements ④ _____ a darkened room upon waking up after 8 hours of sleep; ⑤ _____, uh, not eating food to ensure that ⑥ _____; and lying flat on your back. Okay? The other one that I mentioned is... RMR. RMR stands for Resting Metabolic Rate, and is synonymous with Resting Energy Expenditure, or REE. RMR measurements are typically taken ⑦ _____ than BMR, and do not require that the person spend the night sleeping ⑧ _____.
As you get older, shorter and lose weight, your BMR and RMR will go down and you will ⑨ _____ or exercise more to maintain your current weight. It is tough getting old, right?

|구문해설| **nothing but** …일 따름, …에 지나지 않는(=only)   **주어 + would + 동사원형 ~ if + 주어 + were to** (가정법 과거로서 현재 사실의 반대를 의미)   **stand for** ~을 의미하다   **prior to** ~ 이전에

DICTATION

Actual Test 1

🎧 Listen and fill in the blanks.

(P=W)

Professor: So something that's happening more and more in research, especially as technology ① _____ every day, is that there is a lot of shared information ② _____. And this is definitely the case as biologists and computer scientists ③ _____ what's being called the Tree of Life.
Now what is this Tree of Life? Well, you know what a family tree is, right? It's a genealogical tool that ④ _____ your ancestors over past generations, ⑤ _____, who their kids are, and all that? Okay, well, the Tree of Life is like that, just on a much larger, interspecies level. In fact, the goal of this project is to create a family tree for the 1.7 million known species on earth!
It's a huge project. So, not only do the biologists need to be able to provide their expertise to ⑥ _____ to have the tree work, but the computer scientists need to ⑦ _____ the machines and software that will enable this to actually become a reality. And so what this will give us, when we're done, is ⑧ _____ exactly ⑨ _____, and how it keeps evolving on this planet. And then this, in turn, is going to benefit our overall understanding of our own bodies; ⑩ _____ new predictive, diagnostic, and treatment abilities.

|구문해설| **move forward** 진보하다 **a family tree** 가계도 **when we're done** 완수했을 때

Actual Test 2

🎧 Listen and fill in the blanks.

(P=M / S=W)

Professor In the late 1950s and early 1960s, a kind of revolution in the world of film-making occurred, called the French New Wave or La Nouvelle Vague.

Student It doesn't seem like it was very influential... French films aren't very popular today.

Professor Well, actually, though this movement in many ways was really ①_____, a type of film that ②_____, rather than a piece of popular entertainment. Well, its influence can still be seen in film today, even in the most mainstream movies. This was ③_____. The New Wave directors were very unhappy with the formulaic, glossy Hollywood movies that had dominated cinema for the past few decades. What the New Wave directors really ④_____ was getting their films ⑤_____... like painting or literature... so, they experimented a lot, stylistically with how things looked. In his film, "Breathless," Jean Luc Godard, for example, one of the directors of this movement, invented what's known as the "jump-cut".... in which the director would ⑥_____ seemingly ⑦_____, or just ⑧_____, into the film. This visual disruption made the story edgier, tenser, more uptight as well as it reminded the viewer that they were watching a movie... Another stylistic innovation was the preference for natural light. Plot-wise, the stories ⑨_____. They tried to avoid happy endings of Hollywood movies, instead, they wanted ⑩_____, and more complex.

|구문해설| **in many ways** 많은 점에서 **A rather than B** B라기 보다 A **seek to** ~하기를 추구하다 **unrelated to** ~와 관련이 없는

Vocabulary Review

Write the meanings of the words in the blanks.

1. decade
2. remarkable
3. forward
4. cause
5. press conference
6. convince
7. labyrinth
8. pilgrim
9. wreak
10. rodent
11. livelihood
12. ecological
13. outlaw
14. critique
15. bias
16. tactic
17. impartial
18. consensus
19. petition
20. perception
21. interfere
22. unfetter
23. prejudice
24. contradict
25. ethnicity
26. cooperate
27. treaties
28. legitimate
29. metabolic
30. expenditure
31. digestive
32. inactive
33. synonymous

Write the meanings of the phrases in the blanks.

34. make up
35. make sure that
36. come up with
37. around the clock
38. cut down on~
39. prior to~
40. when we're done
41. nothing but

Write the correct word or phrase in the blanks.

42. ~을 의미하다
43. 가계도
44. 나타내다
45. B라기 보다 A
46. ~하기를 추구하다
47. 제한하다
48. ~의 측면에서
49. 숨은 측면을 살펴보다
50. 전문적 지식

PROGRESS TEST

Listening Comprehension Section Directions

This section measures your ability to understand conversations and lectures in English. You will hear each conversation or lecture only one time. After each conversation or lecture, you will answer some questions about it. The questions typically ask about the main idea and supporting details. Some questions ask about a speaker's purpose or attitude. Answer the questions based on what is stated or implied by the speakers.

You may take notes while you listen. You may use your notes to help you answer the questions. Your notes will not be scored. If you need to change the volume while you listen, click on the **Volume** icon at the top of the screen. In some questions, you will see this icon: 🎧 This means that you will hear, but not see part of the question.

Some of the questions have special directions. These directions appear in a gray box on the screen. Most questions are worth one point. If a question is worth more than one point, it will have special directions that indicate how many points you can receive. You must answer each question. After you answer, click on **Next**. Then click on **OK** to confirm your answer and go on to the next question. After you click on **OK**, you cannot return to previous questions.

You will have 20 minutes to answer the questions in this section. A clock at the top of the screen will show you how much time is remaining. The clock will not count down while you are listening to test material.

Progress Test 3

TOEFL Listening

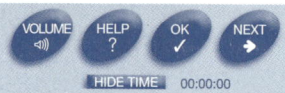

Listen to a discussion on the standardization of time in a western civilizations class. Then answer the questions.

TOEFL Listening

1. What is the discussion mainly about?
   - Ⓐ The history of clocks and watches
   - Ⓑ The role of schedules in the railroad industry
   - Ⓒ The reason for the existence of standardized time
   - Ⓓ The problems with Greenwich Mean Time

2. Why does the professor mention New York?
   - Ⓐ To explain it was the first location to use standardized time
   - Ⓑ To show what he means by the term, standardized time
   - Ⓒ To suggest that this location does not use standardized time
   - Ⓓ To note that New Yorkers use both standard and local time

138 TOEFLing Listening Level 3

3 How does the professor explain standardized time's emergence?
- Ⓐ By giving background information on the first timepieces in Britain
- Ⓑ By explaining the different methods of time keeping over history
- Ⓒ By describing the process by which factories instituted time
- Ⓓ By contrasting standard time with the way local time was kept before in history

4 According to the professor, what was one problem with local time?
- Ⓐ There were discrepancies in keeping local time.
- Ⓑ Railroads were always running late.
- Ⓒ The sun looked different from different locations.
- Ⓓ Factories were unable to create schedules.

5 According to the professor, why was standardized time instituted?
- Ⓐ The railroad industry felt it would be more efficient.
- Ⓑ Trains wanted to have a reliable schedule.
- Ⓒ Factories wanted to ensure more productivity.
- Ⓓ People were bothered by the lack of consistency.

6 Why does the professor mention London?
- Ⓐ To imply that standard time was really random
- Ⓑ To note that it was the seat of the British rail industry
- Ⓒ To illustrate a place that was hesitant to standardize clocks
- Ⓓ To indicate that its time was used as the standard time

Progress Test 4

TOEFL Listening

Listen to a conversation about campus housing. Then answer the questions.

TOEFL Listening

1 Why does the woman go to see the man?
  Ⓐ To compare different campus dorms
  Ⓑ To ask about the new apartments
  Ⓒ To discuss several housing options
  Ⓓ To ask him to be her housemate

2 Where does the man want to live next year?
  Ⓐ He wants to rent an off-campus apartment.
  Ⓑ He wants to live in a dorm on-campus.
  Ⓒ He wants to get into an on-campus apartment.
  Ⓓ He wants to move into the woman's house.

3. According to the woman, why is her house a good choice?
   - Ⓐ It is much cheaper than the on-campus apartments.
   - Ⓑ It has the qualities he is looking for in a home.
   - Ⓒ It is closer to classes than the apartments.
   - Ⓓ It gives him an opportunity to make new friends.

4. Indicate whether each phrase below is a step in the process of the man's housing plan. Check the correct box.

	Yes	No
Put his name on the waiting list		
Participate in a lottery		
Apply to the woman's campus house		
Apply for a dorm near the lecture hall		
Put an ads on a classified for an apartment		

5. What does the woman say about the junior or senior apartments?
   - Ⓐ She contradicts the man's characterization of them.
   - Ⓑ She agrees with the man's opinion about the new apartments
   - Ⓒ She indicates that he hasn't seen them up close.
   - Ⓓ She implies that they are more expensive than off-campus apartments.

6. Why does the woman mention "Plan B"?
   - Ⓐ To indicate that she thinks he'll get an apartment
   - Ⓑ To remind the man that getting an apartment is not easy
   - Ⓒ To convince him to forget about the apartments and move to her house
   - Ⓓ To imply that she believes he will choose a low number in the lottery

DICTATION

Progress Test 3

🎧 Listen and fill in the blanks.

(P=M / S=W)

Professor Now, we take the existence of standardized time ① _____ today... We know that if, say, we were in New York and wanted to call California, ② _____ three hours earlier... not two hours later, or four hours and ten minutes earlier or whatever... But this is actually ③ _____. Anybody know what brought it about?

Student Was it business? I know that time is really ④ _____, so maybe factories or something like that wanted to standardize time ⑤ _____ over the country?

Professor Not a bad answer, but actually, it was the British railroad that really made ⑥ _____. Until this point, different localities measured their time based on where the sun was in the sky, like man has been doing ever since ⑦ _____ into these minutes and hours.

The town's main clock would be set according to the sun, and then people would set their own clocks and watches to that. And so everybody was more or less on the same schedule within one town, but ⑧ _____ _____ or anything. And it wasn't exactly precise. And so it could be five o'clock in one town, five thirty in another, and four forty-five in another. In those days, such disparities or noticeable differences didn't really bother people much. But the railroad ⑨ _____, and so it was important that each town, ⑩ _____, had the same time. So, by 1855 most public clocks in Britain were set to the time in London, which was Greenwich Mean Time or GMT, still the standard we use today when referring to world time schedules.

|구문해설| take 목적어 for granted ~을 당연히 여기다 be linked to~ ~와 관련이 있다 come into being 탄생하다, 존재하게 되다

Progress Test 4

🎧 Listen and fill in the blanks.

(S1=W / S2=M)

Student 1 Hey, John... Where are you going to live next year? ① _____ or getting an apartment off campus?

Student 2 I'm definitely staying on... ② _____ to live in campus housing than to try and find a place to rent. I really want to get into the new junior and senior apartments on campus. They're really nice, and are ③ _____ my dorm is now.

Student 1 Well, I was gonna tell you to apply to live in my house, if you want... It's on-campus housing, but only ten of us live there. ④ _____ ... And some of the people are graduating this semester and moving out, so...

Student 2 Oh, thanks, but I really want to try to get into that new apartment, first...

Student 1 Yeah, they are nice. A friend of mine lived there this year. But it's ⑤ _____ , isn't it?

Student 2 Well, since it is very competitive, they give you a number. If you ⑥ _____ , you are pretty well assured of getting an apartment. But the higher it is, the more likely you won't get a place... I draw my number tomorrow.

Student 1 Well, do you have a plan B?

Student 2 What do you mean?

Student 1 I mean, what if you get a high number? What will you do then?

Student 2 Well, I'll keep my name on the waiting list and hope that ⑦ _____ at the last minute, so I can move in!

Student 1 Still, there's not a great chance that'll happen...

Student 2 I'll sign up for your house if the apartment ⑧ _____ . Thanks so much for the information!

|구문해설| **get a spot** 장소를 구하다　**be assured of** ~을 확신하다　**it's pretty tough to** ~하는 것이 상당히 어렵다　**keep one's name on the waiting list** 이름을 명단에 올려놓다

Vocabulary Review for Progress Test

Choose the correct synonym of the given words or phrases.

Progress Test 3

1. Her explanation sounded <u>fairly</u> plausible and nobody disagreed with her.
   a. honestly   b. unfaithfully   c. tolerably   d. contradictorily

2. My goal is to make a <u>noticeable</u> difference in human-centered technology.
   a. striking   b. generous   c. superficial   d. integral

3. A tailor must take <u>precise</u> measurements before making a suit.
   a. vague   b. incorrect   c. accurate   d. suffocate

4. She threatened to call the police if he didn't stop <u>bother</u>ing her.
   a. agitating   b. releasing   c. reviling   d. feigning

Progress Test 4

1. If the company approves, the business person may buy or <u>rent</u> the store for a period of years.
   a. suppress   b. lease   c. hire   d. resolute

2. What is the most popular sightseeing <u>spot</u> in this area?
   a. flaw   b. place   c. remains   d. cliche

3. To <u>assure</u> seating for dinner, please make your reservations before 5 o'clock.
   a. reserve   b. replace   c. forbear   d. confirm

4. As the job market becomes more <u>competitive</u>, education and training become more important.
   a. violent   b. aggressive   c. solitary   d. insure

OVERVIEW

Inference / Stance

Inference는 말한 내용을 토대로 또 다른 사실이나 결론을 추론해 내는 것을 말하며 Stance는 내용에 대한 Speaker의 생각이나 입장을 유추하는 것이다. 특히, Replay Question으로 전체의 일부를 들려주고 그 중 다시 특정 부분에 나타난 화자의 입장이나 태도를 묻는다.

Question Types

What can be inferred from the lecture/conversation?
What does the professor imply when she says this ~?
What will the man probably do next?
What is the professor's attitude toward ~?
How does the man feel about ~?
What is the woman's opinion of ~?

General Strategies

1 Inference

Speaker가 한 말에 근거하여 어떤 것을 추론할 수 있는가(Inference), Speaker는 무엇을 암시하는가(Implication), 또 어떤 것을 예상할 수 있는가(Prediction)를 질문한다. 자신의 생각이나 이론으로 재해석한 지나친 억측은 피해야 하며, 본문에 근거가 확실히 드러나지 않거나 반박 가능한 것은 추론이라고 볼 수 없다.

2 Stance

Speaker의 말이나 표현에 드러난 느낌이나 입장을 판단하는 문제로, 언급한 내용 자체는 물론이고, 그 말을 하게 된 이유나 배경까지 파악하고 있어야 보다 정확한 답을 찾을 수 있다. 같은 말이나 표현이라도 그 말을 한 상황에 따라 긍정적인지 부정적인지, 신뢰하는지 의심하는지, 회의적인지 적극적인지가 달라질 수 있다.

- positive / negative / neutral
- favorable / critical / objective
- amused / upset
- pleased / worried
- respectful / defiant
- humorous / outraged

Pre Test

TOEFL Listening

Pre Test 1

Listen to a conversation in the library. Then answer the question.

What can be inferred about the interlibrary loan book?
- Ⓐ It hasn't been requested mistakenly.
- Ⓑ It is not needed immediately.
- Ⓒ Its title is not on the computer.
- Ⓓ It will be used in his class.

Pre Test 2

Listen to a conversation in the student center. Then answer the question.

How does the man feel about going to the library?
- Ⓐ He feels that there are no other choices to choose from.
- Ⓑ He thinks that the library should be aware of the problem.
- Ⓒ He is not sure whether they could get a room for them.
- Ⓓ He is positive that the library can provide a space for them.

VOCABULARY
1. **recall** 회수 신청하다 **see if** ~인지 아닌지를 확인하다 **interlibrary loan** 상호대차 **look up on the computer** 컴퓨터상에서 찾아보다
2. **expand** 확장하다 **disturb** 방해하다 **concentrate** 집중하다 **You've got a point.** 제대로 핵심을 짚다

Dictation Listen and fill in the blanks.

Pre Test 1
(S=M / L=W)

Student I wanted to _____ I had recalled. The library sent me _____ .

Librarian Sure. What's your last name?

Student Jones. Also, _____ an interlibrary loan book has come in for me, too? I ordered it almost two weeks ago.

Librarian Two weeks, huh? That's usually enough time to get interlibrary loans. Hold on... Okay, _____ . You can keep this out for three weeks. But I didn't see your loan book... If you wait I can _____ on the computer.

Student Don't worry about it, but it would be nice if I could find out _____ _____ .

Librarian I've got it.

Pre Test 2
(S1=W / S2=M)

Student 1 Wow! There are so many people in here today...

Student 2 I know... I wish they would _____ . It's always too crowded! _____ , but we can't even sit down!

Student 1 Maybe we should just go to the library.

Student 2 But we really can't talk in the library, and we need to discuss our project.

Student 1 That's true... I'm going to suggest to the library director _____ _____ especially for students working on projects. _____ _____ than the student center, but we won't disturb the other students in the library.

Student 2 That's a good idea... _____ ... I guess we just have to sit here though and try to concentrate despite the noise.

Student 1 You know what, though? I think they might have some other options for us. How many students do you think there are like us?

Student 2 _____ .

Vocabulary Preview for Mini-Exercise

Listen and choose the correct definition of the given words or phrases.

Mini-Exercise 1

1.
  1. expel — a. ☐ b. ☐
  2. colony — a. ☐ b. ☐
  3. dialect — a. ☐ b. ☐

2.
  1. ratify — a. ☐ b. ☐
  2. diverse — a. ☐ b. ☐
  3. address — a. ☐ b. ☐

3.
  1. declaration — a. ☐ b. ☐
  2. definitely — a. ☐ b. ☐
  3. analysis — a. ☐ b. ☐

Mini-Exercise 2

1.
  1. cultivate — a. ☐ b. ☐
  2. barren — a. ☐ b. ☐
  3. accumulation — a. ☐ b. ☐

2.
  1. produce — a. ☐ b. ☐
  2. depict — a. ☐ b. ☐
  3. conservation — a. ☐ b. ☐

3.
  1. assignment — a. ☐ b. ☐
  2. expand — a. ☐ b. ☐
  3. cost — a. ☐ b. ☐

Mini-Exercise 1 Inference

Lecture 1 Listen to a lecture about the expulsion of the Acadians. Then answer the questions.

1 What can be inferred about the Canadian Acadians?
(A) They voluntarily moved from Canada to the southern U.S.
(B) They did not get along with the English settlers in Canada.
(C) They completely lost the ability to speak French.
(D) They came to America to seek riches, peace, and more freedom.

» **Comprehension Question** «

2 Which of the following is true about French settlers in the United States?
(A) They were small in number but came from geographically diverse regions.
(B) They soon spoke English primarily, but still Acadian at home.
(C) Their distinct culture can be found in certain places in the United States.
(D) They had a serious conflict with the English settlers in the United States.

Dictation Listen again and fill in the blanks. (P=M)

Professor By the 18th century, the land that would become the United States _____ English and German speakers... How is it, then, that French speakers were living in Louisiana? Well, the Acadians, _____ today, _____ their homes in a region of eastern Canada known as Acadia... The English there felt that these French settlers _____ English security and demanded they leave. Some _____ New England, and some to the southern colonies of South Carolina or Georgia... Others, however, _____ Louisiana. Today there are still residents who speak a French dialect called Cajun, and many aspects of Cajun culture, from food to music, reflect the French culture of Acadia.

Mini-Exercise 1

Talk in a class 2 Listen to a talk about the Federalist Papers. Then answer the questions.

1 What does the professor mean when she says this: 🎧
(A) She agrees that it is much different in modern government.
(B) She feels it was responsible for the creation of the Bill of Rights.
(C) She implies that things have not changed very much even today.
(D) She thinks that it is much worse than it was in 1787.

» **Comprehension Question** «

2 Which of the following is a concern of ratifying the US Constitution? Choose TWO answers.
(A) Some of the states were opposed to the US Constitution.
(B) Many different groups of people had very diverse opinions.
(C) The nation was too wide to be controlled by one universal rule.
(D) The series of Federalist Papers were not completed properly.

Dictation Listen again and fill in the blanks. (P=W / S=M)

Professor Before the US Constitution _____ in 1787, there was great concern that the new nation of the time was _____ _____ under a single democratic rule... In other words... there were too many factions — organized groups of people within the nation. They opposed the ideas of the nation and _____, and... and... there would never be enough general agreement _____. This sounds, uh, _____, doesn't it? (*sarcastically*) yeah right... Anyway, this problem of factions was the subject of Federalist No. 10. This essay was written by James Madison as a series of the Federalist Papers... What are these papers?

Student A series of arguments for the ratification of the United States Constitution.

Professor Right, Madison made the case that ultimately a republican democracy was _____. Why? Any ideas?

Inference / Stance

Mini-Exercise 1

Conversation 3 Listen to a conversation between two students. Then answer the questions.

1 What will the man likely do next?
(A) Go to meet with his premed advisor.
(B) Discuss his decision with his family.
(C) Talk to the parents after declaration.
(D) Get an extension on declaration due.

» **Comprehension Question** «

2 What does the man say he wants to do?
(A) Go to a medical school.
(B) Pursue history as a major.
(C) Become a historical fiction writer.
(D) Teach history in high school.

Dictation
Listen again and fill in the blanks. (S1=M / S2=W)

Student 1 _____ our major declaration forms tomorrow... but I'm still not really sure _____.

Student 2 Really? I thought you were definitely going to do premed. What happened?

Student 1 Yeah, that's what my parents want, but _____, the more I realize I'm not very interested in medicine. I don't think _____ _____. What I'm really interested in is history. But I'm not sure that's a very practical subject.

Student 2 I think it could be okay... You could go on to teach or to do some type of job _____ ... You really have to be sure what you can do later... But there are plenty of options. It's your choice after all but then again, it could be one of the most important matters to your parents, too. I mean, _____ before you make any decisions, tell them what you really want to study... I'm sure they would understand.

Student 1 Thank you so much for your kind advice.

152 TOEFLing Listening Level 3

Mini-Exercise 2   Stance

Talk in a class 1   Listen to a talk in an ecology class. Then answer the questions.

1 How does the professor feel about bogs?
(A) He is enthusiastic about their products.
(B) He considers them useful in some capacity.
(C) He feels they have excellent, unrealized potential.
(D) He is negative about how much labor is required to farm them.

» Comprehension Question «

2 What does the decay of a bog's plant matter result in?
(A) Wet and muddy ground
(B) Useless land to farm
(C) A highly acidic area
(D) Changes in berry species

Dictation   Listen again and fill in the blanks.   (P=M / S=W)

Professor   Humans have managed to cultivate some of _____ places on earth. This can be seen in the various industries that _____ ... Now, what can you tell me about bogs?

Student   Well, areas of land which are very _____, so they're not good for building, and they're usually in colder climates, right? And, uh... _____, so not great for agriculture. Basically, pretty unforgiving places, you might say.

Professor   Good, yeah. Plants do grow in bogs, but _____ their highly acidic conditions. The acidity comes from the accumulation of peat, _____. However, blueberries, cranberries, and lingonberries all thrive in these conditions, and have been harvested in bogs for centuries, _____ for farmers in bog areas. So despite the seeming uselessness of the land, it does actually produce.

* bog 늪, 습지

Mini-Exercise 2

Discussion 2 Listen to a discussion about John James Audubon in an art history class. Then answer the questions.

1 What is the woman's attitude toward Audubon?
(A) She is impressed with his output but unsure of its validity.
(B) She is indifferent toward his efforts but is nonetheless curious.
(C) She is critical of the methods he used to create art.
(D) She is negative about his artwork because it lacks realism.

» **Comprehension Question** «

2 What can be inferred about Audobon's artwork?
(A) It was not created to accomplish scientific purposes.
(B) The color used in it is outdated by today's standards.
(C) Its use of stuffed subjects is currently under question.
(D) It is little known outside of academia until recent time.

Dictation   Listen again and fill in the blanks.   (P=M / S1=M / S2=W)

Professor John James Audubon is best known for his series of 435 nature engravings, pictures that _____ on which designs have been cut. They are called *The Birds of America* in which he depicted the birds of this continent _____ and _____.

Student 1 But it's not like he wrote about birds that didn't even exist or were really separate species. I mean why is it so important?

Student 2 And I also read that he killed thousands of birds to study for his drawings while making this book, which seems pretty bad to me _____ _____ him as a conservationist.

Professor Whoa! Hold on, hold on! Now, it's true that Audubon sometimes _____, but more often killed the birds, yes. And from today's perspective, that does seem pretty bad. But _____ is still widely admired today, _____, not for its scientific value, though, as you mentioned.

* engraving 조각(술), 판화

Mini-Exercise 2

Conversation 3 Listen to a conversation between two students talking about an assignment. Then answer the questions.

1 What does the man mean when he says this: 🎧
(A) He is interested in starting his own business.
(B) He is sure that he understands the business plan.
(C) He is not sure whether he has enough knowledge to formulate a plan.
(D) He wants to make a plan for his real business.

» Comprehension Question «

2 What is the man's attitude toward the assignment at first?
(A) He is confused because he lacks experience in the field.
(B) He is receptive because he knows it will help him later.
(C) He is first anxious because the due date is very soon.
(D) He is negative because the instructions are ambiguous.

Dictation Listen again and fill in the blanks. (S1=M / S2=W)

Student 1 I don't really understand what I'm supposed to do for this assignment. How am I supposed to _____ when I don't even have a business?

Student 2 Well, you don't have to have a real business... _____ that you'd like to have and then create a plan for it.

Student 1 Well, even so. Say I wanted to have a, uh, a cosmetics business. What do I do? What's the business plan _____?

Student 2 Oh, OK...it's really the information you'd need to supply to investors — people _____ to help you start it or expand it — so that they know that you have a plan to make money, sell things, deal with competition, control costs... those kinds of things. I'm sure you learned these... from your class.

Student 1 I really need to have a business first.

Student 2 Come on...

Inference / Stance

Vocabulary Preview for Practice

Listen and choose correct definition of the given words or phrases.

Practice 1

1. boost   a. ☐   b. ☐
2. feature   a. ☐   b. ☐
3. promote   a. ☐   b. ☐
4. generate   a. ☐   b. ☐

Practice 2

1. explosion   a. ☐   b. ☐
2. structure   a. ☐   b. ☐
3. perceive   a. ☐   b. ☐
4. imperceptible   a. ☐   b. ☐

Practice 3

1. traditional   a. ☐   b. ☐
2. tension   a. ☐   b. ☐
3. direction   a. ☐   b. ☐
4. burst   a. ☐   b. ☐

Practice 4

1. cover letter   a. ☐   b. ☐
2. be supposed to   a. ☐   b. ☐
3. passionate   a. ☐   b. ☐
4. help out with   a. ☐   b. ☐

Vocabulary Preview for Actual Test

Choose the best word to complete each sentence.

Actual Test 1

1. His main income comes from _____ cattle.
   a. breeding   b. nurturing   c. adopting   d. forging

2. Architects are questioning assumptions they made earlier about the _____ strength of future earthquakes.
   a. prevalent   b. potential   c. permanent   d. persistent

3. Much of the coast has been _____ by nuclear waste.
   a. notified   b. contaminated   c. accelerated   d. compelled

4. As a teacher you have to _____ your methods to suit the needs of slower children.
   a. jeopardize   b. ensure   c. adjust   d. disregard

Actual Test 2

1. The Ministry of Culture and Tourism plans to launch a project this year to _____ folk songs and musical instruments.
   a. block   b. conserve   c. deter   d. enlist

2. Pupils in our school have the _____ of taking Japanese, Chinese, or French.
   a. option   b. negotiation   c. legacy   d. fidelity

3. Our 75-year-college has recently expanded to _____ the influx of overseas students.
   a. maltreat   b. accommodate   c. mangle   d. induce

4. The price includes travel and accommodation but meals are _____.
   a. scanty   b. pecuniary   c. touching   d. extra

Practice 1

Lecture

Listen to a lecture in a travel and tourism class.

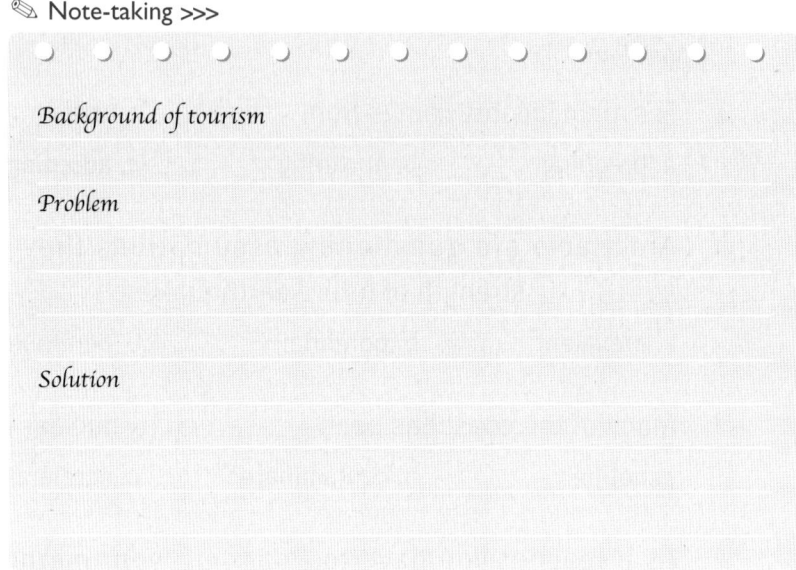

Note-taking >>>

Background of tourism

Problem

Solution

Now answer the questions.

1 What is the professor's attitude toward traditional tourism?

(A) He is upset that it is criticized.
(B) He is worried it is in decline.
(C) He is concerned about its negative impact.
(D) He is critical of its slow growth.

2 What can be inferred about the size of tourism?

(A) It will constantly increase at the same rate it has increased.
(B) Many countries saw the economical potential in tourism.
(C) It is considered to be small compared to other industries.
(D) The world's economic output greatly depends tourism.

3 What can be inferred about the ecotourist industry?

(A) It costs much less than traditional tourism.
(B) It will only introduce unknown cultures around the world.
(C) It is not preferred by many tourists for its inconvenience.
(D) It doesn't require any artificial development of nature.

Practice 2

Discussion

Listen to a discussion in a physics class.

Note-taking >>>

Past century

One theory

Criticism

* multiverse 다중우주론

Now answer the questions.

1 According to the professor, what can be inferred about the structure of the universe?

(A) We are far from understanding the structure of our universe yet.
(B) There has been much study on the universe over the past century.
(C) Previous theories about the universe have been proved to be wrong.
(D) Only a few theories can explain the structure of the universe now.

2 What is the student's attitude toward multiverse theory?

(A) She is skeptical about its approach.
(B) She is confused about what its implications are.
(C) She is critical of the lack of clarity surrounding it.
(D) She is ambivalent about its relevance to her studies.

3 What does the professor mean when he says this: 🎧

(A) Many other students have asked the question before.
(B) There is much criticism about the multiverse theory.
(C) The student needs to do more research on the theory.
(D) He has already answered the question earlier in the class.

Practice 3

Conversation

Listen to a conversation between two students.

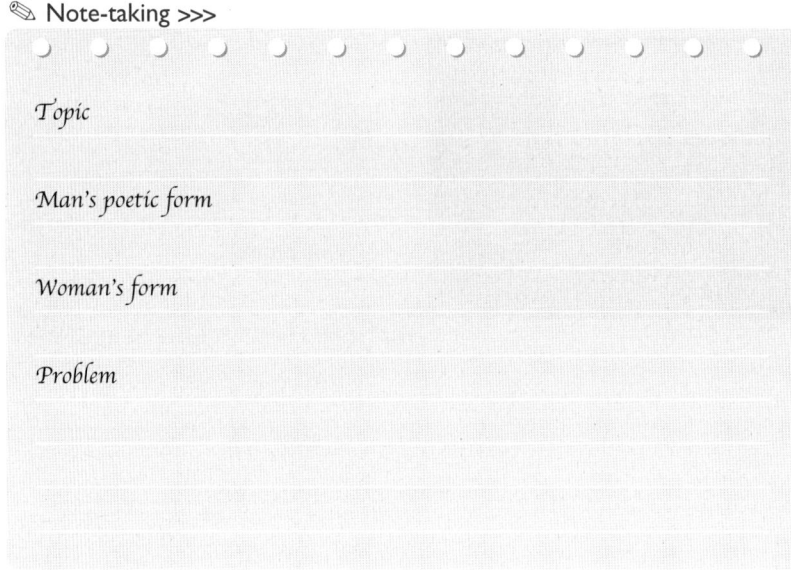

Note-taking >>>

Topic

Man's poetic form

Woman's form

Problem

Now answer the questions.

1 What can be inferred about 19-line poems?

(A) Shakespeare didn't like using the 19-line forms.
(B) This form was created in 20th century in English.
(C) Many poets started to use the form in 20th century.
(D) Shakespeare didn't know about this type of peom.

2 What does the man mean when he says this: 🎧

(A) He is asking the woman to come with him to confirm what a sonnet is.
(B) He is assuming that the woman did okay on the exam.
(C) He is sure that the woman is mixed up with a sonnet.
(D) He is persuading the woman to admit that she knew that.

3 What can be inferred about the woman?

(A) She will find out what sonnets are.
(B) She might have to talk to the professor.
(C) She can expect a decent grade on this exam.
(D) She will probably get a low grade on the exam.

Practice 4

Conversation

Listen to a conversation between two students.

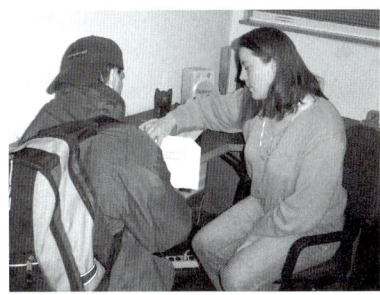

✎ Note-taking >>>

Problem

Solution

        suggestion 1

        suggestion 2

Now answer the questions.

1 What does the man mean when he says this: 🎧

(A) He doesn't think that she's qualified for the job.
(B) He thinks that the letter is not convincing enough.
(C) He is confident that the woman gets accepted.
(D) He thinks she needs to cut out some of the information.

2 What can be inferred about the length of the cover letter?

(A) It should be some lines of self-introduction.
(B) It could be more than a page if is necessary.
(C) It may not exceed a page with efficient information.
(D) It should be less than a half page of brief biography.

3 What is the man's opinion of the woman's cover letter?

(A) He thinks it is more or less complete.
(B) He feels she should include more details in it.
(C) He believes she needs to start over.
(D) He considers it to be slightly dishonest.

Inference / Stance 161

Actual Test 1

TOEFL Listening

Listen to a discussion on genetically modified foods.

Note-taking >>>

Controversy

Concern

Now answer the questions.

1 What is the discussion mainly about?
  A The flaws in protests about genetically modified foods
  B The history of agricultural manipulation of crops and foods
  C The problems and effects of genetically modified foods
  D The impact of genetically modified foods on human health

2 What can be inferred about two students?
  A They both agree that genetically modified foods are debatable.
  B They both agree that genetically modified foods should be prohibited.
  C They both disagree that genetically modified foods have negative affects.
  D They don't agree with each other on the affects of genetically modified foods.

3. What does the professor mean when she says this: 🎧
   Ⓐ She thinks that it is the main issue over genetically modified foods.
   Ⓑ She wants to encourage students to mention more problems.
   Ⓒ She implies that the student mentioned something not very important.
   Ⓓ She wants to see if students remember the issues from previous lecture.

4. Which of the following is true about genetically modified crops?
   Ⓐ They cannot be cultivated on a large scale.
   Ⓑ They are not as healthy as natural foods.
   Ⓒ They are not discussed very much in some countries.
   Ⓓ They are not able to produce fruits continuously.

5. Which of the following can be a problem with sterile seeds of genetically modified crops?
   Ⓐ If they are not sterile, they cannot reproduce seeds next year.
   Ⓑ If they are sterile, they can contaminate other crops.
   Ⓒ If they are sterile, they can endanger genetic diversity.
   Ⓓ If they are not sterile, they maybe more dangerous to the environment.

Actual Test 2

TOEFL Listening

Listen to a conversation in the international students office.

✎ Note-taking >>>

What he wants

Option   1.

          2.

Now answer the questions.

1 Why does the student go to the woman?
- Ⓐ To discuss the possibility of getting a job
- Ⓑ To inquire about financial aid for the summer
- Ⓒ To find out about housing options over the vacation
- Ⓓ To complain about his current living situation

2 Why do the dorms close over break?
- Ⓐ To give the maintenance staff a chance to do repairs
- Ⓑ To save on costs and keep the campus safe
- Ⓒ To discourage students from remaining on campus
- Ⓓ To increase business for local hotels and boardinghouses

3 Why doesn't the man want to stay with his friend?
- Ⓐ He lives too far away from the school.
- Ⓑ He doesn't want to inconvenience him.
- Ⓒ He is nervous about meeting his family.
- Ⓓ He doesn't have much room in his house.

4 What does the man mean when he says this: 🎧
- Ⓐ He is not sure since he has not seen the house yet.
- Ⓑ He is not certain whether he could afford the money.
- Ⓒ He is not fully satisfied with the choice.
- Ⓓ He thinks the boardinghouse is quite reasonable.

5 What does the woman mean when she says this: 🎧
- Ⓐ She asks if he understood the option correctly.
- Ⓑ She is not certain whether food is provided.
- Ⓒ She doubts if he could save more money.
- Ⓓ She is a little concerned about the man's choice.

DICTATION

Practice 1

🎧 Listen and fill in the blanks.

(P=M)

Professor In places where there is little material industry, many governments ① _____ tourism ② _____ the economy. Tourist industry accounts for more than... uh, ten percent of the world's economic output, which used to be around 1 or 2 percent in 1980s... Now traditional tourism often comes at the expense of local traditions and the surrounding environment... What happens is that, at the beginning, tourists ③ _____. I mean the natural features, the clean beaches, the wildlife, and even the customs and cultures of the places, right? And what happens next is that the industry will try to develop their natural features to bring more tourists. And then, ④ _____ _____ in the process of tourist development. Not just destruction of the economy, ⑤ _____ our environment, too. There must be something done to stop this... right? Now, let's take a look at this new type of tourism called... umm, the ecotourism industry. Well, you can guess what it is from the name, right? Okay... ⑥ _____ ... is the idea that tourism should actually help preserve these features. This ecotourism is really about providing travel opportunities for people that ⑦ _____, directly, the nature and culture of ⑧ _____. Unlike traditional tourism, it doesn't need to have some westernized hotels on a beach somewhere, but meeting the people and ⑨ _____ ... The idea behind this is ⑩ _____ and preserve the natural resources of a place, but also to promote interactions among people of different cultures.

|구문해설| account for ~을 차지하다   at the expense of ~을 이용하여   let's take a look at ~을 보다   in the past two decades 과거 20년 동안

Practice 2

🎧 Listen and fill in the blanks.

(P=M / S=W)

Professor We've seen a real explosion of different ideas about the structure of the universe over the past century, as we discover more and more about how, really, um, complicated things are... much more than we thought. Alright, one of these ideas is that our physical universe, ① _____ _____, is really only part of the entire physical reality of, uh, existence. I mean there are many other universes and our universe is ② _____ ... You know what I mean... that there are many different worlds out there that, even though ③ _____ _____ . This is the multiverse theory.

Student But I thought that one of the main tenets of science was that we could observe and test that which ④ _____ . If we can't perceive other aspects of the universe, is it really scientific to claim that they exist?

Professor ⑤ _____ ... If we can't perceive it, how can we know it's there? However, ⑥ _____ , is the discovery over the past few decades of stuff like dark matter... matter that ⑦ _____ , but in fact we know it exists ⑧ _____ . So, as I said, things are really very complicated.

|구문해설| **make a claim for** ~을 주장하다 **You're not alone in~** 하는 것은 당신만이 아닙니다

DICTATION

Practice 3

🎧 Listen and fill in the blanks.

(S1=W / S2=M)

Student 1 Wow, ① _____ in literature class today, wasn't it? But I think I did all right, actually. So which type of poetic form did you ② _____ _____?

Student 2 I chose the one about villanelles, I mean the traditional 19-line poem... Which one did you choose?

Student 1 The same one. I wrote about how Shakespeare used 19-line poems to ③ _____ regarding the relationships of people within the poems, ④ _____... well, I just hope that the professor likes what I wrote.

Student 2 ⑤ _____, but...uh...Shakespeare didn't write 19-line poems at all... ⑥ _____ not common in English until the 20th century... Remember we read one of those by Dylan Thomas in the textbook? I think you're talking about Shakespeare's sonnets.

Student 1 What do you mean?

Student 2 The professor said that a sonnet has fourteen lines, ⑦ _____ _____, the direction of the poem changes.

Student 1 No... that's got to be 19-lines... I mean, are you sure?

Student 2 Uh... Come on... Susan...

|구문해설| **burst one's bubble** 찬물을 끼얹다

Practice 4

🎧 Listen and fill in the blanks.

(S1=W / S2=M)

Student 1 Hey, Mitch, will you ① _____ for me? ② _____ _____ at a law firm for the spring, and I'm really worried ③ _____ , though I really want to. Can you tell me what you think?

Student 2 Sure... Okay... hmmm... well, I think that ④ _____ . But you really don't provide a lot of information about yourself in this. Why should the law firm choose you as an intern?

Student 1 What do you mean? I have a resume, too that has ⑤ _____ _____ . I thought cover letters ⑥ _____ , anyway.

Student 2 Well, you usually want to ⑦ _____ . But it should do the job of "selling" you to the potential employer. I mean, all you say here is that you are interested in going to law school after you graduate. But why?

Student 1 Well, because I'm really ⑧ _____ the environment and I think that I could really ⑨ _____ . Also I think this law firm does a lot of good work in this area. I'd like to ⑩ _____ some experience.

Student 2 You see?

Student 1 What? ⑪ _____ ?

Student 2 Way more.

|구문해설| **be supposed to** ~하기로 되어 있다 **help out with** ~에 대해 도움을 주다

Inference / Stance 169

DICTATION

Actual Test 1

🎧 Listen and fill in the blanks.

(P=W / S1=W / S2=M)

Professor There's been a lot of controversy over the past few years over the introduction of ① _____ into our food supply. Now, of course, man has been, uh, ② _____ of his foods ever since the Neolithic agrarian revolution. Using selective breeding to get a certain type of corn or apple... so what's the difference now? I mean ③ _____? Why are people so upset about this?

Student 1 Well, some people claim that there's not really been any research ④ _____ of these modifications. There could be a negative impact on the human body that we haven't really seen before.

Professor Yeah. That's one concern...

Student 2 Well, in the past, farmers could collect the seeds from their ⑤ _____. But, uh, since a lot of the genetically modified crops are sterile, meaning that these crops are not able to produce seeds... um, the farmers ⑥ _____ each year from the seed companies or something... and they become like slaves in a way...

Student 1 Yeah. And ⑦ _____, there is a chance that they can contaminate other seed crops, ⑧ _____. At some point, this could endanger genetic diversity, making crops a lot more dangerous to disease and so on...

Professor Okay...so, despite the fact that ⑨ _____ is not a new human pursuit, we definitely have ⑩ _____ because of recent laboratory modifications.

|구문해설| **be forced to** 하는 수 없이 ~하다   **at some point** 어떤 점에서

Actual Test 2

🎧 Listen and fill in the blanks.

(S=M / D=W)

Student I want to save money to go home this summer, so I'm thinking that ① _____ if I can. But I read that my dorm will be closed for three weeks.

Director Yes. For safety reasons, ② _____ , most of the student dorms do close...

Student Is there any other way I could stay on campus?

Director Well, do you have a friend whose family you could stay with ③ _____ ?

Student Well, my roommate ④ _____ his family. But, I have a job here that I don't want to ⑤ _____ if possible, and he lives several hours away.

Director I see. Okay, one thing you can do is... well, all right... you could stay in a boardinghouse near campus. Many international students choose this option because the woman ⑥ _____ provides breakfast and dinner for boarders... It'll probably run you 150 dollars for the whole time... How does that sound?

Student Well, I don't know... but ⑦ _____ ...

Director Well, there is this one dormitory building that stays open on campus ⑧ _____ students. It's fifty extra dollars for the entire break, but there are no cooking or laundry facilities, so you have to ⑨ _____ . Also it might cost you more than you think it would..

Student Since I work in a restaurant, food is free for me... so... I think I could save even more. ⑩ _____ .

Director (concerned) Are you sure?

|구문해설| **take time off** 시간을 빼앗기다　**one thing you can do** 당신이 할 수 있는 한 가지　**more than you think** 당신이 생각하는 이상으로

Inference / Stance　171

Vocabulary Review

Write the meanings of the words in the blanks.

1. recall _____
2. notice _____
3. expand _____
4. disturb _____
5. concentrate _____
6. expel _____
7. colony _____
8. ratify _____
9. diverse _____
10. address _____
11. declaration _____
12. analysis _____
13. cultivate _____
14. barren _____
15. accumulation _____
16. depict _____
17. conservation _____
18. expand _____
19. boost _____
20. feature _____
21. promote _____
22. generate _____
23. structure _____
24. perceive _____
25. imperceptive _____
26. tension _____
27. passionate _____
28. breed _____
29. potential _____
30. contaminate _____
31. adjust _____
32. accommodate _____
33. extra _____

Write the meanings of the phrases in the blanks.

34. see if _____
35. at the expense of _____
36. burst one's bubble _____
37. help out with _____
38. at some point _____
39. figure out _____
40. You've got a point _____
41. be supposed to _____

Write the correct words or phrases in the blanks.

42. 하는 수 없이 ~하다 _____
43. ~을 주장하다 _____
44. 농업의 _____
45. 메마른 _____
46. 개량, 수정 _____
47. 헌법 _____
48. 거주자 _____
49. 농업 _____
50. 추수, 추수하다 _____

Chapter 06
FUNCTION

OVERVIEW

Function

Function은 Speaker가 어떤 말을 하는 이유나 목적, 즉 그 말이 하는 기능을 말한다. 앞뒤 문맥을 파악하여 Speaker가 그 말을 하게 된 배경을 알고, 말에 나타나는 억양이나 어조를 통해 속에 담긴 의미까지 파악해야 제대로 이해할 수 있다.

Question Types

Why does the professor say this?
Why does the professor mention ~?
Why does the man say this?
What does the advisor mean when he says this?
What does the professor mean when she says this?

General Strategies

Function-Purpose

Speaker가 왜 이 말을 했는가, 즉 그 말의 기능을 파악하는 것으로 Speaker의 목적과 동기를 생각하도록 한다. 예를 들어, Speaker가 특정 말을 한 것이 사과를 하려는 것인지, 불평을 하려는 것인지, 제안을 하려는 것인지를 파악하는 것이다. Speaker의 Tone과 Intonation을 듣고 의도된 의미를 파악하도록 한다.

- To give direction or instruction
- To recommend, suggest, advice, or persuade
- To complain, apologize or forgive
- To give opinion, agree or disagree
- To request
- To invite

Pre Test

TOEFL Listening

Pre Test

Listen to a lecture on fashion. Then answer the question.

Why does the professor mention the women who broke their ribs or passed out?
- Ⓐ To imply that wearing a corset can cause a serious health problem
- Ⓑ To emphasize how difficult it was to conform the ideal beauty of the 18th century
- Ⓒ To show that the material used to make in corsets was hard
- Ⓓ To suggest that corsets were a marginal part of women's life

Listen to part of the lecture again: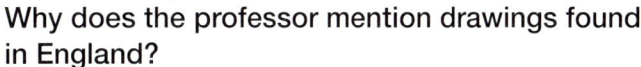

Why does the professor mention drawings found in England?
- Ⓐ To show how men's corsets increased their strength
- Ⓑ To demonstrate how tight men wore their corsets back then
- Ⓒ To indicate a place where corsets were popular among men
- Ⓓ To provide an evidence of men wearing corsets in the past

VOCABULARY | come to mind ~한 생각이 떠오르다 | used to 동사원형 (과거에) 하곤 했다 | tighten 조이다 | appearance 외관 | drawing 그림 | Neolithic 신석기 시대의 | archeological 고고학의 | site 유적지

Dictation Listen and fill in the blanks.

Pre Test

(P=W)

Professor: When we think of corsets, well, images of women _____ _____ probably come to mind... these are the whalebone corsets of the 18th century. Women used to wear these corsets really tight, _____ into a desired shape. Well, some women were known to _____ or _____ _____ just from wearing them! All in the name of beauty! You might be surprised to hear that men also wore corsets! ... to uh... _____ and increase the appearance of strength... _____ the Neolithic archeological site at Brandon, in Norfolk, England, we can see both men and women wearing animal hide corsets...

Listen to part of the lecture again.

You might be surprised to hear that men also wore corsets! ... to uh... to tighten their waists and increase the appearance of strength... in drawings discovered at the Neolithic archeological site at Brandon, in Norfolk, England, we can see both men and women wearing animal hide corsets...

Vocabulary Preview for Mini-Exercise

Listen and choose the correct definition of the given words or phrases.

Mini-Exercise

1
1. embellish   a. ☐   b. ☐
2. toxin   a. ☐   b. ☐
3. specifically   a. ☐   b. ☐

2
1. efficiency   a. ☐   b. ☐
2. productivity   a. ☐   b. ☐
3. deal with   a. ☐   b. ☐

3
1. carnival   a. ☐   b. ☐
2. costume   a. ☐   b. ☐
3. catch up   a. ☐   b. ☐

4
1. inspire   a. ☐   b. ☐
2. chaos   a. ☐   b. ☐
3. ideal   a. ☐   b. ☐

Mini-Exercise 1 Function-Purpose

Discussion 1 Listen to a discussion in an ecology class. Then answer the questions.

1 Why does the professor talk about Hitchcock's movie?
(A) To emphasize the movie was very scary
(B) To suggest that the toxin mostly damages birds
(C) To explain how a toxin can influence birds' behavior
(D) To find out if students have seen the movie

» **Comprehension Question** «

2 What will the class do next time?
(A) View portions of a Hitchcock movie
(B) Debate the validity of the explanation
(C) Discuss the attacks in small groups
(D) Learn about domoic acid's composition

Dictation Listen again and fill in the blanks. (P=M / S1=W / S2=W)

Professor I don't know how many of you have ever watched that movie, "The Birds..."
Student 1 The one where all the birds _____?
Professor That's it! Now, Hitchcock _____ to make the movie scary, one night, _____ windows and sides of houses, dived bombing cars, and fell out of the sky into the streets, dead...
Student 2 I didn't see the movie but I think I remember the scenes from TV or something.
Professor Probably... but in fact, it really _____ that happened in 1961 in Santa Cruz, California. What caused this completely unusual action? Well, we've discovered _____ by a naturally occurring toxin that acts _____, called domoic acid, which was eaten by the anchovies, uh... small fish that the birds fed on. We don't have time to _____ this toxin today, but we'll look at how it works next time.

Mini-Exercise

Discussion 2 Listen to a discussion in a business class. Then answer the questions.

1 Why does the professor say this: 🎧
(A) To ask students the basic meaning of inefficiency
(B) To encourage students to discuss the Taylor's idea
(C) To check if the students have done the assignment
(D) To explain what Taylor's main philosophy really is

» Comprehension Question «

2 What can be inferred about two students?
(A) They both agree with Taylor's philosophy on efficiency.
(B) They both disagree with Taylor's idea for efficiency.
(C) The man thinks that the idea makes sense in a way.
(D) The woman doesn't agree with the man's opinion.

Dictation Listen again and fill in the blanks. (P=W / S1=M / S2=W)

Professor "Scientific management," was _____ to try and increase the efficiency of... uh... factories and businesses in the early 20th century. Frederick Winslow Taylor was really _____, and his main philosophy was that... _____, managers had to put the system of production ahead of people. We had to get rid of the causes of inefficiency — workers wasting time. Did that mean workers had to work like machines?

Student 1 _____ wasting time... _____ of production means, I guess, I mean, it seems like he didn't realize he was dealing with people and not machines.

Student 2 I don't think Taylor meant that workers should work like machines. Well, maybe that's part of it... _____.

Mini-Exercise

Conversation 3 Listen to a conversation between two students. Then answer the questions.

1 Why does the man mention the last classes?
(A) To imply that the final will not be that difficult
(B) To suggest a way to catch up on the readings
(C) To find out whether the woman will go to the classes
(D) To remind the woman that they'll get to know what's going to be on the exam

» Comprehension Question «

2 Which of the following is mentioned as being used in carnivals held in Brazil and Louisiana?
(A) Special clothing
(B) Rhythmic dance
(C) Political debate
(D) Childish plays

Dictation
Listen again and fill in the blanks.   (S1=M / S2=W)

Student 1 So, are you ready for the history final exam?

Student 2 Sort of ... but I'm really _____ . What questions do you think he'll ask?

Student 1 Well, the big thing is going to be _____ the different carnival traditions in African-influenced cultures... so Brazil, Haiti, and Louisiana for example... well, he... I think... he wants us to look at the ways that people in those places, particularly in Brazil and Louisiana, used uh, used costumes and skits _____ the larger power structures... it's all in the readings...

Student 2 Man... I missed the week that we _____ ... and I never did _____ the readings...

Student 1 He pretty much will let us know what's gonna be on the exam _____ ... you know...

Student 2 I know... but still...

Student 1 Oh come on, you did well on the mid-term.

Mini-Exercise

Lecture 4 Listen to a lecture about the Haitian slave revolt. Then answer the questions.

1 Why does the professor say this: 🎧
(A) To explain how little slave revolts succeeded in the 18th century
(B) To emphasize the European power over slaves at the time
(C) To introduce a successful revolt and the reason behind it
(D) To ask students the reason why the revolts failed

» Comprehension Question «

2 What was the result of L'Ouverture's revolt?
(A) The death of L'Ouverture
(B) The French abolishment of slavery in all of its colonies
(C) Autonomy for Haiti and its people
(D) Driving every European away from Haiti

Dictation
Listen again and fill in the blanks. (P=M)

Professor Okay, so we've, we've uh seen that the slave revolts of the 18th century _____ and, uh, well, usually executed... Well, why is that, though? Is this always the case? Let's take a look at one revolt, on the Caribbean island of Haiti.... Uh, that was successful at _____. This was led by Toussaint L'Ouverture, who was a, uh, a former slave. We would like to take a look at the primary factors that _____. As you all read in the book, L'Ouverture was inspired, um greatly inspired, by the ideals of the French Revolution. A brief, uh, _____ followed by a reinstatement of it led to mass chaos on the island, on Haiti, and, uh, so soon the French _____ with the slaves, led by L'Ouverture. Finally, it was Napoleon Bonaparte who _____ L'Ouverture, granting independence to the island and its people.

Vocabulary Preview for Practice

Listen and choose the correct definition of the given words or phrases.

Practice 1
1. mark   a. ☐   b. ☐
2. hypothesize   a. ☐   b. ☐
3. hold   a. ☐   b. ☐
4. exceptional   a. ☐   b. ☐

Practice 2
1. virtue   a. ☐   b. ☐
2. flatter   a. ☐   b. ☐
3. convey   a. ☐   b. ☐
4. at hand   a. ☐   b. ☐

Practice 3
1. embody   a. ☐   b. ☐
2. philanthropist   a. ☐   b. ☐
3. mistreatment   a. ☐   b. ☐
4. motivation   a. ☐   b. ☐

Practice 4
1. frustrate   a. ☐   b. ☐
2. pressure   a. ☐   b. ☐
3. priority   a. ☐   b. ☐
4. committee   a. ☐   b. ☐

Vocabulary Preview for Actual Test

Choose the best word to complete each sentence.

Actual Test 1

1. He suffered a stroke two years ago, which left him unable to speak, but his mental _____ wasn't affected.
   a. custody   b. insanity   c. entity   d. capacity

2. The government plans to cut taxes in order to _____ the economy.
   a. stimulate   b. abound   c. weave   d. absorb

3. The court ruled the parents are partially _____ their children's car accidents.
   a. related to   b. responsible for c. blamed for   d. resigning from

4. It's very difficult to _____ yourself into a society whose culture is so different from your own.
   a. cohere   b. contend   c. integrate   d. annihilate

Actual Test 2

1. The doctors have _____ the cause of the illness to an unknown virus.
   a. forced   b. attributed   c. advocated   d. entitled

2. He tried to _____ an opportunity to ask questions.
   a. invoke   b. capture   c. revitalize   d. seize

3. In short, you occupy several different positions in the complex _____ of society.
   a. structure   b. option   c. influx   d. command

4. Because of the severe recession, many companies in the movie industry have lost a lot of money recently, and _____ this has caused unemployment.
   a. primarily   b. in turn   c. chiefly   d. for the time being

Function 183

Practice 1

Lecture

Listen to a lecture about Van Gogh.

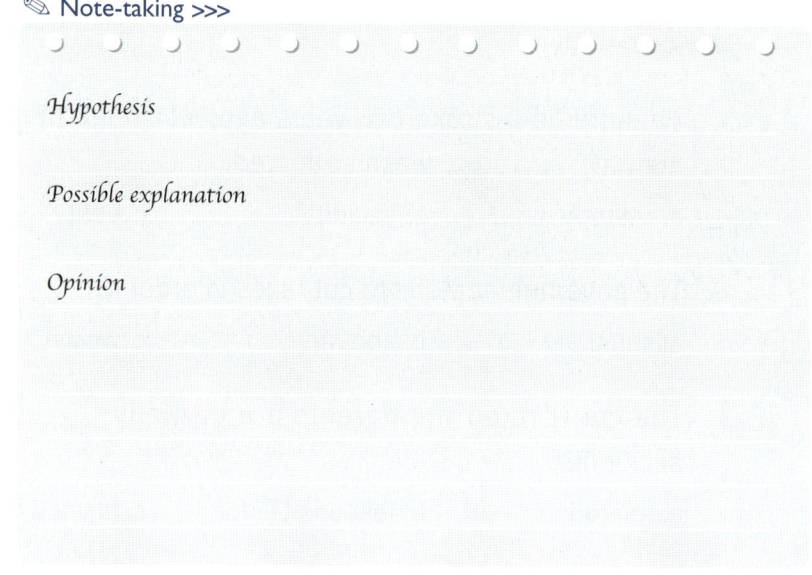

Note-taking >>>

Hypothesis

Possible explanation

Opinion

* digitalis (식물) 디기탈리스   halo effect 후광 효과

Now answer the questions.

1 Why does the professor mention the Impressionists?

(A) To indicate Van Gogh was a member of that school
(B) To illustrate Van Gogh's distinctive style
(C) To emphasize the influences on Van Gogh's work
(D) To imply that Van Gogh disliked Impressionism

2 Why does the professor mention Van Gogh's doctor?

(A) To indicate a person who claimed the hypothesis
(B) To imply that Van Gogh's illness had not affected his art
(C) To describe Van Gogh's emphasis on yellow color and the halo effect
(D) To introduce the possible explanation for Van Gogh's mental illness

3 Which of the following is NOT true about the theory?

(A) Van Gogh's art style may have been influenced by his eye problem.
(B) Van Gogh's blurry halo vision was caused by an herb.
(C) Van Gogh used yellow and blue filters when he was painting.
(D) Van Gogh's use of yellow and halo effects is the basis of the theory in question.

Practice 2

Discussion

Listen to a discussion about international business.

✎ Note-taking >>>

Business letter

      case 1

      case 2

Lesson to learn

Now answer the questions.

1 Why does the professor say this: 🎧

(A) To introduce common statements in business with other countries
(B) To exemplify a business letter with a great complimentary introduction
(C) To give an example of a letter that can be misunderstood
(D) To point out the importance of the first paragraph of a letter

2 Why does the professor mention this: 🎧

(A) To ask students to guess which would be better for business writing
(B) To imply that either case would not be considered proper in business letters
(D) To indicate that there are two common types of business letters
(D) To show his point about international business letter writing

3 Which is NOT a reason to learn subtle ways to show respect in other cultures?

(A) So you can get a business with desired partners.
(B) So you will not be offending to people from different cultures.
(C) So you can get straight to the point in your letter.
(D) So you will not be considered rude in business situations.

Function 185

Practice 3

Discussion

Listen to a discussion about Andrew Carnegie.

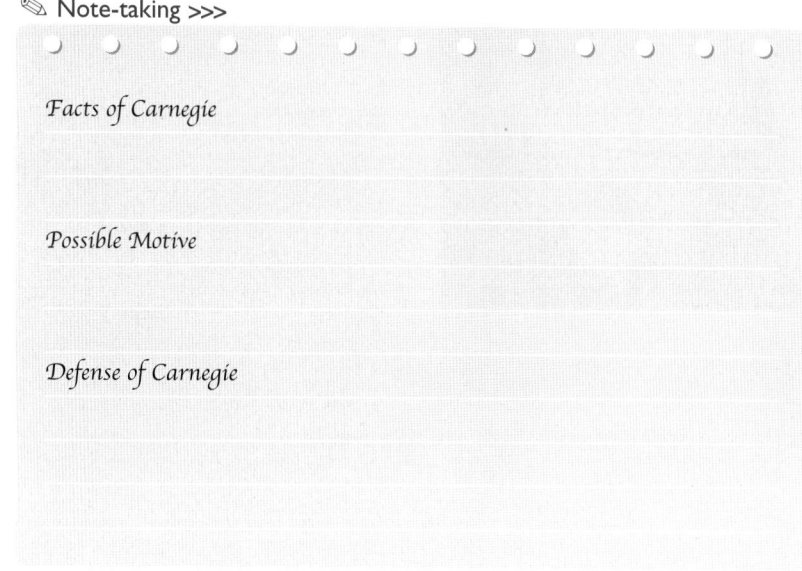

📝 Note-taking >>>

Facts of Carnegie

Possible Motive

Defense of Carnegie

Now answer the questions.

1 Why does the professor mention the American rags-to-riches myth?

(A) To imply that Carnegie exploited workers, and gave little back in return
(B) To explain that Carnegie was able to make his fortune from nothing
(C) To show a possible reason why he gave help to needy people
(D) To indicate that the myth came from the success of Carnegie

2 Why does the professor say this: 🎧

(A) To point out that this is a subject of intense public argument
(B) To see if students want to support that Carnegie is a philanthropist
(C) To explain that there are other views on Carnegie as a philanthropist
(D) To encourage students to express their opinions on Carnegie

3 What can be inferred about the two students?

(A) They both agree that Carnegie's motives were misunderstood.
(B) The woman agrees that Carnegie was an unselfish person.
(C) The man agrees that Carnegie was a sincere philanthropist.
(D) They both don't agree that Carnegie was all about self-glorification.

Practice 4

Conversation

Listen to a conversation between two students.

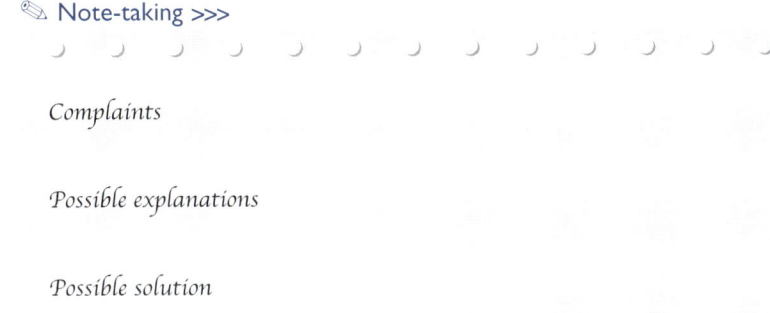

Complaints

Possible explanations

Possible solution

Now answer the questions.

1 Why does the man mention making an appointment?

(A) To tell the man that's the only way to see the professor
(B) To suggest that it is necessary even in the office hours
(C) To suggest the best way to get together with the professor
(D) To ask if the man called the professor for the appointment

2 What does the woman mean when she says this: 🎧

(A) She feels that an appointment is not necessary when the professor is in his office.
(B) She thought she could visit the professor anytime within the office hours.
(C) She doens't have to visit the professor during the office hours.
(D) She didn't know that she could make an appointment with the professor.

3 Why does the woman say this: 🎧

(A) To ask whether the man heard the announcements about the office hours
(B) To question if the newly announced office hours are reliable
(C) To wonder if the announcements about the office hours are important to pay attention
(D) To ask whether the professor ever makes the announcement in class

Actual Test 1

TOEFL Listening

Listen to a lecture on education.

✎ Note-taking >>>

Montessori program

Best way

Now answer the questions.

1 What is the lecture mainly about?
- Ⓐ Problems with educating all children in the United States
- Ⓑ The goal and major elements of the Montessori education program
- Ⓒ Differences between Maria Montessori and Bronson Alcott
- Ⓓ Comparisons between traditional education and Montessori

2 Why does the professor say this: 🎧
- Ⓐ To start an overview of Montessori's opinion on child education
- Ⓑ To find out if students have done their reading assignment
- Ⓒ To imply that Montessori's philosophy is well-known among people
- Ⓓ To encourage students to think of the basic concept of the Montessori educational philosophy

3. Why does the professor mention instructors in traditional programs?
   - Ⓐ To explain that their roles were comparably important also
   - Ⓑ To imply that the role of teachers in Montessori program is weakened
   - Ⓒ To contrast with the role of teachers in Montessori programs
   - Ⓓ To suggest that teachers were essential in both programs

4. How does the professor explain the Montessori program?
   - Ⓐ By comparing it with the features of traditional programs
   - Ⓑ By explaining the main principles of the Montessori program
   - Ⓒ By listing some advantages of the Montessori program
   - Ⓓ By pointing out three major elements of the Montessori program

5. Which of the following is NOT an explanation of the Montessori program?
   - Ⓐ The role of teachers is to help children by providing them with a guide for the lesson.
   - Ⓑ Each child is aware that they are mainly responsible for their own learning.
   - Ⓒ Children will have to bring study materials to the class for each day's lesson.
   - Ⓓ A stimulating environment is provided to create interest in a child's world.

Actual Test 2

TOEFL Listening

Listen to a discussion on music history.

Note-taking >>>

American art

Jazz   characteristic

Now answer the questions.

1   What is the discussion mainly about?
- Ⓐ Features of the arts in early American history
- Ⓑ The emergence of the first American art form
- Ⓒ Jazz influenced from the African slave culture
- Ⓓ The origin of jazz music and its development

2   Why does the professor say this: 🎧
- Ⓐ To emphasize the reasons of Jazz as part of an American culture
- Ⓑ To persuade students to have group discussions on the origins of jazz
- Ⓒ To have students discuss the reasons why jazz is so unique to American culture
- Ⓓ To suggest that the class should focus on talking about the reasons

3 Why does the professor say this: 🎧
   Ⓐ To show that he is surprised by students' answers
   Ⓑ To indicate that both opinions are relevant
   Ⓒ To suggest that the issue is very controversial
   Ⓓ To imply that further discussion won't be necessary

4 According to the professor, which of the following is true about jazz? Choose TWO answers.
   Ⓐ Some of the musical features are influenced by African culture.
   Ⓑ Instruments used in jazz music have influenced American cultures.
   Ⓒ Jazz was influenced by two cultures that existed in two separated states.
   Ⓓ Different cultural elements in jazz make it very American.

5 What does the professor say about American culture?
   Ⓐ Much of American culture is influenced by different European cultures.
   Ⓑ American culture is a mixture of many different elements.
   Ⓒ Many aspects of American culture deal with slavery.
   Ⓓ Only Europeans are responsible for the development of American culture.

DICTATION

Practice 1

🎧 Listen and fill in the blanks.

(P=W)

Professor: Vincent Van Gogh's paintings ① _____. His style ② _____ from the Impressionists who came before him. There are some experts who hypothesize that Van Gogh's style was the result of a vision disorder — the paintings represent ③ _____. Now, we'll take a look at some slides of his work in a minute, but let's first talk about this idea... Alright, ④ _____ that Van Gogh's doctor ⑤ _____ the painter's infamous bouts of mental illness with digitalis. These might cause problems in a person's yellow-blue vision — ⑥ _____ the world through a yellow filter and the sufferer is also seeing a blurry halo around objects. Many of Van Gogh's paintings ⑦ _____, and the halo effect can be seen quite clearly in many of his paintings as well. However, ⑧ _____, Van Gogh's expertise as a painter is well documented by his exceptional output. But come on, that his distinctive style was the result of a disease rather than a brilliant artistic mind ⑨ _____.

|구문해설| **in a minute** 잠시 후에 **A rather than B** B라기 보다 A **far from** ~와는 거리가 먼

Practice 2

🎧 Listen and fill in the blanks.

(P=M / S=W)

Professor Okay, so say you, you got a letter from a businessperson from another country who was obviously interested in ① _____ _____. Let's suppose that the first paragraph of the letter ② _____ _____, praising the virtues of your company... umm... "I admire what you have, uh, accomplished and heard a lot about your creative and innovative works and so on..." Now, ③ _____ as a businessperson?

Student Suspicion! If somebody is ④ _____, I feel like they're trying to sell me something I don't want. I like it much better when people ⑤ _____ .

Professor Yet in this, uh, this person's culture, it's expected that business letters begin with a fair amount of compliment and flattery before ⑥ _____ _____. In fact, to just "jump right in" to what you want ⑦ _____ .... just like you had a negative feeling to overly complimented beginning.

So what am I getting at here? Should it be directly to the point? Or complimentary? What I'm saying is that these things are relative to your culture. Before ⑧ _____ people from other cultures for business purposes, it's an absolute necessity — if you want their business — ⑨ _____ in which, uh, respect and consideration are conveyed in writing.

|구문해설| **go into great detail** 상세한 내용을 다루다 **begin with** ~로 시작하다 **So what am I getting at here?** 자, 내가 여기서 말하려는 것이 무엇일까요? **directly to the point** 단도직입적으로 말하다

DICTATION

Practice 3

🎧 Listen and fill in the blanks.

(P=W / S1=W / S2=M)

Professor: Andrew Carnegie was a Scottish-born industrialist who really embodies ① _____ . Now in addition to being highly skilled at making money, Carnegie was also quite a philanthropist who freely gave money away and helped people ② _____ . Not only did he employ countless workers, he gave back to society, ③ _____ the creation of over 2,800 free libraries in the U.S. and Britain. I know you guys might want to ④ _____ .

Student 1: Yeah, I think he is ⑤ _____ from the donations. I mean, it just made him look good in the public's eye, which made them ⑥ _____ of his workers.

Student 2: Well, I've seen a few Carnegie libraries... They don't even have his name on them, the way that today's philanthropists want their name all over everything... It doesn't seem like it was all about self-glorification.

Professor: It's true that he didn't want his name on the buildings. On the other hand, it's also true that ⑦ _____ who gave the grant for the construction of these buildings. So, what we can see is that the motivations of this famous industrialist ⑧ _____ .

구문해설 | **rags-to-riches** 가난했던 사람이 부자가 되는, 출세하는   **in addition to** ~ 뿐만 아니라   **on the other hand** 다른 한편으로

Practice 4

🎧 Listen and fill in the blanks.

(S1=W / S2=M)

Student 1 You know, ① _____ I've gone to Professor Brown's office during his office hours and he wasn't there... It's really ② _____ and have him not be there.

Student 2 I know ③ _____, so he has many meetings, which add a lot of pressure to a professor's schedule.

Student 1 I guess, but his priority should be his students, don't you think? My roommate says that her professor cancelled an appointment three times!

Student 2 ④ _____. But, did you make an appointment to meet with the professor?

Student 1 No... ⑤ _____ when I had a question. Why would I have to when there are office hours?

Student 2 You may be right. But if you know he's often not there when he's supposed to be, it probably makes sense to make an appointment if you want to talk to him.

Student 1 I guess that's what I'll do from now on.

Student 2 And he announces in class ⑥ _____ or if there is any change in his office hours... ⑦ _____?

Student 1 No, I didn't, I mean I did... but I didn't pay much attention... (*doubtly*) You did?

Student 2 I don't want to waste my time going to the professor's office when he is not there...

|구문해설| **make sense** 이치에 맞다, 일리가 있다 **make an appointment** 시간 약속을 하다

DICTATION

Actual Test 1

🎧 Listen and fill in the blanks.

(P=W)

Professor: As it became more and more common in the United States to educate all children, ① _____ about how best to educate all of these children. One of these ② _____ an Italian physician named Maria Montessori... Well, you've probably heard the name before... Alright! So, what basically is it? I mean what does she say is the best way to educate children? She greatly ③ _____ _____ as the keys to helping children of all different talents and capacities ④ _____. One of the, uh, the main components of Montessori's program were to provide children ⑤ _____ _____ that would ⑥ _____ the world around them. They were encouraged to explore and ask questions ⑦ _____. They were, uh, also made aware of the fact that they were responsible for their own learning, which required self-discipline and respect for others around them. A third principle of the Montessori method was ⑧ _____. In traditional programs, teachers were instructors, telling the students exactly what it is, what to do and even what they learned... but Montessori teachers were more of facilitators, helping the children as they discovered new things. What were children expected to, uh, come out of the Montessori program with? Well, the memorization of facts, ⑨ _____ many schools, ⑩ _____. Rather, Montessori, uh, ⑪ _____ _____ children to know ⑫ _____ knowledge throughout their lives. If you open your textbooks, we can take a look at how this compares with the educational philosophies of Bronson Alcott...

|구문해설| **key to** ~에 대한 열쇠   **be responsible for** ~에 대해 책임이 있다

Actual Test 2

🎧 Listen and fill in the blanks.

(P=M / S1=W / S2=M)

Professor The arts in early American history ① _____ their European predecessors. So...uh...basically, white writers, painters, and musicians were constantly ② _____ themselves from the Europeans. ③ _____ to create a uniquely "American" art, black American musicians ④ _____ their own cultural traditions to create the truly American music style known as jazz. Now, we should spare some time to think about why many people believe that jazz is truly a product of American culture, OK?

Student 1 But wasn't so much of what influenced jazz music really a product of African culture, ⑤ _____ ? The drumming, for example, and syncopated rhythms?

Student 2 On the other hand, though, jazz music ⑥ _____ , and traditional jazz really stays pretty close to the standard structure of European style music, with melody and harmony and all that.

Professor Yes... and yes! This is the point. What emerged out of the convergence of the two cultures was ⑦ _____ . This new kind of music was very much influenced by the blues music that ⑧ _____ the slaves' songs, ⑨ _____ Africa. But, as you'll hear on this next recording, the instruments were primarily of European influence. ⑩ _____ is very American as American culture is very much about the blending of many different influences. And I think that's why we can say that jazz was the first truly American art form.

|구문해설| **attribute to** ~ 덕분이라고 생각하다   **search for** ~을 추구하다   **distinguish A from B** A와 B를 구별하다   **in turn** 차례로, 번갈아, 이번에는

Function 197

Vocabulary Review

Write the meanings of the words in the blanks.

1. tighten _____
2. appearance _____
3. archeological _____
4. embellish _____
5. toxin _____
6. specifically _____
7. efficiency _____
8. productivity _____
9. carnival _____
10. costume _____
11. catch up _____
12. inspire _____
13. chaos _____
14. ideal _____
15. hypothesize _____
16. hold _____
17. exceptional _____
18. virtue _____
19. flatter _____
20. convey _____
21. embody _____
22. philanthropist _____
23. committee _____
24. motivation _____
25. priority _____
26. pressure _____
27. capacity _____
28. component _____
29. memorization _____
30. acquire _____
31. interpret _____
32. philosophy _____
33. convergence _____

Write the meanings of the phrases in the blanks.

34. come to mind _____
35. A rather than B _____
36. got straight to the point _____
37. begin with _____
38. in addition to _____
39. make sense _____
40. attribute to _____
41. distinguish A from B _____

Write the correct words or phrases in the blanks.

42. ~을 다루다 _____
43. 미묘한 _____
44. ~에 대해 책임이 있다 _____
45. 상세한 내용을 다루다 _____
46. 차례로, 번갈아, 이번에는 _____
47. 원리 _____
48. 패배시키다 _____
49. 지독한 _____
50. 독특한, 탁월한 _____

PROGRESS TEST

Listening Comprehension Section Directions

This section measures your ability to understand conversations and lectures in English. You will hear each conversation or lecture only one time. After each conversation or lecture, you will answer some questions about it. The questions typically ask about the main idea and supporting details. Some questions ask about a speaker's purpose or attitude. Answer the questions based on what is stated or implied by the speakers.

You may take notes while you listen. You may use your notes to help you answer the questions. Your notes will not be scored. If you need to change the volume while you listen, click on the **Volume** icon at the top of the screen. In some questions, you will see this icon: 🎧 This means that you will hear, but not see part of the question.

Some of the questions have special directions. These directions appear in a gray box on the screen. Most questions are worth one point. If a question is worth more than one point, it will have special directions that indicate how many points you can receive. You must answer each question. After you answer, click on **Next**. Then click on **OK** to confirm your answer and go on to the next question. After you click on **OK**, you cannot return to previous questions.

You will have 20 minutes to answer the questions in this section. A clock at the top of the screen will show you how much time is remaining. The clock will not count down while you are listening to test material.

Progress Test 5

TOEFL Listening

Listen to a lecture on Zoos. Then answer the questions.

TOEFL Listening

1. What is the lecture mainly about?
   - Ⓐ A history of royal animal collections in Europe
   - Ⓑ The evolution of keeping animals in zoos
   - Ⓒ A criticism of modern zoos with barred cages
   - Ⓓ A biography of the first modern zookeeper

2. Why does the professor mention the use of moats?
   - Ⓐ To imply that most modern zoos have moats
   - Ⓑ To suggest the ideal surroundings for animals
   - Ⓒ To give an example of of Carl Hagenbeck's contributions
   - Ⓓ To show how animals are kept in many zoos

3 Why does the professor say this: 🎧
- Ⓐ To imply that there is no clear evidence of the exact time
- Ⓑ To encourage students to participate in the class
- Ⓒ To emphasize the importance of the time of change
- Ⓓ To explain when the circumstances in zoos started to change

4 What can be inferred about past zoos?
- Ⓐ The various animals were frequently abused by monarchs.
- Ⓑ The purpose of zoos has changed over the past 400 years.
- Ⓒ European climates were not healthy for most exotic animals.
- Ⓓ It was one of the most popular places among many people.

5 According to the professor, what did Hagenbeck accomplish?
- Ⓐ He changed the way zoos treated animals at the time.
- Ⓑ He gathered an impressive collection of animals.
- Ⓒ He improved the cages animals were kept in.
- Ⓓ He educated the public on the care and feeding of animals.

6 Which of the following is NOT part of a modern zoo's mission?
- Ⓐ Creating new breeds of animals through cloning
- Ⓑ Protecting animals that are in danger of dying out
- Ⓒ Helping the build up the populations of endangered animals
- Ⓓ Adding to the general knowledge of animals

Progress Test 6

TOEFL Listening

Listen to a conversation between two students. Then answer the questions.

TOEFL Listening

1 Why does the woman go to see the man?
- Ⓐ To complain about the difficulty of the assignment
- Ⓑ To ask him about the main points of the assignment
- Ⓒ To find out if the man has taken the class before
- Ⓓ To persuade him to work on the assignment together

2 Why does the man mention Bob Dylan's or Joan Baez's songs?
- Ⓐ To imply that they are the most popular folk song writers
- Ⓑ To encourage her to listen to folk music for the assignment
- Ⓒ To ask if she knows some folk singers and their songs
- Ⓓ To remind the woman of the contents of the 60's folk songs

3. Why does the woman say this: 🎧
   A. To show that she is satisfied with the man's comment
   B. To hide her disappointment of the man's suggestion
   C. To encourage the man to continue on the first point
   D. To imply that the man told her enough information

4. Why does the man mention the non-political folk songs?
   A. To give a reason why most folk songs are respected
   B. To explain how early political folk songs had evolved
   C. To point out another theme of 60's folk music
   D. To conclude the major points that he made so far

5. Why does the woman say this: 🎧
   A. To confirm if the man is done with the comments
   B. To summarize the main points for the assignment
   C. To suggest that there may be an additional point
   D. To point out the problem with the man's comments

6. According to the conversation, what is one way this music differed from other music?
   A. It relied on old-fashioned instruments.
   B. It used political issues as its central theme.
   C. It was not played on the radio very much.
   D. It was not widely appreciated by young people.

DICTATION

Progress Test 5

🎧 Listen and fill in the blanks.

(P=W)

Professor: Almost every major city today has a zoo. Today's zoos usually ① _____, not only to educate the visitor about the species, but also to ensure the animal's health and happiness. They're quite different from zoos of the past. Zoological collections ② _____, and by the Middle Ages in Europe, ③ _____ gifts of exotic creatures... and, well, large collections of wild animals grew up this way. Of course, the lives of the animals in these zoos were really pretty miserable. ④ _____ were pretty poorly understood, and so they would often ⑤ _____. So, when did this change? In the 17th century? Or 18th century? Well, ⑥ _____ that the value of trying to recreate the animals' habitats was really seen. Carl Hagenbeck, a new manager at Jardin des Plantes Zoological Gardens, uh... it's a zoo in Paris, he uh... introduced the idea of making the animals' surroundings as natural and familiar as possible. You know... animals in many zoos ⑦ _____, right? But he was the first person to institute the use of moats, ⑧ _____ dug around the perimeter of the zoo and filled with water, in order to prevent the animals from escaping or to protect them from any possible attack from others... This enabled the zoo keepers to create much nicer, bigger environments for the animals. Today's zoos, in addition to providing education and entertainment for people, see ⑨ _____ as part of their mission, as well. Breeding programs for animals ⑩ _____ are part of this mission. They also really demonstrate how far zoos have come from their initial roles as simple entertainment and symbols of power for kings and queens.

|구문해설| **attempt to** ~하기를 시도하다   **not only A but also B** A 뿐 아니라 B도   **go back to** ~로 거슬러 올라가다   **not until** ~하고 나서야 비로소 …하다   **enable ~ to...** ~가 …할 수 있게 하다   **as well** 도 또한

Progress Test 6

🎧 Listen and fill in the blanks.

(S1=W / S2=M)

Student 1 Hey, Mike, you got a minute?

Student 2 Sure, what is it?

Student 1 I just wanted to ask you something for my assignment ① _____ . You have probably done this before... It's about 60's folk music...

Student 2 Oh, I think I remember something about that from last semester. So, what is the problem?

Student 1 Oh, ② _____ what points I really have to focus on... I mean, I don't understand why the professor was making such a big deal about the 60's folk music revival. I mean ③ _____ it was such an important moment, but I don't get it.

Student 2 Well, I think he was saying there are ④ _____ . I think it's really important to think about it in terms of the protest movement. You probably know some of those... uh... Bob Dylan's or Joan Baez's songs, right? Don't they seem like ⑤ _____ _____ ? Their songs are offering critical comments about power and ideology... That folk music was really something that ⑥ _____ _____ before. And anti-war songs really ⑦ _____ a lot of the concerns of the young.

Student 1 (In content) Not bad! That's definitely a point, go on, what else?

Student 2 Well, we can also look at the stuff that wasn't political. Folk songs that really just revived the roots of the music of rural America. ⑧ _____ _____ specific political policies, it was making a kind of protest against modern life such as wasteful consumption and materialism. The songs kind of ⑨ _____ a simpler way of life.

Student 1 Nice, basically both of these things really, I guess, point to a kind of dissatisfaction with the way things were, on the part of young people. Okay... ⑩ _____ .

|구문해설| **have a hard time ~ing** ~하는 데 어려움을 겪다   **figure out** 이해하다   **in terms of** ~의 관점에서

Vocabulary Review for Progress Test

Choose the correct synonym of the given words or phrases.

Progress Test 5

1. The computer doesn't <u>mimic</u> human thought, but it reaches the same ends by different means.
   a. criticize   b. overthrow   c. transfer   d. imitate

2. The Chancellorship of the University was <u>bestowed upon</u> her in 1981.
   a. presented to   b. contributed to   c. reconciled to   d. involved with

3. They have survived under <u>miserable</u> and inhuman conditions for thirty years.
   a. delighting   b. keen   c. wretched   d. firm

4. The museum is full of <u>rare</u> and precious treasures.
   a. affordable   b. uncommon   c. genuine   d. variable

Progress Test 6

1. The President's support was <u>critical</u> to this project, but it was neglected by many of them.
   a. important   b. skillful   c. dominant   d. minor

2. Traditional skills are being <u>revived</u> by local craftsmen.
   a. renewed   b. released   c. recovered   d. reissued

3. The money is intended to be used for <u>specific</u> purposes.
   a. uncertain   b. particular   c. common   d. general

4. Have you <u>definitely</u> decided to go to Paris?
   a. dreadfully   b. alternatively   c. steadily   d. certainly

FINAL TEST

Listening Comprehension Section Directions

This section measures your ability to understand conversations and lectures in English. You will hear each conversation or lecture only one time. After each conversation or lecture, you will answer some questions about it. The questions typically ask about the main idea and supporting details. Some questions ask about a speaker's purpose or attitude. Answer the questions based on what is stated or implied by the speakers.

You may take notes while you listen. You may use your notes to help you answer the questions. Your notes will not be scored. If you need to change the volume while you listen, click on the **Volume** icon at the top of the screen. In some questions, you will see this icon: 🎧 This means that you will hear, but not see part of the question.

Some of the questions have special directions. These directions appear in a gray box on the screen. Most questions are worth one point. If a question is worth more than one point, it will have special directions that indicate how many points you can receive. You must answer each question. After you answer, click on **Next**. Then click on **OK** to confirm your answer and go on to the next question. After you click on **OK**, you cannot return to previous questions.

You will have 20 minutes to answer the questions in this section. A clock at the top of the screen will show you how much time is remaining. The clock will not count down while you are listening to test material.

Final Test 1

TOEFL Listening

Listen to a lecture on translating poetry in a class. Then answer the questions.

* etymological 어원적인

TOEFL Listening

1 What is the lecture mainly about?
- Ⓐ The function of translation in the history of poetry
- Ⓑ The role of the translator in influencing interpretation
- Ⓒ The varieties of translation in English and Spanish poetry
- Ⓓ The various approaches to translating a poem

2 According to the lecture, which of the following are considered elements of poetry translation? Choose TWO answers.
- Ⓐ Conveying the meaning to the reader
- Ⓑ Providing information the reader can act on
- Ⓒ Getting across the author's intention
- Ⓓ Providing a cultural context for the work

3 How does the professor explain the choices of translators?
- Ⓐ By pointing to a famous poem in Spanish
- Ⓑ By offering examples of three different possibilities
- Ⓒ By suggesting sound is more important than sense
- Ⓓ By implying that good translators don't need to choose

4 Why does the professor mention Ezra Pound?
- Ⓐ To demonstrate one of the ways to translate a poem
- Ⓑ To show how many concerns can be dealt with at once
- Ⓒ To illustrate a translator who prized meaning over sound
- Ⓓ To highlight the risks inherent in translation

5 What does the professor mean when she says this: 🎧
- Ⓐ Translators often have to give up rhyme of a poem.
- Ⓑ It is difficult to translate some poetic features.
- Ⓒ Rhyme or sound shouldn't be translated easily.
- Ⓓ A poem should have the same sound as the original.

6 Why does the professor say this: 🎧
- Ⓐ To explain that words are more important than rhyme most of the times
- Ⓑ To indicate that translators are responsible for exact meaning of the words
- Ⓒ To show how translators decide whether to translate meaning or sound
- Ⓓ To suggest that the rhyme of a poem should be considered prior to meaning

Final Test 2

TOEFL Listening

Listen to a discussion about alternative fuels. Then answer the questions.

* tidal power 조력 발전   fusion power 핵융합 발전

TOEFL Listening

1. What is the discussion mainly about?
   - Ⓐ An overview of research into renewable energy resources
   - Ⓑ A comparison of different types of alternative fuels
   - Ⓒ A survey of problems with fusion-generated energy
   - Ⓓ A look at a potential solution to the energy problem

2. Why does the professor mention oil?
   - Ⓐ To imply that the alternative anergy is similar to it
   - Ⓑ To indicate the main source of energy at this time
   - Ⓒ To suggest that it has similar problems to fusion energy
   - Ⓓ To point out what shoud be developed as an alternative

3 Which of the following is NOT mentioned as a benefit of fusion?
- Ⓐ It is cleaner than other energy sources.
- Ⓑ It is technologically simple to achieve.
- Ⓒ Its environmental impact is minimal.
- Ⓓ It requires readily available resources.

4 How does the professor explain the fusion power?
- Ⓐ By describing the principle of fusion reaction
- Ⓑ By comparing it to other forms of energy
- Ⓒ By explaining the chemical formula for it
- Ⓓ By pointing to an illustration in the textbook

5 Listen to the part of the lecture again:
Why does the professor say this:
- Ⓐ To find out if students have read the article in the book
- Ⓑ To encourage the students to give their opinions
- Ⓒ To imply that there is a great deal of criticism on fusion
- Ⓓ To suggest that the reasons are too obvious and easy

6 What does the professor mean when he says this:
- Ⓐ Fusion reaction is very sensitive to even soft contact.
- Ⓑ Fusion can cause a great loss of energy.
- Ⓒ Fusion is less likely to fail because the reaction just stops.
- Ⓓ Fusion is not dangerous and wouldn't cause disaster.

Final Test 3

TOEFL Listening

Listen to a conversation between a professor and a student. Then answer the questions

* shorthand 속기   abbreviation 약어

TOEFL Listening

1 Why does the man go to see the professor?
- Ⓐ To get notes for a class he's missed
- Ⓑ To talk about a deadline he can't meet
- Ⓒ To find out if he can participate in the study session
- Ⓓ To ask how to improve his note-taking skills

2 Why will the man attend tomorrow's office hours?
- Ⓐ He wants to return a book to the professor.
- Ⓑ He wants to have to find out if the book is there.
- Ⓒ He wants to get a book from the professor.
- Ⓓ He wants to see the professor's notes again.

3 Why does the professor say this: 🎧
- Ⓐ To assure him that she knows he's doing the assignments
- Ⓑ To indicate that she will change tonight's assignment
- Ⓒ To find out whether he is prepared to understand the lecture
- Ⓓ To encourage the man to pay closer attention to the assignments.

4 What does the professor mean when she says this: 🎧
- Ⓐ Her note-taking skills weren't always good in college.
- Ⓑ She will show him her notes from her college years.
- Ⓒ Her note-taking was great from her first year in college.
- Ⓓ She would prefer not to show the student her notes.

5 Indicate whether each phrase is the professor's suggestion. Check the correct box for each phrase.

	Yes	No
Be prepared for the class by reading textbook.		
Study with a classmate		
Record the lecture and do the the note-taking after class		
Improve the note-taking skills by practicing with a partner		
Participate in the class by asking questions		

6 What does the man mean when he says this: 🎧
- Ⓐ He is not sure that's a good idea.
- Ⓑ He is wondering whether asking questions is good.
- Ⓒ He is determined that he will participate more in the class.
- Ⓓ He is not comfortable with asking questions in the class.

MEMO

MEMO

성공적인 학습을 위한 단계별 전략!
Development & Progress for Completion

NEXUS TOEFL® iBT
넥서스영어교육연구소

정답 및 해설

Listening 3
Level

TOEFL® is a registered trademark of Educational Testing Service.
This publication is not endorsed or approved by ETS.

NEXUS Edu

성공적인 학습을 위한 단계별 전략!
Development & Progress for Completion

NEXUS TOEFL® iBT

정답 및 해설

Listening

3

Level

NEXUS Edu

CHAPTER 01
MAIN IDEA

Pre Test 1

초(超)심리학에 대한 강의를 듣고, 질문에 답하시오.

🎧 스크립트

P   As, uh, as we've looked at the way that scientific inquiries have evolved over the centuries, we've seen how, how, uh, a lot of questions have been answered. For example, the wobble of the moon's orbit... okay? Then again, a lot of explanations were rethought primarily due to oddities in the data. Yeah, so when something seems strange, it doesn't add up, then scientists tend to take a closer look at it. Actually there are many questions that are thought to be odd or strange... and for many of them, we don't have the answers. Okay, so uh, let's look at a completely different branch of science today — one that not everyone would even agree it is a science — that primarily focuses on explaining oddities, things we can't explain, things we can't even see. This is parapsychology. Parapsychologists, uh, do two things: they, uh, investigate and try to find a scientific basis for things that most other scientists don't even believe in — psychic communication, telepathy, those kinds of things... and they attempt to apply scientific methods to understanding these phenomena...

교수   수 세기에 걸쳐서 과학 연구가 발전해왔던 방식을 살펴보면서, 우리는 많은 의문점들에 대한 해답을 어떻게 찾았는지 알아 보았습니다. 예를 들면, 달 궤도의 흔들림 같은 것... 그렇죠? 그리고 이 가운데 많은 설명들이 주로 자료가 기이하다는 이유로 재검토되었습니다. 그래서 무언가가 이상한 것 같으면 이치에 맞지 않고, 그렇게 되면 과학자들은 그것을 더 면밀하게 살펴보는 경향이 있습니다. 실제로 터무니 없거나 이상하다고 생각되는 질문이 많이 존재합니다. 우리는 그 가운데 많은 질문에 대한 해답을 가지고 있지 않습니다. 그렇습니다. 어, 오늘날 과학의 완전히 다른 부문을 살펴봅시다. 즉 그것이 과학이라는 것조차 부정하는 사람이 있고, 주로 이상한 현상, 우리가 설명할 수도 심지어 볼 수도 없는 것에 주력을 하는 부문 말이죠. 이것이 바로 초심리학입니다. 초심리학자는 다음의 두 가지 일을 합니다. 대부분의 다른 과학자들은 믿지도 않는 심령의 의사소통, 텔레파시 등에 대한 과학적인 근거를 조사하고 발견하려 노력합니다. 그리고 그들은 이러한 현상을 이해하는 데 과학적 방법을 적용하려 시도합니다.

주로 어떤 내용의 강의인가?
(A) 행성의 특이한 움직임
(B) 과학적 방법을 사용하는 데 따르는 허점
(C) 과학의 서로 다른 분야끼리의 비교
(D) 알려지지 않은 현상에 대한 조사

정답 (D)

해설   우리가 설명할 수도 심지어 볼 수도 없는 이상한 현상들을 연구하는 초심리학에 대한 내용을 다루고 있다.

Pre Test 2

교수의 사무실에서 이루어지는 대화를 듣고, 질문에 답하시오.

🎧 스크립트

S   Hi Professor. Could I talk to you about this assignment for a minute?
P   Sure. What's the problem?
S   Well, um, you told us that we should bring a water sample into lab on Friday, but I was late for class last time and didn't hear the explanation about that.
P   Oh. Well, uh, really it's pretty simple. You just have to do two things: get a small sample of water — you can even put it in a plastic bag. Secondly, it must be from any source on campus.
S   Even, like, the sink in my dorm?
P   Sure, that would be fine. Or the pond, or the fountain outside of this building. Then, uh, then just bring it to class and we'll examine it in lab.
S   Oh. Okay. Well, that makes sense.

학생   안녕하세요, 교수님. 과제물에 대해 잠깐만 이야기할 수 있을까요?
교수   그럼. 무엇이 문제인가?
학생   그게요. 금요일에 실험실로 물 샘플을 가져와야 한다고 말씀하셨는데, 지난 번 수업에 지각하는 바람에 그것에 대한 설명을 듣지 못했습니다.
교수   그래. 그것은 매우 간단해. 두 가지만 하면 되는 거야. 물 샘플을 약간 가져오면 돼. 비닐봉지에라도 넣어와도 되고. 다음으로, 그것은 교내에 있는 것이어야 해.
학생   심지어 기숙사에 있는 싱크대에서 물을 받아와도 되나요?
교수   그럼. 그래도 좋아. 아니면 연못이나 이 건물 바깥에 있는 분수도 좋고. 그리고 그 물 샘플을 수업시간에 가져와서 실험실에서 조사해 볼 거야.

학생 예, 잘 알겠습니다.

학생이 교수를 찾아간 이유는 무엇인가?
(A) 결석한 수업에 대해 교수와 의논하기 위해서
(B) 수업의 과제물을 제출하기 위해서
(C) 과제물에 대한 더 많은 정보를 얻기 위해서
(D) 금요일 연구실 모임을 확인하기 위해서

정답 (C)

해설 지난 번 수업시간에 지각을 하는 바람에 듣지 못한, 과제물 제출에 대한 설명을 듣기 위해서 교수를 찾아갔다.

Vocabulary Preview for Mini-Exercise

Mini-Exercise 1

1-1. consequence (결과)
 ✓ a. a result or effect of something
   b. the state of being awake

1-2. literacy (읽고 쓰는 능력)
   a. of its most basic sense
 ✓ b. the ability to read and write

1-3. subscribe to (~에 동의하다)
 ✓ a. agree with an idea
   b. make a statement

2-1. perspective (시각, 견지)
   a. likely or expected to happen
 ✓ b. a way of thinking about something

2-2. evolutionary (진화의)
 ✓ a. connected with the scientific theory of evolution
   b. the act of taking part in an activity

2-3. heritage (유산)
 ✓ a. the art and beliefs that a society considers important to its history and culture
   b. the genetic process by which a parent's qualities or diseases pass to their child

3-1. hangover (숙취)
   a. a place where a particular group of people like to spend time
 ✓ b. being tired and sick because of too much drinking

3-2. alternative (대체의)
 ✓ a. able to be used instead of it
   b. happening or coming one after another

3-3. immunity (면역)
   a. the act of copying someone's behavior
 ✓ b. the protection that someone's body gives them against a particular disease

Mini-Exercise 2

1-1. permanent (영구한)
   a. allowing someone a large amount of freedom
 ✓ b. happening or existing for a long time or for all time in the future

1-2. enrollment (등록자수)
 ✓ a. the number of people who are taking a course at a school
   b. the process of making something larger

1-3. burst at the seams (매우 붐비다)
   a. to stop being useful or effective
 ✓ b. to be very full of people or things

2-1. all of a sudden (갑자기)
 ✓ a. quickly and without any sign that it is going to happen
   b. in a condition similar to sleep in which you do not sense

2-2. be broke (파산하다)
   a. to make something separate into two or more pieces
 ✓ b. to have no money

2-3. get somebody down (실망시키다)
   a. to support an idea, project, etc.
 ✓ b. to make someone feel sad or lose hope

3-1. participate (참여하다)
   a. to go past something
 ✓ b. to take part in something

3-2. semester (학기)
 ✓ a. one half of an academic year
   b. one of four equal parts of something

3-3. at ease (편하게)
   a. to make a problem less severe
 ✓ b. confident and relaxed

Mini-Exercise 1 Finding Topics of Lectures

1 미디어 해석능력배양 교육에 대한 강의를 듣고, 물음에 답하시오.

🎧 스크립트

P Children in this, uh, in this country watch, on average, about 20 hours a week of television. <u>Seems like a lot</u>? Well, there're some pretty serious physical consequences, but <u>I'm not gonna get into</u> those, at least not today. Instead, I want to look at media literacy — the movement to, uh, educate young people in, uh, interpreting and making intelligent judgments about media. What do media literacy educators do? Okay, there're two parts to this field that I'd like to spend much time on today. So, the first one is, uh, to talk to kids about the ways that television shows and commercials are, uh, constructed. Educators feel that it's a very early, but important step. Secondly, they also try to get kids to think about what the show or ad is trying to get the person to do — is it going to make you buy something? Or subscribe to a certain ideology? And so on...

교수 이 나라의 아이들은 평균적으로 일주일에 약 20시간 동안 텔레비전을 시청합니다. 많은 시간처럼 생각되나요? 텔레비전 시청에는 매우 심각한 신체적 결과가 따르지만 나는 최소한 오늘만은 그것에 대해서는 말하지 않을 것입니다. 대신, 미디어 해석능력 문제, 즉 미디어를 해석하고 이에 대해 지성적인 판단을 하도록 젊은이들을 교육시키는 운동에 대해 살펴보고 싶습니다.
미디어 해석능력 교육자가 하는 일은 무엇입니까? 그렇습니다. 오늘 내가 많은 시간을 투자하고 싶은 이 분야에는 두 가지 부분이 있습니다. 첫 부분은 아이들에게 텔레비전 쇼와 광고의 구성 방법에 대해 말해 주는 것입니다. 교육자들은 이것이 매우 초기이지만 중요한 단계라고 느낍니다. 그리고 두 번째 부분은 텔레비전 쇼나 광고가 사람들에게 어떤 일을 하게 하는지에 대해 아이들이 생각하도록 만들려고 노력하는 것입니다. 무언가를 구매하게 만드는 것인가? 아니면 어떤 이념을 수용하게 하는 것인가? 등이죠...

1 강의는 주로 어떤 내용을 다루고 있는가?
(A) 미디어로 인해 야기된 물리적으로 부정적인 상황
(B) 미디어에 대해 아이들을 교육하는 것
(C) TV 시트콤의 기본적인 줄거리 구조
(D) 아이들의 TV시청 시간의 증가 원인

정답 (B)

해설 매체를 해석하고 지성적인 판단을 내릴 수 있도록 아이들을 가르치는 방법에 대해 설명한다. 'Instead'로 시작하는 문장에서 강의의 주제를 명확히 제시하고 있다.

2 다음 중 매체 교육자의 목적은 어느 것인가?
(A) 사람들에게 TV 시청시간 수를 줄이는 방법에 대해 가르치기
(B) 교육 정보의 해석방법을 학생들에게 보여 주기
(C) TV 광고나 쇼가 어떻게 만들어지고, 무슨 작용을 하는지를 설명하기
(D) TV에서 본 제품은 무조건 사지 말라고 학생들을 부추기기

정답 (C)

해설 매체 교육자의 목적은 두 가지로, 텔레비전 쇼와 광고의 구성방식에 대해 가르치고, 물건을 사게 하는 등의 그 작용에 대해 가르치는 것이다.

2 심리학 수업의 강의를 듣고, 물음에 답하시오.

🎧 스크립트

P Last class we finished talking about the history of psychology. What we're gonna start looking at today is the... the relationship between biology and psychology. In particular, what I'm gonna try to do today are... hmmm... two things. First, I will define what Darwin's theory says. After that, I'll get into some different perspectives of psychologists, particularly, what our evolutionary heritage has to do with our psychological behavior.
As you all know, Charles Robert Darwin achieved lasting fame as the originator of the theory of evolution through natural selection. He first developed his interest in natural history while studying medicine at university.

교수 지난 시간에는 심리학의 역사에 대해 이야기했습니다. 오늘 살펴볼 문제는 생물학과 심리학의 관계입니다.
특히, 오늘 하고자 하는 일은 두 가지입니다. 첫째, 다윈 이론의 주장을 정의할 것입니다. 그런 후에 심리학자들이 가지고 있는 몇몇 다른 관점에 대해서도 이야기할 것입니다. 특별히 우리의 진화적 유산이 심리학적 행동과 어떤 관계가 있는지에 대해서 말입니다.
여러분 모두 알고 있듯이, 찰스 로버트 다윈은 자연적 선택을 통한 진화 이론의 창시자로서 영원한 명성을 얻었습니다. 다윈은 대학에서 의학을 공부하면서 처음으로 자연사에 관심을 갖게 되었습니다.

1 주로 어떤 내용의 강의가 이어지겠는가?
(A) 심리학의 역사와 방법에 대한 개관
(B) 다윈의 진화론에 대한 심리학적 관점
(C) 생물학의 방법과 심리학의 방법의 비교
(D) 진화론과 인간 심리학의 관계

정답 (D)

해설 오늘 강의의 주제는 생물학과 심리학의 관계이다. 그 중 생물학의 예로 다윈의 진화론을 들고 있다. 'What we're gonna start looking at today...'라는 표현이 강의의 주제를 밝히는 signal이 된다.

2 교수의 강의에 따르면, 찰스 다윈이 자연사에 관심을 갖게 된 것은 언제인가?
(A) 교수로서의 경력을 처음 시작했을 때
(B) 전공을 심리학에서 자연사로 변경했을 때
(C) 대학에서 의학을 공부할 때

(D) 약의 효과를 낼 수 있는 자연물질을 연구할 때

정답 (C)

해설 마지막 문장을 보면 다윈은 대학에서 의학을 공부하는 동안 자연사에 관심을 갖게 되었다.

3 동종요법(同種療法, 인체에 질병 증상과 유사한 증상을 유발하는 물질을 소량 투여하여 치료하는 방법)에 대한 강의를 듣고, 물음에 답하시오.

🎧 스크립트

P You've all heard of the saying, "the hair of the dog," right? This idiom <u>is said to have come from</u> the belief that consuming a mixture involving the hair of the dog would effectively treat diseases such as rabies that the dog may have carried. Well, it is frequently used to refer to alcoholic beverages consumed with the intent of lessening the effects of a hangover which was of course caused by the alcohol. Okay, now I wanna talk about homeopathy which has a similar notion in alternative medicine, and, and <u>how it really works to cure</u> certain illnesses, okay?

S So, you <u>kind of use a very small dose</u> that causes a disease? Isn't it a vaccine?

P However, we know why a vaccine works — it creates an immunity in your body. Not like it can actually cure the disease. Well, some conventional physicians claim that <u>if it does work</u>, then it is the human mind that cures the disease.

교수 모두들 "개털"이라는 말에 대해 들어봤겠지요? 이 표현은 개털이 들어간 약을 먹으면, 개가 전염시키는 광견병과 같은 질병을 효과적으로 치료할 수 있다는 통설에서 유래된 것이라고 합니다. 그것은 당연히 알코올로 말미암은 숙취의 영향력을 감소시키려는 의도로 복용되는 알코올 음료를 지칭하기 위해서도 흔히 사용됩니다. 자, 이제 대체의학과 개념이 유사한 동종요법과 이 요법이 어떻게 특정 질병을 치료하는지에 대해 이야기하려 합니다. 알겠죠?

학생 그러니까 어떤 질병을 유발하는 물질의 매우 적은 양을 사용한다는 말씀이신가요? 백신을 말씀하시는 건가요?

교수 하지만 우리는 백신이 작용하는 이유를 알고 있습니다. 백신은 우리 몸에 면역성을 갖게 하는 겁니다. 실제로 질병을 치유할 수 있는 것은 아닙니다. 몇몇 일반 의사들은 백신이 효과가 있는 경우에, 질병을 치유하는 것은 바로 인간의 정신이라고 주장합니다.

1 주로 어떤 내용의 강의가 이어지겠는가?
(A) 알코올 중독 치료에서의 동종요법
(B) 몇몇 질병을 치료하는 동종요법의 효과
(C) 동종요법이 실제로 효과를 발휘하지 못할지도 모르는 이유
(D) 동종요법과 대체의학에 대한 비판

정답 (B)

해설 동종요법과 그 요법을 통해서 어떻게 특정 질병을 치료할 수 있는지에 대한 내용이 전개될 것이다.

2 동종요법에서는 무엇을 주입시키는가?
(A) 질병을 효과적으로 없애는 항생물질
(B) 어떤 약도 포함하지 않은 가짜 약
(C) 그 질병을 일으키는 소량의 바이러스
(D) 무해하고 알려지지 않은 물질

정답 (C)

해설 동종요법은 질병을 일으킬 수 있는 물질을 몸 속에 소량 투입해서 질병을 치료하는 요법이다.

Mini-Exercise 2 Finding Purposes of Conversations

1 두 조교 사이의 대화를 듣고, 물음에 답하시오.

🎧 스크립트

TA1 Can I <u>talk to you for a second</u>?
TA2 Sure, what is it?
TA1 Did you hear that they are closing down the TA's lounge? I mean permanently. I was just told they're turning it into office space for the new professors.
TA2 Well, I do see the need for more office space; enrollment is up, classes <u>are bursting at the seams</u>, so yeah, they need more space.
TA1 Don't you think we need the lounge to relax between classes? I think we should appeal to someone that we do need some place for this. Now <u>there's nowhere to go</u> to relax.
TA2 I think you're right, but what if there really is no room or <u>space available at all</u>?
TA1 Hey, I just thought of something — the English Department is moving to a new building. There must be some space available there.
TA2 Oh, we'll have to go see to <u>make sure</u>.

조교1 잠시 이야기 좀 할 수 있을까?
조교2 그럼, 뭔데?
조교1 학교에서 조교 휴게실을 폐쇄한다는 소식을 들었니? 영구히 폐쇄한대. 그리고 신임 교수를 위한 사무실 공간으로 바꾼다는 이야기를 막 들었어.
조교2 사무실 공간이 더 필요하기는 하지. 학교 등록인원이 늘어났고, 교실은 터져나갈 정도로 꽉 차 있고 말이야. 그러니 더 많은 공간이 필요하겠지.
조교1 조교들에게도 공강 시간에 휴식을 취할 휴게소가 필요하다고 생각하지 않니? 우리에게 이런 장소가 필요하다는 사실을 누군가에게 호소해야 한다고 생각해. 이제 쉬러 갈 곳이 없잖아.
조교2 네 말이 옳다고 생각해. 하지만 사용할 수 있는 방이나 공간이 정말 전혀 없다면 어떡하지?
조교1 음, 지금 막 생각이 떠올랐어. 영문학과가 새 건물로 이사를 나갈 거잖아. 거기에 틀림없이 사용할 수 있는 공간이 있을 거야.
조교2 그렇지, 가서 확실하게 알아봐야겠다.

1 남자가 여자에게 말걸고 싶었던 이유는 무엇인가?
(A) 영문학과의 구조에 대해 토론하기 위해
(B) 여자에게 조교 휴게실이 생길 거라는 사실을 알리기 위해
(C) 조교 휴게실을 대체할 수 있는 장소에 대해 말하기 위해
(D) 자신의 의견에 여자가 동의하는지 알아 보기 위해

정답 (C)

해설 조교 휴게실이 폐쇄되리라는 소식을 듣고 조교 휴게실의 필요성에 공감하고 대체 장소에 대해 말하기 위해서이다.

2 그들은 이후에 무엇을 할 것인가?
(A) 조교 휴게소를 마련해 달라고 요청하기 위해 사무실에 갈 것이다.
(B) 휴게소로 사용할 수 있는 적절한 장소가 나올 때까지 기다릴 것이다.
(C) 조교 휴게실을 위한 공간이 있는지 알아 보러 갈 것이다.
(D) 휴게실의 필요성에 대해 교수들에게 말할 것이다.

정답 (C)

해설 조교 휴게실로 사용할 수 있는 공간을 찾다가, 영문학과가 새 건물로 이전한다는 사실을 생각해내고 공간이 있는지 알아 보러 갈 것이다.

2 두 학생 사이의 다음 대화를 듣고, 물음에 답하시오.

🎧 스크립트

S1 So, what did you want to see me for?
S2 Well, I wanted to ask you about the job you had at the cafeteria.
S1 Why, all of a sudden?
S2 You know, I never have any money. It seems like I'm always broke. And, it's really getting me down. The only thing I can do is make more money. And I wanted to ask if it was okay... I mean, did you have enough time for the school work?
S1 What do you think? You work 4 to 5 hours a day and 4 days a week. And after work, you're so exhausted.
S2 But still, you've managed to have a good grade and money at the same time, right? How did you do that?
S1 Well, there are some things you should have in mind when you think about getting a job.

학생1 그래서, 무엇 때문에 나를 보고 싶어했니?
학생2 응, 네가 카페테리아에서 했던 일에 대해 물어 보고 싶었어.
학생1 갑자기 왜?
학생2 있지, 내게 돈이 하나도 없거든. 언제나 무일푼으로 지내는 것 같아. 그래서 정말 우울해져. 내가 할 수 있는 유일한 일이란 돈을 더 많이 버는 거야. 그래서 괜찮은지 물어 보고 싶었어... 내 말은, 학교 공부를 할만한 시간이 있었니?
학생1 네 생각은 어때? 하루에 4~5시간씩 일주일에 4일을 일하는 거야. 일이 끝나면 아주 녹초가 되지.
학생2 하지만 너는 여전히 좋은 성적과 돈을 동시에 해냈잖아? 어떻게 했는데?
학생1 일을 가지려고 생각할 때 명심해야 하는 몇 가지가 있어.

1 남자가 여자를 만나고 싶어한 이유는 무엇인가?
(A) 자신이 할 수 있는 일이 있는지 물어 보려고
(B) 시간당 얼마나 받을 수 있는지 알아 보려고
(C) 그녀가 일과 공부를 어떻게 해내는지 들어 보려고
(D) 카페테리아의 근무조건에 대해 알아 보려고

정답 (C)

해설 남학생은 일하면서 학교공부를 할 시간이 있었는지, 여학생이 일하면서 어떻게 좋은 성적을 유지할 수 있었는지 궁금해한다.

2 여성은 일하는 것에 대해 어떻게 느꼈는가?
(A) 교내에서 일하는 것을 좋아하지 않았다.
(B) 일이 복잡하다고 생각했다.
(C) 공부할 시간이 부족했다.
(D) 일한 후에 공부하기가 쉽지 않다고 느꼈다.

정답 (D)

해설 대화에 따르면 하루에 4~5시간씩 일주일에 4일을 일하느라 일이 끝나면 아주 녹초가 되었다.

3 교수와 학생 간의 대화를 듣고, 물음에 답하시오.

🎧 스크립트

S Hi, do you have a second? I want to talk about my group project.
P Have a seat. So, what about it?
S Well, I'm a leader of this project and there are 5 other members in my group. The thing is... every time we have a discussion, it's like pulling teeth trying to get them to talk!

P What do you mean?

S I really <u>have a hard time getting</u> other members to participate. I don't know how we could finish the project this semester.

P Umm, well, so, all together, it's 6 people in your group, right? Okay... why don't you just make them work in even smaller groups, like two or three of them to ask and answer uh... some questions. You know, I think, since it's beginning of a semester, students might be uncomfortable to talk, but this seems to <u>put them at ease</u>. Then, they could return to the larger group and give a mini-presentation.

학생 안녕하세요. 잠깐 시간 좀 있으세요? 그룹 프로젝트에 대해 말씀드릴 것이 있는데요.

교수 앉게나. 그래, 무슨 일인가?

학생 제가 이 프로젝트의 통솔자이고 제 그룹에는 5명의 구성원이 더 있습니다. 문제는... 우리가 토론을 할 때마다, 그들을 말하게 만드는 것이 마치 이를 잡아당기는 것 같아요!

교수 그것이 무슨 뜻인가?

학생 다른 구성원을 토론에 참가하게 하는 것이 정말 힘들어요. 우리가 프로젝트를 이번 학기에 끝마칠 수 있을지 의문이에요.

교수 음, 자네 그룹에는 모두 6명이 있지, 맞나? 그럼, 2~3명으로 이루어진 훨씬 작은 그룹으로 나누어 질문을 묻고 대답하는 일을 하게 하지 그러나? 내 생각에는 학기 초이기 때문에 학생들이 말하기를 불편해할 수 있어. 하지만 이렇게 하면 그들이 편안해질 거야. 그리고 나면 더 큰 그룹으로 되돌아가서 짧게 발표를 하는 거지.

1 학생이 교수를 찾아간 이유는 무엇인가?
(A) 그룹 토론 중 학생들이 받는 긴장을 감소시킬 수단에 대해 물어 보려고
(B) 소 그룹 토론과 관련 있는 문제에 대해 교수에게 알리려고
(C) 프로젝트를 위해 그룹으로 활동하는 것의 장단점에 대해 토론하려고
(D) 학생들의 그룹 토론 참여를 향상시키기 위한 조언을 구하려고

정답 (D)

해설 여학생은 프로젝트의 리더로, 그룹 구성원이 토론에 참여하지 않는 문제로 어려움을 겪고 있기 때문에 이에 대해 교수의 조언을 구하고 싶어한다.

2 교수가 더 작은 그룹을 제안한 이유는 무엇인가?
(A) 학생들이 이야기할 시간을 좀더 많이 가질 수 있도록
(B) 학생들이 스스로 기준선을 만들 수 있도록
(C) 학생들이 좀 더 편안하게 느낄 수 있도록
(D) 소 그룹 관리가 좀더 쉽기 때문에

정답 (C)

해설 교수는, 학기 초이기 때문에 학생들이 말하는 것에 대해 불편해할 수 있으므로 더 작은 그룹으로 쪼개라고 제안했다.

Vocabulary Preview for Practice

Practice 1

1. distinguish (구별하다)
   ✓ a. to make one thing seem different from another
   b. to consider similarities
2. deficient (결함이 있는)
   ✓ a. not good enough
   b. to refuse to obey
3. exceedingly (대단히)
   a. in a way that is successful
   ✓ b. to a very great degree
4. utilize (활용하다)
   ✓ a. to use something in an effective way
   b. to keep something for a particular purpose or time

Practice 2

1. figure out (해결하다)
   a. to become noticeable
   ✓ b. to find the solution to a problem
2. infection (전염병)
   ✓ a. a disease caused by bacteria or a virus
   b. consisting of facts
3. pasteurize (저온 살균하다)
   ✓ a. to heat to a high temperature to kill the harmful bacteria
   b. to stop feeling angry after an argument
4. crucial (중대한)
   ✓ a. extremely important or necessary
   b. able to be believed or trusted

Practice 3

1. excessive (과도한)
   a. a way of approaching a place
   ✓ b. more than is required, expected, or considered reasonable
2. examine (검토하다)
   ✓ a. to inspect or evaluate thoroughly
   b. to make something seem larger, more important, better or worse than it really is
3. imply (암시하다)
   ✓ a. to communicate an idea without saying it directly
   b. to show or point out

4. result in (~한 결과를 낳다)
   a. to solve or end a problem or difficulty
   ✓ b. to cause a particular situation to happen

Practice 4

1. involve (종사시키다)
   ✓ a. to make them take part in
   b. to move something to move round a central point
2. cover (떠맡다)
   a. the reporting of a particular important event
   ✓ b. to take responsibility for
3. congress (의회)
   ✓ a. a formal meeting of representatives
   b. advancement to an improved or more developed state
4. doable (행할 수 있는)
   a. able to last a long time without becoming damaged
   ✓ b. able to be done

Vocabulary Preview for Actual Test

Actual Test 1

1. a 인간을 복제하는 것은 가능할지 모르지만, 윤리적인 것일까?
2. c 등산가들은 높은 고도에 이르게 될 때, 산소를 사용한다.
3. b 그들은 "당신은 2등이다. 더 열심히 노력하라."라는 기치를 내걸고 캠페인에 착수했다.
4. d 용의자들이 침묵을 지켜왔다는 이유만으로, 그들이 유죄라고 추정할 수 없다.

Actual Test 2

1. b 의사들은 서로 다른 질병들의 증상을 알아볼 수 있도록 훈련 받는다.
2. d 때때로 할아버지는 상당히 어리둥절해져, 무슨 요일인지도 알지 못하신다.
3. d 금년에는 조지 오웰의 어떤 소설 작품들이 강의 계획서에 포함되어 있나?
4. a 이 좌석들은 노인과 아기를 동반한 여성들을 위해 준비되어 있다.

Practice 1

1 (C)   2 (D)   3 (C)

미술 수업의 강의를 들으시오.

🎧 스크립트

P So, today, I wanna examine the, uh, way that a physical disability can play into, and often, uh, help create, a new kind of artistic expression. I know a lot of people, when they think of physical disabilities, they automatically think of the word "handicap." But you know, you might be surprised to learn that, well, this isn't necessarily the case. Yeah, we're so accustomed to thinking about people with physical limitations as being held back from creativity, but for an artist like Christy Brown, it was his limitations that really distinguished him from other, um, visual artists.

Brown had cerebral palsy or CP, a permanent disorder with developmental brain injuries that... uh... occur during fetal development, birth, or shortly after birth. Anyway, his doctors assumed he was mentally deficient, as well as his speech was, uh, seriously impaired. However, one day, while... uh... watching his sister write with some chalk, Brown grabbed the piece of chalk with his left foot, the only part of his body that he could, uh, really control, and began drawing! From then on, he... he began painting using his left foot to hold the brushes. The work was exceedingly expressive and really utilized a personal vocabulary that came out of his own experience of having CP.

교수 오늘은 신체적인 장애가 새로운 종류의 예술표현을 창조하는 데 도움이 될 수 있는 방식에 대해 검토해 보려 합니다. 신체적 장애를 생각할 때 자동적으로 '불리한 조건'이라는 단어를 생각하는 사람이 많습니다. 그러나 여러분이 놀랄지도 모를 일이지만, 꼭 그렇지만은 않습니다. 우리는, 신체적 한계를 가진 사람들을 창의성이 위축되어 있는 사람으로 생각하는 데 너무나 익숙해져 있습니다. 그러나 Christy Brown과 같은 예술가에게는 자신을 다른 시각예술가들과 구별시키는 점이 바로 그의 한계였습니다.

Brown은 뇌성마비 혹은 CP를 앓고 있었습니다. 이는 태아가 발달하는 동안 또는 출생할 때나 출생 직후에 발생하는 발전성 두뇌손상을 동반하는 영구 질환입니다. 어쨌거나 Brown의 담당의사들은 언어능력이 심각하게 손상을 입었을 뿐만 아니라 정신적으로 결함이 있다고 추정했습니다. 그러나 어느 날 누이가 분필을 가지고 쓰고 있는 것을 지켜 보던 Brown은 자신의 신체부위 중에서 유일하게 스스로 통제할 수 있는 왼쪽 발로 분필을 잡고 그림을 그리기 시작한 겁니다! 그 후로 Brown은 왼쪽 발에 붓을 잡고 그림을 그리기 시작했습니다. 그의 작품은 표현이 대단히 풍부하고, CP를 앓는 개인적인 경험에서 나오는 개인적인 표현 형식을 사용했습니다.

1 강의는 주로 어디에 중점을 두게 되는가?
 (A) 장애인에 의해 표현되는 예술형식
 (B) CP가 브라운 같은 예술가에게 부정적으로 미치는 영향
 (C) 한 예술가에게 미친 CP의 예상치 못한 영향
 (D) 질병을 치료하기 위한 예술 치료법의 활용

해설 강의의 주제는 첫 문장에 나와 있듯이 신체 장애가 예술표현에 미치는 영향으로, 오히려 장애를 통해 다른 화가와 구별될 수 있었던 Christy Brown의 예를 들었다.

2 다음 중 Christy Brown에 대해 사실이 <u>아닌</u> 것은 무엇인가?
 (A) 심각한 언어장애가 있었다.
 (B) 움직일 수 있는 신체범위가 제한되었다.
 (C) 손을 사용하지 않고 그림을 그렸다.
 (D) 그림을 그릴 때 대개 분필을 사용했다.

해설 처음에 분필을 이용해서 그림을 그리기 시작했지만, 후에는 붓을 사용했다

3 교수는 Brown의 작품들에 대해 어떻게 말하는가?
 (A) 몇몇 작품은 걸작으로 간주된다.
 (B) 그의 누이가 그의 작품에 크게 영향을 미쳤다.
 (C) 작품들은 질병을 겪은 경험을 반영한다.
 (D) 작품들을 통해 Brown은 부분적으로 질병에서 회복하게 되었다.

해설 Christy Brown의 장애는 그를 다른 화가와 구별시키게 만든 요소이다. 그의 작품의 특징은 표현이 대단히 풍부하다는 점과, 뇌성마비를 앓는 개인적인 경험을 반영한다는 점이다.

Practice 2

1 (C)   2 (B), (D)   3 (A)

화상치료에 사용되는 꿀에 대한 토의를 들으시오.

🎧 스크립트

P Many new therapies have been, uh, developed over the past century or so… to help repair skin and tissue damaged by fire. However, as we've seen, as our technology has progressed, we haven't found any treatment that is as effective as honey, yet. It's not completely, um, clear why, but let's look at the data and try to figure it out for ourselves, shall we? So, yeah, of all the conventional dressings for burns, honey seems to work better to treat infection and protect the healing skin.

S Is the honey prepared or processed in any special way before it's put on the burn?

P Actually, no, it isn't. It only seems to be, uh, unpasteurized honey that works well. Pasteurization is the process of heating food for the purpose of killing harmful organisms such as bacteria and viruses. But, I guess the pasteurizing might actually remove some useful chemical or uh… enzyme. So, it must be those enzymes in the honey that clean out the wound and keep the infection at bay.
The other thing about honey is that it really works to keep the wound moist, which is, uh, crucial to healing a burn. I guess no matter how hard we try to improve upon nature, it still does the best job.

교수 화상에 의해 손상을 입은 피부와 조직을 치료하기 위해서 지난 세기에 걸쳐 다수의 새로운 치료법이 개발되어왔습니다. 그러나 우리가 보아왔듯이, 기술이 발달을 거듭했음에도 불구하고 우리는 아직 꿀만큼 효과적인 치료법을 찾지 못했습니다. 그 이유가 완전히 밝혀진 것은 아니지만, 이제 자료를 보면서 우리가 직접 그 이유를 찾아보도록 합시다. 화상에 사용하는 통상적인 치료제 중에서도 꿀은 감염을 치료하고 회복 중인 피부를 보호하는 데 더욱 효과적인 것 같습니다.

학생 화상에 사용하기 전에 꿀을 특별한 방법으로 준비하거나 처리해야 하나요?

교수 사실 그렇지 않습니다. 단지 저온 살균하지 않은 꿀만이 효능이 있는 것 같습니다. 저온 살균은 박테리아와 바이러스와 같은 유해한 생물을 죽일 목적으로 식품을 가열하는 공정입니다. 그러나 저온 살균이 유용한 화학물질이나 효소를 실질적으로 제거할지도 모른다고 추측하고 있습니다. 그래서 상처를 치유하고 감염을 저지하는 것은 바로 꿀 속에 들어있는 그러한 효소임에 틀림이 없습니다.
꿀이 가진 또 다른 장점은 상처를 촉촉하게 유지시켜 주는 데 정말 효과가 있다는 점입니다. 이것이 화상치료에 결정적으로 중요합니다. 내가 생각하기에는, 우리가 자연을 더 좋게 하기 위해 얼마나 노력하는가에 관계없이 자연은 여전히 최상의 일을 합니다.

1
강의의 주된 내용은 무엇인가?
(A) 전통적 화상치료법과 현대 화상치료법과의 비교
(B) 꿀 치료법을 향상시키기 위한 기술의 사용
(C) 꿀이 화상치료에 효과가 있는 이유
(D) 주로 균질화로 인해 꿀 치료법이 변하는 방식

해설 새로운 화상치료법이 꾸준히 개발되고 있지만 아직까지는 저온 살균을 거치지 않은 꿀만큼 효과적인 치료법은 없다. 꿀이 화상치료에 효과가 있는 이유로, 꿀 안에 함유된 효소가 상처를 치유하고 감염을 저지한다는 점과 상처를 촉촉하게 유지시켜 준다는 점을 들고 있다.

2
교수에 따르면, 꿀에 대해 사실인 것은 무엇인가? 정답 두 개를 고르시오.
(A) 꿀은 1천년 동안 화상과 상처의 치료에 사용되었다.
(B) 꿀은 바이러스 감염을 막으면서 상처를 깨끗하게 유지시켜 준다.
(C) 꿀은 감염된 화상부위에서 효소를 제거하는 데 도움이 된다.
(D) 꿀은 치료를 촉진하기 위해 화상을 입은 부위에 습기를 제공한다.

해설 꿀이 화상치료에 효과가 있는 이유로, 꿀 안에 함유된 효소가 상처를 치유하고 감염을 저지한다는 점과 상처를 촉촉하게 유지시켜 준다는 점을 들고 있다.

3
교수는 저온 살균에 대해 무엇이라 말하는가?
(A) 꿀에 있는 유용한 성분을 파괴할지도 모른다.
(B) 공정을 거치는 동안 꿀의 효험이 증가한다.
(C) 화상을 치료할 때 저장수명을 연장시킨다.
(D) 유익한 화학물질을 꿀에 주입시킨다.

해설 저온 살균은 박테리아와 바이러스와 같은 유해한 생물을 제거하기 위해 식품을 가열하는 과정이지만, 이로 인해 꿀에 함유된 화상치료에 효과적인 화학물질이나 효소가 제거될 수도 있다.

Practice 3

1 (D)   2 (D)   3 (C)

병리학 수업의 토의를 들으시오.

🎧 스크립트

P   It's becoming the, uh, exception these days not to be able to pull out one's cell phone anywhere at anytime, right. And yet, as convenient as these useful devices may be, they also, uh, come with a host of potential dangers. There are some cases that show, uh, excessive cell phone uses being linked to brain cancer..., and well, have any of you thought about that?

S1 Well, why would a cell phone cause brain cancer but a regular phone wouldn't?

S2 Isn't it the radiation that cell phones emit right toward the brain? It's obvious that the two are connected.

P   Well, I don't think that, uh, either side has made a conclusive case yet. We will examine various cases, today, that might have something to do with this electromagnetic energy. All right? Now, it's true that cell phones do emit a low level of electromagnetic energy, excessive exposure to, uh, which some claim results in brain tumors. But many devices use electromagnetic energy, yet there's not evidence that implicates them in negative health. So... it's not quite so cut and dried.

교수   요즈음은 (오히려) 시간과 장소에 따라 휴대폰을 꺼낼 수 없는 것이 예외가 되어가고 있습니다. 하지만 이런 유용한 장비들이 편리하기는 하지만 많은 잠재적 위험성 또한 안고 있습니다. 과도한 휴대폰 사용이 뇌암과 관련이 있다는 사실을 보여 주는 사례가 있습니다. 여러분 중에서 이 문제에 대해 생각해 본 사람이 있나요?

학생1   일반전화는 그렇지 않은데 휴대폰은 왜 뇌암을 유발할까요?

학생2   휴대폰에서 방출하는 방사선이 곧바로 두뇌를 향하기 때문이 아니겠습니까? 두 가지가 연관성이 있다는 것은 명백합니다.

교수   두 학생 어느 쪽도 아직은 명확한 결론을 내렸다고는 생각되지 않습니다. 우리는 오늘 이 전자기 에너지와 관련이 있을지도 모르는 다양한 사례를 조사할 것입니다. 알겠죠? 자, 휴대폰에서 낮은 수준의 전자기 에너지가 방출된다는 것은 사실입니다. 또한 일부 사람들은 여기에 지나치게 노출이 된다면 뇌종양을 일으킬 수 있다고 주장합니다. 그러나 전자기 에너지를 사용하는 장비는 많지만, 건강에 부정적이라는 증거는 없습니다. 그래서... 그렇게 결정적인 이야기는 아닙니다.

1
토의에서 주로 다루어질 내용은 무엇인가?
(A) 다양한 장치에서 방출되는 전자기 에너지의 유형
(B) 세포기술의 사용을 지배하는 규칙의 증가 필요성
(C) 휴대폰 관련 종양발생의 증가를 보여 주는 의학적 자료
(D) 휴대폰 사용과 연관되어 있다고 주장되는 건강상의 문제점들

해설 교수는 오늘 전자기 에너지와 관련되어 있을지도 모르는 다양한 사례들을 검토할 것이라고 했다.

2
두 학생에 대해 추론할 수 있는 점은 무엇인가?
(A) 그들은 교수의 의견에 동의하지 않는다.
(B) 그들은 교수가 제안한 아이디어에 동의한다.
(C) 남학생은 교수의 의견에 동의하지 않는다.
(D) 여학생은 암과 휴대폰 사용이 관계가 있다는 데 동의한다.

해설 여학생은 암과 휴대폰 사용이 관련이 있다는 데에 동의하고 있다.

3 교수에 따르면, 다음 중 사실이 <u>아닌</u> 것은 무엇인가?
  (A) 휴대폰은 두뇌에 해로울 수 있는 에너지를 방출한다.
  (B) 휴대폰이 뇌암을 유발하는지 아닌지는 아무도 확신하지 못한다.
  (C) 휴대폰은 서로 다른 에너지를 방출한다.
  (D) 기타 몇몇 장비는 휴대폰과 같은 형태의 에너지를 방출한다.

해설 휴대폰에서는 낮은 수준의 전자기 에너지가 방출된다.

Practice 4

1 (C)   2 (B)   3 (C)

캠퍼스 신문 사무실에서의 대화를 들으시오.

🎧 스크립트

S1 Hi. I was wondering if you'd be able to help me.
S2 I can try. Were you interested in writing for the campus paper?
S1 Yes. I was editor of my high school newspaper and I'd really like to get involved with the campus paper, but I don't know how to make it happen.
S2 Well, your best bet would be to come to the assignment meeting tonight. Our editor has a list of stories she wants to cover for this week's paper, and we can always use another writer.
S1 Okay… I'd be particularly interested in covering the student congress and stuff. I wrote a lot about school politics in high school.
S2 Well, that's probably doable. It might be a good idea to bring a clipping of something you've written to the meeting. To show her what you can do. Maybe come a little early to talk to the editor?
S1 Okay, I will. That's really helpful. Thanks. See you tonight.

학생1 안녕, 나 좀 도와 줄 수 있을지 모르겠다.
학생2 해 볼게. 캠퍼스 신문에 글을 쓰는 데 관심이 있었지?
학생1 응. 고등학교 다닐 때 편집자였고, 캠퍼스 신문을 만드는 일을 정말 하고 싶어. 하지만 어떻게 하면 그럴 수 있을지 모르겠어.
학생2 최선의 방법은 오늘 저녁에 열릴 기사 할당 회의에 가는 거야. 우리 신문 편집자는 이번 주 신문에서 다루고 싶은 기사의 목록을 가지고 있기 때문에 언제나 작가가 필요하거든.
학생1 알았어… 나는 특히 학생회 등에 관심이 있어. 고등학교 시절에는 학교 정치에 대한 기사를 많이 썼거든.
학생2 아마도 그런 일을 할 수 있을 거야. 네가 썼던 기사를 오려서 회의에 가져오는 것도 좋은 생각일지 몰라. 네가 할 수 있는 것을 편집자에게 보여 주는 거지. 좀 일찍 와서 편집자와 이야기하는 것은 어때?
학생1 알았어, 그렇게 할게. 정말 도움이 되었어. 고마워. 오늘 저녁에 보자.

1 여학생이 남학생에게 말하고 싶어한 이유는 무엇인가?
  (A) 기사 할당 회의의 주제를 알아내려고
  (B) 회의에 참석하기 위해 준비해야 할 자료에 대해 물으려고
  (C) 캠퍼스 신문에 작가로 합류하려면 어떻게 해야 하는지 물으려고
  (D) 캠퍼스 신문에 기사를 쓰는 것에 대해 더욱 많이 배우려고

해설 여학생은 평소 학교신문에 글을 기고하고 싶어서, 남학생에게 그 방법에 대해 조언을 구하고 있다.

2 남학생은 여학생에게 회의에 올 때 무엇을 가져오라고 말하는가?
  (A) 신문 편집자와 인터뷰
  (B) 그녀가 썼던 기사의 견본
  (C) 그녀가 쓰고 싶은 기사의 목록
  (D) 모교 고등학교 편집자의 추천장

해설 예전에 썼던 기사를 가져와서 편집자에게 여학생이 무엇을 할 수 있는지 보여 주라고 조언한다.

3 다음 중 사실인 것은 무엇인가?
  (A) 여학생은 신문을 만들기 위한 기사 할당 회의에 참석했다.
  (B) 여학생은 오늘밤 편집자와의 인터뷰 일정을 잡았다.
  (C) 여학생은 학생회에 관해 보도하는 데 관심이 있다.
  (D) 여학생은 자신이 편집자로 있던 때 고등학교에서 남학생을 만났다.

해설 여학생은 대학친구의 조언에 따라 편집자가 주관하는 기사 할당 회의에 참석할 예정이고, 학교 내 정치 문제에 관심이 있다.

Actual Test 1

1 (C)   2 (A)   3 (C)   4 (C)   5 (B)

우주과학 수업의 강의를 들으시오.

🎧 스크립트

P Since we've been successfully launching people and objects into space, we've pretty much assumed that all the space transportation methods would involve some kind of spacecraft, right? Well, but one of the future of space transport could

Main Idea 11

actually involve an elevator.

Now... first... let me define what I mean by an elevator before I get into the nuts and bolts of the thing, okay? Um, I'm not talking about some metal box that takes you to the top of a skyscraper. What I'm talking about is a long cable that goes from the earth's surface out into space, and that has its center at an orbiting station that's about 20,000 miles in altitude. And so what would happen would be that these electromagnetic vehicles, carrying anything from people to objects, could travel up and down this cable. Everyone got the picture? Now, what makes us consider this space elevator as a possible transportation method while there are spacecrafts that we are familiar with, launching so many times? What, uh, what would this accomplish? Well, it would cut down on the costs of launching individual vehicles. It takes a lot less fuel to run up the side of a cable than it does to blast off. And so this would make commercial space travel—for both tourism and exploration, a lot more economically feasible. Now there's a lot we still need to work on here, obviously. Lots of logistics to work out. But it's definitely within the realm of possibility.

교수 우리가 사람과 물체를 우주에 성공적으로 발사해왔기 때문에, 우주에서의 모든 운송방법은 일종의 우주선과 관련이 있으리라고 가정하고 있습니다. 그렇죠? 음, 그러나 우주운송의 미래 가운데 하나는 실제로 엘리베이터와 관련이 있습니다.

자... 우선... 실제적인 이야기로 들어가기 전에 엘리베이터가 무엇을 의미하는지 정의하겠습니다. 내가 엘리베이터라고 말할 때는 고층건물의 꼭대기까지 사람들을 실어 나르는 금속 상자를 말하는 것이 아닙니다. 내가 말하는 것은 지구 표면에서 우주로 뻗어 나가고, 고도 2만 마일쯤에 위치한 궤도 상의 정거장에 중심을 두고 있는 기다란 케이블을 말합니다. 그래서 앞으로 일어날 수 있는 일은, 사람부터 물건에 이르기까지 무엇이든 운반하는 전자석 차량이 이 케이블을 따라 위아래로 이동하는 겁니다. 모두들 무슨 말인지 알겠어요?

자 이제, 우리가 그토록 여러 번 발사했기 때문에 우리에게는 우주선이 친숙한데, 이런 우주 엘리베이터를 가능한 운송수단으로 생각하게 된 이유가 무엇일까요? 이를 사용하면 무엇을 달성할 수 있겠습니까? 음, 개별 운송수단의 발사에 드는 비용을 줄일 수 있습니다. 발사하는 것보다 케이블을 따라 달리게 하면 연료도 훨씬 덜 소모됩니다. 그래서 여행이나 탐험 목적을 위한 상업적인 우주여행을 훨씬 더 경제적으로 실현 가능하게 만들 것입니다. 이제 이 문제에 대해 좀 더 해야 할 일이 여전히 많이 남아 있습니다. 해결해야 할 실질적인 문제도 많고요. 그러나 이 모든 것이 실현 가능한 것은 분명합니다.

---

1 주로 무엇에 관한 강의인가?
(A) 인간의 우주탐험의 역사
(B) 우주 엘리베이터 기술의 활용 가능성
(C) 이전의 기술을 능가하는 우주 엘리베이터의 장점
(D) 우주 여행에 대한 관심의 증가

해설 미래 우주 운송수단으로서 우리에게 친숙한 우주선을 누르고 엘리베이터가 부각되는 이유를 열거하고 있다.

2 다음 중 우주 엘리베이터에 속한 것이 아닌 것은 무엇인가?
(A) 금속 상자
(B) 기다란 케이블
(C) 궤도 상의 정거장
(D) 전자석 차량

해설 우주 운송수단으로서의 엘리베이터는 고층건물의 꼭대기까지 사람들을 실어나르는 금속 상자가 아니다.

3 우주 엘리베이터에 드는 비용에 대해 다음 중 사실인 것은 무엇인가?
(A) 우주 엘리베이터는 연료가 필요없기 때문에 비용이 저렴해서 경쟁력이 있다.
(B) 정거장까지 케이블이 뻗어야 하기 때문에 우주선보다 비용이 더 들 것이다.
(C) 기존의 우주 운송수단에 드는 비용보다 훨씬 더 저렴하다.
(D) 매 여행시 절약되는 시간을 고려해 보면 비싸지 않다.

해설 우주 엘리베이터가 가진 비용상 장점은 개별 운송수단의 발사에 드는 비용을 줄일 수 있고, 연료가 훨씬 덜 소모된다는 점이다.

4 우주 엘리베이터 기술에 대해 다음 중 사실은 무엇인가?
(A) 실현 가능하지만 군사적 용도를 위해 몇몇 과학자에게 극도로 제한된다.
(B) 우주 엘리베이터에 사용하는 케이블은 현재 사용할 수 있지만 정거장은 준비되어 있지 않다.
(C) 이론적으로는 가능하다고 입증되었지만 여전히 해야 할 일이 더 많다.
(D) 다른 기술의 발달 없이는 완성되지 못할 것이다.

해설 실현 가능한 것은 확실하지만 그러기 위해서는 해야 할 일과 해결해야 할 문제가 많다. (D)에 대한 언급은 없다.

5 교수는 우주 엘리베이터에 대해 어떠한 태도를 견지하고 있는가?
(A) 엘리베이터의 불완전한 기술에 대해 회의적이다.
(B) 엘리베이터 덕분에 더욱 저렴한 비용으로 우주여행이 가능해진다는 것에 대해 상당히 긍정적이다.
(C) 엘리베이터로 인해 발생할 수 있는 알려지지 않은 잠재적 위험에 대해 걱정한다.
(D) 상업적 우주여행의 편의성으로 인해 즐거워한다.

해설 교수는 기존의 우주선에 비해 저렴한 비용으로 우주여행을 가능하게 할 우주 엘리베이터에 대해 긍정적인 태도를 보이고 있다.

Actual Test 2

1 (C)　　2 (D)　　3 (A)　　4 (C)　　5 (B)

두 학생 사이의 대화를 들으시오.

🎧 스크립트

S1　Hey, you're in my media studies class, aren't you?
S2　Yes, right. I recognize you, too. I'm June.
S1　Nice to meet you, June. I'm Peter. Well, listen, I'm a little confused about something on the syllabus and I wonder if maybe you could help me.
S2　Well, sure. What is it?
S1　Okay, so see here, where Professor Wilson tells us to read an article from *Listening to Media* for next Monday? But that's not one of the textbooks he told us to get.
S2　Oh, yeah. No, that's on reserve in the library.
S1　Ah, I see... um... what does that mean? What's reserve?
S2　That's when the professor has the library put aside certain books for students to use. They can't be checked out of the library, but you can read them in the library, or photocopy what you need to read and take it home.
S1　Oh, okay! I've seen the reserve desk. I just didn't know what it was for!
S2　Right, just go up there and tell them your class and what book you want. I think you can use it for up to three hours at a time. But it should only take you about an hour to read the article.

학생1　안녕, 너 나랑 같이 미디어 수업 듣지, 그렇지?
학생2　그래, 맞아. 나도 네 얼굴이 눈에 익어. 내 이름은 June이야.
학생1　만나서 반가워, June. 나는 Peter야. 그런데, 강의계획서에 약간 혼동되는 부분이 있어서 그러는데 나를 좀 도와 줄 수 있겠니?
학생2　그럼. 뭔데?
학생1　응, 여길 봐. Wilson 교수님께서 다음 주 월요일 수업 때 읽어오라고 한 『미디어 청취』에 난 기사를 어디에서 읽어오라는 거지? 교수님이 우리에게 준비하라고 말한 교재에는 없거든.
학생1　아, 그것. 아니야. 그 책은 도서관에 예약되어 있어.
학생2　아, 그래... 음... 무슨 뜻이야? 예약되어 있다니?
학생1　그건 교수님이 어떤 책들을 학생들이 사용할 수 있도록 도서관 측에 따로 빼놓게 하는 거야. 학생들은 책을 도서관에서 대출해갈 수는 없지만, 도서관 안에서 읽을 수 있고, 아니면 읽을 필요가 있는 부분을 복사해서 집에 가져갈 수 있어.
학생2　아, 알겠어! 예약 도서대를 본 적이 있어. 하지만 무엇인지 몰랐지!
학생1　맞아, 그곳에 가서 강의명을 말하고 어떤 책을 원하는지 말해. 내 생각에는 한 번에 3시간까지 책을 볼 수 있어. 하지만 단지 한 시간 정도면 그 기사를 읽을 수 있을 거야.

1 남학생이 여학생에게 말걸고 싶은 이유는 무엇인가?
(A) 수업시간에 받은 강의계획서에 대해 도서관에서 의논하려고
(B) 도서관에서 찾아볼 교과서의 이름을 알아내려고
(C) 수업을 위해 지정된 책을 어디서 구할 수 있는지 물어 보려고
(D) 수업을 위해 준비해갈 교과서를 제대로 찾고 있는지 확인하려고

해설 교수가 강의계획서에서 기사를 읽어오는 과제를 주었는데, 그 기사를 찾지 못해 수업을 같이 듣는 여학생에게 묻고 있다.

2 여학생은 책에 대해서 무엇이라고 말하는가?
(A) 그녀는 강의계획서에 지정된 책을 보지 못했다.
(B) 그녀는 그 책이 읽을 가치가 있다고 생각하지 않는다.
(C) 학생들이 책을 사는 것은 강제적이 아니다.
(D) 도서관에서 찾을 수 있다.

해설 교수님이 기사가 수록된 책을 도서관에 예약해 놓았다고 일러 주면서, 기사를 볼 수 있는 방법을 자세히 가르쳐 주고 있다.

3 예약된 책에 대해 사실이 아닌 것은 무엇인가?
(A) 예약된 책은 대출할 수 있다.
(B) 예약된 책은 복사할 수 있다.
(C) 예약된 책은 도서관에서 읽어야 한다.
(D) 예약된 책은 도서관 밖으로 가지고 나갈 수 없다.

해설 예약된 책은 도서관 안에서만 열람할 수 있다.

4 Peter는 예약 데스크에 대해 무엇이라 말하는가?
(A) 그것이 어디에 있는지 모른다.
(B) 거기서 일하는 친구가 있다.
(C) 무엇을 하는 곳인지 몰랐다.
(D) 사서들이 도움이 안 된다는 것을 깨달았다.

해설 Peter는 예약 데스크를 본 적이 있지만 무엇을 하는 곳인지 몰랐다.

5 June은 기사의 길이에 대해 무엇이라 말합니까?
(A) 읽는 데 3시간이 걸린다.
(B) 읽는 데 시간이 그다지 오래 걸리지 않을 것이다.

(C) 거의 책만큼의 분량이다.
(D) 약 30분이면 읽을 수 있다.

해설 June 생각으로는, 책을 한 번에 3시간까지 열람할 수 있고, 과제물인 기사를 읽는 데는 단지 한 시간 정도로, 오래 걸리지 않는다.

Dictation

Practice 1

① know a lot of people
② might be surprised to learn
③ we're so accustomed to thinking about
④ really distinguished him from
⑤ shortly after birth
⑥ with his left foot
⑦ From then on
⑧ came out of his own experience

Practice 2

① over the past century or so
② as effective as honey
③ let's look at the data
④ figure it out
⑤ seems to work better
⑥ honey that works well
⑦ for the purpose of
⑧ The other thing about honey
⑨ no matter how hard

Practice 3

① as convenient as
② come with a host of
③ being linked to brain cancer
④ the two are connected
⑤ have something to do with
⑥ some claim results in
⑦ it's not quite so cut and dried

Practice 4

① if you'd be able to help me
② like to get involved with
③ how to make it happen
④ would be to come to
⑤ I'd be particularly interested in

⑥ that's probably doable
⑦ what you can do

Actual Test 1

① we've pretty much assumed
② let me define what I mean
③ takes you to the top of
④ in altitude
⑤ what makes us consider
⑥ we are familiar with
⑦ It takes a lot less fuel to
⑧ than it does to blast off
⑨ we still need to work

Actual Test 2

① I'm a little confused about
② if maybe you could help me
③ he told us to get
④ put aside certain books
⑤ be checked out of the library
⑥ take it home
⑦ what it was for
⑧ take you about an hour to

Vocabulary Review

1 발전시키다, 전개하다
2 궤도
3 심령의, 영혼의
4 ~에(서명하여) 동의하다
5 진화의, 발달의
6 숙취
7 대체의
8 등록자수
9 대단히
10 결함이 있는
11 전염, 감염
12 검토하다
13 종사시키다
14 떠맡다
15 의회
16 (업무의) 세부 계획
17 읽고 쓰는 능력, 해독
18 비틀거림, 흔들림
19 과도한
20 가능한
21 고도
22 발사하다, 착수하다
23 추정하다
24 알아보다
25 당황한
26 강의 계획서
27 연구
28 현상(복수형태)
29 기이함
30 분과, 부문
31 지시하다
32 구성하다
33 해석하다
34 이치에 맞다, 이해되다
35 매우 붐비다
36 ~를 실망시키다
37 위축시키다
38 ~을 저지하다, 궁지에 몰리게 하다
39 ~와 관련되다
40 (사물의) 기본, 요점
41 별도로 마련해 놓은

42 focus on
44 permanent
46 be broke
48 ideology
50 originator
43 distinguish A from B
45 participate
47 at ease
49 theory

CHAPTER 02
SUPPORTING DETAILS

Pre Test 1

수업에서 있었던 토의를 듣고, 질문에 답하시오.

🎧 스크립트

P There are, uh, always people out there who doubt science... who think the earth is flat, who think the moon landing was faked... and those who suggest that dinosaurs and humans <u>lived side-by-side</u>, closely together...

S I thought it was common knowledge that humans <u>didn't show up until</u> about... 60 million years after dinosaurs became extinct.

P Well, that's the mainstream scientific consensus. <u>But for a period of time</u>, the so-called Paluxy man tracks of Paluxy River seemed to contradict this. The river <u>is best known for</u> numerous dinosaur footprints found in its bed near Glen Rose, Texas. Also... there were some other tracks that some claimed to be human, in the same fossil bed. This seemed irrefutable proof that man and dinosaur coexisted. However, close study has shown they were the result of numerous different phenomena — <u>stretched out</u> dino tracks, erosion, and some contemporary carvings — not prehistoric man.

교수 과학을 의심하는 사람은 항상 있기 마련입니다... 즉 지구가 평평하다고 생각하는 사람, 달 착륙이 가짜라고 생각하는 사람... 그리고 공룡과 인간이 매우 가까이에 나란히 살았다고 제안하는 사람들도 있습니다.

학생 저는 공룡이 멸종되고 약 6천만 년이 지나서까지도 인간이 지구상에 출현하지 않았다는 것이 일반화된 지식이라고 생각했습니다.

교수 그것이 주류를 이루는 과학계의 지배적인 의견입니다. 그러나 기간에 대해서는, 팔럭시 강에 남아 있는 소위 팔럭시 인간의 발자국은 그 의견에 상반되는 것 같이 보였습니다. 텍사스 주 클렌 로즈 근처에 있는 그 강은 강 바닥에서 발견된 수많은 공룡 발자국으로 잘 알려져 있습니다. 그리고... 몇몇 사람들이 인간의 것이라고 주장하는 발자국도 같은 화석 바닥에 있었습니다. 이는 인간과 공룡이 공존했었다는 사실에 대한 반박할 수 없는 증거처럼 보였습니다. 그러나, 자세하게 연구를 해 본 결과, 그 발자국은 선사시대 인간의 발자국이 아니라, 여러 가지 다른 현상에 따른 결과였습니다. 즉 공룡의 발자국이 나 있는 곳에, 부식이 발생하고 당시에 있던 조각들이 합쳐진 것이었습니다.

교수에 따르면, 공룡 이후에 인간이 출현했다는 연대기에 의문을 갖게 한 것은 무엇인가?
(A) 몇몇 공룡 화석이 가짜였다는 사실이 밝혀진 것
(B) 고생물학자가 화석의 나이를 측정하는 방법의 변화
(C) 공룡 화석 바닥에서 인간의 것으로 보이는 발자국의 발견
(D) 가능한 것 같아 보이는 것보다 훨씬 더 오래된 인간 화석의 발견

정답 (C)

해설 팔럭시 강 바닥에서 공룡과 인간의 것으로 추정되는 발자국이 발견되어서 인간과 공룡이 공존했었을지도 모른다는 의심을 갖게 되었다.

Pre Test 2

캠퍼스 견학 동안 있었던 대화를 듣고, 물음에 답하시오.

🎧 스크립트

S1 This is the campus library. It's one of the oldest buildings at the school, dating back to the 1850s. The library itself has one of the largest collections in the state — over 1.5 million books, periodicals, and recordings.
S2 Wow. It looks like a mansion or something.
S1 Actually, the library used to be the college president's house in the 19th century. It's large, because during those days, people usually had large families. In fact, the last president to live there before the building was renovated had 8 kids!
S2 Um, so what do we need to do to get a library card? Will they be given out at orientation later today, or...?
S1 Actually, bring your student ID, which you should already have, and bring it to the front desk at the library. They'll scan your bar code into the computer and then you can use your ID as your library card. It's pretty easy, actually.

학생1 여기가 대학 도서관이야. 1850년대까지 거슬러 올라가는 건물로, 학교에서 가장 오래된 건물 중 하나지. 도서관 자체만으로도 이 주에서 장서를 가장 많이 가지고 있는 도서관 중의 하나야. 150만권 이상의 도서와 정기 간행물, 녹음기록 등이 있거든.
학생2 와! 꼭 저택처럼 생겼다.
학생1 실제로 이 도서관은 19세기에는 총장공관으로 사용되었어. 그 시절에는 대부분 대가족이 살았기 때문에 건물이 이렇게 컸던 거지. 사실 건물을 보수 공사하기 전까지 마지막으로 이곳에 살았던 총장은 자녀가 여덟 명이었다니까!
학생2 음, 그러면 도서관 카드를 받으려면 어떻게 해야 하니? 오늘 이따가 있을 오리엔테이션 시간에 받을 수 있는 거야, 아니면...?
학생1 사실상, 네가 이미 가지고 있는 학생증을 도서관의 접수 데스크에 가져가면 돼. 그들이 컴퓨터에 네 바코드를 긁으면 학생증을 도서관 카드로 사용할 수 있어. 정말 간단해.

남학생은 여학생에게 도서관 카드를 발급 받으려면 무엇을 해야 한다고 말하는가?
(A) 그날 있을 오리엔테이션에 참석해야 한다.
(B) 학생증을 스캔한 복사본을 제출해야 한다.
(C) 도서관에 학생증을 등록해야 한다.
(D) 도서관 카드 신청서를 기입해야 한다.

정답 (C)

해설 남자의 마지막 말에 따르면 학생증을 도서관 접수 데스크에 가져가서 컴퓨터에 바코드를 입력시키면 도서관 카드로도 사용할 수 있다.

Vocabulary Preview   for Mini-Exercise

Mini-Exercise 1

1-1. eternal (영원한)
　　✓ a. continuing forever
　　　b. being or situated at an end
1-2. lofty (고원(高遠)한)
　　　a. a shaped mass of baked bread
　　✓ b. of intellectual value
1-3. successor (후계자)
　　✓ a. a person who inherits some office
　　　b. a person with a record of successes
2-1. offspring (자손)
　　　a. a cruel and frightening person
　　✓ b. someone's child or children
2-2. reproductive (생식의)
　　✓ a. producing new life
　　　b. to take possession of again
2-3. participate (관여하다)
　　　a. a person who takes part
　　✓ b. to be involved in something
3-1. financial (재정상의)
　　✓ a. relating to money
　　　b. happening at the end of the event

3-2. semester (한 학기)
  a. a small class at a university for study and discussion
  ✓ b. one half of an academic year

3-3. tuition (수업료)
  ✓ a. a fee paid for instruction
  b. a person who gives private instruction

Mini-Exercise 2

1-1. remedial (학력 부족을 보충하는)
  a. to recall knowledge from memory
  ✓ b. designed to improve basic scholastic skills

1-2. incur (초래하다)
  ✓ a. to bring upon oneself
  b. to conclude on the basis of evidence

1-3. inability (무능)
  ✓ a. lack of capacity or means
  b. making something possible or giving someone special powers

2-1. theft (도둑질, 절도)
  a. the state of being deep
  ✓ b. an instance of stealing

2-2. notice (인지하다)
  ✓ a. to be aware of
  b. an idea, belief, or opinion in someone's mind

2-3. character (등장인물)
  a. a distinguishing quality
  ✓ b. a person in a novel, play, or the like

3-1. notorious (악명 높은)
  a. able to turn on an axis
  ✓ b. widely known for something bad

3-2. valid (타당한)
  ✓ a. well grounded in logic
  b. degree of merit or usefulness

3-3. definitely (확실히)
  ✓ a. without a doubt
  b. lacking clear definition or limits

Mini-Exercise 1 Important Information

1 연금술에 대한 강의를 듣고, 물음에 답하시오.

🎧 스크립트

P Alchemy, the... ancient art of seeking to harness the power of and transform metals through chemistry, had <u>more or less</u> two goals. One was material: the alchemist wanted to turn a worthless metal into gold. The other was spiritual — if the philosopher's stone — the mysterious substance that would allow the alchemist to <u>transform a metal into gold</u> — was discovered, then it could <u>not only bring wealth, but eternal life</u>. Some pretty lofty goals, don't you think? The first records we have on alchemy are from the Greeks and Egyptians. While these early people like their successors, were unsuccessful at obtaining <u>either unlimited gold or eternal life</u>, what they did manage to do was <u>to learn quite a bit about</u> the properties of different metals, such as lead, mercury and all other kinds of things. In fact, though we would consider their goals highly unscientific today, these alchemists were really our first chemists.

교수 화학을 통해서 금속의 힘을 이용하고 금속을 변형시키는 고대의 기술인 연금술은 대체로 두 가지의 목적을 가집니다. 한 가지는 물질적인 것입니다. 연금술사들은 가치 없는 금속을 금으로 바꾸고 싶어했습니다. 다른 한 가지는 영적인 것입니다. 만약 철학자의 돌 — 연금술사가 금속을 금으로 변화시킬 수 있게 해주는 신비스러운 물질 — 이 발견되었다면, 그것은 재산뿐만 아니라 영원한 삶도 가져올 수 있었습니다. 정말 대단한 목적이었죠, 그렇죠? 우리가 연금술에 대해 갖고 있는 첫 번째 기록은 그리스인과 이집트인에서 찾아볼 수 있습니다. 이 초기 사람들은 자신의 후계자들과 마찬가지로 무한한 양의 금을 얻는 데도 영원한 삶을 얻는 데도 성공하지 못했지만, 납, 수은 등과 같은 다른 금속의 성질에 대해 상당히 많은 지식을 습득했습니다. 사실, 오늘날에는 그들이 세웠던 목적이 매우 비과학적이라는 생각이 들지만, 이 연금술사들이야말로 정말 최초의 화학자들이었습니다.

1 교수는 연금술 실험의 이유를 무엇이라고 밝히는가? 정답 두 개를 고르시오.
  (A) 화학에 대한 정보를 제공할 수 있었다.
  (B) 무한한 부를 제공할 수 있었다.
  (C) 사람들이 죽음을 피할 수 있게 해 주었다.
  (D) 과학적인 지식을 확장시켜 주었다.

정답 (B), (C)

해설 연금술사들은 무한한 양의 금을 얻고, 영원한 삶을 얻기 위해 실험에 몰두했다.

2 이야기에 따르면, 연금술사가 궁극적으로 성공한 것은 무엇인가?
  (A) 다양한 금속의 성질을 변화시키는 방법을 배웠다.
  (B) 이전에 알려졌던 물질의 새로운 용도를 발견했다.
  (C) 최초로 확립된 과학적 방법론을 창안했다.

(D) 금속의 물리적인 특징을 발견했다.

정답 (D)

해설 연금술사는 금속을 금으로 변화시키는 방법과 영원한 삶이라는 원래의 목적을 달성하지는 못했지만, 납, 수은 등과 같은 각기 다른 금속의 특징을 발견했다.

2 동물과 협동에 대한 강의를 듣고, 물음에 답하시오..

🎧 스크립트

P We've been looking at various ways in which animal societies cooperate or don't cooperate and, um, some of the possible reasons for that. Today I want to hone in on eusocial animals, who participate in what, uh, some researchers call "extreme cooperation." Okay, so first let me define what it means to be a eusocial animal. In this type of organization, the majority of members of the society give up their reproductive potential in order to take care of the offspring of a main producer. So, whether the animals are related or not to the main producer, they spend their entire life taking care of the young of the society. We see this in bees and ants and other such creatures. The fact that all sense of individual purpose is sacrificed to the society... well, you can see why we call it extreme cooperation, can't you?

교수 우리는 동물 사회가 협동하거나 협동하지 않는 다양한 방식과 이에 대한 가능한 이유에 대해 검토하고 있습니다. 오늘 나는 몇몇 연구가들이 '극단적인 협동'이라 부르는 것과 관련 있는 진사회성 동물에 대해 살펴보겠습니다. 우선 진사회성 동물이 무엇인지 정의를 내려보겠습니다. 이런 형태의 조직에서, 사회 구성원의 대다수는 주요 생산자의 자손을 돌보기 위해서 자신의 생식 잠재력을 포기합니다. 그래서 주요 생산자와 관련이 있든지 없든지 간에, 그 동물들은 사회의 어린 생명을 돌보는 데 자신의 일생을 보냅니다. 우리는 꿀벌, 개미, 기타 생물들에게서 이런 현상을 볼 수 있습니다... 음, 이제 왜 우리가 이를 극단적인 협동이라 부르는지 알겠죠?

1 교수에 따르면, 다음 중 진사회성 동물의 특징이 아닌 것은 무엇인가?
(A) 무리의 자손 모두를 생산한다
(B) 사회의 어린 생명을 돌본다
(C) 사회를 위해서 자신의 자아를 희생한다
(D) 생식능력을 포기한다

정답 (A)

해설 무리의 자손 모두를 생산하는 것이 아니라 주요 생산자의 자손을 돌보기 위해 자신의 생식 잠재력을 포기한다.

2 진사회성 동물들 중에서, 주요 생산자의 임무는 무엇인가?
(A) 자손에게 먹이를 먹인다
(B) 새끼를 밴다
(C) 은신처를 짓는다
(D) 음식을 만든다

정답 (B)

해설 진사회성 동물 중 주요 생산자는 대다수의 사회 구성원의 지원을 받아 자손의 생산을 담당한다.

3 재정지원에 대한 대화를 듣고, 물음에 답하시오.

🎧 스크립트

S Hi, I was expecting my financial aid check, like, a week ago, and it hasn't shown up.
FAO Hmmm... let's get to the bottom of this... actually, this shows that you haven't completed your paperwork for this semester. That's why we haven't gotten a check for you.
S Excuse me? But I... can you tell me what I didn't hand in?
FAO Um... yes, we never received a tax form.
S Oh no... I must've forgotten it. I can't pay my tuition without the check and I'm afraid I'll be disenrolled if I don't pay soon.
FAO We can expedite the process and have the check to you in two weeks if you get the form to us today. And we can write a note to the registrar, explaining the circumstances, so you won't be disenrolled.
S Thanks so much. I feel a lot better now.

학생 안녕하세요? 일주일 전에 제 재정지원 수표가 도착하리라 예상했었는데 오지 않았어요.
FAO 음... 원인부터 따져봐야겠어요... 실제로, 여기를 보면 당신이 이번 학기에 필요한 서류를 모두 제출하지 않았군요. 그래서 수표를 줄 수 없었던 거죠.
학생 뭐라고요? 하지만, 저는... 제가 어떤 서류를 제출하지 않았는지 말씀해 주시겠어요?
FAO 음... 그래요, 세금 양식을 받지 못했네요.
학생 맙소사... 제가 깜빡 잊었나 봐요. 수표를 받지 못하면 학비를 낼 수 없어요. 학비를 곧 내지 않으면 등록이 취소될 테고요.
FAO 당신이 오늘 우리에게 양식을 갖다 주면 절차를 신속하게 처리해서 2주 후에 수표를 받도록 할 수 있어요. 그리고 상황을 설명하는 쪽지를 우리가 교무직원에게 보내 줄게요. 그러면 등록이 취소되는 일은 없을 거예요.
학생 정말 감사합니다. 이제 훨씬 마음이 놓이는 걸요.

1 학생이 걱정한 것은 무엇인가?
   (A) 학비 부족
   (B) 등록금 체납
   (C) 재정지원을 받을 수 있는 자격
   (D) 복잡한 등록 절차
                                              정답 (B)

해설 학교로부터 재정지원 수표를 받지 못하면 학비를 지불할 수 없어서 등록이 취소될까봐 걱정한다.

2 직원에 따르면, 학생이 수표를 받지 못한 이유는 무엇인가?
   (A) 학교에서 학생의 등록을 취소했다.
   (B) 작년에 세금을 내지 않았다.
   (C) 제출해야 할 서류를 제출하지 않았다.
   (D) 학비를 내지 않았다.
                                              정답 (C)

해설 학비 보조금을 받기 위해 제출해야 할 서류를 제출하지 않았다.

Mini-Exercise 2 True or False

1 기술적인 작문수업의 강의를 듣고, 물음에 답하시오.

🎧 스크립트

P So listen to this: a recent report claims that states are having to spend about a quarter of a billion — that's right, a billion — dollars a year on remedial writing classes for their employees. The inability of state workers to express themselves clearly not only causes all kinds of problems for state agencies, but also for the taxpayers who rely on these employees to get accurate, clear information.
And this doesn't include the cost that the actual bad writing itself is incurring. Okay, so you're asking yourselves how could bad writing itself cost money? Well, think of all the lost time — and time is money — caused by instructions that just don't make sense. The customer has to ask questions that should already be answered, the worker has to take time to answer the questions. Or the time it takes to redo the poor writing. It's not something we really think about much, but the cost really adds up. And it makes good writers to be in high demand in the workplace.

교수 잘 들어 보십시오. 최근 보고서의 주장에 따르면, 주 정부가 직원들의 작문 보충수업을 위해서 일년에 약 2억 5천만 달러를 지불해야만 한답니다. 주 직원들이 자신의 생각을 분명하게 표현할 수 없다는 문제점은 주 소속 기관에 온갖 종류의 문제를 야기할 뿐만 아니라, 이런 직원들에게서 정확하고 명확한 정보를 얻고자 기대하는 납세자에게도 온갖 종류의 문제를 일으킵니다.
게다가 여기에는 실질적으로 글을 잘못 써서 일어날 수 있는 비용문제는 포함되어 있지 않습니다. 알겠습니다. 여러분들은 글을 잘못 쓴 것이 어떻게 비용을 낭비할 수 있는지 스스로에게 묻고 있군요. 자, 말이 되지 않는 지시사항에 때문에 낭비되는 시간을 생각해 봅시다—시간은 돈입니다—고객들은 이미 대답을 들었을 질문들을 다시 물어야만 합니다. 그리고 직원들은 그 질문에 대답하느라 시간을 들여야 합니다. 또는 잘못 쓴 글을 다시 쓰는 데 시간이 낭비됩니다. 우리는 이런 문제에 대해 많이 생각하지 않습니다만, 비용은 점점 늘어나기 마련입니다. 이렇게 되면 직장에서 글을 잘 쓰는 사람에 대한 수요가 증가합니다.

1 형편없는 글쓰기 기술에 대해 교수는 뭐라고 말하는가?
   (A) 세금을 지원받는 직장이 글을 쓸 사람을 더 필요로 하게 된다.
   (B) 정부와 납세자 사이의 의사소통을 얽히게 만든다.
   (C) 직원들이 보충수업 수준 이상으로 진보하는 것을 불가능하게 한다.
   (D) 그런 기술에 상당히 영향을 받는 사람들 대부분이 통상 눈치채지 못한다.
                                              정답 (B)

해설 주 직원의 글쓰기가 형편없는 경우에는 주 기관뿐만 아니라 납세자에게도 문제가 발생해서 정확하고 명확한 정보를 얻을 수 없게 된다.

2 형편없는 글쓰기 자체와 관련이 있는 문제는 무엇인가?
   (A) 납세자의 저하된 동기부여
   (B) 글쓰는 사람이 더 많이 필요하게 되는 것
   (C) 작문수업에 대한 연방 지원금의 감소
   (D) 이로 인해 야기되는 시간 낭비의 증가
                                              정답 (D)

해설 형편없는 글쓰기에 의해 직접적으로 야기되는 문제는 무엇보다 시간 낭비이다. 의사소통이 제대로 이루어지지 않아 질문을 다시 해야 하고, 질문을 다시 답하고 잘못된 글을 다시 쓰는 등 시간이 낭비된다.

2 영화 연구 수업에서의 토의를 듣고, 물음에 답하시오.

🎧 스크립트

P Something that we'll notice as we study these next few films by Alfred Hitchcock, is the use of a plot device that the director referred to as the MacGuffin. Now then... uh — how can we define a MacGuffin? Well, to make a long story short, it's a detail in the plot that isn't nearly as important as it seems — it's just something that advances the story and holds the viewers' attention.

S Oh, so for example, would Janet Leigh's character in *Psycho* stealing the money from her boss be considered a... a... what's it called again?
P MacGuffin. Bingo. The theft of the money is just something Hitchcock does to get the woman to the Bates Motel, where the real story of the movie starts. It really isn't an important part of the film.

교수 앞으로 알프레드 히치콕이 만든 영화 몇 편을 보면서 우리가 보게 될 것은 바로 감독이 맥거핀이라고 부른 줄거리 장치의 사용입니다. 자 그렇다면 맥거핀을 어떻게 정의할 수 있을까요? 자, 간단하게 말해서, 그것은 보이는 것만큼 중요하지 않은 줄거리 상의 세부사항을 말합니다. 그저 이야기를 전개하고 관객의 관심을 끄는 무언가를 뜻합니다.
학생 아, 예를 들어서, '사이코'에서 자넷 리가 맡은 등장인물이 상사에게서 돈을 훔치는 것을 말하는군요... 무엇이라 부른다 하셨죠?
교수 맥거핀이요. 맞았습니다. 돈을 훔친 것은 그저 그 여자를, 영화의 진짜 이야기가 시작되는 베이츠 모텔에 가게 하기 위해 히치콕이 만든 장치입니다. 영화에서 그다지 중요한 부분이 아니지요.

1 교수는 맥거핀에 대해 무엇이라 말하는가?
   (A) 겉보기에는 사소한 줄거리지만 많은 것을 설명한다.
   (B) 이야기 가운데 관심을 끌기 위해 사용되는 사소한 부분이다.
   (C) 영화에서 배우의 행위에 대한 주요한 자극이다.
   (D) 영화의 줄거리에서 배우들이 일종의 범죄를 저지를 때를 뜻하는 용어이다.
   정답 (B)

   해설 맥거핀은 이야기를 전개하고 관객의 관심을 끌기 위해 사용하는 줄거리 상의 세부사항을 의미하고, 보이는 것만큼 중요하지 않다.

2 영화에서 돈을 훔치는 장면을 학생이 언급한 이유는 무엇인가?
   (A) 교수가 말하려는 요점의 예시를 제시하기 위해서
   (B) 예외가 될지도 모르는 예를 들기 위해서
   (C) 맥거핀의 사용에 대한 자신의 지식을 강조하기 위해서
   (D) 관객의 관심을 끌 필요성을 설명하기 위해서
   정답 (A)

   해설 교수가 설명한 맥거핀을 제대로 알고 있는지 확인하기 위해 예를 들었다.

3 두 학생의 대화를 듣고, 물음에 답하시오.
   🎧 스크립트

S1 I'm pretty nervous. I have to give a presentation in class today.
S2 Oh, don't be nervous. I'm sure you'll do fine. Anyway, everyone in our class is really nice — they won't give you a hard time or anything.
S1 I'm not worried about the other students — I'm worried about the professor! He's notorious for being a really tough grader on presentations.
S2 Well, he definitely gives a lot of feedback, but I don't think it's nearly as bad as people say. I had him last semester, and I was super nervous, too, but every comment he made was valid and helpful.
S1 Well, what kinds of things should I do to get a good grade?
S2 Just make sure to make eye contact with the class, speak clearly and slowly, and be ready to answer questions. He'll definitely ask you a lot of questions.
S1 Hmmm... I would never get used to it.

학생1 난 정말 긴장이 되네. 오늘 수업시간에 발표를 해야 하거든.
학생2 긴장하지마. 나는 네가 잘 할 수 있으리라 확신해. 어쨌거나 우리 반 학생들은 모두들 정말 좋잖아. 너를 힘들게 하지 않을 거야.
학생1 다른 학생들 때문에 걱정하는 게 아니야. 교수님 때문에 걱정이라고! 발표 점수를 짜게 주기로 유명하시잖아.
학생2 교수님이 의견을 많이 주시는 것은 확실해. 하지만 사람들이 말하는 것만큼 끔찍하지는 않다고 생각해. 나도 지난 학기에 교수님의 수업을 들었어. 초긴장을 했지만 교수님이 하는 논평은 타당하고 유용했어.
학생1 그럼, 좋은 학점을 받으려면 어떻게 해야 하니?
학생2 교실에 있는 학생들의 눈을 쳐다보면서 분명하고 천천히 말을 하도록 해. 그리고 질문에 대답할 준비를 갖추어야 해. 교수님은 정말 질문을 많이 하시거든.
학생1 음... 결코 익숙해질 수 없을 거야.

1 남학생은 발표에 대해 무엇이라 말하는가?
   (A) 질문에 대답하기 위해 주어진 시간은 매우 짧다.
   (B) 학생들은 발표가 끝나고 질문을 할 수가 없다.
   (C) 발표를 잘하기 위한 몇 가지 조언이 있다.
   (D) 다른 학생이 하지 않는다면 교수님이 질문을 할 것이다.
   정답 (C)

   해설 남학생은 발표점수를 잘 받으려면 교실에 있는 학생들의 눈을 쳐다보면서 천천히 말을 하고, 질문에 대답할 준비를 해야 한다고 추천했다.

2 남학생에 대해 사실이 아닌 것은 무엇인가? 정답 두 개를 고르시오.
   (A) 그는 여자가 지난 학기에 들었던 것과 같은 수업을 듣고 있다.
   (B) 그는 전에 그 교수님의 수업 중의 하나를 들은 적이 있다.
   (C) 그는 발표에 대해 좋은 학점을 받지 못했다.
   (D) 그는 교수님의 의견이 유용하다고 생각했다.
   정답 (A), (C)

해설 남학생은 지난 학기에 그 교수님의 수업 중의 하나를 들었다고 했다. 또한 그가 받은 학점에 대한 언급은 없다.

Vocabulary Preview — for Practice

Practice 1

1. infection (감염)
   - ✓ a. invasion by germs
   - b. a substance that kills germs
2. eliminate (제거하다)
   - ✓ a. to do away with
   - b. to light something and make it brighter
3. withstand (견디다)
   - a. to take back, out, or away
   - ✓ b. to bear or not be changed by something
4. evolve (진화하다)
   - a. to move in circular fashion around a fixed point
   - ✓ b. to change and develop gradually into different forms

Practice 2

1. violence (폭력)
   - a. to act in disregard of laws and rules
   - ✓ b. an act of aggression
2. source (근원, 출처)
   - ✓ a. the origin or cause of something
   - b. a liquid dressing that is served with food to add flavor
3. provoke (야기하다)
   - ✓ a. to cause or incite as a reaction
   - b. to describe in advance as a result of knowledge
4. debate (토론하다)
   - a. to fight or struggle against
   - ✓ b. to discuss or argue

Practice 3

1. behavior (행동)
   - ✓ a. manner of acting yourself
   - b. at or toward the back
2. infancy (유아기)
   - a. a feeling of favorable regard
   - ✓ b. the earliest period in the life
3. integrate (통합하다)
   - a. to determine or explain the meaning of
   - ✓ b. to unite with something else to create a whole
4. crucial (결정적인)
   - ✓ a. of the greatest importance
   - b. to move in or pass through cycles

Practice 4

1. variation (변화)
   - ✓ a. an instance of change
   - b. a number or situation which can change
2. evaporate (증발하다)
   - a. to determine or set the value or worth of
   - ✓ b. to turn from liquid into vapor
3. likelihood (가능성)
   - ✓ a. the state of being likely
   - b. a strong liking or inclination
4. irrefutable (반박할 수 없는)
   - ✓ a. impossible to refute or disprove
   - b. the act or an instance of refusing

Vocabulary Preview — for Actual Test

Actual Test 1

1. c 고대 이집트는 항상 나를 매혹시킨다.
2. b 이 왕국은 놀라운 생명체로 가득 차 있다.
3. d 그는 울고 싶은 충동을 참았다.
4. a 그것들은 종합 검사를 통해서만 감지할 수 있다.

Actual Test 2

1. a 30마일은 매일 출근하기에는 너무 먼 거리이다.
2. b 그 시장의 성장 가능성은 어떻습니까?
3. d 그들의 결혼은 단지 조화를 이루지 못해서 결말을 냈다.
4. d 당신 요즘 들어 과일을 많이 먹는 거 같아요.

Practice 1

1 (B)   2 (C)   3 (B)

생물학 수업의 강의를 들으시오.

🎧 스크립트

P We take antibiotics for granted today... in fact, we overuse them, according to some researchers. But it's only been about 75 years that we've consistently used antibiotics to battle infections of the body. Okay, so everyone knows what antibiotics are, right? — Medicines that kill the bacteria that cause infections. Now, when we first discovered these medicines in the 1930s, we were suddenly able to treat diseases that, until then, had really been considered untreatable, like pneumonia, tuberculosis, and so on. Even a small infection could kill someone. But along come antibiotics, and we gained the upper hand over these bacteria. And so, by the 1970s it started to seem like, wow, we're going to eliminate all infectious diseases from the earth! How great! However, what we've started to notice over the past few decades is not a reduction, or near elimination of these diseases, but an increase in people whose infections aren't responding to antibiotics. This occurs because of antibiotic resistance. Bacteria strains have evolved enough to be able to withstand the effects of antibiotics and so are not slowed down by this medicine. In fact, these bacteria are able to reproduce, creating even stronger strains that are even more resistant to treatment.

교수 우리는 오늘날 항생제를 당연한 것으로 받아들입니다... 몇몇 연구자에 따르면 사실상 우리는 이것을 남용하고 있습니다. 그러나 우리가 신체 감염과 싸우기 위해 항생제를 꾸준히 사용해온 것은 약 75년 정도밖에 되지 않았습니다. 항생제가 무엇인지는 모두들 알고 있죠? — 바로 감염을 일으키는 박테리아를 죽이는 약을 말합니다. 자, 1930년대에 이 약을 처음 발견했을 때, 폐렴, 결핵 등 그때까지만 해도 정말 치료가 불가능하다고 생각했던 질병을 갑자기 치료할 수 있게 되었습니다. 심지어 아주 자그마한 감염에도 사람이 죽을 수 있었습니다. 하지만 항생제가 등장하면서 우리는 이러한 박테리아를 제압할 수 있게 되었습니다. 이렇게 1970년대에 이르게 되자, 와, 모든 감염성 질병을 지구상에서 제거할 수 있을 것처럼 보였습니다! 정말 멋진 일이었습니다! 하지만 과거 수십 년 동안 우리가 목격하기 시작한 것은 이러한 질병의 감소도 제거도 아니었고, 오히려 감염이 항생제에 반응하지 않는 사람들의 수적인 증가였습니다. 이런 현상은 항생제에 대한 내성 때문에 생겨납니다. 박테리아 변종이 항생제의 효과를 견뎌낼 수 있을 정도로 진화하기 때문에 이런 약으로는 활동이 둔화되지 않습니다. 사실상, 이런 박테리아는 치료에 훨씬 더 내성이 강한 더욱 강력한 변종을 만들면서 재생될 수 있습니다.

1 교수는 항생제를 어떻게 정의하는가?
(A) 박테리아의 재생을 둔화시킬 수 있는 약이다.
(B) 심각한 감염을 일으키는 박테리아를 죽이는 치료제이다.
(C) 효험을 상실한 질병 예방 치료법이다.
(D) 지금은 사람들이 거의 사용하지 않는 종류의 약이다.

해설 강의에 따르면, 항생제란 감염을 일으키는 박테리아를 죽이는 약을 뜻한다.

2 교수에 따르면, 1970년대에 가졌던 항생제에 대한 가정은 무엇인가?
(A) 예상치 못한 부작용을 일으켰다.
(B) 가장 심각한 질병에만 사용되어져야 한다.
(C) 감염성 질병을 없앨 것이다.
(D) 모든 질병에 원인을 제공했다.

해설 항생제의 등장으로 모든 감염성 질병을 지구상에서 제거할 수 있을 것처럼 보였다.

3 사람들이 항생제에 반응하지 않는 이유는 무엇인가?
(A) 몇몇 새롭고, 치료가 불가능한 질병이 최근에 발생했다.
(B) 박테리아가 항생제의 효과를 견뎌낼 만큼 진화했다.
(C) 사람들은 어떤 감염에 대한 면역성이 더 이상 없다.
(D) 박테리아는 더 이상 감염의 주요 원인이 아니다.

해설 항생제에 대한 내성이 생겨서, 항생제의 효과를 견뎌낼 만큼 박테리아 변종이 진화했기 때문이다.

Practice 2

1 (C)   2 (B)   3 (C)

미래파에 대한 토론을 들으시오.

🎧 스크립트

P It's no secret that the 20th century was a time of rapid change in technology, transportation, communication and so on... we went from most people walking or using horses to get around at the beginning of the century, to not only being able to travel long distances at a faster speed, but even being able to travel to the moon. Now, there are certainly some problems that have arisen because of these changes, but today I want to look at a group of artists from the early 20th century who really celebrated these developments — the Futurists. Can anybody tell me anything about them?

S Well... they were all about speed and energy, the power of machines, right?

P Yes. The machine was a symbol... for their own energy and power. We can see speed represented in all kinds of interesting ways in their art. But they valued violence and conflict as well, as sources of energy and renewal. And these, of course, made some people angry — as violence is not a good thing. However, for the Futurists, provoking people into debating these issues was more or less the point. They wanted people to seriously think about culture and what made it move.

교수 20세기가 기술, 운송, 의사소통 등의 분야에서 급격한 변화의 시기라는 것은 명백한 사실입니다... 우리는, 20세기 초 이동하기 위해 대부분의 사람이 걸어가거나 말을 사용하여 갔던 시기를 거쳐, 더 빠른 속도로 먼 거리를 여행할 수 있을 뿐만 아니라 심지어는 달까지 여행할 수 있는 시대에 도달했습니다. 이러한 변화 때문에 발생한 문제들이 분명 있습니다. 하지만 오늘은 이런 발달을 정말 축하했던 20세기 초 한 무리의 예술가들, 즉 미래파에 대해 살펴보고자 합니다. 미래파에 대해 말할 수 있는 사람이 있습니까?

학생 그들은 속도와 에너지, 즉, 기계의 힘과 모두 관련이 있었습니다. 그렇죠?

교수 맞습니다. 기계는 그들 자신의 에너지와 힘을 나타내는 상징입니다. 우리는 그들의 예술 속에 속도가 온갖 종류의 흥미로운 방식으로 표현된 것을 볼 수 있습니다. 그러나 그들은 또한 에너지와 재생의 원천으로 폭력과 갈등도 또한 중요하게 생각합니다. 그리고 물론 이러한 점이 몇몇 사람들을 분노하게 만들었습니다. 왜냐하면 폭력은 좋은 것이 아니기 때문입니다. 그러나 미래파에게 있어서는, 사람들이 이런 주제에 대해 토론하도록 자극하는 것이 대체로 그들의 취지였습니다. 그들은 문화와 문화를 움직이게 만드는 것에 대해 사람들이 진지하게 생각하기를 원했습니다.

1 다음 중에서 미래파의 상징으로 생각되는 것은 무엇인가?
(A) 나무와 식물
(B) 고층 빌딩
(C) 자동차와 기차
(D) 돈과 명예

해설 미래파와 관련이 있는 것은 속도, 에너지, 기계의 힘 등이다.

2 다음 중에서 미래파의 특징이 <u>아닌</u> 것은 무엇인가?
(A) 속도 숭배
(B) 기술에 대한 불신
(C) 전쟁에 대한 찬미
(D) 기계에 대한 애정

해설 기계가 미래파의 에너지와 힘을 나타내는 상징인 것으로 보아 미래파는 기술을 숭배한다. 또한 폭력과 갈등을 에너지와 재생의 근원으로 보았다.

3 교수에 따르면, 미래파가 사람들을 자극하려 했던 이유는 무엇인가?
(A) 예술이 좀 더 논쟁적일 필요가 있다고 생각했다.
(B) 사람들이 새로운 기술의 가치를 인정한다고 생각하지 않았다.
(C) 사람들이 문화와 문화의 변화에 대해 심사숙고하기를 원했다.
(D) 그들의 예술에 대한 관심을 끄는 데 흥미가 있었다.

해설 미래파는 폭력과 갈등을 중요하게 생각했고, 이를 통해 사람들을 자극해서 자신이 속한 문화에 대해 생각하게 하려 의도했다.

Practice 3

1 (C)   2 (C)   3 (B)

사회화에 대한 토론을 들으시오.

🎧 스크립트

P How important, really, is the first year of a child's life in its development? Well, let's take a look at a case in India. Two girls, one about 2 years old and the other about 8, were found living with wolves in the wild. It was presumed the girls had been with the animals since infancy... the person who found them tried to integrate the girls into human society, but it was difficult, as neither girl could speak, and each acted far more like an animal than a human. For instance, walking on all fours.

S1 (*negatively*) Can we even really call them human?

S2 You don't have to be able to speak to be human, though. And humans are capable of a wide range of strange behaviors — that doesn't make them less human.

P For many, the ability to connect with others is the most essential element of being human. And these girls really couldn't do that. The younger girl died within a year of being taken away from the wolf pack — much as a wild animal would do. The older girl learned a few words and could walk on two legs but was never able to connect. So in body, she was human, but in spirit, perhaps more like a wolf. So it seems that, in some really crucial ways, we become a member of our species during that first year...

교수 발달과정에서 한 아이의 삶의 첫 해가 얼마나 중요하겠습니까? 인도에서 발생했던 한 가지 사례를 살펴봅시다. 대략 2살과 8살짜리 두 소녀가 황야에서 늑대들과 함께 생활하고 있는 것이 발견되었습니다. 소녀들은 갓난아이였을 때부터 동물들과 함께 있었던 것으로 추정되었습니다... 두 소녀를 발견했던 사람은 그들을 인간 사회에 통합시키려고 애를 썼지만, 이는 어려웠습니다. 두 소녀 모두 말을 할 수 없었고, 사람이라기보다는 동물에 훨씬 가깝게 행동했습니다. 예를 들자면 네 다리로 걸어다녔죠.

학생1 (부정적으로) 우리가 그들을 인간이라고까지 부를 수 있을까요?

학생2 꼭 말을 할 수 있어야 인간이라고 할 수는 없습니다. 그리고 인간은 정말 광범위한 범위의 이상한 행동들을 할 수 있습니다. 그렇다고 덜 인간답게 되는 것은 아닙니다.

교수 많은 사람들에게는, 다른 사람과 관계를 맺는 능력이 인간이기 위한 가장 중요한 요소입니다. 그리고 이 소녀들은 그것을 할 수 없었습니다. 나이가 더 어렸던 소녀는 늑대 무리에서 떨어진 후 일 년이 채 지나지 않아 죽었습니다. 야생동물이 그렇듯이 말입니다. 나이가 많았던 소녀는 몇 마디 단어를 배웠고 두 발로 걸을 수 있었지만 결코 다른 사람과 관계를 맺을 수는 없었습니다. 그래서 육체적으로는 인간이었지만 정신적으로는 늑대에 더욱 가까웠을 것입니다. 그래서 몇 가지 상당히 중요한 점에서, 우리는 그 첫 해 동안에 우리가 속한 종의 구성원이 되는 것 같습니다...

1 그 소녀들을 사회에 통합시키기가 어려웠던 이유는 무엇인가?
(A) 소녀들이 집에서 살기를 거부했다.
(B) 소녀들을 발견했던 남자가 대단히 잔인했다.
(C) 두 소녀 모두 마치 늑대처럼 행동했다.
(D) 사람들이 소녀들의 이상한 행동을 두려워했다.

해설 두 소녀 모두 말을 할 수 없었고, 네 다리로 걷는 등 사람이라기보다는 동물에 훨씬 가깝게 행동했기 때문이다.

2 남학생은 인간에 대해 어떻게 말하는가?
(A) 인간은 두 발로 걷는, 지적이고 말을 할 줄 아는 동물이다.
(B) 인간은 광범위한 범위의 말을 할 수 있다.
(C) 인간은 여러 가지 다른 방식으로 행동할 수 있다.
(D) 인간은 사회와 관련을 맺으며 살아가는 동물이다.

해설 남학생은 인간이 광범위한 종류의 이상한 행동을 할 수 있다고 했다. (D)는 교수의 말이다.

3 교수에 따르면, 몇몇 사람들이 소녀들을 인간이 아니라고 생각하는 이유가 무엇인가?
(A) 그들이 속한 사회의 다른 사람들이 먹는 음식을 먹지 않았다.
(B) 다른 인간과 관계를 맺을 수 없었다.
(C) 한 마디도 할 수 없었다.
(D) 늑대 떼를 떠나 살고 싶어하지 않았다.

해설 교수의 주장에 따르면, 많은 사람들이 생각하기에 인간이기 위한 가장 중요한 요소는 다른 사람과 관련을 맺는 능력인데 소녀들은 전혀 그러지 못했다.

Practice 4

1 (A)   2 (C)   3 (B)

우주에 대한 대화를 들으시오.

🎧 스크립트

S1 Have you read this article? It's just like what the professor was saying in astronomy class last week.
S2 What article are you talking about?
S1 It was in the paper this morning. It's all about how astronomers have confirmed the presence of frozen water in pretty big quantities on Mars. They are fairly certain that the water is there throughout the year 'cause there isn't enough variation in temperature on the planet for it to evaporate or melt...
S2 Okay... but what does that have to do with class?
S1 Well... remember how she was talking about the relationship of water to the likelihood of finding evidence of life? Well, finding irrefutable evidence of water now makes it really just a matter of time before we find traces of living things...
S2 Well... maybe. I mean, how do we know it's not, like frozen carbon dioxide? There's plenty of that on Mars, too, and it looks like water ice. That wouldn't support any life we know...
S1 Actually, they thought of that. But the frozen CO_2 at the pole where they found the water ice is gone — it's a lot more susceptible to evaporation, you know. So they know it's gotta be water left up there. Then... uh... Mars is a lot like Earth in some ways.

학생1	이 기사 읽어 본 적 있니? 지난 주에 교수님이 천문학 수업시간에 말씀하신 것과 똑같아.
학생2	어떤 기사에 대해 말하는 거니?
학생1	오늘 아침 신문에 났어. 천문학자들이 화성에 꽤 많은 양의 물이 언 흔적을 어떻게 확인했는지에 관한 기사야. 그들은 물이 일년 내내 존재한다는 사실을 상당히 확신하고 있어. 물이 증발하거나 녹는다고 하기에는 혹성의 온도변화가 그다지 심하지 않기 때문이야...
학생2	그래... 하지만 그것이 수업과 무슨 관계가 있니?
학생1	물과 생명체가 존재한다는 가능성과의 관계에 대해 교수님이 말씀하셨던 것 기억나? 물이 존재한다는 반박할 수 없는 증거를 발견했기 때문에 이제 생명체의 흔적을 발견하는 것은 정말 시간 문제지...
학생2	그래... 아마도 그렇겠지. 내 말은, 이산화탄소가 언 것처럼 그것이 물이 아닌지도 모르잖아? 화성에는 이산화탄소도 많이 있거든. 그리고 그건 물이 언 얼음처럼 생겼어. 어떤 생명체가 있다는 증거가 되지 못할거야...
학생1	실제로 그들도 그 점에 대해 생각했어. 하지만 언 물을 발견했던 극지방에서는 언 이산화탄소는 사라지고 없었어. 언 이산화탄소는 훨씬 더 증발하기 쉽거든. 그래서 그들은 그곳에 남아 있는 것이 물이라는 사실을 알지. 그리고 화성은 몇 가지 점에서 지구와 많이 비슷해.

1 천문학자들이 화성에 물이 일년 내내 존재한다고 생각하는 이유는 무엇인가?
(A) 화성의 온도가 증발을 허용하지 않는다.
(B) 일년 내내 물의 이미지를 찍었다.
(C) 지구의 상태를 바탕으로 추정했다.
(D) 온도변화가 매우 극단적이다.

해설 화성에서는 온도변화가 심하지 않아서 물이 증발하거나 녹지 않는다.

2 교수에 따르면, 물의 존재는 무엇을 의미하는가?
(A) 물은 생명을 유지하는 데 필요한 몇 가지 중의 하나일 뿐이다.
(B) 물은 혹성에서 흔히 볼 수 있는 특징이지만, 생명이 살고 있다는 증거는 아니다.
(C) 물은 화성에 생명체가 존재할지도 모른다는 표시이다.
(D) 생명체는 물과 이산화탄소가 있는 장소에 있을 가능성이 더 많다.

해설 물이 존재한다는 것은 생명체가 살고 있다는 증거이다.

3 얼음이 이산화탄소가 아닌 물이라는 사실을 천문학자들은 어떻게 아는가?
(A) 화성의 표면에는 이산화탄소가 없기 때문에
(B) 이산화탄소라면 이미 증발했을 것이기 때문에
(C) 물 얼음은 이산화탄소 얼음과 다르게 생겼기 때문에
(D) 우주 탐침으로 가져온 견본이 물이었기 때문에

해설 이산화탄소라면 이미 증발했을 것이기 때문에 남아 있는 것은 물이라는 결론에 도달했다.

Actual Test 1

1 (D) 2 (C) 3 (B) 4 (A) 5 (B), (D)

신체 화학에 대한 강의를 들으시오.

🎧 스크립트

P Every day we experience different emotions, right? Happiness, sadness, even just boredom... but what exactly do they mean? I mean, what is an emotion? Well, this is a question that has pretty much fascinated humans ever since they started to be conscious of their own consciousness. Past explanations have pointed to different organs, like the heart or the spleen, as being the source of emotion. Others have pointed to supernatural creatures like devils or angels being the cause of these things.
So, what do modern scientists think about these impulses that have such a great impact on how we experience and respond to the world? Well, something that we know is that emotion is accompanied by detectable changes in a person's nervous system and body chemistry. Darwin pointed out that many of the physiological accompaniments to emotion — adrenaline spikes, increased heartbeat, and so on — are more or less the same among higher-order mammals, monkeys, dogs, humans. So for him, this meant that emotions were really practical measures taken by the body to ensure survival. Fear is very functional, in other words, in keeping us away from things that might hurt us. Things that make us happy — family, good food, and so on — well, these are things we seek, and are good for us. So, many scientists see these impulses as being functional, if at times mysterious, elements of the body.

교수 우리는 매일 다른 감정을 경험합니다. 그렇죠? 행복, 슬픔, 심지어 권태조차도... 그러나 정확하게 감정은 무엇을 의미합니까? 내 말은, 감정이란 무엇입니까? 이것은 자신의 의식을 인식하기 시작한 이래로 인간을 매우 매혹시켰던 질문입니다. 과거에 시도했던 설명들은 감정의 근원지로 심장이나 비장과 같은 다른 장기를 지목했습니다. 어떤 사람들은 감정의 원인으로

악마나 천사 등과 같은 초자연적인 존재를 지목했습니다. 그렇다면 우리가 경험하는 방식에 세상에 반응하는 방식에 그토록 지대한 영향을 미치는 이러한 충동에 대해 현대 과학자들은 어떤 생각을 가지고 있을까요? 우리가 알고 있는 점은, 사람의 신경계와 신체 화학에서 감지할 수 있는 변화로 인해 감정이 발생한다는 것입니다. 다윈은 감정에 따라오는 많은 생리학적인 현상 즉 아드레날린 분비, 심장박동수의 증가 등은 원숭이, 개, 인간 등 상위를 차지하는 포유류 사이에 대개 공통적으로 일어난다고 지적했습니다... 그래서 다윈에게 이것은 생존을 확실히 하기 위해 신체가 취한 실제적인 조치였습니다. 다른 표현을 사용하자면, 두려움은 우리를 해칠지도 모르는 것으로부터 우리를 멀어지게 만드는 매우 실용적인 감정입니다. 가족, 맛있는 음식 등 우리를 행복하게 만드는 것들은 우리가 찾는 것이고 우리에게 좋은 것입니다. 그래서 많은 과학자들은 이와 같은 충동을 때로 불가사의하기는 하지만, 신체의 기능적인 요소로 생각합니다.

1 강의는 주로 무엇에 대한 내용인가?
(A) 감정적 행동에 영향을 미치려는 과학적 시도
(B) 다윈의 『종의 기원』에 나오는 감정에 관한 연구
(C) 감정을 설명하려는 실패한 과학적 시도
(D) 인간 감정에 대한 과학적 설명

해설 과학자들은 인간 감정이 신체의 기능적인 요소라고 생각한다.

2 강의에 따르면, 감정에 대한 설명이 아닌 것은 무엇인가?
(A) 불가사의한 존재의 영향
(B) 신체의 화학적 활동
(C) 두뇌 안에서 일어나는 전기적 변동
(D) 다른 장기 기능의 결과

해설 과거에는 심장이나 비장 등 장기 또는 초자연적인 존재를 감정의 근원지로 생각했다. 현대 과학자들은 사람의 신경계와 신체의 화학적 활동을 그 원인으로 생각한다. 감정에 따른 충동을 감정의 근원지로 생각했다.

3 교수는 다윈에 대해 무엇이라고 말하는가?
(A) 동물의 감정에 대한 연구에 매우 흥미를 느꼈다.
(B) 감정에 따른 유사한 생리학적 현상을 특정 동물들에게서 보았다.
(C) 감정을 인간 두뇌 구조의 결과로 생각했다.
(D) 감정을 동물의 생존능력을 방해하는 것으로 보았다.

해설 다윈은 감정에 수반되는 많은 생리학적 현상 즉 아드레날린 분비, 심장박동수 증가 등은 원숭이, 개, 인간 등 상위를 차지하는 포유류 사이에 대개 공통적으로 일어난다고 지적했다.

4 교수에 따르면, 감정은 생존과 어떤 관련이 있는가?
(A) 위험이나 피해를 피할 수 있게 돕는다.
(B) 사랑에 빠지고 결혼하는 것을 보증한다.
(C) 다른 사람에게 동정적으로 반응할 수 있게 해 준다.
(D) 우리가 위험한 추구나 행동을 하도록 유도한다.

해설 자신에게 해로운 요소로부터 멀어지게 만들거나, 자신을 행복하게 만드는 것을 추구하게 하는 신체의 기능적 요소이다.

5 다음 중 충동에 대해서 어느 것이 사실인가? 정답 두 개를 고르시오.
(A) 우리의 경험을 다르게 변화시킬 수 있다.
(B) 충동은 신체에서 일어나는 물리적 변화로 인해 발생한다.
(C) 충동은 신체의 반응과 그다지 관련이 없다.
(D) 충동은 인체의 신경에 영향을 미칠 수 있다.

해설 감정에 수반되는 생리적 반응이 포유류에 공통적으로 나타난다는 사실에 근거하여, 과학자들은 충동이 신체적 변화에 의해 야기된다고 주장한다.

Actual Test 2

1 (D)   2 (B)   3 (A)   4 (C)   5 (C)

두 학생의 대화를 들으시오.

🎧 스크립트

S1 Man, gas prices are killing me lately. It's costing me a fortune to commute back and forth to campus...
S2 Why don't you take the bus? It's a lot cheaper, isn't it?
S1 That'd be nice, but the bus stops running at 8 and my last class doesn't end until 8:30! Well, so, I was thinking maybe I could ask you how you found your place. I wish I could afford to move closer to campus.
S2 Well, have you checked out the housing board in the student center? It's got all these flyers for roommates posted on it. The board itself is continually updated. By the way, so the information is really fresh. That's how I found my place. And my rent is actually pretty cheap.
S1 Hmm... I didn't even know there was a housing board. It sure would save me a lot of time and aggravation if I could just bike to class. But the last thing I want to do is move into somebody's house that was always partying and making a lot of noise.
S2 Well, one thing you could do is put up your own sign, saying that you're looking for a cheap, quiet room to rent. That way you could make sure that your conditions are clear.
S1 I guess I could interview any potential roommate, too, to make sure we're compatible.

S2 Right. And frankly, it's nice to have a buddy to chat with at the end of the day.
S1 This is a pretty good idea. Wow, this could really make my life a whole lot easier.

학생1 세상에, 최근에 휘발유 가격 때문에 정말 죽을 지경이야. 학교까지 통학하는 데 정말 돈이 많이 들어...
학생2 버스를 타지 그러니? 훨씬 싸잖아?
학생1 그럼 좋지만, 버스는 8시면 운행을 멈춰. 내가 듣는 마지막 수업은 8시 30분이나 돼야 끝나거든. 그래서 네가 숙소를 어떻게 찾았는지 물어볼 수 있을까 생각했어. 학교에 가까운 곳으로 이사올 만한 여유가 있었으면 좋겠어.
학생2 학생 센터에 있는 주거 게시판에 가봤니? 거기에 룸메이트를 찾는 광고가 잔뜩 붙어 있어. 게시판은 계속적으로 새로운 정보로 교체되고 있어. 어쨌거나 그래서 정말 최신 정보들이야. 나도 그렇게 방을 구했어. 그리고 실제로 내가 내는 방세는 정말 싸.
학생1 음... 주거 게시판이 있는지조차 몰랐어. 그저 자전거를 타고 수업에 갈 수 있다면, 많은 시간을 절약할 수 있고 화도 덜 날 거야. 하지만 정말 원하지 않는 것은 언제나 파티를 열고 소음을 많이 내는 사람 집으로 이사하게 되는 거지.
학생2 네가 할 수 있는 한 가지 방법은 너만의 광고를 붙이는 거야. 방세가 싸고 조용한 방을 찾고 있다고 써서 말이야. 그렇게 하면 네가 원하는 조건을 분명하게 밝힐 수 있어.
학생1 사이 좋게 지낼 수 있을지 확실하게 하고 싶다면 룸메이트가 될 사람을 미리 만나볼 수도 있겠다.
학생2 맞아. 그리고 솔직히, 하루 일과를 끝내고 같이 수다를 떨 친구가 있는 것은 좋아.
학생1 매우 좋은 아이디어구나. 내 생활을 훨씬 편안하게 만들 수 있겠다.

1 여학생은 무엇을 알고 싶어하는가?
  (A) 자동차 소유에 따른 비용을 감소시키는 방법
  (B) 집을 함께 쓰는 데 따르는 문제점
  (C) 현재 집에서 이사 나오는 것
  (D) 학교 근처에 숙박비용이 저렴한 숙소를 알아보는 방법
해설 여학생은 학교까지 통학하는 데 따른 비용문제로 고민해서, 학교 근처에서 숙소를 찾은 남학생에게 방법을 묻고 있다.

2 여학생이 버스를 타지 않는 이유는 무엇인가?
  (A) 그녀는 항상 예정보다 늦는다.
  (B) 마지막 수업이 늦게 끝나서 버스를 탈 수 없다.
  (C) 버스 정류장 근처에 살지 않는다.
  (D) 버스를 타면 학교에 도착하는 데 너무 오래 걸린다.
해설 여학생의 마지막 수업은 8시 30분에 끝나는데 버스는 8시에 운행을 중지하기 때문이다.

3 남학생은 주거 게시판에 대해 뭐라고 말하는가?
  (A) 숙소에 관한 최신 정보가 있다.
  (B) 캠퍼스 내 주거 센터에 위치한다.
  (C) 판매하려고 내놓은 물건을 찾기에 좋은 장소이다.
  (D) 캠퍼스 주거 부서의 정보보다 그곳의 정보가 더 낫다.
해설 주거 게시판은 학생 센터에 있고, 그곳에서는 룸메이트를 찾는 광고를 볼 수 있으며 계속 새로운 정보로 교체된다.

4 룸메이트를 구하는 문제에 대해 여학생이 걱정하는 것은 무엇인가?
  (A) 룸메이트가 그녀를 너무 일찍 깨울까봐.
  (B) 룸메이트가 자전거를 가지고 있지 못하게 할까봐.
  (C) 룸메이트가 너무나 시끄러울까봐.
  (D) 룸메이트가 집 청소를 하지 않을까봐.
해설 여학생은 시끄럽게 하는 사람이 있는 장소를 구하게 될까봐 걱정한다.

5 여학생은 사이 좋게 지낼 수 있는 룸메이트를 어떻게 구할 것인가?
  (A) 친구에게 추천장을 요구할 것이다.
  (B) 주거 게시판에 붙은 광고에 응답할 것이다.
  (C) 주거 게시판에 자신의 광고를 붙일 것이다.
  (D) 남학생의 집으로 이사할 것이다
해설 남학생이 제안한 방법으로, 자신이 원하는 조건을 분명하게 밝힌 자신만의 광고를 붙일 것이다.

Dictation

Practice 1

① it's only been about
② had really been considered untreatable
③ and so on
④ along came antibiotics
⑤ it started to seem like
⑥ over the past few decades
⑦ enough to be able to withstand
⑧ that are even more resistant to

Practice 2

① to get around
② not only being able to
③ but even being able to travel
④ want to look at
⑤ all about speed and energy
⑥ represented in all kinds of
⑦ more or less the point

Practice 3

① let's take a look at a case
② as neither girl could speak

③ far more like an animal
④ don't have to be able to
⑤ the ability to connect with others
⑥ being taken away from
⑦ but in spirit

Practice 4

① It's just like
② for it to evaporate or melt
③ that have to do with
④ remember how she was talking about
⑤ how do we know it's not
⑥ it's gotta be water left up
⑦ in some ways

Actual Test 1

① pretty much fascinated
② being the cause of these things
③ have such a great impact on
④ emotion is accompanied by
⑤ more or less the same
⑥ keeping us away from things
⑦ as being functional

Actual Test 2

① commute back and forth to
② I wish I could afford to
③ actually pretty cheap
④ the last thing I want to do
⑤ is put up your own sign
⑥ to make sure we're compatible
⑦ make my life a whole lot easier

21	정확한	22	결정적인
23	신경 과민한, 불안한	24	확실히
25	항생 물질	26	치료할 수 없는
27	제거하다	28	잘 견디다
29	성나게 하다	30	통합하다
31	이상한	32	확인하다
33	~에 참여하다	34	포기하다
35	~을 돌보다	36	제출하다
37	이치에 닿다	38	~을 살펴보다
39	~할 여유가 있다	40	~할 능력이 있다
41	~을 당연한 것으로 여기다	42	~에 익숙해지다
43	accurate	44	detail
45	consistently	46	variation
47	likelihood	48	save
49	compatible	50	disenroll
51	presentation	52	redo

Vocabulary Review

1	날조하다	2	멸종하다
3	~에 반하는 행동을 하다	4	침식, 부식
5	(데이터를) 훑다	6	꽤
7	실제로	8	이용하다
9	바꾸다	10	연금술사
11	특징	12	협동하다
13	잠재력	14	전체의
15	희생하다	16	극단적인
17	재정적인	18	학기
19	교무직원	20	~할 수 없음, 무능력

Progress Test

Progress Test 1

1 (B) 2 (C) 3 (C) 4 (C) 5 (B) 6 (B)

조라 닐 허스턴에 대한 강의를 듣고, 질문에 답하시오.

🎧 스크립트

P An interesting phenomenon in the world of literature is that people can achieve some measure of, uh, fame... even a great deal of fame... and then disappear from the public's awareness almost completely. In this way it's, uh, not really so different than being a movie star or something... but sometimes, authors are "rediscovered" by scholars decades later, who feel that the author's contribution to literature shouldn't be forgotten. The scholar becomes a kind of, of a champion of the forgotten author, trying to restore his or her place in the, uh, canon, the "must-read" books in a culture.

So, this is certainly the case with Zora Neale Hurston, an African-American novelist who, uh, published a number of stories and novels... primarily in the 1930s and 40s. She achieved a fair bit of fame, not only because she was one of very few females, let alone African-American females, publishing during that time, but also because she was a real stylistic innovator. She employed the, uh, rhythms, cadences, or intonation of African-American folk tales, as well as the Biblical stories that shaped her culture, to tell stories that had an impact on readers across racial and gender lines. At the peak of her career, she was awarded the prestigious Guggenheim fellowship, completed grad work at Columbia University, and published five books within ten years. And then, um, then her career just sort of stopped altogether... yeah... in the end she died penniless and alone. It wasn't really until the 1980s, when novelist Alice Walker stumbled upon Hurston's works and began to promote Hurston as an important American writer, that the contemporary literary establishment acknowledged her contribution. Since then, Hurston has been a, uh, key figure in discussions of both American and African-American literatures of the 20th century.

교수 문학세계에서 흥미로운 현상은, 사람들이 어느 정도의 명성을, 심지어는 상당한 정도의 명성을 달성할 수 있고... 그리고 나서 대중들의 인식으로부터 거의 완전하게 사라질 수 있다는 겁니다. 이런 식이라면, 영화배우가 되거나 유명인사가 되는 것과 별반 다르지 않습니다... 그러나 작가들은, 그들의 문학적 공헌이 잊혀져서는 안 된다고 느끼는 학자들에 의해 수십 년 후에 '재발견' 되기도 합니다. 학자들은 잊혀진 작가들을 위한 일종의 옹호자가 되어, 그들의 작품을 한 문화 안에서의 '필독 도서'로 회복시키려 노력합니다.

아프리카 미국인 소설가로서, 주로 1930년대와 40년대에 많은 이야기와 소설을 출간했던 조라 닐 허스턴의 경우가 그랬습니다. 그녀가 상당한 명성을 구축할 수 있었던 것은, 아프리카 미국인 여성이었던 점을 제외하고도 당시 글을 발표했던 매우 소수의 여성 가운데 하나였던 동시에 진정으로 문체의 혁신을 달성했기 때문입니다. 그녀는 아프리카 미국인에게 전해 내려오는 민화의 리듬과 가락, 억양뿐만 아니라 자신의 문화를 형성한 성서 이야기도 활용하여, 인종과 성별에 관계없이 독자들에게 영향을 주는 이야기를 전달했습니다. 작가로서 전성기 때, 그녀는 신망이 있는 구겐하임 장학금을 받았고, 콜롬비아 대학교에서 대학원을 수료했고, 10년 안에 5권의 책을 펴냈습니다. 그러다가 그녀의 경력이 모두 멈춰 버렸습니다. 그래서 끝에 가서는 무일푼으로 외롭게 죽고 말았습니다. 1980년대가 되어서야 비로소, 소설가인 앨리스 워커가 허스턴의 작품들을 우연히 접하고 허스턴을 미국 중요 작가로 승격시키기 시작하면서, 허스턴이 동시대의 문학 성립에 기여했다는 사실이 인정되었습니다. 그때 이후로 허스턴은 20세기 미국 문학과 아프리카 미국 문학의 주요인물로 거론되고 있습니다.

1 강의의 주된 내용은 무엇인가?

(A) 1930년대와 40년대 아프리카 미국 문학의 다양한 가치와 양상
(B) 다시 중요성을 인정 받게 된 작가와 그들의 작품
(C) 다른 작가들에 의해 재발견된 아프리카 미국인 여성의 소설
(D) 허스턴이 워커를 포함한 다른 동시대 작가들에 미친 영향

해설 문학세계에서 볼 수 있는 흥미로운 현상에 대한 설명으로, 작가는 명성을 얻었다가도 대중에게서 완전히 잊혀지고, 오랜 세월이 흐른 후에 학자에 의해 그 가치가 인정받는 경우가 있다. 본문은 조라 닐 허스턴의 경우를 예로 들고, 그녀의 이력과 작품을 설명한다.

2
교수가 영화배우를 언급한 이유는 무엇인가?
(A) 허스턴이 처음에 아프리카 미국 영화에 출현했었다는 사실을 지적하려고
(B) 허스턴의 이야기 가운데 다수가 할리우드에 대한 것이었다는 사실을 알리려고
(C) 문학적 명성이 영화에서의 명성만큼 덧없을 수 있다는 사실을 말하려고
(D) 여성들이 영화에서 성공할 가능성이 더 높다는 사실을 은연중에 나타내려고

해설 일순간 인기가 사라질 수 있는 영화배우나 유명인처럼 작가가 구축한 명성 또한 갑자기 사라질 수 있다.

3
교수에 따르면, 학자들이 몇몇 작가들을 재발견하는 이유는 무엇인가?
(A) 그들은 대개 문학의 기준에서 가치 없는 작가들을 구별하고 싶어한다.
(B) 그들은 일반적으로 자신의 중요성과 명예를 증가시키고 싶어한다.
(C) 그들은 사람들이 위대한 문학작품을 기억해야 한다고 느낀다.
(D) 그들은 예술과 작품의 특정 아름다움을 높이기를 진정으로 바란다.

해설 학자들은 해당 작가들이 대중에게 잊혀졌지만 그 작가들이 문학에 남긴 공헌까지 잊혀져서는 안 된다고 생각한다.

4
강의에 따르면, 허스턴이 명성을 얻게 된 이유가 아닌 것은 무엇인가?
(A) 아프리카 미국인이었다.
(B) 여성이었다.
(C) 대학원 과정을 수료했다.
(D) 문체가 흥미로웠다.

해설 본문에서 허스턴이 명성을 얻게 된 이유로 제시한 것은 그녀가 아프리카 미국인 여성이었다는 점, 당시에는 소수에 불과했던 여성 작가였다는 점, 문체의 혁신을 달성했다는 점이다.

5
다음 중에서 허스턴의 문학적 문체로 인식된 것은 무엇인가?
(A) 분열된 이야기의 도입
(B) 문화적 특징과 성경적 특징의 통합
(C) 다양한 인종의 내레이터에 대한 의존
(D) 장치로서 성경 이야기의 사용

해설 그녀는 아프리카 미국인에게 전해 내려오는 민화의 리듬과 가락, 억양을 작품에 반영했고, 성경의 특징을 전달했다.

6
다음 중 조라 닐 허스턴에 대한 사실이 아닌 것은 무엇인가?
(A) 첫 여성 작가 중 한 사람이었다.
(B) 말년에 매우 유명해졌다.
(C) 그 시대에 속했던 사람들의 인정을 받았다.
(D) 자신의 작품에 대해 그다지 보상을 받지 못했다.

해설 한 동안 대중의 인기를 얻었지만 갑자기 경력이 정지되면서 말년에는 무일푼이 되어 외롭게 죽어갔다.

Progress Test 2

1 (C) 2 (C) 3 (D) 4 (B) 5 (C) 6 (D)

교수 사무실에서 대화를 듣고, 질문에 대답하시오.

🎧 스크립트

S Good afternoon, professor, can I talk to you for a minute?
P Sure, come in...
S Okay, I wanted to talk to you about the last essay.
P All right, go ahead...
S Um, one thing you commented on was that Jensen's theory about the role of the miniature paintings in Indian royal life was not universally accepted, right? But I read at least three articles that talked about his theory and none seemed to cast any doubt on it.
P Yeah. There are many scholars out there who accept Jensen's idea that the paintings were a way to educate members of the royal court in Indian history and Hindu mythology as gospel... I didn't mean to imply that there wasn't support for it out there.
S But then are there scholars who disagree?
P Yes. The point that I'm trying to make, though, and this is what I don't think I was clear about, is not that I think you have to disagree with Jensen. He does have some support for his claims, and you do too, as you defend him in your paper. But you don't mention the controversy over his ideas at all.
S Well, I thought that might take away from the strength of my claim. If I tell the reader not everyone agrees with him, maybe they won't trust me.
P Actually, by giving the whole picture to your reader, you're building even more trust. It shows that you respect the reader enough to let him or her make up their own mind. You give them the evidence for both sides, give your opinion, and let the readers decide. It's a much more effective strategy than ignoring a part of the argument.

학생	안녕하세요, 교수님. 잠시 말씀 좀 드려도 될까요?
교수	그럼. 어서 들어오게...
학생	예. 지난번 논문에 대해 말씀을 드리고 싶습니다.
교수	알겠네. 말해 보게...
학생	음, 교수님께서는, 인도 왕족의 삶에서 세밀화의 역할에 대한 젠센의 이론이 보편적으로 허용되고 있지는 않다고 논평하셨습니다. 하지만 그의 이론에 대해 주장한 논문을 최소한 세 편 읽었지만 그에 대해 어떤 의문도 던지지 않았습니다.
교수	맞네. 그림이 인도 역사와 절대진리로서의 힌두 신화를 왕족에게 교육시키는 방법이었다는 젠센의 견해를 받아들이는 학자들이 많이 있네... 그의 이론을 지지하는 사람이 없다고 말한 것은 아니었네.
학생	하지만 동의하지 않는 학자들도 있습니까?
교수	그렇지. 내가 분명하게 말하지 않았다고 생각하네만, 내가 말하려 했던 요점이 자네가 젠센의 견해에 반대해야 한다는 것은 아니라네. 젠센의 주장을 지지하는 사람들도 있고, 자네의 논문에서 그를 변호했던 것처럼 자네도 그의 주장을 지지하고 있네. 그러나 자네는 그의 견해에 대한 논쟁에 대해서는 전혀 언급하지 않고 있네.
학생	그렇게 하면 제 주장의 강점이 사라질지도 모른다고 생각했습니다. 모든 사람이 그의 의견에 동의하는 것은 아니라고 독자들에게 말한다면 아마도 독자들은 내 논문을 신뢰하지 않을 겁니다.
교수	실제로는, 자네의 독자들에게 전체 윤곽을 보여 주게 되면 자네는 훨씬 더 큰 신뢰를 구축하게 된다네. 자네가 그만큼 독자들을 존중해서 그들로 하여금 스스로 마음의 결정을 하도록 했다는 사실을 나타내니까 말이네. 독자들에게 양쪽의 증거를 주고, 자네의 견해를 제시해서 독자들이 결정하도록 하는 걸세. 논쟁의 일부분을 무시하는 것보다 훨씬 더 효과적인 전략이지.

1 학생이 교수와 이야기를 하고 싶어한 이유는 무엇인가?
  (A) 지난 논문에 대한 점수에 불만을 표시하기 위해서
  (B) 논문의 주요 주장을 명확히 하고 변호하기 위해서
  (C) 자신의 논문에 대한 교수의 논평에 대해 토론하기 위해서
  (D) 교수의 논평에 반대의 뜻을 나타내기 위해서

해설 학생은, 젠센의 이론을 변호했던 자신의 논문에 대해 젠센의 이론에 반대하는 의견이 있다는 교수의 논평을 듣고 이에 대해 토론하고 싶어한다.

2 남학생은 젠센의 이론에 대해 무엇이라 말하는가?
  (A) 대부분의 학자들에게 널리 알려져 있지는 않았다.
  (B) 단지 이론의 일부에만 동의했다.
  (C) 이론에 대해 광범위한 지지가 있음을 발견했다.
  (D) 논리에 심각한 결함이 있다.

해설 남자가 읽었던 논문의 저자 모두 젠센의 이론을 지지했다.

3 교수는 그 이론에 대해 무엇이라 말하는가?
  (A) 지난 몇 년 동안 거짓으로 판명되어왔다.
  (B) 논문에 포함시키지 말았어야 했다.
  (C) 정확한 해석일 가능성이 많다고 생각한다.
  (D) 그 분야에서 활동하는 대부분의 학자들에게 인정되는 것은 아니다.

해설 젠센의 이론이 보편적으로 받아들여지는 것은 아니어서 이에 반대하는 의견도 있다.

4 교수는 학생이 무엇을 하기를 원하는가?
  (A) 젠센의 이론이 옳다는 점을 보여 주는 증거를 더 제공하기
  (B) 이론에 반대하는 의견을 언급하기
  (C) 논쟁에 대한 언급을 논문에서 제거하기
  (D) 논쟁에 대한 그녀의 견해를 논문에서 제거하기

해설 젠센 이론의 장점만을 논한 학생의 논문에 그 반대편 논쟁 또한 포함시킨다면 더욱 독자의 신뢰를 획득할 수 있다.

5 남학생이 이론을 둘러싼 논쟁을 전혀 언급하지 않은 이유는 무엇인가?
  (A) 논문에 실어야 한다는 사실을 몰랐기 때문에
  (B) 이론이 널리 인정을 받고 있는지 확신할 수 없었기 때문에
  (C) 자신의 요점을 흐리지 않을까 걱정했기 때문에
  (D) 이론에 대한 다른 의견을 인식하고 있었기 때문에

해설 학생은 자신의 논문에서 주장한 이론에 반대하는 의견도 있다고 말하면 논문에 대한 신뢰도가 떨어질지도 모른다고 생각했다.

6 교수는 자신의 제안에 대해 어떤 이유를 대는가?
  (A) 학생의 논문에 길이를 더해 줄 것이고 학점을 향상시킬 것이다.
  (B) 학생이 하고 있는 주장을 단순화할 것이다.
  (C) 학생의 논쟁을 좀 더 명확하게 만들 것이다.
  (D) 저자에 대한 독자의 신뢰를 증가시킬 것이다.

해설 논문에 대한 독자의 신뢰도를 증가시킬 것이다.

Dictation

Progress Test 1

① even a great deal of fame
② not really so different than
③ shouldn't be forgotten
④ let alone
⑤ as well as the Biblical stories
⑥ just sort of stopped
⑦ in the end she died penniless and alone

Progress Test 2

① none seemed to cast any doubt on it
② there wasn't support for it out there
③ does have some support for
④ over his ideas at all
⑤ might take away from

⑥ let him or her make up their own mind
⑦ a much more effective strategy than

Vocabulary Preview   for Progress Test

Progress Test 1

1. a 명성 있는 대학으로서 옥스퍼드는 9세기 동안 존재해왔다.
2. c 어떤 사람들은 살인자들에 대한 사형 제도를 복원시키는 데 찬성한다.
3. b 국립 유럽 미술문화 박물관에서는 이번 한 달 동안, 유럽 현대 미술의 진수를 보여 주는, 주요 유럽 모더니즘 화가 10인의 작품을 전시합니다.
4. b 일반적으로 역사가들은 그녀를 그 분야의 천재로 인정한다.

Progress Test 2

1. a 그 기사는 그에 대해 논평하기로 선정된 편집자에게 제출되어야 한다.
2. d 수상은 실업을 증가시킨 정책을 어떻게 옹호할지에 대해 질의를 받았다.
3. a 그는 성실한 사람이라 그 학과의 모든 사람들에게 존경받고 있다.
4. b 그 상품에 대한 마케팅 전략은 가능한 한 많은 무료 홍보를 얻어내는 것과 관련되어 있다.

CHAPTER 03
PROCESS/CLASSIFICATION

Pre Test 1

동굴 동물에 대한 강의를 듣고, 질문에 답하시오.

🎧 스크립트

P   So... cave inhabiting animals can be categorized as troglobites, troglophiles, trogloxenes. <u>As you all may know</u>, cave-inhabiting animals range from tiny microscopic organisms to huge mammals. However, not all these creatures are cave-limited species. Uh... these cave dwellers or cave limited species are called troglobites, all right? Okay... some cave animals are called troglophiles, umm, animals which <u>are found in the caves</u>..., but can also live outside, such as cockroaches and spiders... okay? And others are trogloxenes; they live in the caves, but <u>go outside to feed</u>. Bats and cave crickets are the examples. Well, people and elephants <u>can be classified as</u> cave visitors. Studies have found that the cave food chain is quite complex, but everything ultimately <u>depends on the bats for survival</u>. Bats are the only creatures which regularly go outside caves to feed. They leave the cave at night to feed on insects, fruits and pollen.

교수   자... 동굴에 거주하는 동물들은 혈거 동물인 트로글로바이츠, 트로글로파일즈, 트로글로신즈 등으로 분류될 수 있습니다. 여러분 모두 알고 있듯이, 동굴에 거주하는 동물들은 아주 미세한 생물에서부터 거대한 포유류까지 분포되어 있습니다. 그러나 이 동물들이 모두 동굴 제한 종인 것은 아닙니다. 이렇게 동굴에 거주하는 동물이나 동굴에 제한된 종은 트로글로바이츠라고 불립니다. 알겠죠? 자... 트로글로파일즈로 불리는 동굴 동물도 있습니다. 이들은 동굴에서 발견되지만, 동굴 바깥에서도 역시 살 수 있는 바퀴벌레나 거미 등을 말합니다. 알겠죠? 그리고 트로글로신즈가 있습니다. 그들은 동굴에 살지만 먹이를 먹기 위해서 동굴 밖으로 나갑니다. 박쥐와 동굴 귀뚜라미가 그 예입니다. 자, 사람과 코끼리는 동굴 방문객으로 분류될 수 있습니다. 연구결과에 따르면, 동굴 먹이사슬은 아주 복잡합니다만, 모든 것의 생존은 궁극적으로 박쥐에 달려 있습니다. 박쥐는 먹이를 먹기 위해서 규칙적으로 동굴 밖으로 나가는 유일한 동물입니다. 박쥐들은 곤충, 과일과 꽃가루를 먹기 위해서 밤에 동굴 밖으로 나갑니다.

아래의 각 문구가 트로글로바이츠, 트로글로파일즈, 트로글로신즈를 설명하는지 표시하시오. 적절한 칸에 체크하시오.

	트로글로바이츠	트로글로파일즈	트로글로신즈
동굴을 떠날 수 없다	✓		
동굴에 살지만 먹이를 먹으러 동굴 밖으로 나간다			✓
대부분 먹이 사슬의 꼭대기에 있다			✓
동굴이나 다른 장소에서도 산다		✓	

해설 트로글로바이츠는 거주가 동굴로 제한된 종이다. 트로글로파일즈는 동굴에 살지만 동굴 바깥에서도 역시 살 수 있는 바퀴벌레나 개미 등이다. 트로글로신즈는 동굴에 살지만 먹이를 먹으러 동굴 밖으로 나간다. 동굴 동물들의 생존이 박쥐에게 달려 있다고 했으므로, 동굴 속 먹이사슬의 꼭대기에 있다고 할 수 있다.

Pre Test 2

교내 서점에서의 대화를 듣고, 질문에 답하시오.

🎧 스크립트

S Excuse me. I'm trying to find a copy of the Economics 210 textbook.
C Okay, ... oh, actually, this book <u>is out of stock</u> right now.
S Out of stock? But I need the book for class this week!
C Well, this happens with popular classes sometimes... umm, well, what you can do is... contact the publisher directly.
S Do I visit their website and <u>place an order</u>?
C Well, that's possible but it would take a few more days. If you just call them up, then, I think it can save a couple of days. Call the publisher's number, then ask for the distributor that is closest to your region, or you can leave your address and number for them to call back, but it will again <u>take a while for them to</u> have the nearest distributor to call you for your order.
S So I should just ask for the number...
C Right, you call the distributor and <u>ask for a person in charge of</u> the textbooks. You will need the name of the author and the exact title of the book.
S All right, I guess all I need to know is the number.
C Oh, you will have to decide on the delivery options, either express or standard. For express, they <u>might charge you extra</u>.

학생 실례합니다. 경제학 210의 교재를 찾고 있습니다.
점원 예, ... 사실 책의 재고가 지금은 다 떨어졌는데요.
학생 품절이라고요? 하지만 이번 주 수업시간에 그 책이 필요해요!
점원 인기 있는 수업인 경우에 이런 일이 가끔 발생하죠... 그렇다면 출판사에 직접 연락을 해 보는 방법이 있어요.
학생 출판사의 웹 사이트를 방문해서 주문을 할까요?
점원 가능한 일이지만 며칠이 더 걸릴 거예요. 출판사에 전화를 하면 이틀을 벌 수 있으리라 생각합니다만. 출판사에 전화를 해서 당신이 사는 지역에서 가장 가까운 배급업자에 대해 문의하세요. 또는 배급자들이 전화를 걸 수 있도록 당신의 주소와 전화번호를 남기세요. 하지만 출판사가 당신 지역에서 가장 가까운 배급업자에게 연락해서 당신의 주문을 받기 위해 전화를 하려면 좀 걸릴 겁니다.
학생 그러면 그냥 전화번호만 물어 봐야 하나요?
점원 예, 배급업자에게 전화해서 교재배급을 담당하는 사람을 찾으세요. 책의 저자명과 정확한 제목을 알고 있어야 합니다.
학생 알겠습니다. 내가 알 필요가 있는 것은 배급업자의 전화번호겠군요.
점원 참, 배달을 어떻게 할 것인지, 급행인지 보통인지 결정해야 할 겁니다. 급행으로 하려면 요금을 추가 부담해야 할지 모릅니다.

아래의 각 문구가 주문 과정의 단계에 속하는지 표시하시오. 적절한 칸에 체크하시오.

	예	아니오
출판사에 주문한다		✓
배급업자가 책을 배달하게 한다	✓	
책의 배달방법을 그들에게 말한다	✓	
자신의 은행계좌 번호를 그들에게 말해 준다		✓
주문하고 싶은 책에 대해 구체적으로 말한다	✓	

해설 출판사에 직접 주문하면 시간이 걸리므로, 출판사에 전화해서 자신의 주거지와 가장 가까운 곳에 위치한 배급업자의 전화번호를 알아낸 후에 그곳에 직접 주문한다. 이때 주문하려는 책에 대한 정확한 정보를 주어야 하고 배달방법을 구체적으로 제시해야 한다.

Vocabulary Preview for Mini-Exercise

Mini-Exercise 1

1-1. target (~를 목표로 정하다)
  ✓ a. to direct advertising, criticism or a product at someone
     b. a group of people gathered to hear and

sometimes to see a performance, speech, or the like

1-2. publish (출판하다)
   a. to prepare a text or film for printing by correcting mistakes
   ✓b. to make information available to people, especially in a book, magazine or newspaper

1-3. broaden (넓히다, 확장하다)
   ✓a. to increase the range of things that someone knows about or has experienced
   b. to send out a programme on television or radio

2-1. abolish (폐지하다)
   a. to remove earth that is covering very old objects buried in the ground in order to discover things about the past
   ✓b. to end an activity or custom officially

2-2. opponent (적, 상대)
   ✓a. a person who disagrees with something and speaks against it or tries to change it
   b. completely different

2-3. desperate (자포자기의, 절망적인)
   ✓a. very serious or bad
   b. not suitable or correct for a situation

3-1. reputed (평판이 있는)
   ✓a. said to be the true situation although this is not known to be certain and may not be likely
   b. to calculate by mathematical operations

3-2. insanity (광기, 정신 착란)
   ✓a. the medical term used for when someone is seriously mentally ill
   b. serious emotional shock and pain caused by an extremely upsetting experience

3-3. severe (엄한, 격심한)
   ✓a. extreme or very difficult
   b. to keep one group of people apart from another and treat them differently

Mini-Exercise 2

1-1. relentless (가차 없는, 혹독한)
   a. connected with what is happening or being discussed
   ✓b. continuing in a severe or extreme way

1-2. progression (전진, 진보)
   ✓a. advancement to an improved or more developed state

b. a series of actions that you take in order to achieve a result

1-3. exclusively (독점적으로)
   ✓a. limited to only one person or group of people
   b. apart from other persons or things

2-1. testify (증언하다)
   ✓a. to speak seriously about something, especially in a court of law
   b. to do something in order to discover if something is safe, works correctly

2-2. identify (신원을 밝히다)
   a. to find information, a place or an object, especially for the first time
   ✓b. to recognize someone or something and say or prove who or what they are

2-3. attorney (법률 대리인)
   a. a legal representative who officially accuses someone of committing a crime
   ✓b. one whose profession is to give legal advice and to act as a representative in court

3-1. astronomy (천문학)
   ✓a. the scientific study of the universe and of objects which exist naturally in space, such as the moon, the sun, planets and stars
   b. a person who is trained for travelling in a spacecraft

3-2. massive (부피가 큰, 대량의)
   ✓a. very large in size, amount or number
   b. to become completely involved in something

3-3. asteroid (소행성)
   ✓a. one of many rocky objects, varying in width from over 900 kilometers to less than one kilometer, which circle the sun
   b. a system of billions of stars held relatively close to each other by gravity

Mini-Exercise 1　Identifying Processes

1 여성 잡지에 대한 강의를 듣고, 물음에 답하시오.

🎧 스크립트

P Ok, everybody, so... uh, there has been a... a definite evolution of magazines targeting women, beginning with a very small number being aimed at women and arriving at the situation today, where 2 out of 3 magazines target women.

In the 18th century, at... uh... the beginning of the magazine publishing industry, there were about fifteen national publications. Had to start somewhere, right? Anyway, these were primarily aimed at men. However, by the end of the 18th century, the first publication aimed at women was launched. Called *the Lady's Magazine and Repository of Entertaining Knowledge*, this journal provided useful information for women regarding housekeeping and other related subjects. First, women became aware that there could be magazines aimed specifically at their interests. The magazine continued putting out useful information and broadened subjects for a variety of women. Then they bought these magazines in droves. The magazine industry responded by creating more and more "ladies' journals" as they were called. Later, there appeared some magazines that provide very specialized information for women, such as fashion, cosmetics. By the end of the nineteenth century, there were as many women's magazines as there were men's.

교수 자, 여러분, 여성을 겨냥했던 매우 소수의 잡지로 시작해서 3권 중 2권의 잡지가 여성을 겨냥하는 오늘날의 상황에 이르기까지, 여성 잡지는 분명한 발전을 이루고 있습니다.

잡지발행 사업이 시작되었던 18세기에, 국내 출판사는 약 15군데가 있었습니다. 시작 단계에서는 어쩔 수 없는 일이었겠죠? 어쨌든, 이 잡지들은 주로 남성을 겨냥했습니다. 그러나, 18세기 말에 이르러 여성을 겨냥한 첫 출판물이 출범했습니다. '여성 잡지와 연예지식의 보고' 라는 제목의 이 잡지는 여성에게 가사활동과 이와 관련된 기타 주제에 대한 유용한 정보를 제공했습니다. 첫째, 여성들은 특별히 자신들의 흥미를 겨냥한 잡지가 있을 수 있다는 사실을 인식하게 되었습니다. 잡지는 계속해서 유용한 정보를 내놓기 시작했고, 다양한 층의 여성을 위해 주제를 확장시켰습니다. 그러자 여성들은 대거 이 잡지를 샀습니다. 잡지 산업은 요구에 따라 점점 더 많은 '여성용 잡지'를 만들어냈습니다. 후에 패션, 화장품 등 여성을 위한 매우 전문적인 정보를 제공하는 몇몇 잡지들이 등장했습니다. 19세기 말에는 여성 잡지가 남성 잡지 수만큼 존재했습니다.

여성 잡지 산업이 일어난 단계는 다음 중 어느 것인가? 각 구절에 적합한 칸에 체크하시오.

	예	아니오
여성들이 잡지 발행을 요구하는 내용의 글을 출판사를 대상으로 썼다		✓
여성의 관심을 끄는 주제가 더 많이 추가되었다	✓	
분화된 여성 잡지 시장이 형성되었다	✓	
산업은 여성 잡지의 시장잠재성을 인식했다	✓	
보다 많은 여성이 고도로 차별화된 정보를 요구했다		✓

해설 남성만을 겨냥하던 잡지가 여성으로 눈길을 돌려 그들의 관심을 끄는 유용한 정보를 제공하기 시작했고, 여기에 여성 독자들이 호응하면서 여성 잡지 산업이 성장하게 되었다. 그 후 잡지는 여성에게 유용한 정보를 계속 적용하고, 다양한 층의 여성을 위해 주제를 확장시켰으며, 후에는 패션, 화장품 등 여성을 위해 매우 전문적인 정보를 제공하는 잡지도 등장했다.

2 미국 역사 수업에서의 토론을 듣고, 물음에 답하시오.

🎧 스크립트

P John Brown was an abolitionist, or an opponent of human slavery, who believed that violence was justified... in the march to end an absolutely horrifying situation. Thus, he conceived of and planned his infamous raid on Harper's Ferry, Virginia.

S I thought most abolitionists believed that violence is wrong...

P John Brown probably had gone through that stage... I mean he had looked for ways to resolve the situation using the law. But he looked at how long slavery had existed in America and had gone on too long that change would not come soon enough. Basically, he felt the situation was too dire and desperate to work within the bounds of the law. Well, so... as the next step, he examined the options available for fixing the situation. Brown's options were: to wait till things get better... or to use force to stop slavery now. Brown chose the latter option and planned a revolt. But how? I mean how could he verify that he could achieve his goal? Of course, he couldn't do it by himself, so he thought he had to motivate people, followers as a next step. So, he planned to increase the number of his followers by providing slaves with guns to overthrow their masters in Harper's Ferry, Virginia. After Harper's Ferry, other slave communities would hear the news and stage their own uprisings.

교수 존 브라운은 노예제도 폐지론자 즉 인간 노예제도의 반대자로, 너무나 끔찍한 상황을 종결시키기 위한 행진에서는 폭력이 정당화된다고 믿었습니다. 그래서 그는 불명예스러운 버지니아 주 하퍼 페리 습격사건을 생각해내고 계획했습니다.

학생 저는 대부분의 노예제도 폐지론자들은 폭력이 잘못된 것이라 믿었다고 생각했습니다.

교수 아마 존 브라운도 그 단계를 거쳤을 것입니다... 내 말은 그가 법을 사용해서 상황을 해결하기 위한 방법을 찾아보려 했을 것이란 뜻입니다. 하지만 미국에서 노예제도가 얼마나 오래 존재했었는지 보았고, 너무나 오래 끌었기 때문에 변화가 금방 오지 않으리라는 점을 깨달았습니다. 기본적으로 그는 법의 테두리 안에서 해결하기에는 상황이 너무 비참하고 절박하다고 느꼈습니다. 그래서 다음 단계로 그는 상황을 바로잡을 수 있는 선택사항들을 검토했습니다. 브라운이 검토했던 선택사항은 다음과 같았습니다. 상황이 호전될 때까지 기다린다. 아니면 당장 노예제도를 중지시키기 위해 힘을 사용한다. 브라운은 후자를 선택하고 폭동을 계획했습니다. 하지만 어떻게 했을까요? 그러니까, 어떻게 자신의 목적을 성취할 수 있을지 확증할 수 있었을까요? 물론 그는 혼자서 그 일을 할 수 없었습니다. 그래서 다음 단계로 사람들 즉 추종자들을 부추겨야 한다고 생각했습니다. 그래서 버지니아 주 하퍼 페리에서 주인들을 타도하라고 노예들에게 총을 제공함으로써 추종자들의 수를 증가시킬 계획을 세웠습니다. 하퍼 페리 사건 이후에 그 소식을 들은 다른 노예 사회는 나름대로의 폭동을 시작했습니다.

하퍼 페리 습격을 수행하는 과정에서 브라운의 단계는 다음 중 어느 것인가? 적절한 칸에 체크하시오.

	예	아니오
정부를 설득하기 위한 외교적 시도를 했다		✓
상황을 바로잡기 위해 사용할 수 있는 다른 수단에 대한 검토를 했다	✓	
자신이 노예를 이끌 훌륭한 새 리더가 될 수 있다는 사실을 입증했다		✓
다른 지역에 있는 추종자들을 한 장소로 모이도록 선동했다		✓
정부의 규칙체계를 사용해서 상황을 바로잡으려 애썼다		✓

해설 Brown은 일단 합법적으로 문제를 해결하기 위한 방법을 강구했었고, 해결책을 찾기 위해 여러 가지 선택 사항을 놓고 고민했다. 결국 그는 폭동을 선택했고, 이를 위해 추종자를 규합하고 이들을 선동했다.

3 조지 3세에 대한 토론을 듣고, 물음에 답하시오.

🎧 스크립트

P King George III of England <u>is probably best known for</u> his reputed insanity. Yep... the guy acted like he was crazy. But what caused his madness? This has been a source of great interest to researchers.

S Well, since he has long been dead, <u>it seems pretty impossible to ever know now</u>, right?

P Posthumous DNA exams can often tell important information. The first step in determining what is wrong with a dead person is to access his or her DNA. For King George, they had to find something from his body to get a DNA sample from it. Fortunately, they found three strands of <u>the king's hair in a wig he wore</u>. They sent the sample containing his DNA to a lab for testing. Researchers carefully removed King George's hairs from the wig and sent them for testing. The second step in determining <u>what might be wrong with</u> a dead person is analyzing the results. For King George, when the tests came back, researchers found that his hair contained over 300 times the toxic level of arsenic! Finally, the researchers went through the diagnosis step to determine what was wrong with the dead person. After further investigation, the researchers discovered the powder <u>used to keep bugs out of</u> wigs was triggering and making more severe a disease the king had called porphyria — the symptoms of which looked like insanity!

교수 영국의 국왕 조지 3세는 아마도 정신이상이라는 평판을 받았던 것으로 가장 잘 알려져 있을 겁니다. 그렇습니다. 마치 미친 사람처럼 행동하는 사람 말입니다. 하지만 무엇 때문에 그가 미치게 되었을까요? 이는 연구가들에게 매우 흥미로운 연구거리가 되어왔습니다.

학생 그가 사망한지 오래됐기 때문에 지금 알기란 매우 어려운 것 같습니다. 그렇죠?

교수 사후 DNA 조사를 통해서 중요한 정보를 알 수 있는 경우가 많습니다. 죽은 사람에게 무엇이 잘못되었는지 판단하는 첫 단계는 그들의 DNA를 입수하는 겁니다. 조지 국왕의 경우에는 DNA 샘플을 얻기 위해서 그의 몸에서 나온 무언가를 찾아야만 했습니다. 다행히 사람들은 국왕이 썼던 가발에서 그의 머리카락 세 가닥을 찾아냈습니다. 그들은 DNA를 포함한 견본을 실험하기 위해 보냈습니다. 연구가들은 가발에서 조지 국왕의 머리카락을 조심스럽게 떼어낸 다음 실험을 위해 보냈습니다. 죽은 사람에게 무엇이 잘못되었는지 판단하기 위한 두 번째 단계는 결과를 분석하는 겁니다. 조지 국왕의 경우에는, 실험결과가 돌아왔을 때, 연구가들은 그의 머리카락에 300배 이상의 비소 독성이 포함되어 있다는 사실을 발견했습니다! 마침내 연구가들은 죽은 사람에게 무엇이 잘못되었는지 판단하기 위해서 진단 과정을 거쳤습니다. 좀 더 조사를 한 결과, 연구가들은 가발에 벌레가 끼지 못하게 하기 위해 사용되었던 가루가, 왕이 '포르피린 대사 이상 질환'이라고 불렀던,

마치 미친 것처럼 보이게 만드는 증상을 일으켰고 더욱 심각한 질병으로 발전시켰다는 사실을 찾아냈습니다!

과정 상의 단계는 다음 중 어느 것인가? 적절한 칸에 체크하시오.

	예	아니오
조사에 근거해서 결과를 해석한다	✓	
필요한 DNA를 추출하기 위해서 시체를 발굴한다		✓
추가적인 DNA 실험을 위해서 결과를 실험실로 다시 보낸다		✓
죽은 사람으로부터 DNA 샘플을 추출할 수 있는 신체 부위를 입수한다	✓	
견본의 구조를 알아내기 위해서 실험실 실험을 가동시킨다		✓

해설　죽은 사람의 신체 부위에서 나온 무언가를 찾아 DNA 샘플을 추출하고 이를 실험실에 보내 실험을 한다. 이때 반드시 시체를 발굴할 필요는 없다. 그 후 실험 결과를 가지고 결과를 분석한다.

Mini-Exercise 2　Classifying Details

1　파블로 피카소에 대한 강의를 듣고, 물음에 답하시오.

🎧 스크립트

P　Pablo Picasso remains one of the most influential painters of the 20th century. Part of his, uh, impact, I think, really stems from his relentless willingness to experiment and innovate, ... and so we have a number of different styles apparent in his work, each capturing a progression in his thinking about what painting could be and do, ... so for instance, early on in his career, when he was still in his late teens, and just out on his own in the world, we had what's now called the "Blue Period." The subjects of these paintings are almost exclusively people, half-starved and depressed looking, with shades of blue highlighting the melancholy mood. His next move saw a kind of lightening up, in which he focused on painting primarily subjects from the circus, using a warm, bright, pinkish color as the main tone. This is referred to as his "Rose Period."

교수　파블로 피카소는 20세기에 가장 영향력 있는 화가의 한 사람으로 남아 있습니다. 내 생각에, 그가 미친 영향력은 그가 몹시 엄격한 태도로 기꺼이 실험하고 혁신하려던 자세에서 비롯되었습니다... 그래서 그의 작품 안에는 분명하게 서로 다른 스타일이 많이 존재합니다. 각 스타일은 그림이 어떤 것이고 무엇을 해야 하는지에 대한 그의 생각의 발전과정을 나타냅니다. 그래서 예를 들어, 화가로서의 경력의 초기, 아직 십대이고 세상에 홀로 서 있을 때, 오늘날 '청색기'라고 부르는 것에 접하게 되었습니다. 이때 그린 그림의 주제는 침울한 분위기를 강조해서 푸른색 그림자를 드리운 반쯤 굶주리고 우울한 표정을 한 사람들이 거의 대부분입니다. 그의 다음 단계는 어느 정도 분위기가 밝아져서, 주로 서커스에서 주제를 선택하고, 따뜻하고 밝은 핑크 계열의 색을 주요 색조로 사용했습니다. 이 시기를 가리켜 '장미기'라고 부릅니다.

1　아래의 각 구절이 피카소의 청색기나 장미기를 설명하는지 표시하시오. 적절한 칸에 체크하시오.

	청색기	장미기
원숭이와 함께 서 있는 어릿광대		✓
광대, 광대의 아내, 광대의 자식을 그린 초상화		✓
기타 위로 몸을 구부린 마르고 창백한 노인	✓	
곡예공연가 단체		✓

해설　청색기는 우울한 분위기의 작품을 남겼던 시기로, 이때 그림에는 침울한 분위기가 강조되어 나타난다. 반면에 장미기는 좀 더 밝은 분위기의 작품을 남겼던 시기로, 주로 서커스에서 주제를 선택했다.

2　다음 중 피카소의 청색기의 주제에 대해 사실인 것은 무엇인가?
(A) 서커스 공연단인 경우가 많았다.
(B) 매우 슬픈 표정을 한 경우가 많았다.
(C) 대개 푸른색 옷을 입고 있었다.
(D) 사람들이 대개 못생기고 더러웠다.

정답 (B)

해설　청색기의 분위기는 푸른색 그림자를 드리운 반쯤 굶주리고 우울한 표정의 사람을 주제로 하는 등 침울하고 어두웠다. 서커스 공연단을 주제로 한 그림은 장미기에 등장한다.

2　범죄 재판 수업에서의 강의를 듣고, 물음에 답하시오.

🎧 스크립트

P　There are two types of suspect identification that are commonly used in police investigations. The first type is called simple recognition. In simple recognition, a witness testifies that he or she can identify aspects of a suspect, either in a live "line-up" or in a photograph. Of course, the more distinct and unchangeable the aspects are, the better. The second type of suspect identification is evidential identification. Evidential identification is based on what a criminal leaves at the scene that is unique to them. Classically, this is the fingerprint, but other items such as hair or body fluids are also unique and good for identification purposes. While not as good, even a string off a sweater may be evidential identification. When going into court, prosecutors prefer that police have both types of identification. Evidence is sometimes rejected due to mishandling, while witnesses are liable to be swayed by defense attorneys. Having both types of evidence makes an airtight case.

교수 경찰조사에서 보통 사용하는 용의자 확인방법에는 두 가지가 있습니다. 첫 번째 형태는 단순인식이라 부르는 것입니다. 단순인식에서 목격자는 한 줄로 늘어선 사람 중에서 또는 사진으로 용의자를 식별할 수 있다고 증언합니다. 물론 용의자의 모습이 좀 더 분명하고 변화하지 않을수록 좋습니다. 두 번째 형태의 용의자 식별은 증거에 의한 식별입니다. 증거에 의한 식별은 범인이 자신에게만 특유한 것을 범죄현장에 남겼을 때 가능합니다. 고전적으로는 지문이 여기에 속하지만 머리카락이나 체액과 같은 기타 요소들 또한 식별 목적에 적합할 정도로 특유하고 충분합니다. 이만큼 좋은 증거는 아니지만, 스웨터에서 떨어져나간 실도 증거에 의한 식별의 대상이 될 수 있습니다. 법정에 설 때 검사는 경찰이 이 두 가지 형태의 식별을 모두 하기를 원합니다. 목격자는 변호사에 의해 흔들리기 쉬운데다가 증거는 취급부주의로 거부되는 경우가 가끔 발생하기 때문입니다. 두 가지 형태의 증거를 갖춘다면 사건을 물샐틈없이 만들 수 있습니다.

1 다음의 구절을 분류하시오. 각 구절에 적합한 칸에 체크하시오.

	단순인식	증거에 의한 식별
발자국		✓
귀 모양	✓	
튄 핏방울		✓
안경	✓	

해설 단순인식은 목격자가 용의자를 식별해내는 것이다. 증거에 의한 식별은 머리카락이나 체액 등 범인에게만 특유한 특징이 범죄현장에 남은 경우에 가능하다.

2 강의에 따르면, 최고의 식별 출처는 다음 중 무엇인가?
(A) 눈동자 색
(B) 헤어스타일
(C) 옷에서 나온 실
(D) 혈액견본

정답 (D)

해설 (A)와 (B)에 의한 목격자 식별은 여러 가지 이유로 거부되는 경우가 가끔 발생하고, 스웨터에서 나온 실은 증거에 의한 식별대상이 된다고 했지만 동시에 그렇게 좋은 증거는 아니라고 했다.

3 천문학 수업에서의 대화를 듣고, 물음에 답하시오.

🎧 스크립트

S1 I don't seem to understand my astronomy class. You're a science major, can you help me?
S2 Sure, what's wrong?
S1 I need to identify some items for my homework as I find them in the sky, but I don't know how to tell if they are stars or "dark matter" objects.
S2 OK, that's easier than it sounds. Stars are any massive objects that have sustained a continual release of heat and light through nuclear reactions. The closest star to us, a small yellow star, is the sun. It just seems larger than the other stars because it is close by. Other stars are red giants and white dwarfs. In contrast to stars, dark matter objects do not generate their own light or significant heat. This is why they are called cold. Some dark matter objects include planets and asteroids. The only reason we see dark matter objects is because light from a star has reflected off of them. Does that help?
S1 You bet! Thanks!

학생1 나는 천문학 수업을 이해 못하고 있는 것 같아. 너는 과학을 전공하고 있으니까, 나를 도와 줄 수 있겠니?
학생2 물론, 무엇이 문젠데?
학생1 숙제를 하려면 하늘에서 볼 수 있는 몇 가지 사항을 식별해내야 하는데, 그것이 별인지 '암흑물질'인지 알 수가 없거든.
학생2 알았어. 그건 보기보다 쉬워. 핵반응을 통해서 계속적으로 열과 빛을 방출하는 커다란 덩어리를 별이라고 해. 우리에게 가장 가까운, 자그마하면서 노란 별이 바로 태양이지. 태양은 가까이 있기 때문에 다른 별보다 더 크게 보이는 것뿐이야. 다른 별들 중에서 큰 것은 붉은색이고 작은 것은 흰색이야. 별과는 대조적으로 암흑물질은 스스로 빛을 만들어내지도 상당한 열을 내지도 않아. 그래서 차갑다고 말하는 거지. 몇몇 암흑물질에는 행성과 소행성이 포함되어 있어. 우리가 암흑물질을 볼 수 있는 유일한 이유는 별에서 방출되는 빛이 반사되기 때문이야. 도움이 되었니?
학생1 물론! 고마워!

1 아래의 구절을 분류하시오. 각 구절에 적합한 칸에 체크하시오.

	별	행성
우주에서 불타는 기체	✓	
빛의 반사		✓
차갑고 어둡다		✓
뜨겁고 열을 방출한다	✓	

해설 별은 핵반응을 통해서 계속적으로 열과 빛을 방출한다. 반면에 암흑물질은 빛을 만들어내지도 않고, 상당한 양의 열을 방출하지도 않기 때문에 어둡고 차갑다. 단지 별에서 방출되는 빛을 반사하기 때문에 볼 수 있을 뿐이다.

2 암흑물질이 차갑다고 생각되는 이유는 무엇인가?
(A) 별에서 방출되는 빛이 반사된다.
(B) 스스로 빛을 내지 않거나 상당한 열을 내지 않는다.
(C) 다른 무거운 물질보다 더 커 보인다.
(D) 계속적으로 핵 반응을 한다.

정답 (B)

해설 암흑물질은 빛을 만들지도 않고 열도 방출하지 않기 때문에 어둡고 차갑다고 생각되고 있다.

Vocabulary Preview — for Practice

Practice 1

1. trend (경향)
   - ✓ a. a general course, direction, or tendency
   - b. describes something that will probably happen or is expected
2. obesity (비만)
   - a. a disease in which the body cannot control the level of sugar in the blood
   - ✓ b. excessively, unhealthily fat
3. responsibility (책임)
   - ✓ a. something that it is your job or duty to deal with
   - b. a specific item of work assigned to one
4. mandate (위임하다)
   - a. a cleverly planned action which is intended to obtain an advantage
   - ✓ b. to give official permission for something to happen

Practice 2

1. literary (문학의)
   - ✓ a. connected with literature
   - b. able to read and write
2. characteristic (특질, 특성)
   - a. a person, especially when you are describing a particular quality that they have
   - ✓ b. a typical or noticeable quality of someone or something
3. preceding (이전의)
   - ✓ a. existing or happening before someone or something
   - b. to move forward or travel in a particular direction
4. fragment (분해하다)
   - a. not solid and firm and therefore not strong, safe or likely to last
   - ✓ b. to break something into small parts or to be broken up in this way

Practice 3

1. class (계급)
   - a. the sphere or scope of activity or functioning of something
   - ✓ b. a group or division based on quality or rank
2. attribute (속성, 특성)
   - ✓ a. a quality or characteristic that someone or something has
   - b. to give something, especially money, in order to provide or achieve something together with other people
3. supply (공급하다)
   - ✓ a. to provide something that is wanted or needed
   - b. to get control or influence
4. vibrate (진동하다)
   - a. to cause the fall or collapse of
   - ✓ b. to shake slightly and quickly, or to cause something to do this

Practice 4

1. undergraduate (대학 학부 재학생)
   - ✓ a. a student who is studying for their first degree at college or university
   - b. a person who has a first degree from a university or college
2. survey (조사하다, 감시하다)
   - ✓ a. to look at or examine all of something, especially carefully
   - b. the careful watching of a person or place, especially by the police or army
3. candidate (후보자)
   - ✓ a. a person who is competing to get a job or elected position
   - b. a person who formally requests something, especially a job, or a place at college or university
4. accomplish (성취하다)
   - a. to go with someone or to be provided or exist at the same time as something
   - ✓ b. to finish something successfully or to achieve something

Vocabulary Preview for Actual Test

Actual Test 1

1. c 그는 예술계의 영역 밖에서 어떤 일이 벌어지고 있는지 보여주려 노력한다.
2. b 인쇄 매체가 여론을 조작하는 것을 쉽게 만들고, 영화와 라디오는 이 과정을 좀 더 심화시켜 수행할 수 있다.
3. a 그 평론으로 인해 경찰력 내부의 확산된 부패가 드러났다.
4. a 인터넷 경매 사이트의 인기가 높아지면서 신고된 사기 건수도 증가했다.

Actual Test 2

1. d 음악가들은 디지털 기술로 인해 사용료도 내지 않고 음악을 복사해서 인터넷 상으로 전송하기가 쉬워졌다고 불평하고 있다.
2. a 그 보조금은 법률 교육의 질을 높이거나, 법률 서비스를 개선하거나 일반 국민에게 법률 정보를 제공하는 지역 사회 프로그램에 지급된다.
3. c 저는 20년 동안 도서 박람회를 조직했고, 그 덕분에 이 일에 대한 자격 요건을 충족시킵니다.
4. b 양국 정상들은 상정된 평화안을 토의하기 위해 회동을 가졌다.

Practice 1

1 (C)   2 (A), (B)   3 Y, Y, N, N, Y

영양 수업에서의 강의를 들으시오.

🎧 스크립트

P Over the past thirty-five years, the average person in the United States has gotten fatter. Obesity is at an all time high. How can America correct the trend and become a healthier nation? It was claimed that the attitudes towards food, first of all, should be changed. Back in the 1970s, a marketing strategy in the food industry convinced people that large portions are a good value. The new attitude that must be created is that healthier food in proper portions is a better value. Therefore, the next step should be taken for a healthier nation is... to reorient people to fitness instead of convenience. Most U.S. citizens believe that convenience and speed are the keys to a better life, but in reality, such convenience often makes people not have much energy or enthusiasm and even make them lazy. After that, a third step in creating a healthier nation is to teach them by repeating the importance of personal responsibility until it is fixed in their mind. Instead of looking to the government, doctors or corporations to fix the trend, each individual American must look to their own life's issues. If each American starts to live healthier and to make healthier choices, business and culture will respond to that trend. But if the government attempts to mandate health, the reactionary, negative choices of the people to the government's pressure can easily cause the U.S. to stay in the rut it currently occupies, which leads its citizens toward ever increasing weight gains.

교수 지난 35년 동안, 미국의 평균적인 사람은 점점 비대해졌습니다. 비만상태가 언제나 높습니다. 어떻게 하면 미국이 이런 경향을 바로잡고 더욱 건강한 나라가 될 수 있겠습니까? 무엇보다 식품에 대한 태도가 바뀌어야 한다고들 주장했습니다. 지난 1970년대에는, 식품산업에서의 마케팅 전략은 많은 것이 가치 있는 것이라고 사람들을 확신시키는 것이었습니다. 새로 창조되어야만 하는 새로운 태도는 더욱 건강에 좋은 음식을 적당량 섭취하는 것이 더욱 가치 있다는 것입니다. 그리고 더욱 건강한 나라를 위해 취해야 할 다음 단계로는 사람들이 편리성 대신에 건강에 초점을 맞추도록 해야 합니다. 대부분의 미국 시민들은 편리함과 속도가 보다 나은 삶의 주요 요소라고 믿고 있지만, 현실에서 이와 같은 편리함은 사람들에게 그다지 많은 에너지나 열정을 갖게 하지 못하고 심지어는 게으르게 만듭니다. 다음으로, 보다 건강한 나라를 이룩하는 세 번째 단계는 마음속에 각인될 때까지 개인 책임의 중요성을 되풀이함으로써 사람들을 가르치는 것입니다. 그러한 경향을 바로잡으려면, 정부, 의사, 기업 등으로 시선을 돌리기보다는 미국인 각자가 자신의 삶의 문제에 시선을 돌려야 합니다. 만약 미국인 각자가 더욱 건강하고 생활하고 보다 건강한 선택을 하기 시작한다면, 사업과 문화도 그 경향에 반응할 것입니다. 그러나 만약 정부가 건강을 위임하려 시도한다면, 사람들이 정부의 압력에 대해 역행하고 부정적인 선택을 하게 되어 미국이 현재 머물러 있는 관례적인 방식에 안주하기가 쉽고, 결과적으로 시민들의 몸무게는 계속 증가하게 됩니다.

1 강의의 주된 내용은 무엇인가?
(A) 1970년대의 마케팅 전략의 결과
(B) 편리함과 속도의 눈에 띄는 효과
(C) 더욱 건강한 나라를 구축하는 단계
(D) 개인적인 책임의 중요성

해설 강의는 국민이 점점 비대해지는 경향을 바로잡아서 더욱 건강한 나라로 거듭나는 단계에 대해 설명한다.

2 강의에 따르면, 다음 어느 것이 사실인가? 정답 두 개를 고르시오.
(A) 현재 미국인의 몸무게는 35년 전보다 더 나간다.
(B) 좀 더 건강한 생활 선택을 하면 사람들을 좀 더 건강하게 한다.
(C) 사람들이 익숙해지면 먹는 양이 증가한다.
(D) 오늘날 사람들은 먹어야 하는 것보다 3배 많이 먹는다.

해설 미국인의 평균 체중은 지난 35년간 꾸준히 증가했다. 과거에는 양에 가치기준을 두었지만 앞으로 건강에 가치를 둔다면 더욱 건강한 나라를 이룰 수 있다.

3 다음 어느 것이 미국의 건강을 회복하기 위한 단계인가? 적절한 칸에 체크하시오.

	예	아니오
쉽고 편안한 것을 피하면서, 운동을 더 많이 하게 한다	✓	
사람들이 좀 더 건강한 생활 방식으로 살 수 있도록 촉구한다	✓	
규칙적으로 건강관리를 받으러 다니도록 사람들을 설득한다		✓
보다 건강한 삶을 위해 전국적인 캠페인을 벌인다		✓
사람들이 소비하는 음식에 대한 사람들의 관점을 변화시킨다	✓	

해설 강의는 건강한 미국을 만들기 위한 단계로 세 가지를 제시한다. 첫째, 음식을 많이 섭취하는 것보다 건강에 더욱 좋은 음식을 적당량 섭취한다. 둘째, 편리성 대신 건강에 초점을 맞춘다. 셋째, 건강문제에 대한 개인의 책임감을 되풀이해서 교육시킨다.

Practice 2

1 (C) 2 (C) 3 M, M, P, P

문학 수업에서의 토의를 들으시오.

🎧 스크립트

P Okay, so we're going to look at both modernist and postmodernist writing this term as a means of understanding the two biggest literary movements of the 20th century.

S They sound so similar — is there really a big difference between them?

P Well, lines aren't always so clear-cut. However, there are some characteristics that should signal to you what is modernist, and what is postmodernist. Modernist novels, modernism in general, tends to break away from the handed down forms of the past. The modernists reject tradition, recent tradition anyway, and seek to find truth through an exploration of, say form and content. Some modernists turned to the ancient world or other cultures to find meaning. Others sought to look at contemporary culture from a different perspective. The belief in a truth, though, is crucial here. This idea of truth, and hence the major point of the preceding literary movement, is something completely rejected by postmodernists. Thus, postmodernist novels are often fragmented, with many different perspectives and voices. The narrative may be hard to follow. This is because post-modernists think there is not just one way of looking at something, and that our perspectives are often the result of our times, not any universal truth.

교수 자, 이번 학기에는 20세기의 가장 커다란 문학운동을 이해하기 위한 수단으로 모더니스트와 포스트모더니스트의 글을 살펴보려고 합니다.

학생 두 부류는 상당히 유사하게 들립니다. 둘 사이에 정말 커다란 차이가 있나요?

교수 글쎄, 항상 그렇게 분명하게 구분되는 것은 아닙니다. 그러나 모더니스트가 무엇이고 포스트모더니스트가 무엇인지 알려주는 특징이 몇 가지 있습니다. 모더니스트 소설, 일반적으로 모더니즘은 과거로부터 전해져 내려오는 형식을 파기하는 경향이 있습니다. 모더니스트들은 전통, 어쨌든 최근 전통을 거부하고, 형식과 내용의 탐구를 통해서 진리를 찾으려 합니다. 몇몇 모더니스트들은 의미를 찾기 위해서 고대 세계나 다른 문화로 눈길을 돌렸습니다. 또 어떤 모더니스트들은 동시대 문화를 다른 관점에서 바라보려 했습니다. 그렇지만 여기서 결정적으로 중요한 점은 진리에 대한 믿음입니다. 진리에 대한 이러한 생각은 포스트모더니즘에 선행한 문예운동(모더니즘)의 주요 핵심을 이루고 있는데, 포스트모더니스트에 의해 완전히 거부되었습니다. 그래서, 포스트모더니스트 소설들은 서로 다른 다수의 관점과 목소리들이 존재하기 때문에, 흔히 파편화된 양상을 띠고 있습니다. 그 서사 구조는 이해하기가 어려울지도 모릅니다. 이는 포스트모더니스트들이 어떤 대상을 바라보는 데에 단 하나의 방식만이 존재하는 것이 아니라고 생각하고, 우리의 관점도 보편적인 진실의 결과물이 아니라 흔히 우리 시대의 결과물이라고 생각하기 때문입니다.

1 강의는 주로 어떤 내용인가?
   (A) 모더니즘과 포스트모더니즘은 거의 구별할 수가 없다는 것
   (B) 모더니스트 글은 포스트모더니스트 글보다 우수하다는 것
   (C) 20세기 글의 두 가지 주요 형식 사이의 비교
   (D) 고대부터 현대까지의 글 쓰는 스타일에 대한 개관

해설 교수는 모더니즘과 포스트모더니즘이 항상 분명하게 구별되는 것은 아니지만 몇 가지 특징에서 차이를 보인다고 주장하면서 두 문예사조를 비교 설명한다.

2 다음 중 두 가지 문예운동에 대해 사실인 것은 무엇인가?
   (A) 같은 특징을 많이 소유하고 있다.
   (B) 하나는 매우 전통적인 반면에 다른 하나는 전통을 파기한다.
   (C) 둘 사이의 차이점이 항상 분명한 것은 아니다.
   (D) 어느 것도 20세기 운동으로 생각되어져서는 안 된다.

해설 두 가지 문예운동 모두 20세기의 최대 문예운동으로 차이점이 있기는 하지만 항상 분명하게 구별되는 것은 아니다.

3 다음 구절을 분류하시오. 각 구절에 적합한 칸에 체크하시오.

	모더니즘	포스트모더니즘
보편적인 진리의 추구	✓	
전통의 거부	✓	
관점의 파편화		✓
다양한 관점의 포용		✓

해설 모더니즘의 특징은 과거의 전통을 파기하고, 형식과 내용의 탐구를 통해서 진리를 찾으려 한다. 무엇보다 진리에 대한 믿음에 가치를 둔다. 포스트모더니즘은 다양한 관점과 이야기를 갖는다. 사물을 바라보는 관점에는 여러 가지가 있을 수 있고, 이 또한 보편적인 진리가 아니라 시대의 결과물이라 생각한다.

Practice 3

1 B, W, B, B   2 (B), (C)   3 (A), (D)

음악학 수업에서의 강의를 들으시오.

🎧 스크립트

P   As most of you know, there are hundreds of different musical instruments, each with a distinct sound. Each of these instruments is part of a class or family of instruments. With some simple examination, it is not too difficult to determine the classification of an instrument.

Okay, woodwind instruments, well, though now made from many different types of materials, share the common attribute that a player must supply air movement through the instrument and the air movement causes the instrument to provide the vibration necessary for sound. Most woodwinds use reeds to provide vibration, but a few, such as flutes, rely on their design instead of a reed.

In contrast, brass instruments require the player to provide air movement and to provide the needed vibrations. In brass instruments, like trumpets, the vibrations come from the player buzzing their lips into the mouthpiece of the instrument. Well, the view of most scholars is that the term brass instrument should be defined by the way the sound is made, as I explained, and not by whether the instrument is actually made of brass. Thus, as exceptional cases one finds brass instruments made of wood, like the cornet, and woodwind instruments made of brass, like the saxophone.

교수 여러분 대부분이 알고 있듯이, 각각 독특한 소리를 가진 수백 종의 서로 다른 악기가 있습니다. 각 악기는 같은 악기 부류나 종류의 일부입니다. 간단한 검사를 해서 악기를 분류하는 일은 그다지 어렵지 않습니다.

자, 목관악기는 현재 다수의 다른 형태의 재료로 제작되고 있지만, 연주자가 악기를 통해 공기의 흐름을 공급해야 하고, 그 공기의 흐름이 악기가 소리를 내는 데 필요한 진동을 공급한다는 공통된 특징을 갖습니다. 대부분의 목관악기는 진동을 공급하기 위해 리드를 사용하지만, 플루트처럼 소수의 목관악기는 리드보다는 디자인에 의존합니다.

이와는 대조적으로, 금관악기는 연주자가 공기흐름과 소리를 내는 데 필요한 진동을 공급해야 합니다. 트럼펫과 같은 금관악기에서 진동은 연주자가 입술을 악기의 마우스피스에 대고 소리를 냄으로써 발생합니다. 이제 대부분 학자들의 견해는, 금관악기라는 용어는 악기가 실제로 놋쇠로 만들어졌는지에 의해 정의되는 것이 아니라, 설명했듯이 소리가 만들어지는 방식에 의해 정의되어야 한다는 것입니다. 예외의 경우로, 코넷처럼 나무로 만들어진 금관악기가 있고, 색소폰처럼 놋쇠로 만든 목관악기가 있습니다.

1 적절한 칸에 체크하시오.

	목관악기	금관악기
연주가는 입술을 사용해서 진동을 만든다		✓
연주가는 진동을 공급하기 위해서 리드나 디자인을 사용한다	✓	
소리를 만드는 리드가 없는 나무 악기		✓
일반적으로 구리나 아연으로 만든 금속을 재료로 함		✓

해설 목관악기는 진동을 공급하기 위해 리드를 사용하거나, 디자인에 의존한다. 반면에 금관악기는 연주자 자신이 입술을 사용해서 진동을 공급한다. 그러므로 나무로 만든 금관악기도 있고, 놋쇠로 만든 목관악기도 있다.

2 다음 중 목관악기에 대한 사실이 <u>아닌</u> 것은 무엇인가? 정답 두 개를 고르시오.
(A) 그들은 원래 나무 제품으로 만들어졌다.
(B) 리드는 나무나 비슷한 제품으로 만들어진다.
(C) 사람들에게 나무를 연상시키는 소리를 갖는다.
(D) 일부 나무 악기는 금관악기로 분류된다.

해설 목관악기는 여러 가지 형태의 재료로 제작되지만 원 재료는 나무이다. 하지만 나무로 만든 금관악기도 있고, 놋쇠로 만든 목관악기도 있다.

3 다음 중에서 금관악기에 대한 설명이 <u>아닌</u> 것은 무엇인가? 정답 두 개를 고르시오.
(A) 소리가 나는 방식에 의해 분류되어서는 안 된다.
(B) 연주가가 입술을 불어서 소리를 낸다.
(C) 대부분은 노란색 금속으로 만들어진다.
(D) 입술이 닿는 악기의 일부분은 리드이다.

해설 금관악기는 연주가가 입술을 사용해서 진동을 만들어 소리를 내고, 대부분 금속으로 만들어지지만 나무를 재료로 한 금관악기도 있다. 그러므로 악기의 분류는 재료가 아닌 소리를 내는 방식에 따라야 한다. D에 대한 언급은 본문에 없다.

Practice 4

1 (B)   2 Y, N, Y, N   3 (B), (D)

두 학생의 대화를 들으시오.

🎧 스크립트

S1 You know, I'm really sick of the way undergraduates are ignored at this university. Most of our classes are taught by grad students — professors make very little time to see us... I really wish I could change this. I heard you ran for student senate... I really want to know what I need to do to run...
S2 Well, the university president attends meetings to get a sense of what's on students' minds. So, that might work... umm... I guess the first thing you should do is to find out what other students think. You know, if they are frustrated by the issue...
S1 Well, how do I do that?
S2 You can uh, do a survey, I guess. And if you're convinced that there are enough people who think there should be something done, then, the next step is to register as a candidate. At our school you need to get two hundred signatures from current students supporting your candidacy and turn them in to the student senate office.
S1 Wow, that sounds like a lot of work.
S2 Yes, it is. Well, that's not the end of it. The next thing to do is to launch your campaign. You'll want to make posters, flyers, and maybe put an advertisement in the paper. You might want to participate in a couple of debates on campus, so people know what issues you stand for and what you want to accomplish. If everything goes smoothly, then you may even be elected to the senate!

학생1 이 대학에서 학부생을 무시하는 것에 정말 진저리가 나. 대학원생들이 우리 수업의 대부분을 가르치고, 교수들은 우리를 볼 시간을 거의 내지 않잖아... 이런 현상을 바꿀 수 있었으면 좋겠어. 네가 학생 대표에 출마했다고 들었어... 출마하려면 내가 무엇을 할 필요가 있는지 정말 알고 싶어...
학생2 대학 총장은 학생들이 어떤 의견을 갖고 있는지 알기 위해, (학생대표) 회의에 참석해. 그러니까 (네가 학생대표가 되어 그 회의에 참석하는 게) 효과가 있을거야. 음... 네가 우선적으로 해야 하는 일은 다른 학생들의 생각을 파악하는 거야. 그들도 그 문제로 실망하고 있다면...
학생1 그러려면 어떻게 하면 되지?
학생2 내 생각에는 조사를 하는 거야. 무슨 조치가 취해져야만 한다고 생각하는 사람이 충분히 있다고 확신한다면 다음 단계는 후보자로 등록하는 거야. 우리 학교에서는 너의 출마를 지지하는 학생 200명으로부터 서명을 받아서, 학생 대표 사무실에 제출할 필요가 있어.
학생1 와, 정말 할 일이 많겠는걸.
학생2 정말 그래. 그게 끝이 아니야. 다음에 할 일은 선거운동을 시작하는 거야. 포스터와 전단지를 만들고 신문에 광고를 게재해야 할 거야. 교내에서 열리는 두 번의 토론에 참가해야, 네가 어떤 문제를 해결하고 싶어하는지, 무엇을 성취하고 싶어하는지 학생들이 알 수가 있어. 모든 일이 순조롭게 진행된다면 대표로도 선출될 수 있어!

1 남학생이 여학생을 만나러 간 이유는 무엇인가?
(A) 교수의 강의 시간이 거의 없는 것에 대해 불평하려고
(B) 학생대표에 출마할 방법을 알기 위해서
(C) 학생대표가 되는 이유에 대해 물어 보려고
(D) 학생대표가 할 수 있는 일과 해야 하는 일을 물어 보려고

해설 남학생은 학교의 문제점을 개선하기 위해 학생대표에 출마하고 싶어한다. 그래서 출마했던 경험이 있는 여학생에게 방법을 물어본다.

2 다음 중 학생대표에 출마하는 과정에서 밟아야 하는 단계는 무엇인가? 적절한 칸에 체크하시오.

	예	아니오
후보출마를 지지하는 사람을 많이 확보한다	✓	
다른 사람이 매우 실망하고 있는 점에 대해 묻는다		✓
교내에서의 다양한 홍보활동	✓	
학생들이 최상의 아이디어를 가지고 있는 후보자에게 투표하도록 동기를 유발한다		✓

해설 학생대표에 출마하기 위한 첫 단계는 학생들의 생각을 파악하는 것이다. 자신의 의견에 공감하는 학생이 많다면 후보자 등록을 하고 출마를 지지하는 학생의 서명을 받아 학생대표 사무실에 제출한다. 그러고 선거운동을 시작해서 다양한 홍보활동을 벌인다.

3 다음 중 사실인 것은 무엇인가? 정답 두 개를 고르시오.
 (A) 공직에 출마하면 선거에 반드시 이길 수 있다.
 (B) 신문광고는 선거운동에 유용하다.
 (C) 총장은 항상 대표들의 말에 귀를 기울인다.
 (D) 200개 이상의 서명이 선거운동에 필요하다.

해설 선거에 출마해서 설득력 있는 선거운동을 펼친다면 대표로 선출될 가능성이 있다. 그런 선거운동에는 포스터와 전단지, 신문광고, 토론회 참석 등이 포함된다. 두 학생이 재학 중인 학교의 경우에 후보자 등록을 하려면 자신을 지지하는 학생 200명 이상의 서명이 필요하다.

Actual Test 1

1 (D)　　2 (C)　　3 S, A, S, D　　4 (D)　　5 (A)

미술사 수업에서의 강의를 들으시오.

🎧 스크립트

P So, since 1836 when the first photographic image was taken, there have been a number of different uses for photography. Some of it has been documentary — the preservation of images of people and places that no longer or will one day not exist. We see this type of photography often in history books, archives, or historical museums.
Another use of photography has been artistic. Artists like Man Ray or Alfred Steiglitz used the camera to create beautiful and unusual images, pushing the boundaries of the medium. And then, we've got this whole genre of photography that I'll call "spirit photography."
Essentially, because of the "real" nature of the camera and film, people would be convinced that a photographic image was showing them a picture of reality. Most people didn't realize, at least not at first, how easy it was to manipulate film and negatives. Double exposures, light leaks in the cameras, and having a subject move during the time the shutter was open to create a ghostly image were common methods of "capturing" the spirit on film. So, when the ghostly image of a person was superimposed upon another image, people really believed they were seeing evidence of the spirit world! Though popular and convincing for many years, by the beginning of the 20th century, spirit photography had been more or less exposed as the fraud it was.

교수 1836년에 첫 사진영상을 촬영한 이후로, 사진은 수많은 다른 용도로 사용되었습니다. 그 중의 일부는 기록물이었습니다. 즉 더 이상 존재하지 않거나 언젠가 존재하지 않게 될 사람이나 장소의 영상을 보존하는 것이었습니다. 우리는 이런 형태의 사진을 역사책에서나 옛 기록에서나 역사 박물관에서 자주 접합니다.
사진의 또 다른 용도는 예술적인 것이었습니다. Man Ray나 Alfred Steiglitz와 같은 예술가는 카메라를 사용해서 아름답고 특이한 형상을 만들어내어, 매체의 경계를 확장시켰습니다. 그리고 나서는 내가 영혼 사진술이라 부를 장르에 도달하게 되었습니다.
본질적으로는, 카메라와 필름의 '진정한' 본질 때문에 사람들은 사진 영상이 실재를 보여 주고 있다고 확신할 것입니다. 대부분의 사람들은 최소한 처음에는 필름이나 사진 원판을 얼마나 조작하기 쉬운지 깨닫지 못했습니다. 카메라에서의 이중노출, 빛의 누설과 셔터가 열려 있는 동안 피사체를 움직이게 해서 유령 영상을 만들어내는 방법 등은 필름에 영혼을 "포착하는" 흔한 방법이었습니다. 그래서 어떤 사람의 유령 영상과 또 다른 영상을 포갰을 때, 사람들은 영혼세계의 증거를 보고 있다고 진심으로 믿었습니다! 20세기 초까지 여러 해 동안 인기를 끌어왔고 설득력을 행사했지만, 영혼 사진술은 대체로 가짜였다는 사실이 드러났습니다.

1 강의의 주된 내용은 무엇인가?
 (A) 사진작가들의 예술적 성취
 (B) 자연 사진작가들이 사용한 방법
 (C) 유령의 존재를 증명하는 사진
 (D) 19세기 사진의 다른 용도

해설 19세기 첫 사진영상이 촬영된 이후로 사진의 다양한 용도를 기록적인 면과 예술적인 측면에서 설명한다.

2 교수가 역사 박물관에 대해 언급한 이유는 무엇인가?
  (A) 대부분의 영혼 사진이 발견될 수 있는 장소를 알려 주기 위해서
  (B) 더욱 연구를 해야만 하는 이유에 대해 학생들에게 이야기해 주기 위해서
  (C) 사진이 기록용으로 사용된 사례를 제시하기 위해서
  (D) 다른 형태의 박물관에서 사용된 사진과 비교하기 위해서

해설 강의는 사진의 다양한 용도를 기록과 예술로 나누어 설명한다. 사람들은 사진을 사용해서 더 이상 존재하지 않거나 언젠가 존재하지 않을 사람이나 장소의 영상을 보존했다. 그리고 이런 장소의 예로 옛 기록이나 역사 박물관을 들었다.

3 다음의 각 구절이 기록 사진, 예술 사진, 영혼 사진 중 어느 것을 설명하는지 표시하시오. 적절한 칸에 체크하시오.

	기록 사진	예술 사진	영혼 사진
초자연적인 영상을 만들기 위해 필름을 조작한다			✓
창조적인 영상을 만들기 위해 사진을 찍으려 한다		✓	
노출시간을 좀 더 늘리기 위해 셔터를 열어놓는다			✓
보존의 목적을 위해서 영상을 사진에 담는다	✓		

해설 사진은 여러 용도로 사용되었다. 첫째 용도는 기록용으로 더 이상 존재하지 않거나 미래에 존재하지 않게 될 사람이나 장소의 영상을 사진을 통해 보존했다. 다음 용도는 예술용으로 사진을 통해 아름답고 특이한 형상을 창조하면서 영혼 사진술에까지 확장되었다. 영혼 사진은 촬영조작을 통해 초자연적인 영상을 만들어내는 분야이다.

4 강의에 따르면, 영혼 사진을 만들어내는 방법이 <u>아닌</u> 것은 무엇인가?
  (A) 사진 속 인물을 움직이게 한다
  (B) 카메라 본체 안에 빛이 들어가게 한다
  (C) 현상할 때 하나의 영상 위에 다른 영상을 겹쳐 놓는다
  (D) 보름달이 떠 있을 때 사진을 찍는다

해설 영혼 사진을 만들어내기 위해 이중노출과 빛의 누설, 셔터가 열려 있는 동안 피사체를 움직이게 하는 방법, 두 사람의 유령 영상을 겹쳐 현상하는 방법 등을 사용했다.

5 교수에 따르면, 영혼 사진이 그토록 인기를 끌었던 이유는 무엇이었는가?
  (A) 사람들은 사진이 조작될 수 있었다는 것을 몰랐다.
  (B) 사람들은 영혼의 존재를 믿고 싶었다.
  (C) 사람들은 카메라에 마법의 힘이 있다고 믿었다.
  (D) 사람들은 사진을 일종의 예술로 생각했다.

해설 사람들은 사진영상이 얼마나 조작하기 쉬운지 깨닫지 못하고 사진 영상이 현실을 보여 준다고 확신했기 때문에 영혼 사진을 보고 영혼세계의 증거를 보았다고 믿었다.

Actual Test 2

1 (B) 2 (C) 3 N, Y, N, Y 4 (A) 5 (C)

교수와 학생 사이의 대화를 들으시오.

🎧 스크립트

S Oh, Dr. Smith. I wanted to say thank you for your kind comments on my last history paper. Well, also I came to ask you for another thing...

P Go ahead, what is the matter?

S Nothing serious, actually, just, there is this meeting that students from all the different disciplines meet once a month to discuss different issues on campus. But the thing is that we always end up complaining about something... and not making much out of this meeting. I mean I just feel like we're wasting our time.

P Hmm... one of the possible reasons I can suspect is poor organization, or planning of the meeting. Many times you wouldn't know where you are going if you're not well organized. The first thing you should do is to decide the issues that you guys want to discuss. That helps you to set your goal of the meeting. Are we here to discuss how little grants you get? Or to discuss library policies? All right? Then, clearly define what the issue is, or the problem is, there could be several problems, but the more important thing is that you focus only on defining the issue or the problem. Don't let others talk about other issues or any details. Once you found out what the problem is, then, now you are ready to move on to the next step, which is proposing solutions. Now, it is important to have all the members add possible ideas. You might be thinking that this could take forever, but don't worry, after several ideas added, you all know which of those are good or bad... you will see what I mean...

학생 Smith 교수님, 제가 지난 번에 제출했던 역사 보고서에 친절하게 의견을 달아 주셔서 감사합니다. 또 부탁드릴 것이 있어서 왔습니다.

교수 말해 보게. 무엇이 문제인가?

학생 사실 심각한 문제는 아닙니다. 모두 다른 학과의 학생들이 한 달에 한 번씩 모여서 대학에서의 다른 주제들에 대해 논의하는 모임이 있습니다. 그러나 문제는 저희가 항상 무언가 불평하는 것으로 끝난다는 것입니다… 모임을 통해서 그다지 많은 것을 얻지 못하고 있습니다. 그저 시간을 낭비하고 있는 것 같은 생각이 들 뿐입니다.

교수 음… 내가 의심하건대, 있을 수 있는 이유 가운데 하나는 모임에 대한 허술한 조직이나 계획일세. 제대로 체계화하지 않는다면 어떤 방향으로 나아가야 할지 모르는 경우가 많지. 내 생각에 자네가 우선적으로 해야 하는 일은 자네들이 토론하고 싶어하는 논쟁거리를 결정하는 거네. 그렇게 하면 모임의 목적을 수립하는 데 도움이 되지. 보조금이 얼마나 적은지에 대해 토론하려고 여기 모인 것일까? 아니면 도서관 정책에 대해 토론해야 할까? 무슨 말인지 알겠나? 그러고 나서는 논쟁거리가 무엇인지, 문제가 무엇인지, 문제가 되는 것이 몇 가지나 될 수 있을지 등을 분명하게 규정하게. 하지만 보다 중요한 것은 논쟁거리나 문제를 정의하는 데만 초점을 맞추어야 한다는 점일세. 다른 논쟁거리나 다른 사항에 대해 다른 사람이 말하지 못하게 해야 하네… 일단 문제점이 무엇인지 파악하고 나면 다음 단계인 해결책을 제안하는 단계로 넘어갈 준비가 된 걸세. 이제 구성원 모두에게 가능한 아이디어를 내게 하는 것이 중요하지. 이 과정이 정말 오래 걸릴 거라고 생각할지 모르지만 걱정하지 말게. 몇몇 아이디어가 덧붙여지고 나면 어떤 아이디어가 좋은지 나쁜지 알게 될 테니까… 내 말 뜻을 이해하게 될 걸세.

1 남학생이 교수를 찾아온 이유는 무엇인가?
(A) 모임에서 토론할 논쟁에 대해 물어 보려고
(B) 모임의 문제에 대해 조언을 구하려고
(C) 의견을 준 것에 대해 감사를 표현하려고
(D) 모임이 얼마나 낭비적인지 불평하려고

해설 남학생은 모임이 항상 학교에 대한 불평을 이야기하는 자리가 되어 시간 낭비라는 생각이 들었다. 이런 문제점에 대해 조언을 구하기 위해 교수를 찾아갔다.

2 다음 중 모임에 대해 사실인 것은 무엇인가?
(A) 구성원 대부분은 같은 학과에 속한다.
(B) 모임은 교내에서 매주 열린다.
(C) 모임에서는 교내 논쟁거리에 대해 토론한다.
(D) 모임은 수년 동안 개최되어 왔다.

해설 모임의 구성원은 각기 다른 학과에서 온 학생들이고, 학교의 여러 주제에 대해 논의하기 위해 한 달에 한 번 정기적으로 모인다.

3 다음 중 과정 상의 단계는 무엇인가? 적절한 칸에 체크하시오.

	예	아니오
모임에서 토론하고 싶은 논쟁거리를 준비한다		✓
문제가 무엇인지 분명하게 파악하고 서로 이야기한다	✓	
많은 문제 가운데 가장 심각한 문제가 무엇인지 결정한다		✓
논쟁거리나 문제를 정의하는 데 초점을 맞춘다	✓	

해설 교수가 제시한 모임 개선 단계는 첫째, 토론하고자 하는 논쟁거리를 결정하고, 둘째, 그것에 따라 모임의 목적을 수립하고, 셋째, 논쟁거리와 문제, 문제의 소지가 있는 것들을 규정한 후에, 넷째, 문제점에 대한 해결책을 제안한다.

4 학생은 모임에 대해 어떻게 말하는가?
(A) 모임이 끝나도 그다지 많은 결론을 맺지 못한다.
(B) 모임시간이 생각했던 것보다 더 오래 걸린다.
(C) 모임이 불필요하게 너무 자주 열린다.
(D) 모임을 준비하는 시간이 많이 든다.

해설 모임이 주로 학교의 문제점에 대해 불평하는 자리가 되어 시간 낭비라는 생각이 들 뿐 얻는 것이 없다.

5 교수가 다음 말을 한 이유는 무엇인가?

> S Are we here to discuss how little grant you get? Or to discuss library policies?

(A) 토론해야 하는 논쟁에 대해 조언하려고
(B) 그들이 모임에서 토론을 하고 잊는지 물어 보려고
(C) 모임의 목적을 수립하는 방법을 보여 주려고
(D) 남학생이 토론하고 싶어하는 논쟁거리가 무엇인지 결정하려고

해설 모임에서 토론하고자 하는 논쟁거리를 결정한 후에 이에 따라 모임의 목적을 수립하라고 조언하면서, 목적을 수립하는 방법을 예로 든 것이다.

Dictation

Practice 1

① has gotten fatter
② at an all time high
③ first of all
④ the next step should be taken
⑤ even make them lazy
⑥ until it is fixed in their mind
⑦ to live healthier and to make healthier choices
⑧ to stay in the rut

Practice 2

① as a means of
② aren't always so clear-cut
③ tends to break away from
④ seek to find truth through an exploration
⑤ from a different perspective
⑥ may be hard to follow

⑦ there is not just one way of looking at something

Practice 3

① each with a distinct sound
② it is not too difficult to determine
③ though now made from
④ rely on their design instead of a reed
⑤ come from the player buzzing their lips
⑥ as I explained
⑦ made of brass

Practice 4

① I'm really sick of
② what I need to do to run
③ is to find out what other students think
④ to register as a candidate
⑤ that sounds like a lot of work
⑥ The next thing to do
⑦ what issues you stand for

Actual Test 1

① a number of different uses
② no longer or will one day not exist
③ has been artistic
④ we've got this whole genre of
⑤ at least not at first
⑥ was superimposed upon
⑦ had been more or less exposed as the fraud it was

Actual Test 2

① once a month to discuss
② we always end up complaining about
③ not making much out of
④ if you're not well organized
⑤ to discuss how little grants you get
⑥ Don't let others talk about
⑦ move on to the next step
⑧ this could take forever

Vocabulary Preview

1 목표
2 확장하다
3 적수, 상대
4 필사적인, 절망적인
5 전진, 진보
6 배타적으로, 독점적으로
7 반란, 폭동
8 광기, 정신 이상
9 조사
10 우울한
11 굶주리다
12 의심하다
13 증명하다
14 식별, 인지
15 검사, 검찰관
16 변호사
17 잘못 다루다, 잘못 조처하다
18 증거의
19 천문학
20 부피가 큰
21 지속시키다
22 난쟁이
23 소행성
24 명령하다, 요구하다
25 문학의, 문예의
26 분명한, 명확한
27 그러므로
28 이야기, 서사
29 결정하다
30 후보자
31 사기
32 조작하다
33 유형, 장르
34 마음속에 각인되다
35 틀(판)에 박힌
36 ~에 대해 이해하다
37 ~에 대한 수단으로서
38 광고를 게재하다
39 ~에 출마하다
40 다음 단계로 넘어가다
41 ~으로 끝나다, ~에 그치다
42 feel like
43 break down
44 set one's goal
45 a key to
46 range from A to B
47 in charge of
48 out of stock
49 substance
50 abolish
51 relentless

CHAPTER 04
ORGANIZATION

Pre Test 1

유전학 수업의 강의를 듣고, 물음에 답하시오.

🎧 스크립트

P Over the past three decades, <u>we've seen a remarkable reduction</u> in the number of measles outbreaks... Obviously this is primarily because of the modern widespread use of the measles vaccines. "Good news" <u>you might be saying</u>. Well, it, uh, it seems so at first glance. However, then we've got these recent studies that show something interesting about the inheritance and immunity of measles. We've discovered that the moms who, <u>who've been vaccinated against</u> this disease are more likely to have kids who are naturally susceptible to contracting measles. In other words, their natural immunity <u>is weakened by their moms' getting vaccines.</u> Based on the, uh, the study, what we've seen is that almost 33 percent of unimmunized babies born after 1963, when the vaccines were first regularly administered, were infected with measles. This figure stands <u>as opposed to</u> the only 12 percent of unimmunized babies born to older moms who hadn't been vaccinated. So this is a pretty interesting consequence of vaccination programs...

교수 지난 30년 동안 홍역 발병 수가 현격하게 감소했습니다. 물론 이런 현상이 발생하게 된 주요 원인은 홍역 백신이 널리 보급되었기 때문입니다. '좋은 소식'이라고 하겠죠. 처음에 언뜻 보기에는 좋은 소식 같습니다. 하지만 최근 연구를 통해 유전과 홍역 면역에 대한 재미있는 사실을 알게 되었습니다. 홍역 예방 백신을 맞은 엄마에게서 태어난 자녀들이 홍역에 걸리기 더욱 쉽다는 점입니다. 달리 말하자면, 엄마가 백신을 맞게 되면 아이들의 타고난 면역성이 약화된다는 겁니다. 연구 결과에 근거해서 목격할 수 있는 사실은, 처음으로 백신을 정기적으로 접종하기 시작했던 1963년 이후에 태어난 아기들 중에 면역성을 받지 못한 아기들의 거의 33%가 홍역에 걸렸다는 점입니다. 이 수치는 예방접종을 맞지 않은 더 나이 든 엄마에게 태어난 아기들 중에 면역성을 받지 못한 아이들의 단지 12%만이 홍역에 걸린 것과는 대조적인 현상입니다. 그러므로 이런 현상은 백신 프로그램의 매우 흥미로운 결과입니다.

교수는 면역성 감소의 문제를 어떻게 강조하고 있는가?
(A) 백신의 상대적인 비효율성을 설명함으로써
(B) 백신 연구에 대한 배경 정보를 제공함으로써
(C) 1963년 전후의 감염율을 비교함으로써
(D) 홍역에 의해 발병하는 합병증의 예를 제시함으로써

정답 (C)

해설 백신의 정기적 접종이 이루어졌던 1963년을 전후로 백신접종을 받은 어머니와 받지 않은 어머니에게서 태어난 아기들의 홍역 발병 여부를 비교했다.

Pre Test 2

교내 건강 센터에서의 대화를 듣고, 물음에 답하시오.

🎧 스크립트

S I feel terrible, doctor. My head aches, my whole body is sore, and <u>I'm completely exhausted</u>. Is there something you can give me to make me feel better?

D Well, by looking at your symptoms and taking your vital signs, it seems the reason for your feeling this way is <u>because you've got the flu</u>. All I can tell you is that you should get a lot of rest, and make sure you drink a lot of liquids until you get well.

S But I can't rest. I've got two exams this week and a presentation in my class. My professors <u>will fail me if I don't show up</u>!

D Well, if you don't go home and get into bed for the next few days, you're going to <u>get much sicker</u>. You'll wind up in the hospital. Your body needs a break, so it can get better. I'll write a note to your professors <u>so they let you make up the missed work</u>. And I'm sure, really, that they'll understand. After all, if you go to class, you'll get them sick!

학생 의사선생님, 몸이 좋질 않아요. 머리가 아프고, 온 몸이 쑤시고, 완전히 탈진상태예요. 몸이 좀 나아질 수 있는 것이 없을까요?

의사 글쎄요. 학생 증상이나 맥박, 혈압 등을 보니까 이런 식으로 아픈 것은 독감에 걸렸기 때문인 것 같군요. 내가 해 줄 말이라고는 몸이 회복될 때까지 휴식을 많이 취하고 수분을 많이 섭취하라는 것밖에 없네요.

학생 하지만 쉴 수가 없어요. 이번 주에 시험이 두 개 있고 수업시간에 발표도 해야 하거든요. 제가 수업시간에 출석하지 않으

면 교수님이 저를 낙제시킬 거예요!

의사 집으로 가서 앞으로 며칠 동안 침대에 누워있지 않으면 훨씬 더 심하게 앓게 될 거예요. 그러면 결국 병원에 입원해야 한다고요. 몸이 나아지려면 휴식이 필요해요. 빠진 공부를 보충할 수 있도록 내가 교수님들께 쪽지를 써 줄게요. 교수님들도 분명 이해하실 겁니다. 결국 수업에 간다면 다른 학생들에게도 전염될 거예요.

의사가 학생에게 충분한 휴식을 취하지 않은 경우의 결과에 대해 말하는 이유는 무엇인가?
(A) 즉시 휴식을 취하는 것이 중요하다는 점을 강조하려고
(B) 방과 후에 휴식을 취할 것을 장려하려고
(C) 남자의 병세를 좀 더 잘 알려진 병과 비교하려고
(D) 수업을 포기할 것을 제안하려고

정답 (A)

해설 휴식을 취하지 않게 되면 더욱 심하게 앓게 되어 병원에 입원해야 할지도 모른다고 말한 것은 그만큼 휴식이 중요하다는 점을 강조하기 위해서이다.

Vocabulary Preview for Mini-Exercise

Mini-Exercise 1

1-1. more or less (대체로)
 ✓ a. usually
  b. nothing more than ~
1-2. ground (근거)
  a. historical or social conditions or events
 ✓ b. the basis of an argument or stated position
1-3. conference (회의)
  a. a source of information
 ✓ b. a meeting to discuss a specific matter
2-1. linguistics (언어학)
 ✓ a. the systematic study of the structure and development of language
  b. writings such as dramas, poems, novels, essays with artistic value
2-2. convince (확신시키다)
 ✓ a. to persuade someone or make them certain
  b. to decide officially in a court of law that someone is guilty of a crime
2-3. thesis (논문)
  a. to offer a possible plan or action
 ✓ b. a long piece of writing on a particular subject, especially for an academic degree

3-1. journey (여행)
  a. to undertake despite potential danger
 ✓ b. the act of travelling from one place to another
3-2. resurrection (부활)
 ✓ a. a return to life after death
  b. the process of intent thought or meditation
3-3. labyrinth (미로)
 ✓ a. an intricate network of passageways
  b. to make something more difficult to deal with

Mini-Exercise 2

1-1. invasive (침입하는)
 ✓ a. moving into all areas of something and difficult to stop
  b. without legal or factual effect
1-2. havoc (무질서)
 ✓ a. confusion and lack of order
  b. a sudden event that causes very great destruction
1-3. livelihood (생계)
  a. to tell someone confidently that something is true
 ✓ b. means of subsistence
2-1. outlaw (불법화하다)
 ✓ a. to make something illegal or unacceptable
  b. to go or reach beyond
2-2. hesitant (주저하는)
 ✓ a. uncertain or in doubt
  b. not wanting to accept something
2-3. come up with (어떠한 생각이 떠오르다)
  a. to reach the usual or necessary standard
 ✓ b. to suggest or think of an idea or plan
3-1. exceptional (예외적인)
  a. freedom from an obligation
 ✓ b. out of the ordinary
3-2. testimonial (추천서)
 ✓ a. a statement about the qualities of something
  b. the evidence presented under oath in a court of law
3-3. average
  a. satisfactory and able to be approved of
 ✓ b. usual or typical

Mini-Exercise 1 Organization

1 여성사 수업시간의 토론을 듣고, 물음에 답하시오.

🎧 스크립트

P Okay, so let's think about <u>some recent presidents' wives</u>. What is it that they do?
S Well, it seems like the first lady always champions some kind of social issue ... health care, literacy, or something like that...
P Right. But this wasn't always the case. In fact, it was really Eleanor Roosevelt, Teddy Roosevelt's wife, who <u>broke the ground for</u> presidents' wives to have a public role. Before that, first ladies were <u>more or less invisible</u>. She turned her focus onto a variety of different issues that affected the people of this country. One of her main interests was <u>advancing the cause of women</u> in this country... What's an example of this? Well, how about the fact that she would hold weekly press conferences, <u>but only allow female journalists to attend</u>? This resulted in many American newspapers hiring their initial female reporters, so that they <u>could gain access to</u> the White House.

교수 자, 최근 역임했던 대통령들의 부인 몇 분에 대해 생각해봅시다. 그들이 하는 일은 무엇입니까?
학생 영부인은 항상 몇 가지 사회 문제, 즉 건강관리나 문맹퇴치 등을 지원하고 있는 것 같습니다.
교수 맞습니다. 그러나 항상 그랬던 것은 아닙니다. 실제로, 대통령의 아내에 대한 견해를 깨고 공적인 역할을 담당했던 사람은 바로 테디 루즈벨트의 아내였던 엘리노어 루즈벨트였습니다. 그 이전에는 영부인들은 대개 모습을 드러내지 않았습니다. 엘리노어는 이 나라 국민들에게 영향을 미치는 다양한 다른 논쟁거리에 초점을 맞추었습니다. 그녀의 주요 관심사 가운데 하나는 이 나라 여성들에게 명분을 조성해주는 일이었습니다. 어떤 예를 들 수 있을까요? 글쎄요, 그녀가 매주 기자회견을 하면서 여성 기자만 참석하게 한 사실은 어떨까요? 이로 인해 이 나라의 많은 신문사에서 백악관 출입을 위해 첫 여성 기자들을 고용하는 결과를 낳았습니다.

1 교수는 어떤 방식으로 영부인의 공적인 역할을 설명하는가?
(A) 사회 문제에 대한 과거 영부인들의 활동을 간단한 전기 형식으로 설명함으로써
(B) 여권신장운동에 대한 엘리노어 루즈벨트의 관심을, 뒤이어 발생하는 다른 사람의 관심과 대조시킴으로써
(C) 과거 영부인들은 하지 않았던 공적 활동을 최초로 시행한 영부인을 지적함으로써
(D) 엘리노어 루즈벨트가 아프리카 미국인의 평등권을 위해 활동했던 예를 제시함으로써

정답 (C)

해설 대부분 대중에 모습을 드러내지 않았던 과거의 영부인들과는 달리 엘리노어 루즈벨트는 대중에게 영향을 미치는 다양한 논쟁거리에 참여했다.

2 엘리노어 루즈벨트가 자신의 기자회견을 여성들에게만 공개한 이유는 무엇인가?
(A) 여성권리라는 명분을 증진시키려고
(B) 언론분야에서의 여성의 역할을 강조하려고
(C) 여성이 보도에 적합하다는 사실을 나타내려고
(D) 여성의 역할에 대한 남편의 견해에 반대하려고

정답 (A)

해설 엘리노어 루즈벨트는 여성의 명분을 조성하는 일에 활동의 중점을 두었다.

2 학생과 조교 사이의 대화를 듣고, 물음에 답하시오.

🎧 스크립트

S Hi, I'm trying to <u>fill out a grant application</u> to help me fund a linguistics research trip to Lithuania next fall... I'm just not really sure it's any good. I've written down what I intend to do, but I really <u>feel like it's missing something</u>.
TA Well, I think that kinda stuff is important to <u>put in there</u>, but on the other hand, grants are competitive. <u>There's only so much to go around</u>. So have you talked about why your project, in particular, <u>should be funded over</u> another student's?
S Um, not really, no... How do I convince the department of that?
TA Why not talk about how your project is different from anything any of the other students are doing, for example? Or how the research will really benefit, not just your thesis, but also <u>your studies in graduate school</u> in the near future.

학생 안녕하세요, 제가 내년 가을에 리투아니아로 떠나는 언어 연구여행의 비용을 충당할 목적으로 장학금 신청서를 작성하고 있습니다. 제대로 작성했는지 영 자신이 없어요. 제가 하고자 하는 일을 적었습니다만 무언가 빠진 것 같다는 생각이 듭니다.
조교 음, 그런 종류의 내용을 적는 것도 중요하지만, 다른 한편으로 장학금을 타기 위한 경쟁이 치열해요. 빙빙 돌려서 말하기에는 경쟁이 너무 심해요. 그러니까 특별히 학생의 프로젝트가 다른 학생 것보다 우선해서 지원금을 받아야 하는 이유에 대해서는 적었나요?
학생 아, 아뇨, 그렇게 까지는 아니요. 어떻게 하면 과에 그 점을 확신시킬 수 있을까요?

조교 예를 들어 학생의 프로젝트가 여느 다른 학생의 프로젝트와 어떻게 다른지에 대해 쓰면 어떨까요? 아니면 이 연구가 학생의 논문에만 유용한 것이 아니라 가까운 머지 않아 대학원 연구에도 유용하리라는 점을 쓰는지요.

1 여자는 남자의 신청서를 개선하기 위해 어떤 방식으로 조언하는가?
(A) 학생의 관심과 성취에 대한 개인적인 정보를 좀 더 많이 제공함으로써
(B) 신청서의 질을 높일 수 있는 사항에 대한 예를 제공함으로써
(C) 학생의 연구와 그의 지도교수의 연구를 비교함으로써
(D) 학생이 포함시킨 정보를 보다 잘 구성할 수 있는 방법을 제시함으로써

정답 (B)

해설 조교는 학생의 프로젝트가 다른 학생 것보다 우선해서 지원금을 받아야 하는 이유에 대해 적으라고 조언하면서 그 구체적인 예를 들고 있다.

2 연구 목적 기입에 대해 여자는 뭐라고 말하는가?
(A) 포함되어야만 하는 사항은 아니다.
(B) 신청서에 기입하는 것은 괜찮지만 반드시 필요하지는 않다.
(C) 기입하도록 요구되어진 사항이다.
(D) 기입해야 할 중요한 정보 가운데 하나이다.

정답 (D)

해설 무엇을 하고자 하는지에 대해 적은 것이 중요하다고 말하면서, 덧붙여 경쟁이 치열하므로 좀 더 내용을 보완하라고 조언한다.

3 세계사 수업시간의 토론을 듣고, 물음에 답하시오.

🎧 스크립트

P What is a pilgrimage, anyway?
S1 It's a religious journey of some kind, isn't it?
S2 Yeah, like when pilgrims go to <u>the capital of their religion</u>?
P Right. For European Christians during the Middle Ages, Jerusalem was <u>the spiritual center</u>, but most people couldn't go that far, so they'd go to closer places, like France's Chartres Cathedral. There was a labyrinth that <u>consisted of a complicated series of</u> paths or passages, with a single path leading to the center. It was just 260 meters, but that's not the point. The pilgrims who came to Chartres <u>saw the labyrinth as a symbolic journey</u> in two ways. Essentially for them, the labyrinth's path to the center was the path of our long, hard lives — from birth to death. As the pilgrim then <u>walks from the center back out</u>, the journey symbolizes personal resurrection — you know, <u>being "born again,"</u> so to speak, which is a central belief of the Christian religion.

교수 자, 성지순례가 무엇입니까?
학생1 일종의 종교적인 여행이 아닌가요?
학생2 그렇습니다. 순례자들이 자신이 속한 종교세계의 중심지를 찾아가는 것이지요?
교수 맞습니다. 중세시대에 유럽의 기독교인에게 예루살렘은 영적인 중심지였습니다. 하지만 대부분의 사람들은 그렇게 멀리까지 여행할 수가 없었습니다. 그래서 프랑스의 샤르트르 대성당처럼 좀 더 가까운 장소로 갔지요. 그곳에는 길이나 통로가 복잡하게 얽혀 있고 중앙으로 가는 길이 단 하나인 미로가 있었습니다. 미로의 길이는 260미터에 불과했지만 그 점이 중요한 것은 아닙니다. 샤르트르에 왔던 순례자들은 이 미로를 두 가지 면에서 상징적인 여행으로 보았습니다. 본질적으로 순례자들에게 중앙으로 통하는 미로의 길은 출생에서 죽음에 이르는 우리의 힘들고 긴 인생의 길을 의미했습니다. 순례자가 중앙에서 다시 걸어 나오게 되면 그 여행은 개인적인 부활을 상징합니다. 즉, 기독교의 본질적인 신앙인으로 "다시 태어남"을 의미합니다.

1 교수는 어떤 방식으로 샤르트르의 미로에 대해 설명하는가?
(A) 사람들이 이곳을 방문할 때마다 행하는 가장 흔한 종교활동을 제시함으로써
(B) 샤르트로 미로의 복잡한 구조를 예루살렘의 미로의 구조와 비교함으로써
(C) 상징적인 중요성에 대한 기본적인 정의와 확장된 정의를 제시함으로써
(D) 기독교의 중심 신앙이 되는 원인으로 건축의 세부 사항을 제시함으로써

정답 (C)

해설 미로는 출생에서 죽음에 이르는 사람의 길고 힘든 삶의 여정을 의미한다는 기본적인 정의와, 미로의 통과가 종교적으로 다시 태어나는 개인적인 부활을 상징한다는 확장된 의미를 제시했다.

2 초기 기독교인에게 미로는 무엇을 상징했는가? 정답 두 개를 고르시오.
(A) 샤르트르로의 성지순례
(B) 인생의 행로(여정)
(C) 예수의 부활
(D) 재탄생의 개념

정답 (B), (D)

해설 초기 기독교인에게 미로는 길고 힘든 인간 삶의 여정인 동시에 기독교인으로서 다시 태어나기 위한 길이었다.

Mini-Exercise 2　Rhetorical Connection

1　환경연구 수업의 강의를 듣고, 물음에 답하시오.

🎧 스크립트

P　Invasive species are a, uh, a major problem globally. Uh, what do I mean by invasive species, anyway? Plants and animals that wind up in a place where they aren't originally from, and then <u>proceed to wreak havoc with</u> the environment, throwing things out of balance...
You guys know what nutria is, right? Well, it's a furry rodent. And, in the 1930s, a bunch of these nutrias <u>were accidentally released into</u> the marshlands of Louisiana. Good for the nutria, maybe, but bad for the marshes. <u>They wound up really destroying</u> a lot of the native plants as well as the surrounding sugar cane fields... so <u>the ecological balance of the marshes was threatened</u> as well as the livelihood of the farmers. However, by using nutria fur in coats and hats, people have been keeping the population down. But, <u>it's not a blanket solution for</u> all invasive species problems.

교수　침입 종은 에, 음... 세계적으로 중대한 문제입니다. 어쨌거나 침입 종이 무엇이냐고요? 원래 서식하던 곳이 아닌 장소로 이주하면서 사물의 균형을 깨뜨리고 환경을 황폐하게 만드는 동식물을 말합니다.
여러분은 뉴트리아가 무엇인지 알고 있겠죠? 털로 덮인 설치류 동물을 뜻합니다. 그리고 1930년대에 이 뉴트리아 떼가 우연히 루이지애나의 늪지대에 방출되었습니다. 뉴트리아 입장에서는 좋은 일일지 모르지만 늪지대에는 좋지 않은 일이었습니다. 뉴트리아는 주변을 둘러싸고 있던 사탕수수 밭뿐만 아니라 그곳이 원산지인 많은 식물을 파괴했습니다. 그래서 농부들의 생계는 물론 늪지대의 생태학적 균형까지 위협을 받았습니다. 그러나 사람들이 뉴트리아의 털을 코트로 모자로 사용함으로써 그 수가 줄어들고 있습니다. 그러나 이것은 침입 종이 일으키는 모든 문제점에 대한 일괄적인 해결책은 아닙니다.

1　교수가 루이지애나에 뉴트리아가 방출된 사건에 대해 학생들에게 말한 이유는 무엇인가?
(A) 그 동물의 외모와 행동을 묘사하려고
(B) 이 침입 종의 원래 서식지에 대한 배경 정보를 주려고
(C) 이 침입 종이 어떻게 문제점을 발생하는지를 나타내려고
(D) 뉴트리아와 다른 형태의 침입 종을 대조하려고

정답 (C)

해설　침입 종이 환경을 황폐하게 만들 수 있다는 점을 나타내기 위해 뉴트리아를 예로 들었다.

2　교수는 뉴트리아의 수를 줄인 방법에 대해 무엇이라고 말하는가?
(A) 침입 종에게 그 방법을 사용한 것은 처음이었다.
(B) 장기간에는 효과를 발휘할 수 없는 단기 해결책이다.
(C) 모든 침입 종에게 효과를 발휘하지는 못할 것이다
(D) 모든 침입 종에 대한 이상적인 해결책이다.

정답 (D)

해설　교수에 따르면 털을 코트와 모자 등으로 사용해서 뉴트리아의 수를 줄이는 방법은 뉴트리아가 일으키는 모든 문제에 대한 일괄적인 해결책이 될 수 없다.

2　정치학 수업에서 인형극에 관한 토론을 듣고, 물음에 답하시오.

🎧 스크립트

P　In times and places where <u>free expression is outlawed</u>, people may be hesitant to speak freely because of fear of their government, or those in power. Well, so, people come up with some pretty creative ways of <u>critiquing the system</u>. Most common ways we can think of <u>are through various art forms</u>, cartoons, and so on. Now, one of the unique methods <u>used to criticize those in power was puppetry</u>. You know what a puppet is, right? A doll that you can move, either by pulling strings... or by putting your hand inside its body and moving your fingers. Allright, the history of puppetry, in fact, is really <u>tied up with this political expression</u>.
S　Well, because it's a lot easier for a puppet to make a political statement than a person? It seems less dangerous to those in power, maybe?
P　Exactly. Let's, uh, let's look at Punch, a puppet character who was the star of many puppet shows in both England and France starting in the 17th century.

교수　자유로운 의사표현이 금지된 시대와 장소에서는 사람들이 정부나 권력자를 두려워해서 자유롭게 말하는 것을 주저할지 모릅니다. 그래서 사람들은 체제를 비판할 수 있는 매우 창의적인 방법을 창안합니다. 우리가 흔하게 생각할 수 있는 방법은 여러 예술 형태, 만화 등을 통하는 것입니다. 자, 권력자들을 비판하는 독특한 수단 가운데 하나는 바로 인형극입니다. 인형극이 무엇인지는 모두들 알고 있죠? (인형에 달린) 줄을 잡아 당기거나 인형의 몸 속에 손을 넣어서 손가락을 움직임으로써 움직이게 할 수 있는 인형입니다. 자, 실제로 인형극의 역사는 이런 정치적 표현과 관련이 있습니다.

학생　그게, 사람이 정치적 발언을 하기 보다 인형이 하는 편이 훨씬

더 쉽기 때문인가요? 아마도 권력자들에게 덜 위험한 것 같습니다만?

교수 정확합니다. 17세기에 영국과 프랑스에서 시작됐던 여러 인형극의 스타 캐릭터였던 Punch를 봅시다.

---

1 교수가 자유로운 의사표현이 금지되었던 시대와 장소에 대해 설명한 이유는 무엇인가?
(A) 인형극이 정치적 발언의 수단으로 사용된 배경을 설명하려고
(B) 인형이 만들어지게 된 가능한 설명을 제시하려고
(C) 과거 비판의 수단과 현대 비판의 수단을 대조하려고
(D) 인형극이 그러한 시대와 장소에서 인기를 끌게 된 이유를 제시하려고

정답 (A)

해설 자유로운 의사표현이 금지되었던 시대와 장소에서 사람들은 체제를 비판할 수 있는 매우 창의적인 방법으로 다양한 예술 형태를 사용했다. 그 가운데 하나가 인형극이었다.

2 교수에 따르면 Punch는 무엇인가?
(A) 17세기 인형극에 등장하는 유명한 등장인물
(B) 유명한 인형 조작인
(C) 유명한 인형극의 명칭
(D) 인형극의 또 다른 이름

정답 (A)

해설 17세기 영국과 프랑스에서 시작됐던 인형극의 주인공이었다.

3 마케팅 수업의 강의를 듣고, 물음에 답하시오..

🎧 스크립트

P Okay. You've got a product that <u>nobody's heard of</u>, um, say this new soap. You know that it's exceptional soap. It's really gonna change people's perceptions about <u>what soap can be.</u> But, uh, well nobody's heard of it. If they see it on the shelves at the store, and nobody's told them about it, chances are <u>they'll mistrust it and stick with</u> their own soap. This is where advertising comes in — how to convince people to buy a certain product. A really effective way to do this is <u>by using testimonials in your ads</u>. A famous person people know and trust, or even just <u>an average person from the area</u> that people can relate to... If you include these kinds of people talking about <u>why your soap is so good</u>, your customers are going to be much more likely to trust the product and therefore, buy it.

교수 자, 이제 여러분에게 아무도 들어본 적이 없는 제품, 음 예를 들어 새로운 비누가 있다고 합시다. 여러분은 이것이 아주 특별한 비누라는 사실을 압니다. 이 제품은 비누에 대한 사람들의 인식을 바꿔놓을 것입니다. 하지만 음, 글쎄요, 아무도 이 비누에 대해 들어본 적이 없습니다. 사람들은 상점 선반에 진열되어 있는 비누를 보았더라도, 그 비누에 대해 말해주는 사람이 없다면 비누를 신뢰하지 않을 것이고, 자신이 현재 사용하고 있는 비누를 고집할 가능성이 큽니다.

이 시점이 바로 광고가 개입하는 시기입니다. 사람들에게 제품을 사라고 확신시키는 겁니다. 이를 위해 정말 좋은 방법은 다른 사람의 추천을 광고에 사용하는 겁니다. 사람들이 알고 신뢰하는 유명인이나, 심지어는 사람들이 관련되어 있는 지역에 사는 보통 사람의 추천을 말입니다. 이런 사람들이 이 비누가 좋은 이유에 대해 말한다면 고객들이 제품을 신뢰해서 이를 구매할 가능성이 훨씬 커집니다.

1 교수는 어떤 방식으로 자신의 강의를 시작하는가?
(A) 비누제조업자의 최근 광고 활동을 묘사함으로써
(B) 처음으로 추천제를 사용한 예를 제시함으로써
(C) 신제품에 대한 가상 시나리오를 제시함으로써
(D) 학생들에게 책에 있는 사례연구를 검토하라고 지적함으로써

정답 (C)

해설 사람들이 전에 들어본 적이 없는 새 비누가 있다고 가정하고 있다.

2 사람들이 새 비누를 좋아하지 않을지도 모른다고 교수가 말한 이유는 무엇인가?
(A) 비누의 품질이 낮으리라 추측할 것이기 때문에
(B) 비누에 대해 아는 것이 없기 때문에
(C) 비누가 너무 비싸다고 생각할 것이기 때문에
(D) 비누 사용이 안전하지 못하다고 느낄지도 모르기 때문에

정답 (B)

해설 새 비누에 대해 아는 것이 없기 때문에 제품을 신뢰하지 않는다.

Vocabulary Preview for Practice

Practice 1

1. competition (경쟁)
   ✓ a. to try to be more successful than someone else
   b. to make something finished
2. benefit (혜택)
   a. desiring to do good for others
   ✓ b. anything given to provide an advantage
3. bias (편견)
   ✓ a. an inclination or preference that influences judgment
   b. the most important facts, ideas from which something is formed and developed

4. gender (성(性))
   a. to treat a person or particular group of people differently
   ✓b. the sex of a person or an animal

Practice 2

1. conflict (갈등)
   ✓a. a disagreement between people with opposing opinions
   b. to make an arrangement or meeting certain
2. tactic (전술)
   a. a plan for how something will happen
   ✓b. a planned way of doing something
3. impartial (공정한)
   ✓a. not supporting any of the sides involved in an argument
   b. to give all or a part of
4. consensus (합의)
   ✓a. a generally accepted opinion or decision among a group of people
   b. to talk about a subject and tell each other their opinions

Practice 3

1. frustrated (좌절감이 드는)
   ✓a. disappointed at being thwarted
   b. firmly set in one's ideas or habits
2. petition (진정서)
   a. a suggestion that something is suitable for a particular purpose
   ✓b. a document signed by many people demanding some action from an authority
3. signature (서명)
   ✓a. your name written by yourself
   b. a signature of a famous person
4. submit (제출하다)
   ✓a. to give something for a decision to be made by others
   b. to put or plunge under water or other fluid

Practice 4

1. represent (묘사하다, 기술하다)
   ✓a. to show or describe something or someone
   b. to not allow something to be expressed

2. metabolism (물질대사, 신진대사)
   a. an expression which describes a person or object in a literary way
   ✓b. all the chemical processes causing food to be used for energy and growth in your body
3. measurement (측정, 측량)
   ✓a. to discover the exact size or amount of something
   b. a method or way of doing something
4. restrict (제한하다, 한정하다)
   a. an area having fixed borders that are used for official purposes
   ✓b. to limit the movements or actions of someone

Vocabulary Preview for Actual Test

Actual Test 1

1. b 오늘날 교육을 담당하는 대부분의 교사들의 주요 관심사는 학생 훈육을 어떻게 개선하는가이다.
2. d 새로운 분석 방법의 예상되는 가치는 아직 입증되지 않고 있다.
3. b Brad의 전문지식과 느긋한 태도는 그 자리에 이상적인 지원자로 보이게 한다.
4. c 의사들은 환자를 치료할 때, 최근의 증상, 수술이나 치료의 필요성, 그리고 회복 가능성 같은 광범위한 진단 사항들을 설명해야 한다.

Actual Test 2

1. a 새로운 법안은 더 많은 장애우들이 미국 사회의 주류에 편입되도록 허락해야 한다.
2. d 그들은 3년 이내에 아시아 영화 시장을 점령하기를 희망한다.
3. d 그는 끊임없는 혁신으로 인해 그 상을 받을 자격이 있다.
4. b 그 배우는 자신감도 있고, 겉보기에는 최근의 문제로 인해 괴로워하는 것 같지 않다.

Practice 1

1 (A)   2 (C)   3 (C)

경제학 수업의 토론을 들으시오.

🎧 스크립트

P Okay, so we've been looking at the different ways in which competition is fostered by the free market, creating benefits for both workers and employers; in terms of wages, conditions, and so on. What I want to do today is look at the flip-side, discussing a couple of issues that interfere with unfettered competition; market and pre-market discrimination. Let's start with market discrimination. Anyone know what that means?

S Well, I know that, at different time periods, different groups of people would be prevented from getting decent jobs, depending on the society's biases at the time.

P Right. So, we have the idea that prejudice or bias based on people's characteristics, such as a person's race, ethnicity, gender, or even political views might cause prospective employers to not hire them. So, this kind of contradicts the free market promise that you can get a good wage by working hard... If you can't even get in the pool of good jobs to compete, you're kind of stuck, right? And since your job choices are severely limited, you wind up getting very little say about the conditions you work under. You can't just quit and get another job if there really aren't any other jobs for you, right?

교수 우리는, 자유시장에 의해 경쟁이 조장되고, 임금, 근로조건 등의 측면에서 노동자와 고용인 모두에게 혜택이 돌아가는 여러 가지 방법을 살펴보고 있습니다. 오늘은 그 숨은 측면을 살펴보고, 자유 경쟁을 방해하는 두 가지 논쟁, 즉 시장 차별과 선(先) 시장 차별에 대해 얘기해보려 합니다. 우선 시장 차별 문제부터 시작해봅시다. 이것이 무엇을 뜻하는지 아는 사람 있나요?

학생 시대에 따라 각 그룹의 사람들은 그 당시 사회의 편견 때문에 적절한 직업을 구할 수 없다는 의미로 알고 있습니다.

교수 맞습니다. 그래서 우리는 인종, 민족성, 성별, 또는 심지어 정치적 견해 등과 같은 개인의 특징에 대한 편견이나 선입견을 가지고 장래 고용인들이 사람들을 고용하지 않을지도 모른다는 생각을 가지고 있습니다. 이는 열심히 일하면 좋은 임금을 받을 수 있다는 자유 시장의 약속에 상반됩니다. 만약 여러분이 경쟁하기에 좋은 직업 군에 포함될 수 없다면 여러분은 오도가도 못하는 처지가 되는 거겠죠? 여러분의 직업 선택이 극도로 제한되기 때문에 일하는 조건에 대해서는 거의 따지지 않게 됩니다. 다른 직업을 선택할 수 없는데 현재 직업을 그냥 그만두고 다른 일자리를 찾을 수는 없지 않겠습니까?

1 교수는 토론을 어떤 방식으로 시작하는가?
(A) 지난 강의에서 경쟁에 관해 어떤 토론을 했는지를 언급함으로써
(B) 경쟁이 주는 불이익의 예를 듦으로써
(C) 스미스의 경쟁 이론을 설명함으로써
(D) 경쟁이 궁극적으로 실패로 돌아가는 이유에 대해 토론함으로써

해설 자유시장에 의해 경쟁이 조장되는 방법을 살펴보았던 지난 강의의 내용에 대해 언급함으로써, 그 숨은 측면과 무제한 경쟁의 방해 요소에 대해 살펴보려는 이번 강의를 시작하고 있다.

2 교수는 강의를 어떤 방식으로 구성하고 있는가?
(A) 시장 차별 과정을 묘사함으로써
(B) 시장 차별의 두 가지 예를 비교함으로써
(C) 자유 시장의 혜택과 문제점을 대조함으로써
(D) 시장이 가진 다른 여러 종류의 문제점을 분류함으로써

해설 교수는 우선 자유 시장의 혜택에 대한 지난 시간 강의 내용에 대해 언급하고, 무제한 경쟁을 방해하는 시장 차별로 인한 문제점을 제시한다.

3 교수가 개인의 특징에 대해 언급한 이유는 무엇인가?
(A) 자유 시장에서는 모든 견해가 환영 받는다는 사실을 보여주려고
(B) 고용 관행과 정치가 무관하다는 것을 강조하려고
(C) 고용에 부정적인 영향을 미칠지 모르는 요인을 설명하려고
(D) 고용인들이 사람들을 모집할 때 주로 고려하는 것을 보여주려고

해설 인종, 민족, 성별, 정치적 견해 등 개인의 특징에 대한 편견이나 선입견 때문에 장래 고용인이 그런 특징을 가진 사람을 고용하지 않을지도 모르기 때문이다.

Practice 2

1 (D)   2 (D)   3 (B)

자원 관리 수업의 토론을 들으시오.

🎧 스크립트

P If we want to limit the occurrence of violent conflict in the future, we've got to figure out ways for groups to cooperate on resource distribution. Well, so, there are treaties and laws for these conflicts... but... the problem with these is that they are often broken... and because these things tend to be imposed top-down — the government telling people, "hey this is how it is," these are not always seen as legitimate or lawful, which in the end doesn't cut down on conflict. But there is a more effective tactic known as "preventative diplomacy." How this works is that first, you bring together a variety of different people — experts on the resource as well as the people who are directly affected — and then create an impartial environment where competing needs are assessed and dealt through cooperation and consensus.

S Yeah, but come on... people are emotional, especially when they perceive that their livelihood or way of life is threatened. How can we get past that?
P Well, the idea is that at all times, you focus on the resource, not people's emotions. We want to come up with something that will, if not satisfy everyone, at least not cause anyone to feel that someone got a better deal, because that's where violent conflict most often arises.

교수 앞으로는 격렬한 분쟁 발생을 제한하려면 각 집단은 자원 분배를 위해 협동하는 방법을 생각해내야 합니다. 그리고, 음... 이런 갈등을 해결하기 위한 조약과 법칙이 존재합니다. 하지만... 이런 조약과 법률이 가진 문제는 이것이 종종 파기된다는 점입니다. 그리고 이런 것들은 정부가 사람들에게 "이건 이런 식으로 하는 거야."라고 말하는 것처럼 위에서 아래로 부과되기 때문에, 항상 합법적이거나 적법하게 보여지는 것은 아닙니다. 그리고 결국 갈등을 줄이지도 못합니다. 그러나 "예방 외교"로 알려진 좀 더 효과적인 전술이 있습니다. 이 전술의 적용방법은 우선, 직접적으로 영향을 받는 사람뿐만 아니라 자원 전문가 등 다양하게 여러 사람을 모으는 겁니다. 그리고 나서 서로 충돌하는 요구를 협동과 합의를 통해 평가하고 해결될 수 있는 공정한 환경을 조성하는 겁니다.

학생 알겠습니다. 하지만... 사람들은 감정적입니다. 특히 자신의 생계나 생활방식이 위협을 받을 때는 더더욱 그렇습니다. 그 문제를 어떻게 피할 수 있겠습니까?

교수 언제나 사람들의 감정이 아닌 자원에 초점을 맞추는 겁니다. 모든 사람을 만족시킬 수는 없더라도 최소한 누군가가 더 나은 대우를 받았다는 생각이 들지 않게 할 무언가를 생각해내야 합니다. 바로 거기서 격렬한 갈등이 가장 많이 일어나기 때문입니다.

1 교수는 어떤 방식으로 강의를 시작하는가?
(A) 조약과 법률에 대한 배경 지식을 제공함으로써
(B) 자원 전문가의 분석을 제시함으로써
(C) 자원 분쟁의 예를 묘사함으로써
(D) 예방 외교의 목적에 대해 언급함으로써

해설 예방 외교의 목적 즉 미래에 있을 격렬한 갈등의 제한을 위해 자원분배에 협동하는 방법을 생각해내야 한다고 했다.

2 교수가 조약에 대해 언급한 이유는 무엇인가?
(A) 자원 분쟁에 대응할 때 조약을 사용하라고 제안하려고
(B) 사람들이 조약에 대한 언급을 게을리 했다는 사실을 암시하려고
(C) 자신이 읽었던 분쟁해결에 대한 사례연구를 묘사하려고
(D) 이런 장치가 적절하게 사용될 경우 문제를 해결할 수 있다는 점을 나타내려고

해설 여러 사람의 협동과 합의를 통해 갈등을 해결하는 방법은 사람들이 감정적이어서 효과가 없을 수 있기 때문에 강제적인 조약이나 법률을 사용해야 한다고 주장한다.

3 교수는 어떤 방식으로 예방 외교에 대해 설명하는가?
(A) 다양한 노력의 중요성에 대해 설명함으로써
(B) 예방적 외교 장치의 단계를 묘사함으로써
(C) 수단에 대한 다른 견해를 제시함으로써
(D) 예전 법률을 비교함으로써

해설 예방적 외교의 적용방법을 구체적으로 제시함으로써 설명한다.

Practice 3

1 (D)   2 (C)   3 (A), (B)

두 학생 사이의 대화를 들으시오.

🎧 스크립트

S1 I'm so frustrated... my dorm is way too noisy to study in... Most people are finished with finals, so they're relaxing and having a good time, but I still have two exams left! I don't blame them for having fun, but...
S2 Yeah, that's pretty annoying... My dorm is really loud, too.
S1 So, actually I was gonna ask you if you want to go to the library to study.
S2 But the library is closing in 30 minutes. You didn't know they close at midnight?
S1 Are you sure?
S2 Yeah, I don't understand why the library closes so early... Most college libraries stay open 24 hours during final weeks.
S1 Why does ours close? It would be so helpful to have a place to go to get some peace and quiet.
S2 Well, I guess because they don't have the

money to keep it open around the clock.

S1 It's only for two weeks each semester. It seems to me that they could find the money somewhere. It's really important to students. I know lots of people who feel like we do.

S2 Well, maybe we should do something about it...

S1 Like what? Break into the library?!

S2 No, but we could start a petition. We could get a lot of signatures from students who want expanded hours, and then submit it to the president. If we made an issue of it, something might change.

S1 That could work. It won't help me this semester, but maybe it'll make a difference.

학생1 정말 좌절감이 들어. 기숙사가 너무 시끄러워서 공부할 수가 없어. 대부분의 사람들은 학기말 시험이 끝났기 때문에 휴식을 취하면서 재미있게 지내고 있지만, 나는 아직 시험이 두 개나 남았다고! 사람들이 재미있게 지내는 것을 탓하는 건 아니지만...

학생2 맞아, 정말 화가 나. 내가 있는 기숙사도 정말 시끄러워.

학생1 그래서 말인데, 네가 공부하러 도서관에 갈 마음이 있는지 물어보려 했어.

학생2 하지만 도서관은 30분 후에 문을 닫아. 도서관이 자정에 문 닫는지 몰랐니?

학생1 정말이야?

학생2 응, 도서관이 왜 그렇게 일찍 문을 닫는지 모르겠어. 대부분의 대학 도서관은 학기말 시험 주간에는 하루 종일 개방하는 데 말이야.

학생1 어째서 우리 대학 도서관은 문을 닫는 거지? 차분하고 조용하게 있을 장소가 있다면 정말 도움이 될 텐데 말이야.

학생2 내 추측으로는, 아마도 하루 종일 도서관 문을 열만한 돈이 없기 때문일 거야.

학생1 학기마다 단 2주일인 걸. 다른 곳에서 돈을 마련할 수 있을 것 같은데 말이야. 학생들에게는 정말 중요한 일이잖아. 우리와 마찬가지로 생각하는 사람이 많아.

학생2 아마도 이 문제에 대해 우리가 뭔가를 해야겠어.

학생1 어떤 일 말이야? 도서관에 쳐들어가라고?!

학생2 아니, 하지만 진정서에 서명하는 일을 시작할 수 있어. 도서관 시간 연장을 원하는 학생의 서명을 많이 받아서 총장에게 제출하는 거야. 우리가 이 문제를 논쟁화한다면, 변화가 일어날지도 몰라.

학생1 효과가 있을 수 있겠다. 이번 학기에는 도움을 받지 못하겠지만 다음 학기에는 달라질 수 있을 거야.

1 여학생은 자신의 해결책을 어떤 방식으로 제안하는가?
   (A) 대학 총장에게 편지를 씀으로써
   (B) 다른 대학에서 벌이고 있는 비슷한 운동에 대해 설명함으로써
   (C) 항의 중인 남자와 함께 도서관에 쳐들어가자고 제안함으로써
   (D) 제안을 하는 과정을 설명함으로써

해설 여학생은 기숙사가 너무 시끄러워 공부를 할 수 없다는 남학생의 불평을 들어주고 반응을 하는 과정에서 진정서에 대한 학생의 서명을 받아 총장에게 제출하자는 해결책을 제시한다.

2 대화에 따르면, 학기말 시험 기간 동안 도서관이 문을 열지 않는 이유는 무엇인가?
   (A) 대부분의 대학에서 시행하는 관례가 아니다.
   (B) 학생들 대부분이 도서관 개방을 원하지 않는다.
   (C) 재정적 자원이 충분하지 않다.
   (D) 사서가 자정 넘게 일하기를 거절하고 있다.

해설 여학생은 그 이유로 학교가 도서관의 문을 하루 종일 열만한 돈이 없기 때문이라 추측한다.

3 여학생은 자신이 무엇을 해야 한다고 말하는가? 정답 두 개를 고르시오.
   (A) 자신의 의견에 동의하는 학생들에게 진정서에 서명하게 한다.
   (B) 학기말 기간 동안 도서관의 문을 열도록 학교에 호소한다.
   (C) 그 문제에 대해 다수의 다른 학생과 총장과 함께 토론한다.
   (D) 학교 총장과 함께 시간 연장에 대해 고려해달라고 도서관에 요청한다.

해설 도서관 시간 연장을 요청하는 진정서에 학생의 서명을 받아 총장에게 제출함으로써 그 필요성을 학교에 호소하려 한다.

Practice 4

1 (B)   2 (C)   3 (A)

생물학 수업의 강의를 들으시오.

🎧 스크립트

P Okay... so both BMR and RMR are estimates of how many calories you would burn if you were to do nothing but rest for 24 hours. They represent the minimum amount of energy required to keep your body functioning, the body's normal metabolic activity including your heart beating, lungs' breathing and maintenance of body temperature, etc.

BMR stands for Basal Metabolic Rate, and it is synonymous with Basal Energy Expenditure, or BEE. BMR measurements are typically taken in a darkened room upon waking up after 8 hours of sleep; 12

hours of fasting, uh, not eating food to ensure that the digestive system is inactive; and lying flat on your back. Okay? The other one that I mentioned is... RMR. RMR stands for Resting Metabolic Rate, and is synonymous with Resting Energy Expenditure, or REE. RMR measurements are typically taken under less restricted conditions than BMR, and do not require that the person spend the night sleeping in the test facility prior to testing. As you get older, shorter and lose weight, your BMR and RMR will go down and you will need to eat less or exercise more to maintain your current weight. It is tough getting old, right?

교수 자, BMR과 RMR 모두, 24시간 동안 휴식만 취하고 아무 것도 하지 않을 경우 얼마만큼의 열량을 태우는지를 측정한 것입니다. 이는 몸의 기능 즉 심장박동, 폐 호흡, 체온유지 등을 포함한 신체의 정상적인 신진대사 활동을 하는 데 필요한 최소한의 에너지 양을 나타냅니다. BMR은 기초 대사율(Basal Metabolic Rate)의 약자이고, 기초에너지 소비(Basal Energy Expenditure) 즉, BEE와 동의어입니다. BMR은 일반적으로 소화기가 분명히 활동하지 않도록 12시간 동안 음식을 먹지 않은 상태에서 8시간 동안 잠을 자고 난 다음, 어두운 방에서 똑바로 누워서 측정합니다. 알겠죠? 제가 언급한 또 다른 수치는 RMR입니다. RMR은 휴식 대사율(Resting Metabolic Rate)의 약자이고, 휴식에너지 소비(Resting Energy Expenditure) 즉, REE와 동의어입니다. RMR은 전형적으로 BMR 보다 덜 제한된 조건에서 측정하며, 실험에 참가하는 사람이 실험 전에 실험 설비에서 밤을 지낼 필요가 없습니다. 여러분이 나이 들고 키가 작아지고 체중이 빠지면, 여러분의 BMR과 RMR은 감소합니다. 그래서 현재 몸무게를 유지하려면 덜 먹거나 운동을 더 할 필요가 있을 겁니다. 늙는다는 것이 보통 일이 아니죠?

1 교수는 어떤 방식으로 두 가지 측정을 소개하는가?
(A) 측정이 이루어진 장소를 비교함으로써
(B) 두 가지 측정을 통해 알 수 있는 점을 지적함으로써
(C) 서로를 구분 짓는 주요 특징을 제시함으로써
(D) 의학분야에서 두 가지 측정이 인기도를 지적함으로써

해설 서두에서 BMR 과 RMR 의 측정을 통해 24시간 동안 아무 것도 하지 않은 상태에서 신체의 정상적인 신진대사에 필요한 최소한의 에너지 양을 알 수 있다는 점을 지적하였다

2 교수는 어떤 방식으로 BMR을 설명하는가?
(A) 다양한 연령대에 속한 다른 사람들의 결과를 비교함으로써
(B) 대사율을 알아내는 과거 방법의 규칙과 대조함으로써
(C) 정확한 측정에 필요한 조건을 설명함으로써
(D) 이를 설명하는 수학적 방정식을 설명함으로써

해설 BMR 은 소화기가 분명히 활동하지 않도록 12시간 동안 음식을 먹지 않은 상태에서 8시간 동안 잠을 자고 난 다음, 어두운 방에서 똑바로 누워서 측정한다는 측정조건을 제시함으로써 이에 대해 설명한다.

3 교수에 따르면, 다음 중 BMR과 RMR에 대한 설명으로 사실이 아닌 것은 무엇인가?
(A) 사람의 키는 대사율과는 관계가 적다.
(B) 사람이 나이 들어감에 따라 대사율은 낮아진다.
(C) 체구가 크면 대사율은 높다.
(D) 운동을 하면 대사율이 낮아지는 것을 방지할 수 있다.

해설 사람의 키는 대사율과 관계가 있다. 나이가 들어 키가 작아지고 체중이 빠질수록 BMR 과 RMR 은 감소한다. 그러므로 현재 몸무게를 유지하려면 음식 섭취량을 줄이거나 운동을 더 해야 한다.

Actual Test 1

1 (C)   2 (B)   3 (D)   4 (B)   5 (A), (C)

생물학 시간의 생명나무에 대한 강의를 들으시오.

🎧 스크립트

P So something that's happening more and more in research, especially as technology continues to move forward every day, is that there is a lot of shared information between two different academic disciplines. And this is definitely the case as biologists and computer scientists work together to help assemble what's being called the Tree of Life.
Now what is this Tree of Life? Well, you know what a family tree is, right? It's a genealogical tool that enables you to map out your ancestors over past generations, to see who you're related to, who their kids are, and all that? Okay, well, the Tree of Life is like that, just on a much larger, interspecies level. In fact, the goal of this project is to create a family tree for the 1.7 million known species on earth!
It's a huge project. So, not only do the biologists need to be able to provide their expertise to enter the data needed to have the tree work, but the computer scientists need to keep building on, and improving the machines and software that will enable this to actually become a reality. And so what this will give us, when we're done, is

a much clearer picture of exactly how life evolved, and how it keeps evolving on this planet. And then this, in turn, is going to benefit our overall understanding of our own bodies; giving rise to new predictive, diagnostic, and treatment abilities.

교수 특히 기술이 매일 진보하면서 연구 분야에서 더욱 많이 발생하는 현상은 서로 다른 원칙 사이에 공유되는 점이 많아진다는 겁니다. 그리고 생물학자와 컴퓨터과학자가 공동 연구를 통해서 생명나무라 불리는 것을 조합하는 경우도 분명 여기에 속합니다.

그렇다면 생명나무란 무엇일까요? 여러분은 가계도가 무엇인지는 알고 있죠? 이것은 과거 세대에 속한 자신의 조상을 자세하게 나타낼 수 있는 계보상의 수단입니다. 즉 자신의 친척이 누구인지, 그들의 자녀가 누구인지 등을 나타냅니다. 좋아요. 생명나무도 이런 것입니다만, 그 규모는 더 커서 종 사이의 수준을 표시한 것입니다. 실제적으로, 이 프로젝트의 목적은 지구상에 알려진 170만 종에 대한 가계도를 만드는 것입니다!

이는 거대한 프로젝트입니다. 그래서 생물학자들은 나무를 완성하는 데 필요한 자료를 입력하기 위해 자신이 가진 전문적 지식을 제공할 필요가 있고, 컴퓨터과학자들은 이것이 실질적으로 현실로 이루어질 수 있도록 기계와 소프트웨어를 구축하고 향상시킬 필요가 있습니다. 그래서 프로젝트를 끝낸 후에 우리가 얻게 되는 것은 생명체가 이 지구상에서 어떻게 진화했고 어떻게 계속 진화해갈 것인지에 대한 훨씬 분명한 그림입니다. 그러고 나면 새로운 예언적, 진단적 능력과 처리능력이 부상하면서 우리 자신의 몸에 대한 전반적인 이해에 도움을 줄 것입니다.

1 강의의 주된 내용은 무엇인가?
(A) 전 세계적으로 과학자들의 계보의 역사
(B) 의학적 진단을 단순화하는 컴퓨터 프로그램
(C) 생물의 역사를 추적하는 야심찬 프로젝트
(D) 좀 더 컴퓨터 사용 기술을 배우려는 과학자들의 노력

해설 수행하고자 하는 프로젝트는 거대한 규모로 지구상에 알려진 170만 종에 대한 계보를 만드는 것이다.

2 교수는 어떤 방식으로 생명나무에 대한 이야기를 시작하는가?
(A) 학생들에게 하나의 모델을 보여줌으로써
(B) 가계도와 비교함으로써
(C) 게놈 지도와 대조시킴으로써
(D) 진화 과정을 묘사함으로써

해설 학생들이 익숙하게 알고 있는 가계도를 예로 들어 생명나무의 개념을 설명하고 있다.

3 교수는 어떤 방식으로 생명나무 프로젝트를 묘사하는가?
(A) 양측에 해당하는 프로젝트의 구체적 정의를 제공함으로써
(B) 양측 과학자들에게 부과되어야 하는 역할을 제안함으로써
(C) 성공에 필요한 요소를 나열함으로써
(D) 생물학자와 컴퓨터과학자의 역할을 분류함으로써

해설 프로젝트의 수행을 위해 생물학자가 할 일과 컴퓨터 과학자가 할 일을 구분해서 설명함으로써 프로젝트를 설명한다.

4 교수에 따르면, 이 프로젝트에서 컴퓨터과학자의 역할은 무엇인가?
(A) 컴퓨터를 통해 정보를 분배할 것이다.
(B) 필요한 기술을 만들 것이다.
(C) 생명나무의 결과를 해석할 것이다.
(D) 필요한 자료를 입력할 것이다.

해설 프로젝트에서 컴퓨터과학자가 해야 할 일은 생명나무를 완성하는 데 필요한 자료가 입력되도록 기계와 소프트웨어를 구축하고 향상시키는 것이다.

5 다음 중 프로젝트가 완성되었을 때 얻게 되는 혜택은 무엇인가? 정답 두 개를 고르시오.
(A) 생명 진화에 대한 보다 나은 지각
(B) 혹성에 대한 보다 나은 이해
(C) 우리의 몸에 대한 더욱 많은 지식
(D) 알려지지 않은 바이러스에 대한 보다 명확한 그림

해설 생명체가 이 지구상에서 어떻게 진화했고 어떻게 계속 진화해갈 것인지에 대해 보다 분명하게 파악할 수 있고, 이를 통해 우리 자신의 몸에 대해 전반적으로 이해할 수 있다.

Actual Test 2

1 (C)   2 (D)   3 (B)   4 (A)   5 (C)

영화학 수업의 토론을 들으시오.

🎧 스크립트

P In the late 1950s and early 1960s, a kind of revolution in the world of filmmaking occurred, called the French New Wave or La Nouvelle Vague.

S It doesn't seem like it was very influential... French films aren't very popular today.

P Well, actually, though this movement in many ways was really limited to art house film, a type of film that is intended to be a serious artistic work, rather than a piece of popular entertainment. Well, its influence can still be seen in film today, even in the most mainstream movies. This was both a stylistic and a plot oriented change. The New Wave directors were very unhappy with the formulaic, glossy Hollywood movies that had dominated cinema for the past few decades. What the New Wave directors really sought to get was getting their films recognized as an art... like painting or literature... so, they experimented a lot, stylistically with how things looked. In his film, "Breathless," Jean Luc Godard, for example, one of the directors of this movement, invented what's known as the "jump-cut"... in which the director would edit in either images seemingly unrelated to the scene, or just a sudden break in a continuous image, into the film. This visual disruption made the story edgier, tenser, more uptight as well as it reminded the viewer that they were watching a movie... Another stylistic innovation was the preference for natural light. Plot-wise, the stories were also more realistic. They tried to avoid happy endings of Hollywood movies, instead, they wanted something darker, negative, and more complex.

교수 1950년대 말과 1960년대 초, 영화 제작의 역사에 프랑스 뉴 웨이브 또는 누벨 바그로 불리는 일종의 혁명이 발생했습니다.
학생 그 운동이 그다지 영향력을 미쳤던 것 같지는 않습니다. 프랑스 영화는 요즘 그다지 인기가 없으니까요.
교수 사실상 이 운동이 많은 점에서, 인기 있는 오락물이라기보다는 진지한 예술작품이기를 의도했던 예술극장 영화에 한정되기는 했지만, 그 영향력은 오늘날 영화, 심지어 대부분의 주류영화에 여전히 남아 있습니다. 이는 양식상의 변화와 줄거리에 근거한 변화입니다. 뉴 웨이브 운동에 속한 감독들은, 지난 수 십 년간 영화를 지배해온 틀에 박히고 겉만 번지르르한 할리우드 영화를 매우 불만스러워 했습니다. 뉴 웨이브 운동의 감독들이 정말 추구하고 싶어했던 것은 자신들이 만든 영화가 그림이나 문학작품처럼 하나의 예술로 인정받는 것이었습니다. 그래서 그들은 사물이 어떻게 보이는지에 대해 형식상으로 많은 실험을 했습니다. 예를 들어 이 운동에 속한 감독의 한 사람인 장 뤽 고다르는 자신의 영화 '브레스리스(네 멋대로 해라)'에서 '점프컷(연속성이 없어지도록 하는 필름 절단법)'을 고안해냈습니다. 이 방법을 통해 감독은 겉보기에는 영화 장면과 관련이 없는 영상이나 계속 이어지는 영상에 갑작스런 단절을 영화 속에 편집합니다. 이와 같은 시각적인 붕괴를 통해 관객에게 자신이 영화를 보고 있다는 사실을 상기시켜줄 뿐만 아니라 줄거리를 더욱 예리하고, 긴장 넘치고, 긴박하게 만들었습니다. 형식상의 또 다른 진보는 자연광을 선호하는 것입니다. 줄거리에 관해 말하자면, 이야기 또한 더욱 현실적이었습니다. 할리우드 영화의 해피 엔딩을 피하려 노력하면서, 더욱 어둡고, 더욱 부정적이고, 더욱 복잡한 결말을 원했습니다.

1 토론의 주된 내용은 무엇인가?
(A) 예술 극장 영화의 정의와 예
(B) 할리우드에서 성공한 프랑스 감독들
(C) 새로운 종류의 영화 제작의 특징
(D) 1950년대 말과 1960년 대 초의 프랑스 영화 역사

2 교수는 뉴 웨이브 운동의 영향력에 대해 무엇이라 말하는가?
(A) 사람들이 영화를 즐기는 방법에 지대한 영향을 미친다.
(B) 영화 평론가들만이 뉴 웨이브 영화에 대해 관심을 기울인다.
(C) 현대 예술 극장 영화가 인기를 끄는 데 역할을 담당했다.
(D) 뉴 웨이브 운동의 효과를 현대 영화에서 볼 수 있다.

해설 프랑스 뉴 웨이브 또는 누벨 바그로 불리는 운동의 영향력은 오늘날 대부분의 주류 영화에 남아 있다.

3 교수는 어떤 구성으로 뉴 웨이브 운동에 대해 설명하는가?
(A) 혁명의 과정을 묘사함으로써
(B) 변화를 두 가지 요소로 분류함으로써
(C) 미국 배우와 프랑스 배우를 비교함으로써
(D) 운동의 주요 특징을 나타내기 위해 '브레스리스'를 사용함으로써

해설 형식상의 변화와 줄거리에 근거한 변화로 분류함으로써 뉴 웨이브 운동에 대해 설명한다.

4 교수가 장 뤽 고다르를 언급한 이유는 무엇인가?
(A) 뉴 웨이브 운동으로 대표되는 형식상의 혁신을 보여주려고
(B) 그의 작품과 기타 뉴 웨이브 운동 감독들의 작품을 대조시키려고
(C) 그의 촬영술이 할리우드에 영향을 미쳤다는 사실을 암시하려고
(D) 그가 운동을 주도했던 가장 잘 알려진 뉴 웨이브 감독이라는 사실을 암시하려고

해설 뉴 웨이브 운동의 특징인 형식상의 혁신을 보여주기 위해서, 점프컷을 고안해서 작품 활동을 한 장 뤽 고다르에 대해 언급했다.

5 교수에 따르면, 뉴 웨이브 운동의 영화 줄거리는 어떻게 다른가?
(A) 전위적인 영화를 위한 자연주의 연기 기술을 기피했다.
(B) 등장인물이 가진 모든 문제점의 해결을 거부했다.
(C) 대개 긍정적으로 이해되지도, 쉽게 이해되지도 않았다.
(D) 그들은 관객이 영화 기술을 이해해주길 기대했다.

해설 더욱 현실적이면서, 더욱 어둡고, 더욱 부정적이고, 더욱 복잡한 결말을 맺었다.

Dictation

Practice 1

① is fostered by the free market
② look at the flip-side
③ interfere with unfettered competition
④ would be prevented from getting decent jobs
⑤ prejudice or bias based on
⑥ can't even get in the pool of good jobs
⑦ you're kind of stuck
⑧ can't just quit and get

Practice 2

① figure out ways
② there are treaties and laws
③ tend to be imposed top-down
④ not always seen as legitimate or lawful
⑤ competing needs are assessed and dealt through
⑥ their livelihood or way of life is threatened
⑦ someone got a better deal
⑧ violent conflict most often arises

Practice 3

① is way too noisy
② don't blame them for having fun
③ that's pretty annoying
④ is closing in
⑤ Why does ours close
⑥ to keep it open around the clock
⑦ start a petition
⑧ and then submit it
⑨ made an issue of it
⑩ It won't help me

Practice 4

① you would burn if
② required to keep your body functioning
③ it is synonymous with
④ are typically taken in
⑤ 12 hours of fasting
⑥ the digestive system is inactive
⑦ under less restricted conditions
⑧ in the test facility prior to testing
⑨ need to eat less

Actual Test 1

① continues to move forward
② between two different academic disciplines
③ work together to help assemble
④ enables you to map out
⑤ to see who you're related to
⑥ enter the data needed
⑦ keep building on, and improving
⑧ a much clearer picture of
⑨ how life evolved
⑩ giving rise to

Actual Test 2

① limited to art house film
② is intended to be a serious artistic work
③ both a stylistic and a plot oriented change
④ sought to get
⑤ recognized as an art
⑥ edit in either images
⑦ unrelated to the scene
⑧ a sudden break in a continuous image
⑨ were also more realistic
⑩ something darker, negative

Vocabulary Review

1 10년간
2 현격한
3 진척시키다, 전송하다
4 명분
5 기자회견
6 확신시키다
7 미로
8 순례자
9 (위해 등을)가져오다 (원수를) 갚다
10 설치류의 동물
11 생계
12 생태학적
13 불법화하다
14 비평하다
15 편견
16 전술
17 공정한
18 합의
19 진정서
20 인식
21 방해하다
22 석방하다
23 편견
24 부정하다, ~와 모순되다
26 협력하다
25 민족
27 조약, 협정
28 합법의
29 신진대사의
30 소비(량)
31 소화의, 소화를 돕는
32 활동하지 않은
33 동의어의, 유사어의
34 보충하다
35 반드시 ~하다
36 어떠한 생각이 떠오르다
37 24시간 계속하여

38 ~의 [수량]을 줄이다	39 ~ 이전에
40 완수했을 때	41 …에 지나지 않는
42 stand for	43 a family tree
44 represent	45 A rather than B
46 seek to	47 restrict
48 in terms of	49 look at the flip-side
50 expertise	

PROGRESS TEST

Progress Test 3

1 (C) 2 (B) 3 (D) 4 (A) 5 (B) 6 (D)

서구문명 수업에서의 시간 표준화에 대한 토론을 듣고, 물음에 답하시오.

🎧 스크립트

P Now, we take the existence of standardized time for granted today… We know that if, say, we were in New York and wanted to call California, it'd be only three hours earlier… not two hours later, or four hours and ten minutes earlier or whatever… But this is actually a fairly recent occurrence. Anybody know what brought it about?

S Was it business? I know that time is really linked to efficiency, so maybe factories or something like that wanted to standardize time as they spread out over the country?

P Not a bad answer, but actually, it was the British railroad that really made standardized time come into being. Until this point, different localities measured their time based on where the sun was in the sky, like man has been doing ever since we've been breaking our day down into these minutes and hours.
The town's main clock would be set according to the sun, and then people would set their own clocks and watches to that. And so everybody was more or less on the same schedule within one town, but it wasn't standard in a region or anything. And it wasn't exactly precise. And so it could be five o'clock in one town, five thirty in another, and four forty-five in another. In those days, such disparities or noticeable differences didn't really bother people much. But the railroad ran on a schedule, and so it was important that each town, each stop along the railroad, had the same time. So, by 1855 most public clocks in Britain were set to the time in London,

which was Greenwich Mean Time or GMT, still the standard we use today when referring to world time schedules.

교수 자, 오늘날 우리는 표준화된 시간의 존재를 너무나 당연하게 받아들이고 있습니다. 예를 들어 우리가 뉴욕에서 캘리포니아에 전화를 걸고 싶다면, 시간은 3시간이 이를 겁니다. 두 시간이 늦은 것도 아니고, 4시간 10분이 이른 것도 아니고 말입니다. 하지만 시간의 표준화는 사실상 매우 최근에 이루어졌습니다. 시간이 어떻게 표준화 되었는지 아는 사람 있나요?

학생 사업 때문이었습니까? 제가 알기로 시간이 효율성과 밀접하게 관련을 맺고 있습니다. 그러니까 아마도 공장이나 그와 유사한 곳이 전 지역으로 확장되면서 시간을 표준화하고 싶었던 것이 아닐까요?

교수 괜찮은 답변이었습니다만, 사실 표준화된 시간을 탄생시킨 것은 바로 영국 철도였습니다. 이때까지 각 지역은 태양이 하늘에 떠 있는 위치에 근거해서 각자 시간을 측정했습니다. 우리가 하루를 분과 시간으로 쪼갠 이래로 사람들이 해오고 있는 방법처럼 말입니다.
마을의 중심 시계를 태양의 위치에 따라 맞추면, 사람들은 그 시계에 따라 자신의 시계와 손목시계를 맞췄습니다. 그래서 한 마을 안에서는 모든 사람들이 어느 정도 같은 시간에 따를 수 있었습니다. 그러나 그것은 지역의 표준이 아니었고, 완전히 정확하지도 않았습니다. 그래서 한 마을에서는 5시인데, 다른 마을에서는 5시 30분, 또 다른 마을에서는 4시 45분이 될 수 있었습니다. 당시 사람들은 이런 불일치나 눈에 띄는 차이점에 그다지 구애 받지 않았습니다. 그러나 철도는 계획대로 운행되었기 때문에 철도가 지나가는 각 마을과 각 정거장의 시간을 일치시키는 것이 중요했습니다. 그래서 1855년까지 영국에 있는 대부분의 공공 시계를 런던 시간, 그러니까 그리니치 표준시간 또는 GMT에 맞췄습니다. 그리고 이 시간이 현재 우리가 세계 시간으로 사용하는 표준시간입니다.

1 토의의 주된 내용은 무엇인가?
(A) 시계와 손목시계의 역사
(B) 철도산업에서의 일정표의 역할
(C) 표준시간의 존재 이유
(D) 그리니치 표준시간의 문제점

해설 본문은 편의를 위해 표준화한 시간에 대해 이야기한다.

2 교수가 뉴욕을 거론한 이유는 무엇인가?
(A) 표준시간을 사용한 최초의 장소라는 사실을 설명하려고
(B) 표준시간이란 용어의 의미를 실증하려고
(C) 이 지역은 표준시간을 사용하지 않는다는 사실을 암시하려고
(D) 뉴욕 사람들은 표준시간과 지역시간을 모두 사용한다는 사실을 나타내려고

해설 표준시간이 무엇인지 설명하기 위해 뉴욕과 캘리포니아의 시간 차를 예로 들었다.

3 교수는 어떤 방식으로 표준시간의 제정에 대해 설명하는가?
(A) 영국의 첫 시계에 대한 배경정보를 제시함으로써
(B) 역사적으로 시간을 맞추던 여러 방법을 설명함으로써
(C) 공장이 시간을 맞췄던 과정을 묘사함으로써
(D) 역사상 지역시간이 맞춰졌던 방식과 표준시간을 대조함으로써

해설 지역시간과 표준시간을 대조해서 설명하고 철도의 원활한 운행을 위해 시간의 표준화가 필요했다고 설명했다.

4 교수에 따르면, 지역시간의 한 가지 문제점은 무엇인가?
(A) 일정하지 않게 변경될 가능성이 많았다.
(B) 철도가 항상 지연 운행되었다.
(C) 태양은 다른 장소에서 다르게 보였다.
(D) 공장에서 일정표를 짤 수가 없었다.

해설 해당 지역의 표준시간도 아니었고, 완전히 정확한 것도 아니었다.

5 교수에 따르면, 표준시간이 제정된 이유는 무엇인가?
(A) 철도산업계에서는 그것이 좀 더 효과적이 될 것이라 생각했다.
(B) 기차를 타려면 믿을 수 있는 시간표가 있어야 했다.
(C) 공장은 더 많은 생산성을 확보하고 싶었다.
(D) 사람들은 일관성이 부족해서 불편을 겪었다.

해설 표준화된 시간을 탄생시킨 것은 바로 영국 철도로, 열차는 계획대로 운행되었기 때문에 철도가 지나가는 각 마을과 각 정거장의 시간을 같게 만드는 것이 중요했다.

6 교수가 런던을 언급한 이유는 무엇인가?
(A) 표준시간이 아무렇게나 결정되었다는 점을 암시하려고
(B) 영국 철도산업의 중심지였다는 점을 나타내려고
(C) 표준시계의 사용을 꺼려하던 장소라는 점을 나타내려고
(D) 그 지역의 시간이 표준시간으로 사용되었다는 점을 나타내려고

해설 런던 시간이 현재 우리가 세계 시간으로 사용하는 표준시간이다.

Progress Test 4

1 (D)   2 (C)   3 (B)   4 Y, Y, Y, N, N   5 (B)   6 (B)

학교 숙소에 대한 대화를 듣고, 물음에 답하시오.

🎧 스크립트

S1 Hey, John... Where are you going to live next year? Are you staying on campus or getting an apartment off campus?

S2 I'm definitely staying on... it's a lot cheaper for me to live in campus housing than to try and find a place to rent. I really want to get into the new junior and senior apartments on campus. They're really nice, and are much quieter and cleaner than my dorm is now.

S1 Well, I was gonna tell you to apply to live in my house, if you want... It's on-campus housing, but only ten of us live there. We're all pretty studious and neat... And some of the people are graduating this semester and moving out, so...

S2 Oh, thanks, but I really want to try to get into that new apartment, first...

S1 Yeah, they are nice. A friend of mine lived there this year. But it's pretty tough to get a spot, isn't it?

S2 Well, since it is very competitive, they give you a number. If you draw a low number, you are pretty well assured of getting an apartment. But the higher it is, the more likely you won't get a place... I draw my number tomorrow.

S1 Well, do you have a plan B?

S2 What do you mean?

S1 I mean, what if you get a high number? What will you do then?

S2 Well, I'll keep my name on the waiting list and hope that someone backs out at the last minute, so I can move in!

S1 Still, there's not a great chance that'll happen...

S2 I'll sign up for your house if the apartment doesn't come through. Thanks so much for the information!

학생1 안녕, John. 내년에는 어디서 살 거니? 교내에서 지낼 거니, 아니면 학교 밖에 아파트를 구할 거니?

학생2 물론 교내에서 지내야지. 밖에서 세 들어 생활하는 것보다 학교 숙소에서 생활하는 것이 훨씬 더 싸거든. 교내에 새로 지어진 3, 4 학년용 아파트에 들어가고 싶어. 그곳은 지금 내 기숙사보다 훨씬 시설이 좋은데다 조용하고 깨끗하거든.

학생1 음, 네가 원한다면 내가 지금 살고 있는 집에 지원하라고 말하려 했어. 학교 숙소이긴 하지만 겨우 10명만 살고 있거든. 우리 모두 열심히 공부하고 환경도 깨끗해. 그런데 그 중 몇 명은 이번 학기에 졸업을 해서 이사를 가거든. 그래서...

학생2 고마워, 하지만 나는 새 아파트에 정말 들어가고 싶어. 우선...

학생1 맞아, 그곳이 좋긴 하지. 내 친구 하나가 올해 그곳에 살았거든. 하지만 방을 구하기가 정말 어려워, 그렇지 않니?

학생2 경쟁이 아주 심해서 번호를 주더라. 낮은 숫자를 뽑으면 확실히 아파트를 얻을 수 있대. 하지만 숫자가 높을수록 아파트를 얻지 못할 가능성이 커. 내일 숫자를 뽑으려고.

학생1 다른 계획은 가지고 있니?

학생2 무슨 뜻이야?

학생1 그러니까... 높은 숫자를 뽑으면 어떡해? 그러면 어떻게 할 거니?

학생2 글쎄, 대기자 명단에 이름을 올려놓고 누군가가 마지막 순간에 포기해서 내가 들어갈 수 있기를 바라야지!

학생1 하지만 그렇게 될 가능성은 적어.

학생2 만약 아파트를 구할 수 없다면, 네가 살고 있는 집을 신청할게. 정보를 줘서 정말 고마워!

1 여자가 남자를 보러 간 이유는 무엇인가?
  (A) 서로 다른 교내 기숙사를 비교하려고
  (B) 새 아파트에 대해 물어보려고
  (C) 숙소에 관련된 몇 가지 선택사항에 대해 의논하려고
  (D) 자신이 살고 있는 집에 여럿이 함께 살자고 얘기하려고

해설 자신이 살고 있는 집에서 몇 명이 나갈 예정이므로 신청하라고 말해주러 갔다.

2 남자는 내년에 어디에서 살고 싶어 하는가?
  (A) 학교 밖에 아파트를 얻고 싶어 한다.
  (B) 교내에 있는 기숙사에서 살고 싶어 한다.
  (C) 교내 아파트에 들어가고 싶어 한다.
  (D) 여자가 사는 집에 들어가고 싶어 한다.

해설 교내에 새로 지어진 3, 4 학년용 아파트에 들어가고 싶어한다.

3 여자의 말에 따르면, 남자가 그녀가 사는 기숙사를 선택하는 것이 좋은 이유는 무엇인가?
  (A) 교내 아파트보다 훨씬 싸다.
  (B) 남자가 원하는 주거 환경을 갖고 있다.
  (C) 수업에 출석하기가 아파트보다 더 가깝다.
  (D) 새 친구를 사귈 기회를 준다.

해설 남자는 생활비가 싸고, 조용하고, 시설이 좋은 곳을 원한다.

4 남학생이 집을 구하는 과정의 단계를 나타내는 구절에 Yes 또는 No에 체크하시오.

	Yes	No
이름을 명단에 올려놓고 누군가가 포기하기를 기다린다	✓	
추첨에 참가한다.	✓	
여자가 살고 있는 교내 주택을 신청한다.	✓	
강의실에 가까운 기숙사를 신청한다.		✓
아파트를 구하는 광고를 낸다		✓

해설 강의실에서 가까운 기숙사를 신청하는 것은 본문에 언급되어 있지 않다.

5 3, 4 학년 아파트에 대해 여자는 무엇이라 말하는가?
  (A) 남자가 말하는 특징에 반대 의견을 갖고 있다.
  (B) 남자의 의견에 동의한다.
  (C) 남자가 그곳을 자세히 보지 않았다는 점을 지적한다.
  (D) 학교 밖 아파트에 비해 비용이 더 비싸다는 점을 암시한다.

해설 자신의 경험으로 새 아파트가 좋기는 하지만 구하기가 정말 어렵다고 말한다.

6 여자가 '다른 계획'을 언급한 이유는 무엇인가?
   (A) 남자가 아파트를 얻게 되리라 생각한다는 점을 나타내려고
   (B) 아파트를 얻는 것이 보장되지는 않는다는 사실을 남자에게 상기시키려고
   (C) 아파트에 대해서는 잊고 자신이 사는 집으로 들어오라고 설득하기 위해서
   (D) 남자가 추첨에서 낮은 번호를 선택하리라 믿고 있다는 점을 암시하려고

해설 아파트에 들어갈 수 있는 확률이 낮기 때문에, 들어가지 못했을 경우를 대비해 다른 계획을 세워놓았는지 묻는다.

4. a 그녀는 그에게 자신을 계속 괴롭힌다면 경찰에게 전화하겠다고 협박했다.

Progress Test 4

1. b 회사의 승인 하에 사업주는 체인점을 매매하거나 일정 기간 동안 임대할 수 있습니다.
2. b 이 지역에서 가장 인기 있는 관광지는 어디입니까?
3. d 저녁 식사 자리를 확보하려면 5시 전에 예약을 완료해 주십시오.
4. b 구직 시장에서의 경쟁이 점점 치열해짐에 따라, 교육과 훈련이 점점 중요시되고 있다.

Dictation

Progress Test 3

① for granted
② it'd be only
③ a fairly recent occurrence
④ linked to efficiency
⑤ as they spread out
⑥ standardized time come into being
⑦ we've been breaking our day down
⑧ it wasn't standard in a region
⑨ ran on a schedule
⑩ each stop along the railroad

Progress Test 4

① Are you staying on campus
② it's a lot cheaper for me
③ much quieter and cleaner than
④ We're all pretty studious and neat
⑤ pretty tough to get a spot
⑥ draw a low number
⑦ someone backs out
⑧ doesn't come through

Vocabulary Review   for Progress Test

Progress Test 3

1. c 그녀의 설명이 상당히 그럴듯하게 들려서, 어느 누구도 그녀의 주장에 대해 반대하지 않았다.
2. a 내 목표는 인간 중심의 기술에 혁격한 변화를 가져오는 것이다.
3. c 재단사는 옷을 짓기 전에 정확한 치수를 재야한다.

CHAPTER 05
INFERENCE/STANCE

Pre Test 1

도서관에서의 대화를 듣고, 물음에 답하시오.

🎧 스크립트

S   I wanted to pick up a book I had recalled. The library sent me a notice that it was in.
L   Sure. What's your last name?
S   Jones. Also, could you check and see if an interlibrary loan book has come in for me, too? I ordered it almost two weeks ago.
L   Two weeks, huh? That's usually enough time to get interlibrary loans. Hold on... Okay, here's your recalled book. You can keep this out for three weeks. But I didn't see your loan book... If you wait I can look it up on the computer.
S   Don't worry about it, but it would be nice if I could find out when to expect it in my email.
L   I've got it.

학생   제가 회수 신청했던 책을 가지러 왔는데요. 책이 들어왔다고 도서관에서 통지서가 왔습니다.
사서   알겠어요. 성이 무엇이죠?
학생   Jones입니다. 그리고 도서관 상호대차 도서가 들어왔는지도 확인해주시겠어요? 거의 2주일 전에 주문했는데요.
사서   2주일 되었다고요? 대개는 충분한 시간인데. 기다리세요. 여기 회수 신청한 책이 있어요. 3주일간 대출할 수 있어요. 하지만 대차 도서는 보이지 않네요... 기다리신다면 제가 컴퓨터로 조회해볼게요.
학생   괜찮습니다. 대신 이메일로 언제 받아볼 수 있을지 알려주시면 좋겠어요.
사서   알겠어요.

도서관 상호대차 도서에 대해 추론할 수 있는 점은 무엇인가?
(A) 실수로 신청이 이루어지지 않았다.
(B) 당장 필요한 것은 아니다.
(C) 책 이름이 컴퓨터에 기록되어 있지 않다.
(D) 수업시간에 사용될 것이다.

정답 (B)

해설   학생은 컴퓨터 조회 결과를 이메일로 받아보고 싶다고 말한다.

Pre Test 2

학생 회관에서의 대화를 듣고, 물음에 답하시오.

🎧 스크립트

S1   Wow! There are so many people in here today...
S2   I know... I wish they would expand the student center. It's always too crowded! Our fees pay for it, but we can't even sit down!
S1   Maybe we should just go to the library.
S2   But we really can't talk in the library, and we need to discuss our project.
S1   That's true... I'm going to suggest to the library director that they open up a room especially for students working on projects. It'll be less noisy than the student center, but we won't disturb the other students in the library.
S2   That's a good idea... not that it'll help us now... I guess we just have to sit here though and try to concentrate despite the noise.
S1   You know what, though? I think they might have some other options for us. How many students do you think there are like us?
S2   Maybe you've got a point.

학생1   와! 오늘 여기 정말 사람 많다.
학생2   그러게 말이야. 학교에서 학생 회관을 넓혀줬으면 좋겠어. 항상 너무 붐비잖아! 학비를 내서 비용을 대고 있는데 심지어 앉지조차 못하니 말이야!
학생1   아마도 그냥 도서관에 가야 할까 봐.
학생2   하지만 도서관에서는 이야기를 할 수가 없어. 우리는 프로젝트에 대해 이야기를 나눠야 하잖아.
학생1   그건 그렇지... 프로젝트를 수행하는 학생들을 위해서 특별히 방을 하나 마련해달라고 도서관장에게 요청할 생각이야. 그렇게 되면 학생 회관보다 조용하면서도, 도서관에 있는 다른 학생들에게도 방해가 되지 않을 거야.
학생2   좋은 생각이야. 당장은 도움이 되지 않겠지만 말이야. 시끄럽기는 하지만 그냥 여기 앉아 집중을 해 보자.
학생1   이건 어때? 도서관 측에서 우리들을 위해 달리 해줄 수 있는 방법이 있을지도 몰라. 우리 같은 학생들이 얼마나 될 거라고 생각하니?
학생2   네가 제대로 핵심을 짚은 것 같아.

남학생은 도서관에 가는 것에 대해 어떻게 느끼는가?
(A) 달리 선택할 수 있는 방법이 없다고 생각한다.
(B) 도서관 측이 문제점을 인식해야 한다고 생각한다.

(C) 도서관 측이 자신들에게 방을 마련해줄 수 있을지 확신하지 못한다.
(D) 도서관 측이 공간을 제공할 수 있다는 데 대해 긍정적이다.

정답 (D)

해설 남학생이 마지막 말을 들어보면 두 사람처럼 생각하는 사람이 많기 때문에 도서관 측에서 달리 방법을 강구해줄 지도 모른다고 생각함을 알 수 있다.

Vocabulary Preview for Mini-Exercise

Mini-Exercise 1

1-1. expel (내쫓다, 쫓아버리다)
  ✓ a. to drive out forcibly
  b. to reach the end of a fixed term

1-2. colony (식민지)
  a. an enclosed area in which residential units and other facilities are provided
  ✓ b. a territory governed by a distant country

1-3. dialect (사투리, 방언)
  a. an exchange of opinions in an effort to reach mutual understanding
  ✓ b. a variety of a language that is peculiar to a region, social class, or occupation

2-1. ratify (승인하다, 비준하다)
  a. to make something clear or easier to understand
  ✓ b. to make an agreement official

2-2. diverse (다양한, 다른 종류의)
  ✓ a. of various types or sorts
  b. existing everywhere or involving everyone

2-3. address (~에게 말을 걸다)
  ✓ a. to communicate with
  b. to declare something good or right

3-1. declaration (발표, 포고)
  ✓ a. an announcement that is often written and official
  b. to give official permission for something to happen

3-2. definitely (명확히, 확실히)
  ✓ a. without any doubt
  b. a description of the features and limits of something

3-3. analysis (분석, 해석)
  ✓ a. the process of considering something in detail
  b. the scientific study of the body and how its parts are arranged

Mini-Exercise 2

1-1. cultivate (경작하다, 재배하다)
  ✓ a. to prepare land and grow crops
  b. to cause something to start

1-2. barren (불모의, 열매를 맺지 못하는)
  a. producing abundant growth of farm crops
  ✓ b. unable to produce plants or fruit

1-3. accumulation (축적)
  ✓ a. increase in number or amount
  b. a place to live or to be stored in

2-1. produce (생산하다)
  ✓ a. to make something or bring something into existence
  b. to be passed along by inheritance

2-2. depict (그리다, 묘사하다)
  a. to show something and explain how it works
  ✓ b. to represent or show something in a picture or story

2-3. conservation (보존, 보호)
  ✓ a. to protect creatures and natural areas, from the damaging effects of human activity
  b. to keep someone in an enclosed place

3-1. assignment (과제, 숙제)
  a. a share or amount of something that is given to you
  ✓ b. a piece of work given to someone, typically as part of their studies or job

3-2. expand (확장(확대)하다, 넓히다)
  a. to gradually and imperceptibly weaken and destroy
  ✓ b. to increase in size, number or importance

3-3. cost (비용, 경비)
  ✓ a. the amount of money needed to buy something
  b. a collection or mass especially of something which cannot be counted

Mini-Exercise 1 Inference

1 아카디아인의 추방에 대한 강의를 듣고, 물음에 답하시오.

🎧 스크립트

P By the 18th century, the land that would become the United States <u>was primarily settled by</u> English and German speakers... How is it, then, that French speakers were living in Louisiana? Well, the Acadians, <u>as these folks are still called</u> today, were <u>expelled from</u> their homes in a region of eastern Canada known as Acadia... The English there felt that these French settlers <u>posed a threat to</u> English security and demanded they leave. Some <u>were removed to</u> New England, and some to the southern colonies of South Carolina or Georgia... Others, however, <u>made the long journey to</u> Louisiana. Today there are still residents who speak a French dialect called Cajun, and many aspects of Cajun culture, from food to music, reflect the French culture of Acadia.

교수 18세기까지는 미국이 될 영토에 정착하는 사람들은 주로 영어와 독일어를 모국어로 사용하는 사람들이었습니다. 그렇다면 프랑스 어를 사용하는 사람들이 어떻게 루이지애나에 살게 되었을까요? 지금도 여전히 같은 이름으로 불리는 아카디아인은 동부 캐나다의 아카디아라는 지역에 위치한 자신들의 고향에서 추방당했습니다. 영국인들은 이 프랑스 정착민이 자신들의 안전을 위협하는 존재라고 느꼈기 때문에 그곳에 살던 그들에게 떠나라고 명령했습니다. 그 중에는 뉴 잉글랜드로 추방된 사람도 있었고, 남부 캐롤라이나나 조지아의 남부 식민지로 추방된 사람도 있었습니다. 그러나 어떤 사람들은 루이지애나까지 먼 여행을 했습니다. 오늘날에도 여전히 케이준이라는 프랑스 사투리를 말하는 거주민이 있고, 음식에서 음악에 이르기까지 케이준 문화의 여러 면에서 아카디아의 프랑스 문화를 반영하고 있습니다.

1 캐나다에 거주하던 아카디아인에 대해 추론할 수 있는 것은 무엇인가?
(A) 자발적으로 캐나다를 떠나 남아메리카로 갔다.
(B) 캐나다의 영국인 정착민들과 잘 지내지 못했다.
(C) 프랑스 어를 말할 능력을 완전히 잃어버렸다.
(D) 이들은 부와 평화, 그리고 더 많은 자유를 찾아서 미국으로 갔다.

정답 (B)

해설 캐나다에 거주했던 아카디아인은 영국인들에 의해 강제로 추방되었지만, 자신의 언어와 문화를 현재까지 간직하고 있다.

2 다음 중 미국 내 프랑스 정착민에 대해 사실인 것은 무엇인가?
(A) 인구 수는 작지만 지리학상으로 다양한 지역 출신이다.
(B) 주로 영어를 사용하나 집에서는 여전히 아카디아 말을 쓴다.
(C) 이들의 독특한 문화는 미국의 특정 지역에서 발견된다.
(D) 미국 내 영국 거주자들과 심각한 갈등을 일으켰다.

정답 (C)

해설 미국에는 오늘날에도 여전히 프랑스 어가 남아 있고, 음식에서 음악에 이르기까지 프랑스 문화의 잔재가 남아있다.

2 Federalist Papers에 대한 이야기를 듣고, 물음에 답하시오.

🎧 스크립트

P Before the US Constitution <u>was approved and ratified</u> in 1787, there was great concern that the new nation of the time was <u>too big and too diverse to really function</u> under a single democratic rule... In other words... there were too many factions — organized groups of people within the nation. They opposed the ideas of the nation and <u>fought for their own ideas</u>, and... and... there would never be enough general agreement <u>to govern peaceably</u>. This sounds, uh, <u>really different from today</u>, doesn't it? (*sarcastically*) yeah right... Anyway, this problem of factions was the subject of Federalist No. 10. This essay was written by James Madison as a series of the Federalist Papers... What are these papers?

S A series of arguments for the ratification of the United States Constitution.

P Right, Madison made the case that ultimately a republican democracy was <u>ideal for addressing the problem of factionalism</u>. Why? Any ideas?

교수 1787년 미국 헌법이 승인 받고 인준되기 전에는, 당시의 새 국가가 지나치게 비대하고 다양해서 하나의 민주 통치 아래서는 기능할 수 없다고 크게 우려하는 목소리가 있었습니다. 다시 말해서... 국가 안에 사람들의 조직인 파벌이 너무 많다는 것이었죠. 그들은 국가의 의견에 반대하면서, 자신들의 의견을 관철시키기 위해 싸웠습니다. 그리고, 에... 평화로운 통치가 이루어질 수 있을 만큼 전반적인 동의가 성립될 수 없을 것 같습니다. 이는 오늘날과는 정말 상황이 다르지 않습니까? (빈정대듯이) 그렇습니다... 어쨌거나 파벌로 인한 문제는 《Federalist Papers》 중 열 번째 논평의 주제였습니다. 이 글은 《Federalist Papers》의 시리즈로서 James Madison이 작성했습니다. 이 논평이 무엇일까요?

학생 미국 헌법의 인준을 위한 일련의 논평 시리즈입니다.

교수 그렇습니다. Madison은 파벌의 문제를 해결하는 데는 궁극적으로 공화제 민주주의가 이상적이라고 주장했습니다. 이유가 무엇일까요? 아는 사람 있나요?

1 교수가 다음과 같이 말한 것은 무슨 의미인가?

P This sounds, uh, really different from today, doesn't it... (*sarcastically*) yeah right...

(A) 현대 정부와 매우 다르다는 점에 동의한다.
(B) 그것이 권리장전 성립의 동기가 되었다고 생각한다.
(C) 오늘날에도 (과거와 비교할 때) 많이 달라지지 않았다는 것을 암시한다.
(D) 1787년보다 현재가 훨씬 심각하다고 생각한다.

정답 (C)

해설 당시 상황이 현재 상황과 다르다는 점을 인정하는 속뜻은 당시 국가의 이상에 대한 전반적인 동의가 부족했기 때문에 평화로운 통치가 이루어지기 힘들다는 것이었다.

2 다음 중 미국 헌법 인준 당시의 우려사항은 무엇인가? 정답 두 개를 고르시오.

(A) 일부 주에서 미국 헌법에 반대했다.
(B) 다수의 다른 그룹 사람들은 매우 다른 견해를 가졌다.
(C) 국가가 너무 넓어서 한 가지 보편적인 규칙으로는 통제할 수 없었다.
(D) Federalist Papers 시리즈가 제대로 완성되지 않았다.

정답 (B), (C)

해설 새 국가의 규모가 커서 민주적인 규칙을 가지고 통제할 수 없으리라는 점과 국가 안에 다른 견해를 가진 파벌이 많아서 평화로운 통치를 위한 전반적인 동의를 이끌어내기 힘들다는 점이었다.

3 두 학생 사이의 대화를 듣고, 물음에 답하시오.

🎧 스크립트

S1 <u>We're supposed to submit</u> our major declaration forms tomorrow... but I'm still not really sure <u>what I ought to choose.</u>
S2 Really? I thought you were definitely going to do premed. What happened?
S1 Yeah, that's what my parents want, but <u>the more classes I take</u>, the more I realize I'm not very interested in medicine. I don't think <u>I can see myself going on to medical school</u>. What I'm really interested in is history. But I'm not sure that's a very practical subject.
S2 I think it could be okay... You could go on to teach or to do some type of job <u>that involves writing and analysis</u>... You really have to be sure what you can do later... But there are plenty of options. It's your choice after all but then again, it could be one of the most important matters to your parents, too. I mean, <u>you should talk it over</u> before you make any decisions, tell them what you really want to study... I'm sure they would understand.
S1 Thank you so much for your kind advice.

학생1 내일 전공선택 신청서를 제출해야 하는데 아직 무엇을 선택해야 할지 확신이 서질 않아.
학생2 정말? 나는 네가 분명 의예과에 갈 거라고 생각했는걸. 무슨 일이야?
학생1 응, 그건 부모님이 원하는 거야. 하지만 수업을 들을수록 내가 의학에 관심이 별로 없다는 생각을 하게 됐어. 의과대학에 진학하는 내 모습을 그려볼 수가 없어. 내가 정말 관심을 가지고 있는 분야는 역사야. 하지만 그것이 실용적인 과목인지 확신이 서질 않아.
학생2 괜찮을 거라고 생각해. 학생들을 가르칠 수도 있고 집필이나 분석에 종사하는 직업을 가질 수도 있어. 네가 나중에 무엇을 할 수 있을지에 대해 정말 확신이 서야만 해. 하지만 선택사항은 많아. 결국 이건 네 선택에 달린 문제야. 하지만 그건 또 네 부모님에게도 가장 중요한 문제 가운데 하나일 수 있어. 내 말은, 네가 어떤 결론을 내리기 전에 대화를 해서 네가 정말 공부하고 싶어하는 것을 말씀 드려야 한다는 거야. 부모님들도 분명 이해하실 거야.
학생1 친절하게 충고해주어서 정말 고맙다.

1 남자는 이후로 어떤 일을 할 것인가?

(A) 의예과 지도교수를 만나러 간다.
(B) 가족과 자신의 결정에 대해 의논한다.
(C) 전공을 결정한 후에 부모님에게 말한다.
(D) 전공 결정 기한을 연장한다.

정답 (B)

해설 여자는 남자에게 전공선택은 자신이 확신을 가지고 결정해야 하는 문제일 뿐만 아니라 부모님에게도 중요한 문제니까 일방적으로 결론을 내리기 전에 부모님께 자신이 하고 싶은 일에 대해 말씀 드리라고 조언했다.

2 남자는 무엇을 하고 싶다고 말하는가?

(A) 의과대학에 들어가고 싶다.
(B) 역사를 전공하고 싶다.
(C) 소설가가 되고 싶다.
(D) 고등학교에서 역사를 가르치고 싶다.

정답 (B)

해설 부모님은 남자가 의과대학에 진학하기를 바라지만 그는 역사에 관심이 많다.

Mini-Exercise 2 Stance

1 생태학 수업의 강의를 듣고, 물음에 답하시오.

🎧 스크립트

P Humans have managed to cultivate some

of the most seemingly barren places on earth. This can be seen in the various industries that have sprung up around bogs... Now, what can you tell me about bogs?

S Well, areas of land which are very wet and muddy, so they're not good for building, and they're usually in colder climates, right? And, uh... they're really acidic as well, so not great for agriculture. Basically, pretty unforgiving places, you might say.

P Good, yeah. Plants do grow in bogs, but they have evolved to thrive in their highly acidic conditions. The acidity comes from the accumulation of peat, which is a dead plant material. However, blueberries, cranberries, and lingonberries all thrive in these conditions, and have been harvested in bogs for centuries, providing a steady source of income for farmers in bog areas. So despite the seeming uselessness of the land, it does actually produce.

교수 인간은 겉보기에 지구상에서 가장 황폐한 몇몇 지역을 개척해 왔습니다. 이런 현상은 늪지대 주변에서 발생했던 다양한 산업을 통해서도 확인할 수 있습니다. 늪지대에 대해 알고 있는 점을 말해보겠습니까?

학생 음, 매우 습하고 진흙투성이인 땅을 말합니다. 그래서 건물을 짓기에도 적당하지 않고 주로 좀 더 추운 기후에 존재하죠, 맞나요? 또, 음... 토양이 산성이라 농업에도 적절하지 않습니다. 기본적으로 용서 받지 못한 곳이라고나 할까요.

교수 좋아요. 그렇습니다. 늪지대에서도 식물이 자라기는 하지만 이런 식물은 산성이 높은 조건에서 성장 가능하도록 진화했습니다. 땅이 산성인 이유는 죽은 식물 물질인 토탄(土炭)이 축적되기 때문입니다. 그러나 블루베리, 크랜베리, 링건베리 등은 수 세기에 걸쳐 늪지대에서 수확하면서 늪지대 지역 농부들에게 꾸준한 수입원을 제공해왔습니다. 그래서 겉보기에는 쓸모 없는 것처럼 보이는 땅이라도 실질적으로는 생산을 하고 있습니다.

1 교수는 늪지대에 대해 어떻게 느끼는가?
(A) 늪지대에서 생산되는 제품에 대해 열광하고 있다.
(B) 몇 가지 면에 있어서 유용하다고 생각한다.
(C) 인식하지 못한 훌륭한 잠재력을 갖췄다고 느낀다.
(D) 농장을 경작하는 데 얼마나 많은 노동력이 필요할지에 대해 부정적이다.

정답 (B)

해설 늪지대가 지구상에서 가장 황폐한 지역처럼 보이기는 하지만 인간은 이런 늪지대를 개척하기 위해 노력하고 있고, 실질적으로 생산도 이루어지고 있다.

2 늪지대 식물이 부패하면 어떤 결과가 발생하는가?
(A) 축축하고 진흙투성이인 땅
(B) 경작하기에는 쓸모없는 땅
(C) 매우 산성인 지역
(D) 베리 종의 변화

정답 (C)

해설 늪지대 식물이 부패하면 토탄이 축적되어 땅이 산성으로 변한다.

2 미술사 수업 시간에 있었던 John James Audubon에 대한 토론을 듣고, 물음에 답하시오.

🎧 스크립트

P John James Audubon is best known for his series of 435 nature engravings, pictures that have been printed from a plate on which designs have been cut. They are called *The Birds of America* in which he depicted the birds of this continent in their natural habitat and wrote of their habits.

S1 But it's not like he wrote about birds that didn't even exist or were really separate species. I mean why is it so important?

S2 And I also read that he killed thousands of birds to study for his drawings while making this book, which seems pretty bad to me if we're supposed to admire him as a conservationist.

P Whoa! Hold on, hold on! Now, it's true that Audubon sometimes drew from life, but more often killed the birds, yes. And from today's perspective, that does seem pretty bad. But the art that he produced is still widely admired today, for its color and realistic depiction, not for its scientific value, though, as you mentioned.

교수 John James Audubon은 435종의 자연 판화로 구성된 시리즈로 유명합니다. 자연 판화는 도안이 새겨진 판자에서 인쇄한 그림입니다. 그것들은 "미국의 조류" 라고 일컬어지며 자연 서식지에 존재하는 미국 대륙의 새들을 묘사했고 그들의 습성에 대해 기술했습니다.

학생1 존재하지 않았거나 개별적인 종의 새들에 대해 쓴 것은 아니지 않나요? 제 말은 왜 그것이 그렇게 중요하죠?

학생2 게다가 그는 이 책을 만들면서 소묘를 그리기 위해 수천 마리의 새를 죽였다는 사실을 읽었습니다. 우리가 그를 자연보호론자로 존경하는 것에 비추어볼 때 그런 행위는 매우 나쁘다고 생각됩니다.

교수 아! 잠깐만, 잠깐만! Audubon이 때로 산 채로 그렸지만 맞아요, 이보다 더 자주 새를 죽였던 것도 사실입니다. 그리고 오늘날의 관점에서 본다면 이것은 매우 나쁜 일처럼 보입니다. 그러나 그가 만들어냈던 예술은 여러분이 언급했던 것처럼 과학적인 가치 때문이 아니라 그 색채와 사실적인 묘사로 인해서 오늘날에도 여전히 경탄을 받고 있는 것입니다.

1. Audubon에 대한 여자의 태도는 어떠한가?
   (A) 그의 결과물에 대해서는 감명을 받았지만 그 타당성에 대해서는 확신하지 않는다.
   (B) 그의 노력에 대해서는 냉담하지만 그럼에도 호기심은 가지고 있다.
   (C) 그가 예술 창작을 위해 사용했던 방법에 대해 비판적이다.
   (D) 사실주의가 결여되었기 때문에 그의 예술작품에 부정적이다.

   정답 (C)

   해설 Audubon이 책에 들어갈 소묘를 그리기 위해 수천 마리의 새를 죽였다는 사실을 언급하면서 그가 자연보호론자로 존경 받을 가치가 없다고 생각했다.

2. Audubon의 예술작품에 대해 무엇을 추론할 수 있는가?
   (A) 과학적인 목적을 위해 만든 것이 아니다.
   (B) 사용된 색깔은 오늘날의 기준으로 보면 구식이다.
   (C) 박제된 동물시체를 사용한 것이 최근에는 문제가 되고 있다.
   (D) 최근까지도 학계 외부에는 거의 알려지지 않았다.

   정답 (A)

   해설 Audubon의 예술작품이 평가를 받는 것은 과학적인 가치 때문이 아니라 그 색채와 사실적인 묘사 때문이다.

3. 과제물에 대한 두 학생의 대화를 듣고, 물음에 답하시오.
   🎧 스크립트

   S1 I don't really understand what I'm supposed to do for this assignment. How am I supposed to <u>draw up a business plan</u> when I don't even have a business?
   S2 Well, you don't have to have a real business... <u>just invent one</u> that you'd like to have and then create a plan for it.
   S1 Well, even so. Say I wanted to have a, uh, a cosmetics business. What do I do? What's the business plan <u>supposed to be</u>?
   S2 Oh, OK... it's really the information you'd need to supply to investors—people <u>who might put money into the business</u> to help you start it or expand it — so that they know that you have a plan to make money, sell things, deal with competition, control costs... those kinds of things. I'm sure you learned these... from your class.
   S1 I really need to have a business first.
   S2 Come on...

   학생1 이번 과제물은 무엇을 해야 하는지 정말 파악할 수가 없어. 사업체를 가지고 있지도 않는데 어떻게 사업계획서를 쓴단 말이야?
   학생2 글쎄, 사업체를 실제로 가지고 있을 필요는 없지. 그저 네가 해보고 싶은 사업을 하나 만들고, 그 사업을 수행하기 위한 계획을 짜도록 해.
   학생1 음, 그렇다 하더라도 말이야. 내가 어, 그러니까 화장품 사업을 하고 싶다고 치자. 다음엔 무엇을 해야지? 어떤 사업계획이 있을 수 있지?
   학생2 아, 좋아. 사업계획서는 네가 투자가에게 제공해야 하는 정보야. 네가 사업을 시작하거나 확장하는 데 도움이 되도록 사업에 돈을 투입할 사람들에게 말이야. 그래서 네가 수익을 내서 물건을 팔고, 경쟁을 물리쳐 비용을 통제할 수 있는 그런 계획을 가지고 있다고 그들에게 알리는 거야. 이런 점에 대해서는 틀림없이 수업 시간에 배웠으리라 생각해.
   학생1 하지만 우선 진짜 사업체를 가져야 한다니까.
   학생2 세상에, 맙소사 제발...

1. 남자가 다음과 같이 말한 의미는 무엇인가?

   S1 I really need to have a business first.

   (A) 자기의 사업을 시작하는 데 흥미를 갖고 있다.
   (B) 사업계획서가 무엇인지 이해한다고 확신하고 있다.
   (C) 자신이 계획서를 작성할 만한 충분한 지식을 가지고 있는지 확신이 서질 않는다.
   (D) 진짜 사업을 위한 계획서를 작성하고 싶어 한다.

   정답 (C)

   해설 남자는 사업체를 가진 것으로 가정만 한 상태에서 사업계획서를 쓸 수 있을지 자신이 없다.

2. 과제에 대한 남자의 처음 태도는 어떠한가?
   (A) 그 분야에서 경험이 없기 때문에 혼란스럽다.
   (B) 과제가 후에 자신에게 도움이 되리라는 사실을 알고 이를 받아들인다.
   (C) 기한이 곧 다가와서 우선 걱정하고 있다.
   (D) 지시사항이 애매하기 때문에 그는 부정적인 태도를 갖고 있다.

   정답 (A)

Vocabulary Preview   for Practice

Practice 1

1. boost ((사기 등을) 돋우다, 인상하다)
   ✓ a. to improve or increase something
   b. to grow or develop successfully

2. feature (특징, 특성)
   a. the parts, substances, etc. that something is made of
   ✓ b. a typical quality or an important part of something

Inference / Stance

3. promote (증진(촉진)하다)
   ✓ a. to encourage the popularity, sale, development or existence of something
   b. to improve an idea, method, system, etc. by making small changes

4. generate (발생시키다, 낳다)
   ✓ a. to cause something to exist
   b. to come into existence

Practice 2

1. explosion (폭발, 파열)
   ✓ a. when the number of something increases very quickly
   b. to search and discover

2. structure (구조, 구성)
   a. to build something or put together different parts to form something whole
   ✓ b. a thing consisting of a number of elements joined together in a certain way

3. perceive (인식하다, 지각하다)
   ✓ a. to see something or someone, or to become aware of something that is obvious
   b. to give shape to in the mind

4. imperceptible (감지할 수 없는, 눈에 보이지 않는)
   ✓ a. unable to be noticed or felt because of being very slight
   b. not capable of being appeased

Practice 3

1. traditional (전통의, 전설의)
   a. an accepted standard or a way of behaving or doing things that most people agree with
   ✓ b. following the customs or ways of behaving that have continued in a society for a long time

2. tension ((정신적) 긴장, 불안)
   ✓ a. feeling of nervousness before an important or difficult event
   b. eagerness to do something

3. direction (방향; 방침)
   ✓ a. the position towards which someone or something moves or faces
   b. a book which gives a list of names, addresses or other facts

4. burst (터지다, 폭발하다)
   ✓ a. to break open or apart suddenly, or to make something do this
   b. a period of sudden economic growth, especially one that results in a lot of money being made

Practice 4

1. cover letter (첨부 편지, 커버 레터)
   ✓ a. a letter or note which contains information about the thing it is sent with
   b. a letter intended to be read by a lot of people, not just the person it is addressed to

2. be supposed to (~하기로 되어 있다)
   a. to help someone emotionally or in a practical way
   ✓ b. to have a duty or a responsibility to

3. passionate (열렬한, 정열적인)
   ✓ a. having very strong feelings or emotions
   b. not acting to influence or change a situation

4. help out with (~에 대해 도움을 주다)
   a. unable to do anything to help yourself or anyone else
   ✓ b. to do a part of someone's work or give someone money

Vocabulary Preview   for Actual Test

Actual Test 1

1. **a** 그의 주요 수입원은 소를 사육하는 데서 비롯된다.
2. **b** 건축가들은 앞으로 일어날 지진의 강도에 대한 기존 가설에 대해 의문을 제기한다.
3. **b** 대부분의 해안이 핵폐기물로 인해 오염되었다.
4. **c** 교사로서 당신은 학습 성취도가 낮은 학생들의 필요에 부합하는 방법을 채택해야 한다.

Actual Test 2

1. **b** 문화관광부는 올해 민속 음악과 민속 악기의 보존을 위한 프로젝트를 착수할 예정이다.
2. **a** 우리 학교 학생들은 일본어, 중국어, 프랑스 어 중 하나를 선택해서 들을 수 있다.
3. **b** 75년의 역사를 가진 우리 대학은 그 규모를 확대하여 쇄도하는 외국 학생들을 수용하였다.
4. **d** 가격에는 여행비와 숙박비는 포함되어 있지만 식비는 별도이다.

Practice 1

1 (C) 2 (B) 3 (D)

여행과 관광 수업의 강의를 들으시오

🎧 스크립트

P In places where there is little material industry, many governments are turning toward tourism as a way of boosting the economy. Tourist industry accounts for more than... uh, ten percent of the world's economic output, which used to be around 1 or 2 percent in 1980s... Now traditional tourism often comes at the expense of local traditions and the surrounding environment... What happens is that, at the beginning, tourists are attracted by the features. I mean the natural features, the clean beaches, the wildlife, and even the customs and cultures of the places, right? And what happens next is that the industry will try to develop their natural features to bring more tourists. And then, these features get destroyed in the process of tourist development. Not just destruction of the economy, it would cause damage on our environment, too. There must be something done to stop this... right? Now, let's take a look at this new type of tourism called... umm, the ecotourism industry. Well, you can guess what it is from the name, right? Okay... What we've learned in the past two decades... is the idea that tourism should actually help preserve these features. This ecotourism is really about providing travel opportunities for people that allow them to experience, directly, the nature and culture of the place they're traveling to. Unlike traditional tourism, it doesn't need to have some westernized hotels on a beach somewhere, but meeting the people and seeing the land... The idea behind this is not only to generate wealth and preserve the natural resources of a place, but also to promote interactions among people of different cultures.

교수 물질 산업이 거의 존재하지 않는 지역에서는 경제를 부흥시키는 방법으로서 관광사업에 눈길을 돌리는 정부가 많이 있습니다. 관광산업은 1980년대에는 세계 경제 생산의 1~2%정도에 불과했지만 지금은 10% 이상을 차지하고 있습니다. 현재 전통적인 관광사업은 종종 지역 전통이나 주변 환경을 훼손하고 있습니다. 그러니까, 처음에 관광객들은 그 지역의 특징에 관심을 갖습니다. 즉 자연적인 특징, 깨끗한 해변, 야생동물, 심지어는 그곳의 관습과 문화에 말입니다. 그렇죠? 그 다음에 관광산업에서는 더 많은 관광객을 유치하기 위해 그 자연적 특성을 개발하려는 노력을 기울입니다. 그렇게 되면 관광 개발의 과정에서 이러한 자연적 특성이 파괴됩니다. 이는 단지 경제의 파괴에 그치지 않고 우리의 환경도 파괴하게 됩니다. 이를 멈추기 위해 조치를 취해야 하겠죠?

자, 이제 환경관광사업이라는 새로운 형태의 관광사업에 대해 살펴봅시다. 음, 이름만 들어도 무엇인지 알 수 있겠죠? 좋습니다. 우리가 과거 20년 동안 배운 교훈은 관광사업이 사실상 이런 특징을 보존해야 한다는 것입니다. 환경관광사업은 관광객들에게 그들이 여행하는 장소의 자연과 문화를 직접 경험할 수 있는 기회를 제공하는 겁니다. 전통적인 관광사업과는 달리, 환경관광사업은 해변에 서구화된 호텔을 지을 필요가 없습니다. 그저 사람들을 만나고 그 지역을 보는 것입니다. 이 (환경관광사업의) 저변에 깔린 생각은 단지 부를 창출하고 지역의 천연자원을 보존하는 데만 있는 것이 아니라 다른 문화에 속한 사람들 간의 상호교류를 촉진하는 데 있습니다.

---

1 전통적인 관광사업에 대한 교수의 태도는 무엇인가?
  (A) 비판을 받아서 화가 난다.
  (B) 후퇴하고 있어서 걱정스럽다.
  (C) 그 부정적인 영향을 걱정한다.
  (D) 성장이 더딘 것에 대해 비판적이다.

해설 교수는 전통적인 관광산업이 궁극적으로 관광지역의 특징을 파괴하고 환경을 파괴하게 된다고 주장한다.

2 관광사업의 규모에 대해 추론할 수 있는 점은 무엇인가?
  (A) 지금까지와 같은 비율로 꾸준히 증가할 것이다.
  (B) 다수의 국가가 관광사업에서 경제적 잠재력을 보았다.
  (C) 다른 산업에 비해 규모가 작은 것으로 간주되고 있다.
  (D) 세계의 경제적 생산이 관광사업에 크게 의존한다.

해설 많은 정부에서 경제부흥 방법으로 관광에 눈길을 돌리고 있다. 관광산업은 과거의 증가율보다 훨씬 높은 증가율로 성장하고 있다.

3 환경관광산업에 대해 추론할 수 있는 점은 무엇인가?
  (A) 전통적인 관광산업보다 비용이 훨씬 덜 든다.
  (B) 단지 전세계적으로 알려지지 않은 문화만을 소개할 것이다.
  (C) 편리하지 않다는 이유로 많은 관광객들이 선호하지 않는다.
  (D) 자연의 인위적인 발달이 필요하지 않다.

해설 환경관광산업은 관광지의 자연과 문화를 관광객이 직접 경험할 수 있게 하는 것으로 해변에 서구화된 호텔을 짓는 것과 같은 인위적 개발이 필요가 없다.

Practice 2

1 (B)　　2 (A)　　3 (B)

물리학 수업에서의 토론을 들으시오.

🎧 스크립트

P We've seen a real explosion of different ideas about the structure of the universe over the past century, as we discover more and more about how, really, um, complicated things are... much more than we thought. Alright, one of these ideas is that our physical universe, the one that we perceive, is really only part of the entire physical reality of, uh, existence. I mean there are many other universes and our universe is only a part of the entire universe... You know what I mean... that there are many different worlds out there that, even though they are imperceptible to us for now. This is the multiverse theory.

S But I thought that one of the main tenets of science was that we could observe and test that which we were making a claim for. If we can't perceive other aspects of the universe, is it really scientific to claim that they exist?

P You're not alone in asking that... If we can't perceive it, how can we know it's there? However, what complicates this then, is the discovery over the past few decades of stuff like dark matter... matter that we really can't perceive or measure, but in fact we know it exists only by inference. So, as I said, things are really very complicated.

교수　지난 세기 동안 우리는 우주 구조에 대한 서로 다른 견해가 급증하는 것을 목격해왔습니다. 우리가 생각했던 것보다 사물이 훨씬 더 복잡하다는 사실을 발견하게 되면서 말입니다. 무슨 뜻이냐 하면... 이렇게 말해보죠. 이들 견해 가운데 하나는 바로 우리가 지각하는 물질계가 존재의 전체 물질적 실체의 일부분에 지나지 않는다는 겁니다. 그러니까, 여러 개의 우주가 있고 우리가 아는 우주는 그렇게 볼 때 전체의 한 부분이라는 거죠. 이해되나요? 지구 밖에는 최소한 어느 정도는 우리가 감지할 수 없는 다른 세계가 많습니다. 지금 당장은 우리 눈에 보이지 않는다고 하더라도 말이죠. 이것이 바로 다중우주론입니다.

학생　하지만 과학의 주요 신조 중의 하나는 우리가 주장하는 것을 관찰하고 실험할 수 있다는 점이라고 생각합니다. 만약 우리가 우주의 다른 측면을 감지할 수 없다면 그것이 존재한다고 주장하는 것이 진정으로 과학적 태도라 할 수 있습니까?

교수　그렇게 묻는 사람은 학생만이 아닙니다. 우리가 감지할 수 없다면 어떻게 존재한다는 것을 알 수 있겠느냐는 것이죠. 그러나 이 문제를 복잡하게 만드는 것은 바로 우리가 감지할 수도 측정할 수도 없고 사실상 추론만으로 존재한다는 사실을 알고 있는 암흑 물질 등이 지난 수십 년 동안 발견되어왔다는 점입니다. 그래서 제가 말했던 것처럼 상황은 정말 매우 복잡합니다.

1 교수에 따르면, 우주 구조에 대해 추론할 수 있는 점은 무엇인가?

(A) 우리는 아직 우주의 구조에 대해 이해하지 못하고 있다.
(B) 지난 세기에 걸쳐 우주에 대한 연구가 많이 이루어지고 있다.
(C) 우주에 대한 과거 이론은 잘못된 이론으로 판명되고 있다.
(D) 현재 우주의 구조를 설명할 수 있는 이론은 소수에 불과하다.

해설　교수는 강의의 서두에서 지난 세기 동안 우주구조에 대한 서로 다른 견해들이 많았다고 지적한다.

2 다중우주론에 대한 학생의 태도는 무엇입니까?

(A) 그것에 대한 접근법에 회의적이다.
(B) 그것의 함축된 뜻을 혼동하고 있다.
(C) 그것의 불명확함에 대해 비판적이다.
(D) 자신의 연구에 적절한지에 대해 갈등을 느낀다.

해설　과학은 관찰하고 실험할 수 있는 것을 다루어야 하는데 감지할 수조차 없으면서 존재한다고 주장하는 것은 올바르지 않다고 생각한다.

3 교수가 다음과 같이 말한 이유는 무엇인가?

P You're not alone in asking that...

(A) 전에도 많은 학생들이 그와 같은 질문을 했다.
(B) 다중우주론에 대한 비판이 많다.
(C) 학생들은 그 이론에 대해 좀더 연구할 필요가 있다.
(D) 자신은 일찍이 수업시간에 그 질문에 대한 답변을 했다.

해설　다중우주론에 대해 비판하는 사람이 많다는 의미이다.

Practice 3

1 (C)　　2 (C)　　3 (D)

두 학생의 대화를 들으시오.

🎧 스크립트

S1 Wow, that was some test in literature class today, wasn't it? But I think I did all right,

S1 actually. So which type of poetic form did you end up writing about?
S2 I chose the one about villanelles, I mean the traditional 19-line poem... Which one did you choose?
S1 The same one. I wrote about how Shakespeare used 19-line poems to create tension and suspense regarding the relationships of people within the poems, changing the direction of the poem... Well, I just hope that the professor likes what I wrote.
S2 I hate to burst your bubble, but... uh... Shakespeare didn't write 19-line poems at all... Those were an Italian poetic form not common in English until the 20th century... Remember we read one of those by Dylan Thomas in the textbook? I think you're talking about Shakespeare's sonnets.
S1 What do you mean?
S2 The professor said that a sonnet has fourteen lines, and then about halfway through, the direction of the poem changes.
S1 No... that's got to be 19-lines... I mean, are you sure?
S2 Uh... Come on... Susan...

학생1 와, 오늘 문학시험 정말 대단했지, 그렇지 않니? 하지만 괜찮게 봤다고 생각해. 그런데 넌 어떤 시 형식에 대해서 썼니?
학생2 나는 전원시에 대해 썼어. 전통적인 19행 시 말이야. 너는 어떤 것을 선택했니?
학생1 같은 걸로. 나는 어떻게 셰익스피어가 19행 시를 사용해서 사람과의 관계에 대한 불안과 긴장을 조장하고 시의 방향을 바꾸었는지에 대해 썼어. 음, 내가 쓴 글을 교수님께서 좋아하셨으면 하고 바랄 뿐이야.
학생2 찬물을 끼얹기는 싫지만, 음... 셰익스피어는 19행 시를 쓴 적이 한 번도 없어... 그것은 20세기까지 영어에서는 흔하게 볼 수 없었던 이탈리아의 시 형식이거든. 교재에서 Dylan Thomas의 시를 읽었던 기억 나니? 네가 말하는 것은 셰익스피어의 소네트라고 생각해.
학생1 무슨 말이야?
학생2 교수님께서 소네트가 14행이고, 중간쯤에 시의 방향이 바뀐다고 말씀하셨잖아.
학생1 세상에... 19행이 틀림없는데... 너, 확실해?
학생2 잘 생각해 봐, Susna.

1 19행 시에 대해 추론할 수 있는 점은 무엇인가?
(A) 셰익스피어는 19행 형식 사용을 좋아하지 않았다.
(B) 이 형식은 20세기 영어에서 만들어졌다.
(C) 다수의 시인들은 20세기에 이 형식을 사용하기 시작했다.
(D) 셰익스피어는 이 시 형식에 대해 알지 못했다.
해설 전통적인 19행시는 20세기까지 영어에서 흔히 볼 수 없었던 이탈리아의 시 형식으로, 셰익스피어는 19행시를 사용하지 않았다.

2 남자가 다음과 같이 말하는 의미는 무엇인가?
(A) 자신과 함께 소네트가 무엇인지 확인하러 가자고 말하고 있다.
(B) 여자가 시험을 괜찮게 보았다고 생각하고 있다.
(C) 여자가 소네트와 혼동하고 있다고 확신한다.
(D) 그 사실을 알았다는 점을 인정하라고 여학생을 설득하고 있다.
해설 남자는 여자가 19행시와 소네트를 혼동하고 있다고 생각한다.

3 여자에 대해 추론할 수 있는 점은 무엇인가?
(A) 그녀는 소네트가 무엇인지 알아볼 것이다.
(B) 그녀는 교수와 얘기해 보아야 할지 모른다.
(C) 그녀는 이 시험에서 괜찮은 점수를 받기를 기대해도 좋다.
(D) 그녀는 이 시험에서 아마도 낮은 점수를 받을 것이다.
해설 여자는 시험에서 19행시와 소네트를 혼동해서 답안을 작성했기 때문에 아마도 낮은 점수를 받을 것이다.

Practice 4

1 (B)   2 (C)   3 (B)

두 학생 사이의 대화를 들으시오.

🎧 스크립트

S1 Hey, Mitch, will you look at this cover letter for me? I'm applying for an internship at a law firm for the spring, and I'm really worried I won't get it, though I really want to. Can you tell me what you think?
S2 Sure... Okay... hmmm... well, I think that it's a start. But you really don't provide a lot of information about yourself in this. Why should the law firm choose you as an intern?
S1 What do you mean? I have a resume, too that has my grades and class work on it. I thought cover letters were supposed to be short, anyway.
S2 Well, you usually want to keep them to a page. But it should do the job of "selling" you to the potential employer. I mean, all you say here is that you are interested in going to law school after you graduate. But

why?
S1 Well, because I'm really passionate about the environment and I think that I could really make a difference. Also I think this law firm does a lot of good work in this area. I'd like to help out with that and gain some experience.
S2 You see?
S1 What? It sounds stronger now?
S2 Way more.

학생1 안녕, Mitch, 이 첨부 편지 좀 봐줄래? 봄학기에 법률회사 인턴십에 지원하려고 하는데 떨어질까 봐 정말 걱정이야. 합격하길 원하지만 말이야. 네 생각을 좀 말해주겠니?
학생2 그래, 좋아. 음... 시작은 제대로 됐다고 생각해. 하지만 네 자신에 대한 정보가 많이 적혀 있질 않아. 그 법률회사에서 너를 인턴으로 뽑아야 하는 이유가 뭐니?
학생1 무슨 말이야? 들었던 과목과 학점을 기록한 이력서도 첨부했는데. 어쨌거나 첨부 편지는 짧아야 한다고 생각했어.
학생2 그게, 대부분은 첨부 편지를 한 장으로 만들려고 하지. 하지만 첨부 편지는 잠재적인 고용인에게 너를 '판매하는' 역할을 해야 해. 네가 여기에 쓴 것은 졸업한 후에 법과 대학교에 진학하고 싶다는 내용이 다야. 하지만 진학하고 싶은 이유가 뭐니?
학생1 음, 그것은 내가 환경에 대해 대단히 열정적이고 또, 정말 커다란 변화를 일으킬 수 있다고 생각하기 때문이야. 그리고 이 법률회사가 이 분야에서 훌륭한 일을 많이 한다고 생각해서야. 도움을 주고 싶고, 경험도 쌓고 싶어.
학생2 그것 봐?
학생1 뭘? 이제 훨씬 강렬하게 들려?
학생2 아주 많이.

1 남자가 다음과 같이 말한 의미는 무엇인가?

S2 Why should the law firm choose you as an intern?

(A) 그는 여자가 그 직업을 수행할만한 자질이 없다고 생각한다.
(B) 그는 첨부 편지가 충분히 설득력 있다고 생각하지 않는다.
(C) 그는 여자가 채용되리라고 확신한다.
(D) 그는 여자가 정보의 일부를 삭제할 필요가 있다고 생각한다.

해설 남자는 여자가 작성한 첨부 편지에 자신에 대한 정보가 부족하다고 생각하고, 좀 더 구체적으로 작성해야 내용이 더욱 강해지리라 생각하기 때문이다.

2 첨부 편지의 길이에 대해 추론할 수 있는 점은 무엇인가?

(A) 자기 소개가 몇 줄 있어야 한다.
(B) 필요하다면 한 장 이상이 될 수도 있다.
(C) 편지를 적절한 정보로 채우는 데 한 장 이상이 초과되지는 않을 것이다.
(D) 간단한 약력을 쓰는 데 반 장을 초과해서는 안 된다.

해설 남자의 말에 따르면 사람들이 보통 생각하는 첨부 편지의 분량은 한 장 정도이다.

3 여자가 쓴 첨부서에 대한 남자의 의견은 무엇인가?

(A) 어느 정도 완성이 되었다고 생각한다.
(B) 그녀가 첨부 편지에 좀 더 자세한 내용을 포함시켜야 한다고 생각한다.
(C) 그녀가 새로 작성해야 한다고 생각한다.
(D) 약간 정직하지 못한 내용을 담고 있다고 생각한다.

해설 여자가 자신에 대한 정보를 좀 더 기록해야 한다고 생각한다. 예를 들어 졸업 후에 법과 대학교에 진학하고 싶다고만 쓸 것이 아니라 그 이유에 대해 밝혀야 한다.

Actual Test 1

1 (C)   2 (A)   3 (B)   4 (D)   5 (D)

유전자 조작 식품에 대한 토론을 들으시오.

🎧 스크립트

P There's been a lot of controversy over the past few years over the introduction of genetically modified foods into our food supply. Now, of course, man has been, uh, messing with the genes of his foods ever since the Neolithic agrarian revolution. Using selective breeding to get a certain type of corn or apple... so what's the difference now? I mean why not solve hunger? Why are people so upset about this?
S1 Well, some people claim that there's not really been any research about the potential long term effects of these modifications. There could be a negative impact on the human body that we haven't really seen before.
P Yeah. That's one concern...
S2 Well, in the past, farmers could collect the seeds from their previous year's crop. But, uh, since a lot of the genetically modified crops are sterile, meaning that these crops are not able to produce seeds... um, the farmers are forced to buy them each year from the seed companies or something... and they become like slaves in a way...
S1 Yeah. And if the seeds aren't sterile, there is a chance that they can contaminate other seed crops, causing old varieties of plants to disappear. At some point, this could endanger genetic diversity, making crops a

lot more dangerous to disease and so on…
P Okay…so, despite the fact that adjusting the genes of plants is not a new human pursuit, we definitely have some new issues that have arisen because of recent laboratory modifications.

교수 유전자 조작 식품이 우리의 식품 공급에 투입된 데 대해 지난 수년 동안 많은 논쟁이 있었습니다. 자, 물론 인간은 신석기 농업 혁명 이래로 식품의 유전자를 조작해왔습니다. 특정 종류의 옥수수나 사과를 얻기 위해 품종을 선택하는 등 말입니다. 그렇다면 지금과의 차이점은 무엇이겠습니까? 제 말은 어째서 굶주림을 해결하지 못하는 겁니까? 어째서 사람들은 여기에 대해 그토록 분노하는 겁니까?
학생1 글쎄요. 어떤 사람들은 이와 같은 식품 변형이 미칠 장기적인 잠재 영향력에 대해 아무런 연구도 이루어지지 않고 있다고 주장합니다. 전에는 한 번도 본 적이 없는 부정적인 영향이 인간에게 미칠 수 있습니다.
교수 그렇습니다. 그것이 한 가지 걱정거리입니다…
학생2 음, 농부들은 과거에는 전년도 농작물에서 씨앗을 거둘 수 있었습니다. 하지만 많은 유전자 조작 농작물이 열매를 맺지 못하기 때문에, 즉 씨앗을 생산하지 못하는 농작물이 많기 때문에 농부들은 종자 회사로부터 매년 씨앗을 사야만 합니다. 그래서 농부들은 어떤 면에서 마치 노예처럼 됩니다.
학생1 맞습니다. 그리고 씨앗이 열매를 맺을 경우에는 다른 종자 농작물을 오염시킬 가능성이 있어서 과거부터 존재했던 다양한 식물을 멸종시키게 됩니다. 어떤 점에서 이는 유전적 다양성을 위태롭게 하고, 농작물이 질병이나 기타 위험에 더욱 증가시킵니다.
교수 자 좋아요. 그래서 식물의 유전자에 적응하는 것이 새삼스럽게 인간이 추구해야 하는 점은 아님에도, 최근 실험실 변형으로 말미암아 몇 가지 새로운 논쟁거리가 발생하고 있는 것이 분명합니다.

1 토론의 주제는 무엇인가?
(A) 유전자 조작 식품에 대한 항의가 가진 결점
(B) 농작물과 식품의 농업적 조작의 역사
(C) 유전자 조작 식품의 문제점과 그 영향
(D) 유전자 조작 식품이 인간 건강에 미치는 영향

해설 품종 개량을 목적으로 생산된 유전자 조작 식품에 의해 신체에 부정적 영향이 발생할 수도 있다. 또한 매번 종자를 사야 하는 농부들은 종자 회사에 대해 종속적인 위치에 놓이게 되고 씨앗이 열매를 맺을 경우 다른 종자 농작물을 오염시킬 위험성도 있다.

2 두 학생에 대해 추론할 수 있는 점은 무엇인가?
(A) 유전자 조작 식품에 대해 논쟁의 여지가 있다는 데 동의한다.
(B) 유전자 조작 식품이 금지되어야 한다고 생각한다.
(C) 유전자 조작 식품이 부정적 영향을 미치고 있다는 점에 동의하지 않는다.
(D) 유전자 조작 식품의 영향에 대해 서로 의견이 다르다.

해설 두 학생 모두 유전자 조작 식품의 영향에 대해 의문을 제기하고 있다.

3 교수는 다음과 같이 말하는 의미는 무엇인가?
P Yeah. That's one concern…
(A) 그것이 유전자 조작 식품에 대한 주요 논쟁거리라고 생각한다.
(B) 좀 더 많은 문제점을 거론하도록 학생들을 격려하고 싶어 한다.
(C) 학생이 언급한 것은 그다지 중요한 점이 아니라는 사실을 암시한다.
(D) 지난 번 강의에서 거론했던 논쟁거리를 학생들이 기억하고 있는지 알고 싶어 한다.

해설 여학생의 의문제기에 대한 교수의 이 언급은 학생들의 견해를 좀 더 끌어내기 위한 것이다.

4 다음 중 유전자 조작 식품에 대해 사실인 것은 무엇인가?
(A) 대규모로 경작될 수 없다.
(B) 자연식품만큼 건강에 좋지는 않다.
(C) 몇몇 나라에서는 그다지 거론되고 있지 않다.
(D) 매년 열매를 맺을 수는 없다.

5 다음 중 열매를 맺지 못하는 유전자 조작 농작물의 씨앗이 가진 문제점은 무엇인가?
(A) 열매를 맺는다면 다음 해에 씨앗을 재생산할 수 없다.
(B) 열매를 맺지 못한다면 다른 농작물을 오염시킬 수 있다.
(C) 열매를 맺지 못한다면 유전적 다양성을 위태롭게 할 수 있다.
(D) 열매를 맺는다면 환경에 보다 더 위험할 수 있다.

해설 씨앗이 열매를 맺는다면 다른 종자 농작물을 오염시킬 가능성이 있어서 다양한 식물을 멸종시키게 되고, 따라서 유전적 다양성을 해치고 농작물이 질병에 걸릴 위험성을 증가시킨다.

Actual Test 2

1 (C)   2 (B)   3 (A)   4 (C)   5 (D)

국제 학생 사무실에서의 대화를 들으시오

🎧 스크립트

S I want to save money to go home this summer, so I'm thinking that I'm staying on campus over the break if I can. But I read that my dorm will be closed for three weeks.
D Yes. For safety reasons, as well as to conserve energy, most of the student dorms do close…

Inference / Stance   77

S Is there any other way I could stay on campus?
D Well, do you have a friend whose family you could stay with while school is closed?
S Well, my roommate offered to let me stay with his family. But, I have a job here that I don't want to take time off from if possible, and he lives several hours away.
D I see. Okay, one thing you can do is... well, all right... you could stay in a boarding-house near campus. Many international students choose this option because the woman who runs the house provides breakfast and dinner for boarders... It'll probably run you 150 dollars for the whole time... How does that sound?
S Well, I don't know.... but if that's the only option I have...
D Well, there is this one dormitory building that stays open on campus to accommodate students. It's fifty extra dollars for the entire break, but there are no cooking or laundry facilities, so you have to pay for all that out of your pocket. Also it might cost you more than you think it would..
S Since I work in a restaurant, food is free for me... so... I think I could save even more. I'll choose the cheaper one.
D (concerned) Are you sure?

학생 이번 여름에 집에 가는 돈을 절약하고 싶어요. 그래서 가능하다면 이번 여름을 교내에서 지낼까 생각 중인데 3주일 동안 기숙사가 문을 닫을 것이라는 글을 읽었어요.
실장 그래요. 에너지를 절약하기 위해서 뿐만 아니라 안전상의 이유 때문에 대부분의 학생 기숙사가 문을 닫습니다.
학생 제가 교내에서 지낼 수 있는 다른 방법이 없을까요?
실장 글쎄요, 학교가 문을 닫는 동안 같이 지낼 만한 친구가 있나요?
학생 룸메이트가 자기 가족과 함께 지내게 해주겠다고 했어요. 하지만 이곳에 일자리가 있기 때문에 가능하다면 시간을 뺏기고 싶지 않아요. 친구는 이곳에서 몇 시간 떨어진 곳에서 살고 있거든요.
실장 알겠어요. 한 가지 할 수 있는 일은... 음, 좋아요... 학교 근처에 있는 하숙집에서 지내는 방법이 있어요. 하숙집을 운영하는 아주머니가 하숙생에게 아침식사와 저녁식사를 제공하기 때문에 많은 외국 학생들이 이렇게 하고 있죠. 비용은 아마도 통틀어 150달러 정도가 들 거예요. 어때요?
학생 글쎄요, 잘 모르겠어요... 하지만 그것이 제가 선택할 수 있는 유일한 방법이라면...
실장 음, 학생들을 수용할 수 있도록 개방되어 있는 기숙사 건물이 하나 있어요. 방학 내내 사용하면 50달러를 추가로 내야 해요. 하지만 거기에는 요리시설도 세탁시설도 없어요. 그러니까 그것도 모두 학생이 부담해야 해요. 학생이 생각하는 것보다 비용이 더 들지도 몰라요.
학생 제가 식당에서 일하기 때문에 식사는 무료에요. 그러니까... 그렇게 하면 더 많이 절약할 수 있으리라 생각해요. 더 저렴한 쪽으로 선택하겠어요.
실장 (걱정스러워하며) 괜찮겠어요?

1 남자가 여자를 찾아간 이유는 무엇인가?
(A) 취직 가능성에 대해 의논하려고
(B) 여름 동안 받을 수 있는 재정 보조금에 대해 문의하려고
(C) 방학 동안의 숙소 선택사항에 대해 알아보려고
(D) 현재 거주 상황에 대해 불평하려고

해설 방학 동안 집에 가지 않고 교내에서 지낼 수 있는 방법이 있는지 알아보기 위해서이다.

2 기숙사가 방학 동안 문을 닫는 이유는 무엇인가?
(A) 관리직원들이 수리를 할 수 있게 하려고
(B) 비용을 절감하고 캠퍼스 안전을 위해서
(C) 학생들이 교내에 머무르지 못하게 하려고
(D) 지역 호텔과 하숙집의 사업을 촉진시키려고

해설 에너지 절약과 안전상의 이유 때문이다.

3 남자가 친구와 같이 지내는 것을 원하지 않는 이유는 무엇인가?
(A) 친구의 집이 학교에서 너무 멀리 떨어져 있어서
(B) 친구에게 불편을 끼치고 싶지 않아서
(C) 친구의 가족을 만나는 것이 긴장이 돼서
(D) 친구의 집에 공간이 많지 않아서

해설 일자리가 있는데 친구 집은 학교에서 몇 시간 떨어져 있기 때문이다.

4 남자가 다음과 같이 말한 의미는 무엇인가?

S Well, I don't know... but if that's only option I have...

(A) 자신이 그 집을 아직 본 적이 없어서 확신이 서지 않는다.
(B) 자신이 그 비용을 감당할 수 있을지 확신하지 못한다
(C) 그 선택이 완전히 만족스럽지 못하다.
(D) 하숙집이 아주 합리적인 방법이라 생각한다

해설 여자가 제안한 하숙집이 자신의 필요에 맞는 곳인지 확신하지 못한다.

5 여자가 다음과 같이 말한 의미는 무엇인가?

D (Concerned) Are you sure?

(A) 남자가 선택사항을 정확히 이해했는지 묻는다.
(B) 식사가 제공되는지 아닌지 확실히 알지 못한다.
(C) 남자가 돈을 더 절약할 수 있을지 의심스러워 한다.
(D) 남자의 선택이 약간 걱정스럽다.

해설 여자가 마지막으로 제안한 기숙사는 50달러를 추가로 내면 머물 수 있지만 요리시설도 세탁시설도 없기 때문에 결국 비용이 더 들지도 모른

다. 여자는 남자가 이 기숙사를 선택한 것에 대해 걱정스럽고 미덥지 못하다.

Dictation

Practice 1

① are turning toward
② as a way of boosting
③ are attracted by the features
④ these features get destroyed
⑤ it would cause damage on
⑥ What we've learned in the past two decades
⑦ allow them to experience
⑧ the place they're traveling to
⑨ seeing the land
⑩ not only to generate wealth

Practice 2

① the one that we perceive
② only a part of the entire universe
③ they are imperceptible to us for now
④ we were making a claim for
⑤ You're not alone in asking that
⑥ what complicates this then
⑦ we really can't perceive or measure
⑧ only by inference

Practice 3

① that was some test
② end up writing about
③ create tension and suspense
④ changing the direction of the poem
⑤ I hate to burst your bubble
⑥ Those were an Italian poetic form
⑦ and then about halfway through

Practice 4

① look at this cover letter
② I'm applying for an internship
③ I won't get it
④ it's a start
⑤ my grades and class work on it
⑥ were supposed to be short
⑦ keep them to a page
⑧ passionate about
⑨ make a difference
⑩ help out with that and gain
⑪ It sounds stronger now

Actual Test 1

① genetically modified foods
② messing with the genes
③ why not solve hunger
④ about the potential long term effects
⑤ previous year's crop
⑥ are forced to buy them
⑦ if the seeds aren't sterile
⑧ causing old varieties of plants to disappear
⑨ adjusting the genes of plants
⑩ some new issues that have arisen

Actual Test 2

① I'm staying on campus over the break
② as well as to conserve energy
③ while school is closed
④ offered to let me stay with
⑤ take time off from
⑥ who runs the house
⑦ if that's the only option I have
⑧ to accommodate
⑨ pay for all that out of your pocket
⑩ I'll choose the cheaper one

Vocabulary Review

1 회수 신청하다
2 공지사항
3 확장하다
4 방해하다
5 집중하다
6 쫓아내다
7 식민지
8 비준하다
9 다양한
10 ~에게 말을 걸다
11 공표
12 분석
13 경작하다
14 불모의
15 축적
16 묘사하다
17 보호, 보존
18 확장하다
19 증대시키다
20 특징
21 진전시키다
22 산출하다
23 구조
24 인지하다
25 감지할 수 없는
26 긴장
27 열정적인
28 사육하다
29 잠재적인
30 오염시키다

31 적응시키다	32 수용하다
33 여분의, 별도의	34 ~인지 아닌지를 확인하다
35 ~을 이용하여	36 찬물을 끼얹다
37 ~에 대해 도움을 주다	38 어떤 시점에서
39 이해하다	40 제대로 핵심을 짚다
41 ~하기로 되어 있다	42 be forced to
43 make a claim for	44 agrarian
45 sterile	46 modification
47 Constitution	48 resident
49 agriculture	50 harvest

CHAPTER 06
FUNCTION

Pre Test

패션에 대한 강의를 듣고, 물음에 답하시오.

🎧 스크립트

P   When we think of corsets, well, images of women <u>in huge skirts with tiny waists</u> probably come to mind... these are the whalebone corsets of the 18th century. Women used to wear these corsets really tight... <u>to mold and shape their bodies</u> into a desired shape. Well, some women were known to <u>receive broken ribs</u> or <u>pass out from lack of air</u> just from wearing them! All in the name of beauty! You might be surprised to hear that men also wore corsets! ... to uh... <u>to tighten their waists</u> and increase the appearance of strength... <u>in drawings discovered at</u> the Neolithic archeological site at Brandon, in Norfolk, England, we can see both men and women wearing animal hide corsets...

교수   코르셋하면, 허리가 잘록하고 풍성한 치마를 입은 여인의 모습을 떠올립니다. 이것은 18세기의 고래수염으로 만든 코르셋입니다. 여성들은 자신의 몸을 원하는 형태로 만들기 위해 코르셋을 정말 꽉 조여 입곤 했습니다. 일부 여성들은 코르셋을 입느라고 갈비뼈가 부러지거나 공기가 부족해서 기절하기도 했다고 알려져 있습니다! 모두 아름다움 때문이었지요! 남성들 또한 코르셋을 입었다는 이야기를 들으면 놀랄지도 모르겠습니다. 그건, 어, 허리를 조이고 힘 있어 보이게 하기 위해서였죠. 영국 Norfolk주 Brandon에 위치한 신석기 시대 고고학 유적지에서 발굴된 그림을 보면 남성과 여성 모두 동물 가죽 코르셋을 입고 있습니다.

1 교수가 갈비뼈가 부러지거나 기절을 했던 여성들에 대해 말한 이유는 무엇인가?
   (A) 코르셋을 입으면 심각한 건강상의 문제를 일으킬 수 있다는 사실을 암시하려고
   (B) 18세기의 이상적인 미(美)를 따르는 일이 얼마나 힘겨웠는지 강조하려고
   (C) 코르셋을 만드는 데 사용했던 재료가 딱딱했다는 사실을 보여주려고
   (D) 코르셋이 여성의 삶에 그다지 중요한 부분은 아니었다는 사실을 암시하려고

정답 (B)

해설 18세기 여성들이 오로지 아름다움 때문에 그토록 힘들게 노력했다는 점을 강조한다.

2 강의의 일부를 다시 들으시오.

🎧 스크립트

P You might be surprised to hear that men also wore corsets! ... to uh... to tighten their waists and increase the appearance of strength... in drawings discovered at the Neolithic archeological site at Brandon, in Norfolk, England, we can see both men and women wearing animal hide corsets...

교수가 영국에서 발견된 그림에 대해 언급한 이유는 무엇인가?
(A) 남성이 착용한 코르셋이 어떻게 그들의 강인함을 증가시켰는지 보여주려고
(B) 당시 남성들이 코르셋을 얼마나 꽉 조여 입었는지 보여주려고
(C) 남성들 사이에 코르셋이 인기 있었던 장소를 나타내려고
(D) 남성들이 과거에 코르셋을 입었다는 증거를 제시하려고

정답 (D)

해설 여성뿐만 아니라 남성도 코르셋을 입었다는 자신의 주장을 입증하기 위해서다.

Vocabulary Preview for Mini-Exercise

Mini-Exercise

1-1. embellish (미화하다, 장식하다)
  ✓ a. to make something more beautiful or interesting by adding something to it
  b. to fix something firmly into a substance

1-2. toxin (독소)
  a. one who depends on or craves a habit-forming substance
  ✓ b. a poisonous substance, especially one which is produced by bacteria and which causes disease

1-3. specifically (특히, 보다 명확히)
  ✓ a. for a particular reason or purpose
  b. to separate one type of things from a group of things

2-1. efficiency (능률, 효율)
  ✓ a. when someone or something uses time and energy well, without wasting any
  b. to destroy or remove it so that it cannot be seen any more

2-2. productivity (생산성, 생산력)
  ✓ a. the rate at which a company or country makes goods
  b. successful or achieving the results that you want

2-3. deal with (~와 관계가 있다)
  a. an agreement or an arrangement, especially in business
  ✓ b. to be about or be on the subject of something

3-1. carnival (카니발, 축제)
  ✓ a. public enjoyment and entertainment involving wearing unusual clothes, dancing, and eating and drinking
  b. a set of fixed actions and sometimes words performed regularly, especially as part of a ceremony

3-2. costume ((민속) 의상, 복장)
  ✓ a. the set of clothes typical of a particular country or period of history, or suitable for a particular activity
  b. a way of behaving or a belief which has been established for a long time

3-3. catch up (따라잡다)
  a. to trick someone into making a mistake
  ✓ b. to do something you did not have time to do earlier

4-1. inspire (격려하다, 고취하다)
  ✓ a. to make someone feel that they want to do something and can do it
  b. to plan secretly with other people to do something bad, illegal or against someone's wishes

4-2. chaos (혼돈, 무질서)
  a. a situation in which a difficult choice has to be made between two different things you could do
  ✓ b. a state of total confusion and lack of order

4-3. ideal (이상의, 이상적인)
  ✓ a. a principle or a way of behaving that is of a very high standard
  b. a system of accepted beliefs which control behavior, especially such a system based on morals

Function

Mini-Exercise Function-Purpose

1 생태학 수업의 토론을 듣고, 물음에 답하시오.

🎧 스크립트

P I don't know how many of you have ever watched that movie, "The Birds".
S1 The one where all the birds <u>start attacking people for no reason</u>?
P That's it! Now, Hitchcock <u>embellished the story</u> to make the movie scary, one night, <u>a huge flock of seabirds slammed into windows and sides of houses, dived bombing cars, and fell out of the sky into the streets, dead...</u>
S2 I didn't see the movie but I think I remember the scenes from TV or something.
P Probably... but in fact, it really <u>is based on a real event</u> that happened in 1961 in Santa Cruz, California. What caused this completely unusual action? Well, we've discovered <u>it was a mass poisoning</u> by a naturally occurring toxin that acts <u>specifically on nerve cells</u>, called domoic acid, which was eaten by the anchovies, uh..., small fish that the birds fed on. We don't have time to <u>get into the structure of</u> this toxin today, but we'll look at how it works next time.

교수 여러분 중에 '새'란 영화를 본 사람이 몇 명이나 되는지는 모르겠군요.
학생1 새들이 아무런 이유 없이 사람들을 공격하기 시작하는 영화 말씀인가요?
교수 맞아요! 히치콕은 영화를 공포스럽게 만들려고 이야기를 재미있게 꾸몄습니다. 어느 날 밤 바다 새 떼가 창문에 부딪히고 집의 측면으로 달리는 차로 내리꽂히며 하늘에서 거리로 떨어져 죽었습니다.
학생2 저는 그 영화를 보지는 못했지만 TV나 다른 곳에서 그 장면을 본 기억이 납니다.
교수 아마 그랬을 겁니다. 하지만 실제로 영화는 1961년 캘리포니아 주 산타 크루즈에서 발생했던 사건에 기초를 두고 있습니다. 새들로 하여금 이렇게 이상한 행동을 하게 한 원인은 무엇이었을까요? 우리가 발견한 바로는 특히 신경세포에 작용하는 자연 발생적 독소에 의한 집단중독 때문이었습니다. 도모이산으로 불리는 이런 독소를 새들중에 먹이로 하는 안초비(멸치 과의 작은 물고기—옮긴이)가 섭취한 것입니다. 오늘은 이 독소의 구조에 대해 검토할 시간이 없지만 다음 번에 그 작용에 대해 살펴보겠습니다.

1 교수가 히치콕의 영화에 대해 말한 이유는 무엇인가?
(A) 영화가 매우 공포스럽다는 사실을 강조하려고
(B) 독소가 주로 새들에게 피해를 입혔다는 사실을 나타내려고
(C) 독소가 새의 행동에 어떻게 영향을 미치는지를 설명하려고
(D) 학생들이 영화를 본 적이 있는지 알아보려고

정답 (C)

해설 영화에 등장했던 새들의 이상한 행동은 실제로 발생했던 것으로, 신경 세포에 작용하는 자연 발생적 독소에 의한 집단 중독이 그 원인이었다.

2 다음 수업 시간에는 무엇을 할 예정인가?
(A) 히치콕 영화의 일부분을 본다.
(B) 설명의 타당성에 대해 토론한다.
(C) 소 그룹으로 나뉘어 (새들의) 공격에 대해 토론한다.
(D) 도모이산의 성분에 대해 배운다.

정답 (D)

해설 본문의 마지막 문장에 따르면, 도모이 산의 작용에 대해 배울 것이다.

2 경영학 수업의 토론을 듣고, 물음에 답하시오.

🎧 스크립트

P "Scientific management," was <u>the name given to efforts</u> to try and increase the efficiency of... uh... factories and businesses in the early 20th century. Frederick Winslow Taylor was really <u>the pioneer of this field</u>, and his main philosophy was that... <u>in order to speed up productivity</u>, managers had to put the system of production ahead of people. We had to get rid of the causes of inefficiency — workers wasting time. Did that mean workers had to work like machines?
S1 <u>Getting rid of workers</u> wasting time... <u>by putting workers into a system</u> of production means, I guess, I mean, it seems like he didn't realize he was dealing with people and not machines.
S2 I don't think Taylor meant that workers should work like machines. Well, maybe that's part of it... <u>strategies to increase efficiency</u>.

교수 '과학적 경영'이란 20세기 초 공장과 사업체의 효율성을 높이려는 시도나 노력에 붙여진 이름입니다. Frederick Winslow Taylor는 이 분야의 개척자로, 그의 주요 철학은... 생산성을 증가시키기 위해 관리자들은 사람보다 생산체계를 우선해야 한다는 것이었습니다. 그러므로 비효율성의 원인 즉, 시간을 낭비하는 노동자를 제거해야 했습니다. 이는 노동자들이 기계처럼 일해야 한다는 뜻일까요?
학생1 노동자를 생산체계 속으로 밀어 넣음으로써 시간을 낭비하는 노동자를 제거해야 한다는 그의 주장으로 보아, 제 추측으로는 그가 기계가 아니라 사람을 다루고 있다는 사실을 깨닫지

못하고 있는 것 같습니다.
학생2 저는 Taylor가 노동자들이 기계처럼 일해야 한다는 의미로 말했다고는 생각하지 않습니다. 아마도 효율성을 증가시키기 위한 전략의 일부였을 겁니다.

1 교수가 다음과 같이 말한 이유는 무엇입니까?

P Did that mean workers have to work like machines?

(A) 학생들에게 비효율성의 기본 의미를 물어보려고
(B) Taylor의 생각에 대해 토론하도록 학생들을 부추기려고
(C) 학생들이 과제를 했는지 점검하려고
(D) Taylor의 주요 철학이 무엇인지 설명하려고

정답 (B)

해설 교수는 Taylor의 철학에 대해 매우 부정적인 결론을 제시함으로써 학생들의 토론을 유도하려 한다.

2 두 학생에 대해 추론할 수 있는 점은 무엇인가?
(A) 둘 다 효율성에 대한 Taylor의 철학에 동의한다.
(B) 둘 다 효율성에 대한 Taylor의 생각에 동의하지 않는다.
(C) 남학생은 어떤 면에서는 Taylor의 주장이 이치에 맞는 다고 생각한다.
(D) 여학생은 남학생의 의견에 동의하지 않는다.

정답 (D)

해설 남학생은 Taylor가 사람보다는 기계에 비중을 둔다는 부정적인 생각을 가지고 있지만, 여학생은 그보다는 효율성을 증가시키기 위한 Taylor의 의도에 비중을 둔다.

3 두 학생의 대화를 듣고, 물음에 답하시오.
🎧 스크립트

S1 So, are you ready for the history final exam?
S2 Sort of... but I'm really <u>behind with my studying</u>. What questions do you think he'll ask?
S1 Well, the big thing is going to be <u>a comparison of</u> the different carnival traditions in African-influenced cultures... so Brazil, Haiti, and Louisiana for example... Well, he... I think... he wants us to look at the ways that people in those places, particularly in Brazil and Louisiana, used uh, used costumes and skits <u>as a means of lodging criticism against</u> the larger power structures... it's all in the readings...
S2 Man... I missed the week that we <u>covered that stuff</u>... and I never did <u>catch up on</u> the readings...
S1 He pretty much will let us know what's gonna be on the exam <u>in the last one or two classes</u>... you know...
S2 I know... but still...
S1 Oh come on, you did well on the mid-term.

학생1 그런데 너, 학기말 역사 시험 준비는 됐니?
학생2 대강은... 하지만 공부가 정말 밀려 있어. 네 생각에는 교수님이 어떤 문제를 낼 것 같니?
학생1 글쎄, 큰 문제는 아프리카의 영향을 받은 문화에 속한 서로 다른 축제의 전통을 비교하는 문제가 될 거야. 그러니까 예를 들어 브라질, 아이티, 루이지애나 등에서 말이지. 내 생각에는... 특히 브라질이나 루이지애나와 같은 지역에서 사람들이 더 큰 권력 구조에 대항해서 비판하는 수단으로 의상과 촌극을 사용했던 방법에 대해 살펴보라고 하실 것 같아. 그 내용은 모두 읽기자료 안에 있어.
학생2 세상에... 그 부분을 배웠던 주에 결석을 했어. 게다가 읽기자료를 미처 다 읽지 못했어.
학생1 아마 교수님께서 마지막 한 두 수업 시간에 시험에 나올 문제에 대해 많이 알려주실 거야.
학생2 알아... 하지만 여전히...
학생1 참 내, 넌 중간고사 때도 잘했잖아.

1 남자가 마지막 수업시간에 대해 언급한 이유는 무엇인가?
(A) 학기말 시험이 그다지 어렵지 않으리라는 점을 암시하려고
(B) 읽기 자료 학습을 만회할 수 있는 방법을 제안하려고
(C) 여학생이 수업에 참석할지 말지를 알아내려고
(D) 마지막 수업 시간에 어떤 시험 문제가 출제될 지 알 수 있을 것임을 여학생에게 상기시키려고

정답 (D)

해설 여학생이 시험에 대해 걱정하자 교수님이 마지막 수업시간에 시험에 나올 문제에 대해 많이 알려주신다는 사실을 상기시키고 있다.

2 다음 중 브라질과 루이지애나의 행사에서 사용되는 것으로 언급된 것은 무엇인가?
(A) 특별 의상
(B) 율동적인 춤
(C) 정치 토론
(D) 어린아이 같은 놀이

정답 (A)

해설 브라질 등에서는 더 큰 권력에 대항하고 이를 비판하는 수단으로 의상과 촌극을 사용했다.

4 아이티 노예 폭동에 대한 강의를 듣고, 물음에 답하시오.
🎧 스크립트

P Okay, so we've, we've, uh seen that the slave revolts of the 18th century <u>ended with the slaves being defeated</u> and, uh, well, usually executed... Well, why is that, though? Is this always the case? Let's take a look at one revolt, on the Caribbean island of Haiti.... Uh, that was successful at driving the Europeans out of power. This was led by Toussaint L'Ouverture, who was a, uh, a former slave. We would like to take a look at the primary factors that led to this successful revolt. As you all read in the book, L'Ouverture was inspired, um greatly inspired, by the ideals of the French Revolution. A brief, uh, outlawing of slavery followed by a reinstatement of it led to mass chaos on the island, on Haiti, and, uh, so soon the French were embroiled in a war with the slaves, led by L'Ouverture. Finally, it was Napoleon Bonaparte who brokered peace with L'Ouverture, granting independence to the island and its people.

교수 자, 18세기에 일어났던 노예 폭동은 음, 결국 노예의 패배로, 그러니까, 주로 노예들의 처형으로 끝이 났습니다. 그런데, 왜 그랬을까요? 항상 이런 식이었을까요? 아이티의 캐러비안 섬에서 일어났던 폭동을 살펴봅시다. 음, 이 폭동은 유럽인들을 권력의 자리에서 몰아내는 데 성공했습니다. 이 폭동을 이끌었던 인물은 과거 노예였던 Toussaint L'Ouverture였습니다. 우리는 이 폭동을 성공적으로 이끌었던 주요 요소를 살펴보고자 합니다. 여러분이 책에서 읽은 것처럼, L'Ouverture는 프랑스 혁명의 이상에 큰 영감을 받았습니다. 프랑스 혁명의 복귀에 따른 노예제도의 금지로 아이티 섬에는 대규모 혼란이 일어났습니다. 그리고 곧 프랑스는 L'Ouverture가 이끄는 노예들과의 전쟁에 휘말리게 되었습니다. 마침내, 섬과 섬 사람들에게 독립을 부여하면서, L'Ouverture와 평화를 중재했던 사람은 바로 나폴레옹이었습니다.

1   교수가 다음과 같이 말한 이유는 무엇인가?

P   Okay, so we've, we've, uh seen that the slave revolts of the 18th century ended with the slaves being defeated and, uh, well, usually executed... Well, why is that, though? Is this always the case?

(A) 18세기에 성공한 노예 폭동이 얼마나 적은지 설명하려고
(B) 당시에 유럽인의 권력이 노예를 압도했다는 점을 강조하려고
(C) 이례적인 폭동과 그 성공 이유를 소개하려고
(D) 학생들에게 폭동이 실패한 이유에 대해 물어보려고

정답 (C)

해설 18세기에 일어났던 노예폭동이 대부분 노예의 패배로 끝이 났다는 점을 지적하면서 마지막 질문을 통해 이와는 대조적으로 마침내 성공을 거둔 노예폭동을 소개한다.

2   L'Ouverture가 이끌었던 폭동의 결과는 무엇인가?
(A) L'Ouverture의 죽음
(B) 모든 식민 국가에서의 프랑스의 노예 제도 폐지
(C) 아이티와 그 국민들의 가치
(D) 유럽인들을 아이티에서 몰아냄

정답 (C)

해설 유럽인들을 권력의 자리에서 몰아냈고 섬은 독립을 이루었으며, 폭동을 일으켰던 노예들은 해방되었다.

Vocabulary Preview for Practice

Practice 1

1. mark (특징짓다, 나타내다)
   a. to say or write something, especially clearly and carefully
   ✓ b. to identify or be a feature of
2. hypothesize (가설을 세우다)
   a. to develop a set of ideas about something
   ✓ b. to give a possible but not yet proved explanation for something
3. hold (지지하다, 받치다)
   ✓ a. to support something
   b. to set free or allow to go
4. exceptional (뛰어난, 예외적인)
   ✓ a. much greater than usual, especially in skill, intelligence, quality
   b. to become involved with or support an activity or opinion

Practice 2

1. virtue (미덕, 선행)
   ✓ a. a good moral quality in a person, or the general quality of goodness in people
   b. almost a particular thing or quality
2. flatter (추켜세우다, 듣기 좋은 칭찬을 하다)
   ✓ a. to praise someone in order to make them feel attractive or important
   b. to make flat
3. convey (전하다, 알리다)
   a. to prevent something from being seen or known about
   ✓ b. to express a thought, feeling or idea so that it is understood by other people
4. at hand (가까이에, 가까운 곳에)
   ✓ a. near in time or position
   b. to act badly towards the person who is helping or has helped you

Practice 3

1. embody (구체화하다, 구현하다)
   a. to fix something firmly into a substance
   ✓ b. to represent a quality or an idea exactly
2. philanthropist (자선가)
   a. someone who studies or writes about the meaning of life
   ✓ b. someone who helps poor people, especially by giving them money
3. mistreatment (학대, 혹사)
   ✓ a. to treat a person or animal badly, cruelly or unfairly
   b. to cause someone to believe something that is not true
4. motivation (유도, 동기 부여)
   a. to make someone very annoyed, usually when they can do nothing to solve a problem
   ✓ b. the need or reason for doing something

Practice 4

1. frustrate (좌절시키다)
   ✓ a. to make someone feel annoyed or discouraged because they cannot achieve what they want
   b. unhappy, unpleasant or of low quality
2. pressure (압력, 압박)
   a. to take action to save something or protect it from damage
   ✓ b. the force you produce when you press something
3. priority (우선적으로 처리해야 할 가장 중요한 것)
   ✓ a. something that is very important and must be dealt with before other things
   b. an advantage that only one person or group of people has
4. committee (위원회)
   ✓ a. a small group of people chosen to represent a larger organization and either make decisions or gather information for it
   b. the people living in one particular area or people who are considered as a unit

Vocabulary Preview for Actual Test

Actual Test 1

1. d 그는 2년 전에 뇌졸중에 걸려서 말을 할 수 없게 되었으나 정신능력에는 영향이 미치지 않았다.
2. a 정부는 경제를 활성화시키기 위해 세금을 삭감하려는 계획을 하고 있다.
3. b 법원은 이 아이들의 자동차 사고에 부모에게도 일부 책임이 있다는 판결을 내렸다.
4. c 자신의 문화와 매우 다른 문화를 가진 사회에 자신을 통합시키는 것은 상당히 어렵다.

Actual Test 2

1. b 의사들은 그 질병의 원인을 알려지지 않은 바이러스의 탓으로 돌렸다.
2. d 그는 질문할 기회를 포착하려고 노력했다.
3. a 요컨대, 당신은 복잡한 사회 구조에서 몇 가지 다른 지위를 차지하고 있는 것이다.
4. b 극심한 경기 침체로 영화 산업 분야에서 많은 회사들이 최근 상당한 금액의 자금을 잃었으며, 이는 곧 실직을 야기했다.

Practice 1

1 (B)   2 (D)   3 (C)

반 고흐에 대한 강의를 들으시오.

🎧 스크립트

P Vincent Van Gogh's paintings are recognizable to most of us. His style marked a real departure from the Impressionists who came before him. There are some experts who hypothesize that Van Gogh's style was the result of a vision disorder — the paintings represent how he literally saw the world. Now, we'll take a look at some slides of his work in a minute, but let's first talk about this idea... Alright, so one theory holds that Van Gogh's doctor attempted to treat the painter's infamous bouts of mental illness with digitalis. These might cause problems in a person's yellow-blue vision — it looks like you are seeing the world through a yellow filter and the sufferer is also seeing a blurry halo around objects. Many of Van Gogh's paintings have a very yellow cast to them, and the halo effect can be seen quite clearly in many of his paintings as well. However, though he was self-trained, Van Gogh's expertise as a painter is well documented by his exceptional output. But come on, that his distinctive style was the result of a disease rather than a brilliant artistic mind seems to me to be far from likely.

교수   우리들 대부분은 빈센트 반 고흐의 그림의 가치를 인정합니다. 그의 스타일은 그의 전 시대에 있었던 인상파 화가들과의 뚜렷한 결별을 뜻합니다. 반 고흐의 스타일이 시각장애의 결과였다는 가설을 세우는 전문가들도 있습니다. 즉, 그림은 말 그대로 화가가 세상을 바라본 방식을 반영하기 때문이죠. 이제 잠시 그의 작품을 담은 슬라이드를 볼 것입니다. 하지만 먼저 이런 견해에 대해 말해봅시다.
자, 한 가지 이론이 주장하는 것은, 반 고흐의 의사가 화가의 지독한 정신질환 발작을 디기탈리스 식물로 치료하려 했다는 겁니다. 그런데 그 식물은 사람의 황청 시각에 문제를 일으킬 수 있다고 합니다. 이는 마치 노란색 필터를 통해 세상을 보고 또한 환자가 물체 주위에 희미한 후광을 보는 것처럼 만든다는 겁니다. 반 고흐 그림 가운데 많은 수가 매우 노란색을 띠고 있고, 후광 효과를 분명하게 볼 수 있는 그림도 많습니다. 반 고흐가 독학을 하기는 했지만 화가로서 전문적인 기술을 소유했다는 점은 그가 남긴 탁월한 결과물에 의해 입증되고 있습니다. 그러나 제가 보기에 그의 독특한 스타일이 탁월한 예술적 정신의 결과가 아닌 질병의 결과라는 주장은 근거가 없습니다.

1 교수가 인상파 화가들을 거론한 이유는 무엇인가?
(A) 반 고흐가 그 화파의 일원이었다는 사실을 나타내려고
(B) 반 고흐 특유의 스타일을 설명하려고
(C) 반 고흐의 작품에 미친 영향력을 강조하려고
(D) 반 고흐가 인상주의를 싫어했다는 사실을 암시하려고

해설   전 시대에 있었던 인상파 화가와도 구별되는 그의 독특한 스타일을 확인하기 위해서이다.

2 교수가 반 고흐의 의사를 언급한 이유는 무엇인가?
(A) 이 가설을 주장했던 사람을 지적하려고
(B) 반 고흐의 질병이 그의 예술에 영향을 미치지 않았다는 사실을 암시하려고
(C) 반 고흐가 노란색에 중점을 둔 것과 후광 효과를 설명하려고
(D) 반 고흐의 정신질환에 대해 타당한 설명을 소개하려고

해설   반 고흐의 스타일이 시각장애의 결과였다는 가설을 주장하는 전문가들이 있다고 소개하면서 이 이론에 대한 가능한 설명을 제시하기 위해서이다.

3 다음 중 이 이론에 대해 사실이 아닌 것은 무엇인가?
(A) 반 고흐의 예술 스타일은 눈의 질병에 영향을 받았다.
(B) 희미한 후광이 나타나는 반 고흐의 시각은 약초에 의해 생겨났다.
(C) 반 고흐는 그림을 그릴 때 노란 색과 파란 색 필터를 사용했다.
(D) 반 고흐가 노란색과 후광 효과를 사용했다는 것이 이 문제의 이론에 대한 기본 바탕이다.

해설   이 이론에 따르면 의사가 조제한 식물은 반 고흐가 노란 색 필터를 통해 세상을 보고 물체 주위에 희미한 후광을 보는 것처럼 만든다. 그러므로 실제로 노란 색과 파란 색 필터를 사용한 것이 아니다.

Practice 2

1 (B)   2 (D)   3 (C)

국제사업에 대한 토론을 들으시오.

🎧 스크립트

P   Okay, so say you, you got a letter from a businessperson from another country who was obviously interested in conducting business with your firm. Let's suppose that the first paragraph of the letter goes into great detail, praising the virtues of your company... umm... "I admire what you have, uh, accomplished and heard a lot about your creative and innovative works and so on..." Now, what's your reaction as a businessperson?

S   Suspicion! If somebody is too flattering, I feel like they're trying to sell me something I don't want. I like it much better when people get straight to the point.

P   Yet in this, uh, this person's culture, it's expected that business letters begin with a fair amount of compliment and flattery before the matter at hand is addressed. In fact, to just "jump right in" to what you want is considered very rude and offending.... just like you had a negative feeling to overly complimented beginning. So what am I getting at here? Shoud it be directly to the point? Or complimentary? What I'm saying is that these things are relative to your culture. Before you begin corresponding with people from other cultures for business purposes, it's an absolute necessity — if you want their business — to find out the subtle ways in which, uh, respect and consideration are conveyed in writing.

교수 자, 여러분이 여러분과 거래를 하고 싶은 의도가 분명한 외국 사업가로부터 편지를 받았다고 합시다. 그가 편지의 첫 문단에 자세한 내용을 실으면서 당신 회사의 가치를 칭찬했다고 가정해보지요. 음. "나는 귀사가 성취한 것에 감탄하고 있으며, 귀사의 창의적이고 혁신적인 일에 대해 많이 들었으며..." 등등 말입니다. 자. 이제 사업가로서 여러분의 반응은 무엇입니까?

학생 의심입니다! 누군가가 지나치게 칭찬을 한다면 내가 원하지 않는 무언가를 내게 팔려고 애를 쓴다는 느낌을 갖게 됩니다. 사람들이 단도직입적으로 본론을 말하는 것이 훨씬 좋습니다.

교수 그러나 이 사람이 속한 문화에서는, 고려 중인 문제를 거론하기 전에 상당량의 칭찬과 겉치레말로 사업편지를 시작하는 것이 보통입니다. 사실상, 자신이 원하는 주제로 '곧장 뛰어드는 것'은 매우 무례하고 불쾌감을 주는 일로 간주됩니다. 지나치게 칭찬하는 말로 편지를 시작한 것에 학생이 부정적인 느낌을 받았던 것과 마찬가지로 말입니다.
자, 내가 여기서 말하려는 것이 무엇일까요? 곧바로 본론으로 들어가야 합니까? 아니면 칭찬으로 시작해야 합니까? 내가 말하려는 점은 이러한 것이 여러분의 문화와 관련이 있다는 사실입니다. 다른 문화에 속한 사람과 사업적인 목적으로 의사소통을 시작하기 전에 여러분이 그들의 사업에 대해 알고 싶다면, 존경심과 배려가 글로 전달될 수 있는 미묘한 방법을 알아내는 것이 절대적으로 필요합니다.

1 교수가 다음과 같이 말한 이유는 무엇인가?

P umm... "I admire what you have, uh, accomplished and heard a lot about your creative and innovative works and so on..."

(A) 다른 나라와 사업을 함께 하는 데에 사용되는 일반적인 표현을 소개하려고
(B) 대단한 칭찬으로 시작한 상업편지의 예를 들려고
(C) 오해의 소지가 있는 편지의 예를 들려고
(D) 편지에서 첫 문단의 중요성을 지적하려고

해설 문화 차이에 따라 본론으로 직접 들어가지 않고 상당량의 칭찬과 겉치레 말로 관계를 맺기 시작하는 편지의 예를 들고 있다.

2 교수가 다음과 같이 언급한 이유는 무엇인가?

P So what am I getting at here? Should it be directly to the point? Or complimentary?

(A) 상업적인 글쓰기에서 어느 편이 더 나을지 학생들에게 추측해 보게 하려고
(B) 어떤 경우도 상업서신에 적절하지 않은 것으로 간주될 것임을 암시하려고
(C) 상업서신에는 두 가지의 일반적인 형태가 있다는 사실을 나타내려고
(D) 국제 상업서신 작문에 대한 자신의 관점을 보여주려고

해설 상업적인 편지를 쓸 때 문화적인 요소를 고려해야 한다는 자신의 강의 요점을 밝히기 위해 질문을 던지고 있다.

3 다음 중 다른 문화에 대한 존중을 나타내는 미묘한 방법을 배워야 하는 이유가 아닌 것은 무엇인가?

(A) 그렇게 하면 원하는 상대와 거래를 할 수 있다.
(B) 그렇게 하면 다른 문화에 속한 사람에게 불쾌감을 주지 않을 것이다.
(C) 그렇게 하면 자신 편지의 본론으로 곧장 들어갈 수 있다.
(D) 그렇게 하면 상업적인 상황에서 무례하게 생각되어지지 않을 것이다.

해설 다른 문화를 존중하면서 솜씨 좋게 그 뜻을 글로 표현한다면 무례함이나 불쾌감을 주지 않고 기분 좋게 원하는 상대와 거래를 할 수 있다.

Practice 3

1 (B)　　2 (D)　　3 (C)

Andrew Carnegie에 대한 토론을 들으시오.

🎧 스크립트

P Andrew Carnegie was a Scottish-born industrialist who really embodies the classic American rags-to-riches myth. Now in addition to being highly skilled at making money, Carnegie was also quite a philanthropist who freely gave money away and helped people who were in need. Not only did he employ countless workers, he gave back to society, donating money for the creation of over 2,800 free libraries in the U.S. and Britain. I know you guys might want to add some different views here...

S1 Yeah, I think he is the one who benefited more than anyone from the donations. I mean, it just made him look good in the public's eye, which made them more tolerant of his mistreatment of his workers.

S2 Well, I've seen a few Carnegie libraries... They don't even have his name on them, the way that today's philanthropists want their name all over everything... It doesn't seem like it was all about self-glorification.

P It's true that he didn't want his name on the buildings. On the other hand, it's also true that it was no secret who gave the grant for the construction of these buildings. So, what we can see is that the motivations of this famous industrialist were quite complicated...

교수 앤드류 카네기는 스코틀랜드 태생 기업경영인으로, 지극히 가난했던 사람이 부자가 되는 고전적인 미국의 신화를 실제로 구현한 사람입니다. 카네기는 돈을 버는 데 고도의 솜씨를 발휘했을 뿐만 아니라 돈이 필요한 사람에게 기꺼이 돈을 주고 그들을 돕는 자선가이기도 했습니다. 무수히 많은 노동자를 고용했고, 돈을 사회에 환원하여 미국과 영국에 2,800 곳이 넘는 무료 도서관을 건립하였습니다. 여러분들이 여기에 일부 다른 견해를 덧붙이고 싶어할지도 모르겠군요.

학생1 그렇습니다. 그는 기부를 통해 그 누구보다도 혜택을 많이 받았다고 생각합니다. 제 말 뜻은 기부를 함으로써 대중의 눈에 좋은 사람으로 보였고, 그 덕택에 그가 노동자를 혹사시켜도 사람들이 관대한 태도를 취하게 된 겁니다.

학생2 저는 카네기 도서관 몇 군데를 가보았습니다만 도서관에는 심지어 그의 이름도 적혀 있지 않았습니다. 오늘날의 자선가는 무엇에든 자신의 이름을 새겨 넣기를 좋아하는 데 말입니다. 그것이 모두 자기미화를 위한 것만은 아닌 것 같아 보입니다.

교수 그가 건물에 자신의 이름을 남기기를 원하지 않았던 것은 사실입니다. 그러나 한편으로 건물의 건축비를 누가 기부했는지 또한 결코 비밀이 아니었습니다. 그래서 우리가 알 수 있는 사실은 바로 이 유명한 기업경영인의 동기가 매우 복잡했다는 것입니다.

1 교수가 지극히 가난했던 사람이 부자가 되는 미국의 신화를 언급한 이유는 무엇인가?
(A) 카네기가 노동자들을 착취하고도 그 대가는 거의 지불하지 않았다는 점을 암시하려고
(B) 카네기가 무일푼으로 출발해서 돈을 벌 수 있었다는 사실을 설명하려고
(C) 그가 궁핍한 사람들에게 도움을 준 데 대한 타당한 이유를 보여주려고
(D) 그 신화가 카네기의 성공에서 비롯되었다는 사실을 나타내려고

해설 카네기는 무일푼에서 출발해서 얼마든지 부자가 될 수 있다는 미국의 신화를 구현한 인물이다.

2 교수가 다음과 같이 말한 이유는 무엇인가?

P I know you guys might want to add some different views here.

(A) 이것이 강력한 공적 논쟁의 주제라는 사실을 지적하려고
(B) 카네기가 자선가라는 점에 학생들이 동의하는지 알아보려고
(C) 자선가로서의 카네기에 대한 다른 견해가 있다는 사실을 설명하려고
(D) 카네기에 대한 견해를 표현하도록 학생들을 부추기려고

해설 카네기가 자선사업에 적극적이었다는 점을 지적하고, 이에 대해 학생들이 자신의 견해를 발표할 수 있게 하기 위해서이다.

3 두 학생에 대해 추론할 수 있는 점은 무엇인가?
(A) 둘 다 카네기의 동기가 오해 받았다는 점에 동의한다.
(B) 여학생은 카네기가 이기심이 없는 사람이라는 점에 동의한다.
(D) 남학생은 카네기가 진실한 자선가였다는 점에 동의한다.
(C) 둘 다 카네기가 자기미화만을 위해서 자선행위를 했다는 점에 동의하지 않는다.

해설 여학생은 카네기의 자선행위가 사업적인 이익추구를 위한 것이었다고 주장하지만, 남학생은 카네기의 행위가 모두 자기 미화만을 위한 것은 아니었다고 생각한다.

Practice 4

1 (C) 2 (B) 3 (C)

두 학생의 대화를 들으시오.

🎧 스크립트

S1 You know, this is the third time this semester I've gone to Professor Brown's office during his office hours and he wasn't there... It's really inconvenient to go over there and have him not be there.
S2 I know he's on a lot of committees and stuff, so he has many meetings, which add a lot of pressure to a professor's schedule.
S1 I guess, but his priority should be his students, don't you think? My roommate says that her professor cancelled an appointment three times!
S2 That's pretty frustrating. But did you make an appointment to meet with the professor?
S1 No... I ran over to his office when I had a question. Why would I have to when there are office hours?
S2 You may be right. But if you know he's often not there when he's supposed to be, it probably makes sense to make an appointment if you want to talk to him.
S1 I guess that's what I'll do from now on.
S2 And he announces in class if he's not going to be there or if there is any change in his office hours... Did you notice that?
S1 No, I didn't, I mean I did... but I didn't pay much attention... (doubtly) You did?
S2 I don't want to waste my time going to the professor's office when he is not there...

학생1 집무시간 중에 Brown 교수님 사무실에 갔는데 자리에 안 계신 것이 벌써 이번 학기 들어 세 번째야. 그곳까지 갔는데 교수님께서 안 계시면 정말 불편해.

학생2 교수님이 관여하는 위원회나 여러 일 등이 많다고 들었어. 그래서 회의가 많기 때문에 교수님 일정에 많은 압박이 되고 있

나 봐.
학생1 그렇겠지. 하지만, 교수님이라면 학생들에게 우선 순위를 두어야 한다고 생각해. 안 그래? 내 룸메이트의 교수님은 약속을 세 번이나 취소했다더라고!
학생2 정말 기운 빠지는 일이지. 그런데 교수님과 만날 약속은 했니?
학생1 아니, 질문이 있으면 연구실로 찾아갔지. 엄연히 집무시간이 정해져 있는데 왜 내가 그래야만 하니?
학생2 네 말이 맞을 수도 있어. 하지만 교수님께서 연구실에 계서야 하는 시간에 자리를 비우시는 일이 많다면, 교수님과 얘기하고 싶은 경우에는 시간 약속을 하는 것이 이치에 맞을 거야.
학생1 이제부터는 그렇게 해야겠다.
학생2 그리고 교수님께서는 당신이 사무실을 비우실 예정이거나 집무 시간이 변경되면 수업시간에 말씀을 하셔. 알고 있었니?
학생1 아니, 몰랐어. 아니, 알고 있었지만, 그다지 주의를 기울이지 않았어. (의심하듯) 너는 알고 있었어?
학생2 그럼. 교수님께서 계시지 않을 때 사무실을 찾아가느라 시간을 낭비하고 싶지는 않거든.

1 남자가 시간 약속에 대해 언급한 이유는 무엇인가?
(A) 그것이 교수를 볼 수 있는 유일한 방법임을 말하려고
(B) 집무시간이 있다 하더라도 시간 약속은 필요하다는 점을 암시하려고
(C) 교수를 만날 있는 최선의 방법을 제안하려고
(D) 여자가 시간약속을 하기 위해 교수에게 전화를 했는지 물어보려고

해설 집무시간 중에 교수님을 찾아갔다가 허탕치고 불평하는 여자에게 남자는 교수님을 만나려면 시간 약속을 하라는 조언을 한다.

2 여자는 어떤 뜻으로 다음과 같이 말했는가?

S1 Why would, I have to when there are office hours?

(A) 교수가 연구실에 있을 때는 시간약속이 필요하지 않다고 느낀다.
(B) 집무시간 내에는 아무 때나 교수를 찾아갈 수 있다고 생각했다.
(C) 집무 시간 중에 교수를 찾아갈 필요가 없다.
(D) 교수와 시간 약속을 할 수 있는지 몰랐다.

해설 집무시간 중에는 교수가 당연히 사무실에 있을 것이기 때문에 시간약속 없이 아무 때나 찾아갈 수 있다고 생각했다.

3 여자가 다음과 같이 말한 이유는 무엇인가?

S1 No, I don't, I mean I do... but I don't pay much attention... (doubtly) You do?

(A) 집무 시간에 대한 공지사항을 보았는지 남자에게 물어보려고
(B) 수업 시간에 공지된 새로운 집무시간이 확실한지 물어보려고
(C) 집무 시간에 대한 공지에 주의를 기울이는 것이 중요한지 의문이 가서

(D) 교수가 수업 시간에 공지를 했는지 물어보려고

해설 교수가 자신의 일정표에 대해 수업시간에 공지를 했음에도 여자는 주의를 기울이지 않았다. 공지에 귀 기울이이 중요한 것이었는지 몰랐기 때문이다.

Actual Test 1

1 (B)   2 (A)   3 (C)   4 (D)   5 (C)

교육에 대한 강의를 들으시오.

🎧 스크립트

P As it became more and more common in the United States to educate all children, a variety of philosophies surfaced about how best to educate all of these children. One of these emerged from the work of an Italian physician named Maria Montessori... Well, you've probably heard the name before... Alright! So, what basically is it? I mean what does she say is the best way to educate children? She greatly prized self-direction and inquiry as the keys to helping children of all different talents and capacities thrive in education. One of the, uh, the main components of Montessori's program were to provide children with a stimulating atmosphere that would arouse their interests in the world around them. They were encouraged to explore and ask questions as a means of gaining education. They were, uh, also made aware of the fact that they were responsible for their own learning, which required self-discipline and respect for others around them. A third principle of the Montessori method was the role of the teacher. In traditional programs, teachers were instructors, telling the students exactly what it is, what to do and even what they learned... but Montessori teachers were more of facilitators, helping the children as they discovered new things. What were children expected to, uh, come out of the Montessori program with? Well, the memorization of facts, as is common in many schools, was not stressed. Rather, Montessori, uh, sought to prepare children to know how to acquire and integrate knowledge throughout their lives. If you open your textbooks, we can take a look at how this compares with the educational philosophies of Bronson Alcott...

교수 미국에서 모든 아이들을 교육시키는 것이 더욱 보편적으로 되어 감에 따라, 이 모든 아이들을 가장 잘 교육시킬 수 있는 방법에 대한 다양한 철학이 대두했습니다. 이러한 철학 중의 하나는 이탈리아 의사인 마리아 몬테소리의 작품에서 파생되었습니다. 여러분도 아마 그 이름을 들어본 적이 있을 겁니다. 좋습니다! 그렇다면 기본적으로 그 철학은 무엇입니까? 그러니까 그녀의 주장에 따르면 학생들을 교육시키는 최상의 방법은 무엇일까요? 그녀는 각기 다른 재능과 능력을 가진 학생들이 교육을 잘 받도록 돕는 열쇠로써 자기 주도성과 탐구를 중요하게 생각했습니다. 몬테소리 프로그램의 주요 구성 요소 가운데 하나는 아이들에게 주변 세상에 대해 관심을 불러일으키는 자극적인 분위기를 제공하는 것입니다. 학습 습득 수단으로써 아이들이 탐색하고 질문을 하도록 부추겼습니다. 또한 학생들에게 자신의 학습에 대해 스스로 책임이 있다는 점과, 그러기 위해서는 자기 수양과 주변에 있는 다른 사람에 대한 존중을 필요로 한다는 점을 가르쳤습니다. 몬테소리 방법의 세 번째 원리는 교사의 역할입니다. 전통적인 프로그램에서 교사는 학생들에게 정확하게 그것이 무엇이고, 무엇을 해야 하는지, 그리고 심지어는 무엇을 배웠는지도 가르치는 지도자였습니다. 그러나 몬테소리 (프로그램의) 교사들은 아이들이 새로운 것을 발견할 수 있도록 도와주는 중재자에 더 가깝습니다. 몬테소리 프로그램을 끝마치는 아이들에게는 어떤 면을 기대하게 될까요? 많은 학교에서 일반적인 사실의 암기는 강조되지 않습니다. 대신에 몬테소리 프로그램은 살아가면서 지식을 습득하고 통합하는 방법을 알 수 있도록 아이들을 준비시킵니다. 여러분의 교재를 펴보면 브론슨 알콧의 교육철학과 비교해볼 수 있습니다.

1 강의의 주된 내용은 무엇인가?
 (A) 미국의 모든 아이들을 교육시키는 문제
 (B) 몬테소리 교육 프로그램의 목적과 주요 요소
 (C) 마리아 몬테소리와 브론슨 알콧의 차이점
 (D) 전통적인 교육과 몬테소리의 (교육 프로그램의) 비교

해설 본문은 주로 몬테소리 교육의 목적과 주요 원리에 관한 내용이다.

2 교수가 다음과 같이 말한 이유는 무엇인가?

> P Well, you've probably heard the name before... Alright! So, what basically is it? I mean what does she say is the best way to educate children?

 (A) 아동교육에 대해 몬테소리가 가진 견해의 개요를 시작하려고
 (B) 학생들이 참고문헌을 읽는 과제를 했는지 알아보려고
 (C) 몬테소리의 철학이 사람들 사이에 잘 알려져 있다는 사실을 암시하려고
 (D) 학생들이 몬테소리 교육 철학의 근본 개념에 대해 생각하도록 격려하려고

해설 몬테소리 교육 프로그램에 대해 정의하고 설명하기 위해서이다.

3 교수가 전통적 프로그램에서의 교사(지도자)에 대해 언급한 이유는 무엇인가?
 (A) 그들의 역할 역시 동등하게 중요했다는 사실을 설명하려고
 (B) 몬테소리 프로그램에서 교사의 역할이 약화되었다는 점을 암시하려고
 (C) 몬테소리 프로그램에서 교사의 역할과 대조시키려고
 (D) 두 프로그램 모두에서 교사가 중요하다는 사실을 암시하려고

해설 전통적 교육 프로그램과 몬테소리 교육 프로그램에서 교사가 담당하는 역할의 차이점을 밝히려 한다.

4 교수는 어떤 방식으로 몬테소리 프로그램에 대해 설명하는가?
 (A) 전통적인 프로그램의 특징과 비교함으로써
 (B) 몬테소리 프로그램의 주요 원칙을 설명함으로써
 (C) 몬테소리 프로그램의 몇 가지 장점을 열거함으로써
 (D) 몬테소리 프로그램의 세 가지 주요 요소를 지적함으로써

해설 몬테소리 프로그램을 구성하는 세 가지 주요 요소를 제시하고 있다.

5 다음 중 몬테소리 프로그램에 대한 설명이 아닌 것은 무엇인가?
 (A) 교사의 역할은 학과에 대한 지침을 제공함으로써 아이들을 돕는 것이다.
 (B) 아이들은 각자 자신의 학습에 대한 주요 책임은 자신에게 있다는 사실을 안다.
 (C) 아이들은 그날 수업을 위해 학습자료를 가져와야 할 것이다.
 (D) 아이들이 세계에 대한 흥미를 가질 수 있도록 자극적인 분위기를 제공한다.

해설 (A), (B), (D)는 몬테소리 프로그램을 구성하는 세 가지 주요 요소를 가리킨다.

Actual Test 2

1 (D) 2 (C) 3 (B) 4 (A), (D) 5 (B)

음악 역사에 대한 토론을 들으시오.

🎧 스크립트

> P The arts in early American history were always attributed to their European predecessors. So... uh... basically, white writers, painters, and musicians were constantly searching for ways to distinguish themselves from the

Europeans. Yet while this battle was going on to create a uniquely "American" art, black American musicians seized upon their own cultural traditions to create the truly American music style known as jazz. Now, we should spare some time to think about why many people believe that jazz is truly a product of American culture, OK?

S1 But wasn't so much of what influenced jazz music really a product of African culture, imported by slaves? The drumming, for example, and syncopated rhythms?

S2 On the other hand, though, jazz music uses a western scale for its notes, and traditional jazz really stays pretty close to the standard structure of European style music, with melody and harmony and all that.

P Yes... and yes! This is the point. What emerged out of the convergence of the two cultures was something entirely new. This new kind of music was very much influenced by the blues music that had grown out of the slaves' songs, which were, in turn, influenced by Africa. But, as you'll hear on this next recording, the instruments were primarily of European influence. This synthesis of the two cultures is very American as American culture is very much about the blending of many different influences. And I think that's why we can say that jazz was the first truly American art form.

교수 초기 미국 역사에서의 예술은 언제나 유럽인 선조들 덕택이라는 것이 사람들의 생각이었습니다. 그래서 기본적으로 에, 백인 작가, 화가, 음악가는 항상 자신들과 유럽인을 차별화할 수 있는 방법을 추구했습니다. 특유의 '미국적' 예술을 창조하려는 이런 투쟁이 계속되는 동안, 흑인 미국인 음악가들은 자신의 문화적 전통을 활용해서 재즈라 불리는 진정한 미국적 음악 스타일을 창조해냈습니다. 이제 우리는 시간을 할애해서 많은 사람들이 재즈를 진정한 미국 문화의 산물이라 믿는 이유에 대해 생각해보려 합니다. 알겠죠?

학생1 하지만 재즈 음악에 영향을 미친 요소의 많은 부분이 노예에 의해 도입된 아프리카 문화의 산물이 아닌가요? 예를 들어 북을 치는 것과 당김음을 사용하는 리듬 등이 말입니다.

학생2 하지만 다른 한 편으로 재즈 음악은 가락을 서구 음계로 표시하고, 전통적인 재즈는 선율과 화성 등에 있어서 실제로 유럽식 음악의 표준 구조에 매우 가깝습니다.

교수 맞습니다. 그리고 그것도 맞습니다! 이것이 핵심입니다. 두 문화가 통합되면서 완전히 새로운 음악이 등장했습니다. 이 새로운 종류의 음악은 아프리카의 영향을 받은 노예들의 노래에서 성장한 블루스 음악에 의해 많은 영향을 받았습니다. 그러나 다음에 들게 될 노래처럼 악기는 주로 유럽의 영향을 받았습니다. 두 문화의 통합은 매우 미국적입니다. 많은 다른 영향을 혼합한 것이 바로 미국 문화이기 때문입니다. 재즈가 최초로 진짜 미국적인 예술 형식이라 말할 수 있는 것도 바로 이런 이유에서라고 생각합니다.

---

1 토론의 주된 내용은 무엇인가?
(A) 초기 미국사에서의 예술의 특징
(B) 최초 미국 예술 형식의 출현
(C) 아프리카 노예 문화의 영향을 받은 재즈
(D) 재즈 음악과 그 발달의 개관

해설 최초의 미국적 예술형식이라 할 수 있는 재즈에 대해 설명한다.

2 교수가 다음과 같이 말한 이유는 무엇인가?

P Now, we should spare some time to think about why many people believe that jazz is truly a product of American culture, OK?

(A) 재즈를 미국 문화의 일부로 보는 이유를 강조하려고
(B) 재즈의 기원에 대한 그룹 토론을 벌이도록 학생들을 설득하려고
(C) 재즈가 미국 문화에 그토록 특별한 이유에 대해 학생들이 토론하게 하려고
(D) 학생들이 그 이유에 대해 토론하는 것에 수업의 초점을 두어야 한다고 제안하려고

해설 이번 수업시간의 주제는 재즈가 진정한 미국문화의 산물로 여겨지는 이유이므로 교수는 이 말을 통해 학생들의 토론을 이끌어내려 한다.

3 교수가 다음과 같이 말한 이유는 무엇인가?

P Yes... and yes! This is the point.

(A) 학생들의 대답에 놀랐다는 점을 나타내려고
(B) 두 가지 의견 모두 연관되어 있음을 지적하려고
(C) 주제가 매우 논쟁거리가 된다는 사실을 지적하려고
(D) 더 이상 토론을 할 필요가 없으리라는 점을 암시하려고

해설 남학생과 여학생 의견 모두 맞는 이야기라는 사실을 표현하고 있다.

4 교수에 따르면, 다음 중 재즈에 대해 사실인 것은 무엇인가? 정답 두 개를 고르시오.
(A) 일부 음악적 특징은 아프리카 문화의 영향을 받았다.
(B) 재즈 음악에 사용된 악기는 미국 문화에 영향을 주었다.
(C) 재즈는 서로 다른 두 개의 주에 존재하는 두 문화의 영향을 받았다.
(D) 서로 다른 문화적 요소가 재즈를 매우 미국적인 음악으로 만들었다.

해설 재즈는 아프리카 문화와 유럽문화가 통합되어 매우 미국적인 음악이 되었다.

5 교수는 미국 문화에 대해 무엇이라 말하는가?
　(A) 미국 문화의 많은 부분은 여러 유럽 문화의 영향을 받았다.
　(B) 미국 문화는 많은 다른 요소의 혼합물이다.
　(C) 미국 문화의 많은 측면은 노예와 관련이 있다.
　(D) 유럽 문화만이 미국 문화 발전에 영향을 미쳤다.

해설　미국 문화는 여러 가지 다른 영향이 혼합한 문화이다.

Dictation

Practice 1

① are recognizable to most of us
② marked a real departure
③ how he literally saw the world
④ so one theory holds
⑤ attempted to treat
⑥ it looks like you are seeing
⑦ have a very yellow cast to them
⑧ though he was self-trained
⑨ seems to me to be far from likely

Practice 2

① conducting business with your firm
② goes into great detail
③ what's your reaction
④ too flattering
⑤ get straight to the point
⑥ the matter at hand is addressed
⑦ is considered very rude and offending
⑧ you begin corresponding with
⑨ to find out the subtle ways

Practice 3

① the classic American rags-to-riches myth
② who were in need
③ donating money for
④ add some different views here
⑤ the one who benefited more than anyone
⑥ more tolerant of his mistreatment
⑦ it was no secret
⑧ were quite complicated

Practice 4

① this is the third time this semester
② inconvenient to go over there
③ he's on a lot of committees and stuff
④ That's pretty frustrating
⑤ I ran over to his office
⑥ if he's not going to be there
⑦ Did you notice that

Actual Test 1

① a variety of philosophies surfaced
② emerged from the work of
③ prized self-direction and inquiry
④ thrive in education
⑤ with a stimulating atmosphere
⑥ arouse their interests in
⑦ as a means of gaining education
⑧ the role of the teacher
⑨ as is common in
⑩ was not stressed
⑪ sought to prepare
⑫ how to acquire and integrate

Actual Test 2

① were always attributed to
② searching for ways to distinguish
③ Yet while this battle was going on
④ seized upon
⑤ imported by slaves
⑥ uses a western scale for its notes
⑦ something entirely new
⑧ had grown out of
⑨ which were, in turn, influenced by
⑩ This synthesis of the two cultures

Vocabulary Review

1 조이다　　　　　2 외관
3 고고학의　　　　4 아름답게 꾸미다
5 독소　　　　　　6 특별히
7 효율성　　　　　8 생산성
9 축제　　　　　　10 의상
11 따라잡다　　　　12 고무시키다
13 혼돈　　　　　　14 이상적인
15 가설을 세우다　　16 지지하다, 받치다

17 예외적인	18 미덕
19 아첨하다	20 전달하다
21 구현하다	22 박애가, 자선가
23 위원회	24 동기부여
25 우선적으로 해야 할 일	26 압박, 중압
27 수용 능력, 재능	28 구성 요소
29 암기	30 획득하다
31 해석하다	32 철학
33 통합	34 ~한 생각이 떠오르다
35 B라기 보다 A	36 단도직입적으로 말하다
37 ~로 시작하다	38 ~ 뿐만 아니라
39 이치에 맞다, 일리가 있다	40 ~ 덕분이라고 생각하다
41 B와 A를 구별하다	42 deal with
43 subtle	44 be responsible for
45 go into great detail	46 in turn
47 principle	48 defeat
49 infamous	50 distinctive

PROGRESS TEST

Progress Test 5

1 (B)　2 (C)　3 (D)　4 (B)　5 (A)　6 (A)

동물원에 관한 강의를 듣고, 물음에 답하시오.

🎧 스크립트

P　Almost every major city today has a zoo. Today's zoos usually attempt to mimic the animal's native habitat, not only to educate the visitor about the species, but also to ensure the animal's health and happiness. They're quite different from zoos of the past. Zoological collections go back to ancient times, and by the Middle Ages in Europe, rulers would frequently bestow gifts of exotic creatures... and, well, large collections of wild animals grew up this way. Of course, the lives of the animals in these zoos were really pretty miserable. Their needs and habits were pretty poorly understood, and so they would often get sick and die. So, when did this change? In the 17th century? Or 18th century? Well, it really wasn't until the 20th century that the value of trying to recreate the animals' habitats was really seen. Carl Hagenbeck, a new manager at Jardin des Plantes Zoological Gardens, uh... it's a zoo in Paris, he uh... introduced the idea of making the animals' surroundings as natural and familiar as possible. You know... animals in many zoos used to be kept in cages with bars, right? But he was the first person to institute the use of moats, a deep, wide channel dug around the perimeter of the zoo and filled with water, in order to prevent the animals from escaping or to protect them from any possible attack from others... This enabled the zoo keepers to create much nicer, bigger environments for the animals. Today's zoos, in addition to providing education and entertainment for people, see the preservation of rare species as part of their mission, as well. Breeding programs for animals that are about to disappear on earth are part of this mission. They also really demonstrate how far zoos have come from their initial roles as simple entertainment and symbols of power for kings and queens.

교수 오늘날 거의 모든 주요 도시에는 동물원이 있습니다. 오늘날의 동물원은 방문객에게 동물의 종에 대해 교육시킬 뿐만 아니라 동물의 건강과 행복을 보장하기 위해 동물 고유의 서식지를 모방하려고 시도하고 있습니다. 그것들은 과거의 동물원과 매우 다릅니다. 동물 수집의 역사는 고대까지 거슬러 올라갑니다. 그리고 유럽에서는 중세에 이르기까지 통치자들이 외래종 동물을 선물로 주는 일이 많았습니다. 이렇게 해서 야생 동물의 수집이 늘어나게 되었습니다. 물론 이런 동물원에 서식하는 동물들의 삶은 정말 매우 비참했습니다. 사람들이 동물들의 필요와 습관을 제대로 파악하지 못했기 때문에 동물들은 자주 병에 걸렸고 죽어갔습니다. 그러면 이런 현상에 변화가 온 것은 언제였을까요? 17세기였을까요? 아니면 18세기였을까요? 동물들의 서식지를 다시 조성하는 것이 중요하다는 점을 깨달은 것은 20세기에 들어서였습니다. 파리에 위치한 동물원인 Jardin 동식물원의 새 관리자로 임명된 Carl Hagenbeck는 동물들이 서식하는 환경을 가능한 한 야생 그대로 친숙하게 만들자는 생각을 도입했습니다. 많은 동물원에 서식하는 동물들은 창살이 있는 우리에 갇혀 있곤 했죠. 하지만 그는 동물들이 도망가지 못하게 하거나 다른 동물로부터 공격 받는 것을 방지하기 위해 동물원을 빙 둘러 깊고 넓은 수로를 파서 물로 채우는 해자의 사용을 처음으로 실시했습니다. 해자를 사용함으로써 동물원 관리인들은 동물이 살기에 훨씬 훌륭하고 더욱 널찍한 환경을 만들 수 있었습니다. 오늘날의 동물원은 사람들에게 교육과 오락을 제공하는 역할에 덧붙여서, 희귀 종의 보존을 사명의 일부로 생각하고 있습니다. 지구상에서 사라지려는 동물들을 위한 번식 프로그램도 이러한 사명의 일부입니다. 이들은 또한 동물원이 단순한 오락과 왕과 왕비를 위한 상징으로써의 초기 역할에서 얼마나 벗어나 있는지를 보여주고 있습니다.

1 강의의 주된 내용은 무엇인가?
  (A) 유럽 왕족의 동물 수집의 역사
  (B) 동물원 동물 사육 방식의 진화
  (C) 창살 쳐진 우리에 동물을 가두는 현대 동물원에 대한 비판
  (D) 최초의 현대 동물원 관리인의 전기

해설 과거 동물원부터 현재 동물원에 이르기까지 동물을 보존하는 방법의 발전에 대해 설명하고 있다.

2 교수가 해자의 사용을 언급한 이유는 무엇인가?
  (A) 대부분의 현대 동물원이 해자를 가지고 있다는 사실을 암시하려고
  (B) 동물에게 이상적인 환경을 제안하기 위해서
  (C) Carl Hagenbeck이 동물원에 공헌한 예를 들기 위해서
  (D) 많은 동물원이 동물을 가두었던 방법을 제시하려고

해설 동물의 서식지를 가능한 한 야생 그대로 친숙하게 만들자는 아이디어를 도입했던 칼 하겐벡의 기여에 대해 설명하기 위해서이다.

3 교수가 다음과 같이 말한 이유는 무엇인가?

P So when did this change? In the 17th century? Or 18the century?

  (A) 정확한 시기에 대한 명확한 증거가 없다는 점을 암시하려고
  (B) 수업에 참여하라고 학생들을 격려하려고
  (C) 변화의 시기의 중요성을 강조하려고
  (D) 동물원 환경이 언제 변화하기 시작했는지를 설명하려고

해설 동물원의 열악한 환경이 변화하기 시작한 시기에 대한 이야기를 꺼내기 위해서이다.

4 과거 동물원에 대해 추론할 수 있는 점은 무엇인가?
  (A) 다양한 동물들이 자주 군주의 학대를 받았다.
  (B) 지난 400년간 동물원의 목적이 바뀌었다.
  (C) 유럽의 기후는 대부분의 외래종 동물들의 건강에 좋지 않았다.
  (D) 많은 사람 사이에 가장 인기 있는 장소의 하나였다.

해설 과거 동물원은 단순한 오락과 왕과 왕비를 위한 상징의 역할을 했다. 반면에 오늘날의 동물원은 사람들에게 교육과 오락을 제공하고, 희귀 종을 보존하고, 이를 번식시키는 역할을 한다.

5 교수에 따르면, Hagenbeck이 성취한 것은 무엇인가?
  (A) 당시의 동물원이 동물을 다루는 방법을 바꾸었다.
  (B) 인상적인 동물들을 수집했다.
  (C) 동물들을 가두는 우리를 개선했다.
  (D) 동물을 관리하고 동물에게 먹이를 주는 일에 대해 사람들을 교육시켰다.

해설 Hagenbeck은 동물의 서식 환경을 가능한 한 야생 그대로 친숙하게 만들자는 생각을 해서 해자를 설치했다. 그럼으로써 동물원 관리인들은 동물이 살기에 훨씬 훌륭하고 더욱 널찍한 환경을 만들 수 있었다

6 다음 중 오늘날 동물원의 사명의 일부가 아닌 것은 무엇인가?
  (A) 복제를 통해 새로운 종의 동물을 만들어내는 것
  (B) 죽어가는 동물을 보호하는 것
  (C) 멸종 위기에 처한 동물 수의 증가를 돕는 것
  (D) 동물에 대한 일반적인 지식을 확장하는 것

해설 본문은 오늘날 동물원의 사명에 대해 세 가지를 제시하고 있다. 즉 동물에 대한 교육과 오락의 제공, 희귀 종의 보존, 멸종 위기에 처한 동물의 번식 등이다.

Progress Test 6

1 (B)   2 (D)   3 (A)   4 (C)   5 (B)   6 (B)

두 학생의 대화를 듣고, 물음에 답하시오.

🎧 스크립트

S1 Hey, Mike, you got a minute?
S2 Sure, what is it?
S1 I just wanted to ask you something for my assignment due this week. You have probably done this before... It's about 60's folk music...
S2 Oh, I think I remember something about that from last semester. So, what is the problem?
S1 Oh, I'm having a hard time figuring out what points I really have to focus on... I mean, I don't understand why the professor was making such a big deal about the 60's folk music revival. I mean he acts like it was such an important moment, but I don't get it.
S2 Well, I think he was saying there are a couple of aspects to it. I think it's really important to think about it in terms of the protest movement. You probably know some of those... uh... Bob Dylan's or Joan Baez's songs, right? Don't they seem like they were much involved with politics? Their songs are offering critical comments about power and ideology... That folk music was really something that hadn't been seen in this country before. And anti-war songs really gave voice to a lot of the concerns of the young.
S1 (*In content*) Not bad! That's definitely a point, go on, what else?
S2 Well, we can also look at the stuff that wasn't political. Folk songs that really just revived the roots of the music of rural America. Even if it wasn't protesting specific political policies, it was making a kind of protest against modern life such as wasteful consumption and materialism. The songs kind of underscored a desire for a simpler way of life.
S1 Nice, basically both of these things really, I guess, point to a kind of dissatisfaction with the way things were, on the part of young people. Okay... You've been a great help.

학생1 안녕, Mike, 시간 좀 있니?
학생2 그럼, 뭔데?
학생1 이번 주가 마감인 과제물 때문에 너에게 부탁 좀 하고 싶어서. 아마도 너는 이미 했을 거야. 60년대 포크 음악에 관한 건데…
학생2 지난 학기에 뭔가 배운 것 같아. 그래 뭐가 문제인데?
학생1 어떤 점에 초점을 맞추어야 하는지 몰라서 힘들어하고 있는 중이야. 내 말은 교수님께서 60년대 포크 음악이 다시 유행하게 된 것을 그토록 중요하게 생각하시는 이유를 이해할 수 없어. 교수님께서는 그것이 굉장히 중요한 시기인 것처럼 말씀하시는데 나는 이해가 가질 않아.
학생2 내 생각으로, 교수님께서는 그것에 두 가지 측면이 있다고 말씀하셨어. 저항 운동이라는 측면에서 생각해보는 것이 정말 중요해. 너도 아마 밥 딜런이나 조안 바에즈 등 몇 가수의 노래를 알고 있을 거야. 그렇지? 그 음악들이 정치와 연관이 많은 것처럼 보이지 않니? 그들의 노래는 권력과 이념에 대한 비판적인 의견을 제시하고 있어. 그러한 포크 음악은 과거에는 이 나라에서 들어본 적이 없던 음악이었어. 그리고 반전 노래는 젊은이들이 가진 많은 걱정거리가 표출되는 통로가 되었어.
학생1 (만족스러워하며) 괜찮은걸! 확실히 정곡을 찌르는 이야기야. 계속해 봐. 또 뭐가 있어?
학생2 음, 정치적이지 않았던 포크음악도 있어. 그런 포크 송은 미국 시골 음악의 뿌리를 재생시킨 거지. 그것이 구체적인 정치 정책에 저항한 것은 아니더라도, 낭비적인 소비와 물질주의 같은 현대 생활에 대해 항의를 하고 있지. 이런 노래들은 좀 더 단순한 삶의 방식에 대한 욕구를 강조하고 있어.
학생1 좋아, 기본적으로 두 가지 모두 젊은 사람 편에서는 세상이 돌아가는 방식에 불만을 표시한 것이구나. 알았어… 정말 큰 도움이 되었어.

1 여자가 남자를 찾아간 이유는 무엇인가?
  (A) 과제가 어렵다고 불평하기 위해서
  (B) 과제의 주요 핵심에 대해 물어보려고
  (C) 남자가 이 수업을 전에 수강한 적이 있는지 알아보려고
  (D) 함께 과제를 해결해보자고 설득하려고

해설 여자는 과제물인 60년대 포크음악의 부활의 어떤 점에 초점을 맞추어야 하는지에 대해 묻고 있다.

2 남자가 밥 딜런이나 조안 바에즈의 노래를 언급한 이유는 무엇인가?
  (A) 그들이 가장 인기 있는 포크송 작곡가라는 사실을 암시하려고
  (B) 과제를 해결하기 위해 포크 음악을 들으라고 여자를 부추기려고
  (C) 여자가 몇몇 포크송 가수와 그들의 노래를 아는지 물어보려고
  (D) 60년대 포크송의 내용을 여자에게 상기시키려고

해설 포크송이 저항음악의 성격을 띄었다고 이야기하면서 두 가수의 노래를 예로 들고 있다. 이로써 여학생에게 권력과 이념에 대한 비판을 담고 있는 포크송의 내용을 상기시키고 있다.

3 여자가 다음과 같이 말한 이유는 무엇인가?

> **S1** Not bad! That's definitely a point, go on, what else?

(A) 남자가 말한 내용에 만족한다는 사실을 나타내려고
(B) 남자의 제안에 대한 실망을 감추려고
(C) 남자에게 첫 번째 핵심에 대해 계속 얘기하게 하려고
(D) 남자가 자신에게 충분한 정보를 말해주었다는 사실을 암시하려고

해설 여자는 포크송에 대한 남자의 설명을 듣고 만족해하고 있다. 과제를 파악하는 데 도움이 되기 때문이다.

4 남자가 정치색 없는 포크송에 대해 말한 이유는 무엇인가?

(A) 대부분의 포크송이 사랑을 받는 이유를 제시하려고
(B) 초기 정치적 포크송이 어떻게 진화했는지 설명하려고
(C) 60년대 포크 음악의 다른 주제를 지적하려고
(D) 자신이 여태껏 설명했던 주요 핵심의 결론을 맺으려고

해설 60년대 포크송에는 권력과 이념에 대한 비판을 표출한 노래가 있었던 반면에 정치색 없는 포크송 또한 있었다는 점을 설명하고 있다.

5 여자가 다음과 같이 말한 이유는 무엇인가?

> **S1** Nice, basically both of these thing really, I guess, point to a kind of dissatisfaction with the way things were on the part of young people.

(A) 남학생의 설명이 끝났는지를 확인하려고
(B) 과제를 해결하기 위한 주요 핵심을 정리하려고
(C) 추가적인 핵심이 있을지 모른다는 사실을 제안하려고
(D) 남학생의 견해가 가진 문제점을 지적하려고

해설 여자는 포크 음악에 대한 설명을 듣고 어떤 점에 맞추어 과제를 해결해야 할지 나름대로 결론을 내리고 있다.

6 대화에 따르면, 포크 음악이 기타 음악과 다른 한 가지는 무엇인가?

(A) 구식 악기에 의존했다.
(B) 정치적 저항을 중심 주제로 사용했다.
(C) 라디오에서 그다지 많이 방송되지 않는다.
(D) 젊은 사람들이 널리 감상하지는 않았다.

해설 포크 음악은 60년대 젊은이들의 권력과 이념에 대한 비판정신을 담았다는 데 의의가 있는 음악이다.

Dictation

Progress Test 5

① attempt to mimic the animal's native habitat
② go back to ancient times
③ rulers would frequently bestow
④ Their needs and habits
⑤ get sick and die
⑥ it really wasn't until the 20th century
⑦ used to be kept in cages with bars
⑧ a deep, wide channel
⑨ the preservation of rare species
⑩ that are about to disappear on earth

Progress Test 6

① due this week
② I'm having a hard time figuring out
③ he acts like
④ a couple of aspects to it
⑤ they were much involved with politics
⑥ hadn't been seen in this country
⑦ gave voice to
⑧ Even if it wasn't protesting
⑨ underscored a desire for
⑩ You've been a great help

Vocabulary Review for Progress Test

Progress Test 5

1. d 컴퓨터는 인간의 생각을 모방하지 않지만, 다른 수단을 활용하여 동일한 결론에 도달한다.
2. a 1981년 그녀에게 그 대학의 명예총장직이 주어졌다.
3. c 그들은 30년 간 처참하고 비인간적인 상황에서 생존해왔다.
4. b 그 박물관은 희귀하고 귀중한 보물들로 가득 차 있다.

Progress Test 6

1. a 이 프로젝트에는 대통령의 지지가 중요했으나 그들 다수는 이에 소홀했다.
2. a 전통 기술이 지역 장인들에 의해 부활되고 있다.
3. b 그 돈은 특정 목적을 위해 사용되기로 계획되어 있다.
4. d 당신은 파리에 가기로 확실히 결정했습니까?

FINAL TEST

Final Test 1

1 (D) 2 (A), (D) 3 (B) 4 (A) 5 (B) 6 (C)

시의 번역에 대한 강의를 듣고, 물음에 답하시오.

🎧 스크립트

P The task of the poetry translation is a difficult one. More difficult, in some ways, than a translation of any other kind of writing. This is in large part because of, uh, the nature of poetry itself. Now, the etymological meaning of "translate" is "to carry across," right? And so normally the job of the translator is to carry the meaning of one thing across to the, um, reader... so that he can understand. Think about sound or rhyme, for example... huh? These things are what makes a poem a poem, right? But how can these ever be translated exactly...? And so, often, translators have some choices they need to make as they, as they go about translating the work. Like, what's going to be more, uh, important? Literal meaning or sound? And different translators will make different choices here. For example, if a poem in the original Spanish rhymes, the translator might be like, "umm.. the rhyme is an important part of the poem... some words might have to be stretched... to get the sound of the rhyme across." You see? Alternately, if he decides the meanings of these words should be carried across exactly... and then sacrifice the sound. Or uh, you might just translate the feeling of the poem... Well, let's take a look at this translator, Ezra Pound, here... in his translation of the Chinese poem "The River Merchant's Wife: A Letter," he decided that the most important is a mood or feeling. Pound didn't feel that he had to carry across much from the original at all, translated... He was translating a feeling.

교수 시를 번역하는 일은 어렵습니다. 어떤 면에서는 다른 어떤 글의 번역보다도 어렵습니다. 이는 대부분 시 자체의 본질 때문에 그렇습니다. '번역하다'의 어원적 의미는 '가로질러 전달하다'입니다. 맞죠? 그러므로 번역가의 통상적인 업무는 하나의 의미를 독자가 이해할 수 있도록 가로질러 전달하는 것입니다. 예를 들어 소리나 라임에 대해 생각해보십시오. 이러한 것들이 시를 시답게 만드는 요소이죠? 하지만 이것을 어떻게 정확하게 번역할 수 있겠습니까?
그래서 종종 번역가들이 작품을 번역하려 할 때는 몇 가지 선택을 해야 할 필요가 있습니다. 무엇이 좀더 중요한지, 즉 문학적인 의미가 더 중요한지 소리가 더 중요한지 등을 결정해야 합니다. 그리고 이에 대한 결정은 번역가마다 다를 것입니다. 예를 들어 원래 스페인식 라임으로 된 시라면, 번역가는 '이 시에서는 라임이 중요한 역할을 하지... 그러니까 라임으로 된 소리를 만들기 위해서 일부 단어들을 신축적으로 사용할 수도 있어.'라고 전달할지 모릅니다. 무슨 말인지 알겠죠? 이번에는 반대로, 번역가가 단어의 의미를 정확하게 전달해야 한다고 결정한다면 소리를 희생시킬 겁니다. 아니면 그저 시의 느낌을 전달할지도 모릅니다. 번역가인 에즈라 파운드의 경우를 살펴봅시다. 그는 중국 시 '강가 상인의 아내: 편지'를 번역하면서 가장 중요한 것은 분위기와 느낌이라는 판단을 내렸습니다. 파운드는 자신이 본래의 작품을 정확하게 전달해야만 한다고 느끼지 않았습니다. 그는 시의 느낌을 전달했습니다.

1 강의의 주된 내용은 무엇인가?
(A) 시의 역사에서 번역의 기능
(B) 해석에 영향을 주는 번역가의 역할
(C) 영어와 스페인 시에서의 번역의 다양성
(D) 시를 번역하는 여러 접근 방식

해설 작품에 따라 번역의 방법이 달라진다.

2 강의에 따르면, 다음 중 시 번역의 요소로 간주되는 것은 무엇인가? 정답 두 개를 고르시오.
(A) 독자에게 의미를 전달하는 것
(B) 독자가 행동을 취할 수 있는 정보를 제공하는 것
(C) 저자의 의도를 이해시키는 것
(D) 작품을 위해 문화적인 배경을 제공하는 것

해설 본문에 따르면 번역가의 통상적인 업무는 시의 의미를 독자가 이해할 수 있도록 전달하는 것이다.

3 교수는 어떤 방식으로 번역가의 선택에 대해 설명하는가?
(A) 스페인 어로 된 유명한 시를 지적함으로써
(B) 세 가지 서로 다른 가능성의 예를 제시함으로써
(C) 소리가 의미보다 중요하다고 제안함으로써
(D) 훌륭한 번역가는 선택할 필요가 없다는 점을 암시함으로써

해설 번역가의 결정에 따라 번역에는 어느 정도 단어를 무리하게 사용하더라도 소리의 전달에 중점을 두는 방법, 소리를 희생시키더라도 단어의 의미를 정확하게 전달하는 방법, 또는 시의 느낌을 전달하는 방법 등 세 가지가 있다.

4 교수가 에즈라 파운드를 언급한 이유는 무엇인가?
(A) 시를 번역하는 여러 방법 가운데 하나를 제시하려고

(B) 얼마나 많은 관심사가 한꺼번에 다뤄질 수 있는지 보여주려고
(C) 소리보다 의미를 중요하게 생각하는 번역가의 예를 들려고
(D) 번역에 내재된 위험성을 강조하려고

해설 번역가가 고려하는 세 가지 측면 중에 셋째 방법은 시의 느낌을 전달하는 방법에 대한 예를 들기 위해서이다.

5 교수는 어떤 뜻으로 다음과 같이 말하는가?

> P Think about sound or rhyme, for example... huh? These things are what makes a poem a poem, right? But how can these ever be translated exactly...?

(A) 종종 번역가는 시의 라임을 포기해야만 한다.
(B) 몇몇 시적 특징은 번역하기가 힘들다.
(C) 라임이나 소리는 쉽게 번역해서는 안 된다.
(D) 시는 원래 시와 같은 소리를 가져야 한다.

해설 번역의 어려움에 대해 이야기하면서 소리나 라임 등 일부 요소를 번역하는 일이 어렵다는 점을 설명하고 있다.

6 교수가 다음과 같이 말한 이유는 무엇인가?

> P the translator might be like, "umm... the rhyme is an important part of the poem... some words might have to be stretched... to get the sound of the rhyme across." You see?

(A) 대부분의 경우 라임보다는 단어가 더 중요하다는 점을 설명하려고
(B) 번역가는 단어의 정확한 의미를 전달할 책임이 있다는 점을 지적하려고
(C) 번역가가 어떻게 의미나 소리를 번역할지를 결정하는가를 보여주려고
(D) 시의 라임을 의미보다 우선해서 고려해야 한다고 제안하려고

해설 번역가는 번역을 할 때 작품의 소리나 의미 중 어느 것에 중점을 두어야 할지 결정할 필요가 있다.

Final Test 2

1 (D)   2 (B)   3 (B)   4 (A)   5 (B)   6 (D)

대체연료에 대한 토론을 듣고, 물음에 답하시오.

🎧 스크립트

> P As we come to the end of the era in which we can rely on a steady, cheap, and plentiful supply of oil, we are, uh, beginning to think about alternative energy sources with much more focus and, and more seriousness. Experiments in renewable energy, such as wind farms, solar power, and even, uh, tidal power are in progress... And this controversial sources of energy such as nuclear power are also being used in this experiments. This is called uh, fusion power.... It, uh, it has long been thought of as the, uh, seeming "answer" to our energy problems. Fusion power is useful energy generated by nuclear fusion reactions. In this kind of reaction two light atoms fuse together and blend to form a heavier atoms and release energy. Well, though technically fusion is a non-renewable resource but these hydrogen atoms are available in great quantity. Anyway, one problem is that it's not a process that we've mastered completely. Still, as you've read in your textbooks, being able to, uh, harness fusion as an energy source would be of benefit to humans for a number of reasons... Let's hear some.
> S1 Well, first of all fusion is a lot cleaner than anything else we've got. For nuclear power, its by-products are always a problem to deal with. Even things like wind power wind up killing birds. But fusion really has no impact on the environment.
> S2 I don't understand, I mean if this process produces these vast amounts of energy, how it isn't a hundred times more dangerous?
> P Well, the thing with fusion is that, if something goes wrong, rather than there being a melt-down or explosion, what happens? Nothing, the reaction just stops. So, though we haven't been able to master this process yet, there are some good reasons to see it as a realistic next step in energy production.

교수 안정적이면서도 값싸고 풍부한 원유 공급에 의존할 수 있는 시대가 끝남에 따라, 우리들은 훨씬 더 집중해서 그리고 훨씬 더 진지하게 대체 에너지원에 대해 생각하기 시작했습니다. 풍력 발전, 태양열 발전, 심지어는 조력발전과 같은 재생 가능한 에너지에 대한 실험이 진행 중에 있습니다. 그리고 핵 발전

과 같은 논쟁의 여지가 있는 에너지원 또한 실험 대상이 되고 있습니다. 이를 우리는 핵융합 발전이라 부릅니다. 오랫동안 이것은 우리가 직면한 에너지 문제에 대한 '해답'인 것처럼 생각되었습니다. 핵융합 발전은 핵융합 반응에 의해 생성되는 유용한 에너지입니다. 이런 종류의 반응에서, 두 가벼운 원자가 함께 융합하고 섞여서 더 무거운 원자를 형성하며 에너지를 방출합니다. 기술적으로 핵융합 전력은 복원되지 않는 자원이기는 하지만, 이런 수소원자를 다량으로 얻을 수 있습니다. 어쨌거나 한 가지 문제점은 우리가 이 과정을 완벽하게 터득하지 못했다는 겁니다. 하지만 여러분이 교재에서 읽는 것처럼 에너지원으로 융합을 동력화할 수 있다면 여러 이유에서 인간에게 이로울 것입니다. 그 중 몇 가지에 대해 여러분의 의견을 들어봅시다.

학생1 무엇보다도 융합은 우리가 가진 다른 어떤 자원보다 훨씬 깨끗합니다. 핵 전력에 있어서는 그 부산물을 다루는 것이 언제나 문제였습니다. 심지어 풍력발전도 새들을 죽입니다. 하지만 핵융합은 환경에 전혀 영향을 미치지 않습니다.

학생2 저는 납득이 되지 않습니다. 이 과정을 통해 그토록 방대한 양의 에너지가 생산된다면 어떻게 100배나 더 위험하지 않을 수가 있단 말입니까?

교수 음, 융합의 경우, 무언가 잘못 돌아간다면 녹아버리거나 폭발하지 않습니다. 대신 어떤 일이 발생하겠습니까? 아무 일도 일어나지 않습니다. 그저 반응이 멈출 뿐입니다. 그래서 우리가 이 과정을 아직 터득하지 못했음에도 불구하고 이를 에너지 생산의 현실적인 다음 단계로 생각할 충분한 이유가 되는 것입니다.

1 토론은 주로 무엇에 관한 것인가?
(A) 복원 가능한 에너지원에 대한 연구의 개요
(B) 다른 형태의 대체 연료의 비교
(C) 융합으로 생성된 에너지의 문제점 조사
(D) 에너지 문제에 대한 잠재적 해결책의 모색

해설 원유공급에 의존하던 시대가 끝나고 있기 때문에 대체 에너지원에 대해 생각해야 한다는 점을 밝히면서 주로 핵융합발전에 대해 토론하고 있다.

2 교수가 원유에 대해 언급한 이유는 무엇인가?
(A) 대체에너지가 원유와 비슷하다는 점을 암시하려고
(B) 현재 주요 에너지 자원을 지적하려고
(C) 융합에너지와 비슷한 문제가 있음을 암시하려고
(D) 대안으로 발전시켜야 하는 것을 지적하려고

해설 대체에너지 개발의 필요성을 제시하면서 지금껏 세계가 의존했던 에너지원으로 원유를 들었다.

3 다음 중 융합의 혜택으로 언급되지 않은 것은 무엇인가?
(A) 다른 에너지원보다 깨끗하다.
(B) 기술적으로 (에너지를) 획득하기가 간단하다.
(C) 환경에 미치는 영향이 최소한이다.
(D) 즉시 사용할 수 있는 자원을 필요로 한다.

해설 핵융합 기술은 과정이 복잡해서 현재까지도 완벽하게 터득하지 못했다.

4 교수는 어떤 방식으로 융합발전에 대해 설명하는가?
(A) 융합 반응의 원칙을 설명함으로써
(B) 다른 형태의 에너지와 비교함으로써
(C) 그것의 화학 공식을 설명함으로써
(D) 교재에 있는 설명을 지적함으로써

해설 두 가벼운 원자가 함께 융합하고 섞여서 더 무거운 원자를 형성하며 에너지를 방출한다는 융합반응의 원칙을 설명하고 있다.

5 강의의 일부를 다시 들으시오.

P Anyway, one problem is that it's not a process that we've mastered completely. Still, as you've read in your textbooks, being able to, uh, harness fusion as an energy source would be of benefit to humans for a number of reasons... let's hear some.

교수가 다음과 같이 말한 이유는 무엇인가?

P let's hear some.

(A) 학생들이 책에 있는 자료를 읽었는지 알아내려고
(B) 학생들이 의견을 내도록 장려하려고
(C) 융합에 많은 비판이 따른다는 점을 암시하려고
(D) 이유가 너무나 분명하고 쉽다는 점을 나타내려고

해설 융합발전으로 에너지를 얻을 경우 어떤 이점이 있는지에 대해 학생들이 자신의 의견을 발표하도록 유도하고 있다.

6 교수는 어떤 뜻으로 다음과 같이 말하는가?

P Well, the thing with fusion is that, if something goes wrong, rather than there being a melt-down or explosion, what happens? Nothing, the reaction just stops.

(A) 융합 반응은 심지어 가벼운 접촉에도 매우 민감하다.
(B) 융합은 막대한 에너지 손실을 초래할 수 있다.
(C) 융합은 단지 반응이 중지할 뿐이므로 실패할 가능성이 적다.
(D) 융합은 위험하지 않고 재앙을 일으키지도 않을 것이다.

해설 융합발전은 융합이 잘못되더라도 그저 반응이 멈출 뿐이므로 위험하지도 않고 심각한 결과를 초래하지도 않는다.

Final Test 3

1 (D)   2 (C)   3 (C)   4 (A)   5 Y, Y, N, N, Y   6 (D)

학생과 교수의 대화를 듣고, 물음에 답하시오.

🎧 스크립트

S Hi, Professor Davies. Got a minute?
P Sure, Bill. What can I do for you?
S Well, I... uh... I have a problem. I'm having a really hard time keeping up in class. I try to take notes, but, whoa... like I said, I can't keep up. I know you can't... er... slow down, so... uh... I don't know what to do.
P (chuckles) Well, no — I can't slow down. But maybe I can help.
S That's good to hear.
P First, I assume you're reading the assigned text every night?
S Well... uh... actually no. I mean I try, but I don't always have the chance.
P You really have to be fully prepared for each class, and that means doing the reading. Also, you should find a study partner. Then, you can exchange photocopies of notes. And of course you can study together.
S Actually, that sounds like fun. Yeah, good idea.
P OK, and you can always do what I used to do in school — use a tape recorder in class. I don't mind at all, and it's a great way to get all the info.
S I'll do that, yeah.
P Great. Let's see, what else...? Oh, right, you have to learn shorthand.
S You lost me there.
P You know, shorthand. Use abbreviations, delete unnecessary words, and so on. I have a book on it at home actually. It improved my note-taking skills. You should have seen my notes as a freshman! I think I will bring it to my office... you can drop by and pick it up during my office hours anytime.
S I think I want to get it tomorrow, will that be okay?
P Sure, and I notice that you... uh... don't participate much in class. (chuckling) I know you're busy taking notes... and asking questions might sound like an extra work... but you really should ask questions.
S Huu... asking questions...
P Well, that's my last suggestion. Speak up in class more. You know, if you're totally lost, this gives you a chance to clarify what I've said. And of course it gives you a moment to catch up.

학생 안녕하세요. Davies교수님. 시간 좀 있으세요?
교수 그럼, Bill. 물론이지. 무엇을 도와줄까요?
학생 저, 문제가 있어서요. 수업을 따라가기가 매우 힘이 들어요. 메모를 하려고 애를 쓰지만, 음, 말씀드렸다시피 따라갈 수가 없어요. 교수님께서는, 어, 천천히 나갈 수는 없다는 걸 알아요. 아... 어떻게 해야 할지 모르겠어요.
교수 (웃으면서) 물론, 안돼요. 천천히 나갈 수는 없어요. 하지만 아마 내가 도와줄 수는 있을 거에요.
학생 안심이네요.
교수 우선, 과제로 내준 자료를 매일 밤 읽고 있을 테죠?
학생 저, 그게... 사실은 아니요. 노력은 하지만 언제나 기회가 없어요.
교수 수업에 들어올 때마다 수업 준비를 철저히 해야만 해요. 그 말은 책을 읽어오라 뜻이에요. 또한 공부할 파트너를 찾아 보아요. 그리고 나서 노트를 복사해서 교환하도록 하는거죠. 물론 함께 공부해도 좋고요.
학생 실제로 재미있을 것 같네요. 알겠어요. 좋은 생각이에요.
교수 그래, 그리고 내가 학교 다닐 때 하곤 했던 방법을 써 봐요. 수업 시간에 녹음을 하는 거지요. 나는 전혀 개의치 않아요. 정보를 모두 받아들일 수 있는 훌륭한 방법이에요.
학생 예, 그렇게 하겠습니다.
교수 좋아. 그럼. 또 뭐가 있을까...? 맞아, 속기를 배워요.
학생 무슨 말씀인지 잘 이해하지 못하겠는데요.
교수 속기 말이에요. 약자를 쓰고, 필요 없는 말을 없애고, 등등. 사실 집에 속기에 대한 책이 한 권 있는데 나는 그것을 가지고 메모하는 기술을 향상시킬 수 있었죠. 내가 일 학년 때 메모한 것을 학생이 봤어야 하는데 말이에요! 그 책을 사무실로 가져올게요. 언제든 내 근무 시간에 들러서 가져가도록 해요.
학생 내일 가져가고 싶은데요. 괜찮으시겠어요?
교수 그럼요. 그리고 학생은 수업 시간에 그다지 많이 참여하지 않더군요. 사실을 눈치 채고 있었죠. (웃으며) 메모하느라 바쁘기 때문에 질문을 하는 것이 별개의 일처럼 생각될지도 모르지만, 정말 질문을 해야 해요.
학생 아, 질문을 하라고요...
교수 그것이 내가 해주는 마지막 제안이에요. 교실에서 좀더 목소리를 내도록 해요. 전혀 이해를 하지 못할 때라도 목소리를 내면 내가 말했던 것을 명확하게 할 수 있는 기회를 얻게 되거든요. 물론 수업을 따라잡을 시간도 얻을 수 있을 테고 말이죠.

1 남자가 교수를 찾아간 이유는 무엇인가?
(A) 빠진 수업의 필기를 얻으려고
(B) 지킬 수 없는 마감에 대해 말하려고
(C) 연구 수업에 참가할 수 있을지 알아보려고
(D) 메모하는 기술을 향상시키는 방법에 대해 물어보려고

해설 수업을 따라가기가 힘들고, 메모조차 하기에 벅찬 문제에 대해 교수와 의논하기 위해서이다.

2 남자가 내일 (교수의) 근무시간에 찾아가는 이유는 무엇인가?

(A) 책을 교수에게 돌려줄 것이다.
(B) 책이 그곳에 있는지 알고 싶다.
(C) 교수에게서 책을 얻고 싶다.
(D) 교수가 한 메모를 다시 보고 싶다.

해설 교수의 메모 기술을 향상시키는 데 도움이 되었던 속기에 대한 책을 가져가기 위해서이다.

3 교수가 다음과 같이 말한 이유는 무엇인가?

P First, I assume you're reading the assigned text every night?

(A) 남자가 과제를 하고 있다는 사실을 자신이 알고 있다는 점을 확인시키려고
(B) 자신이 오늘 과제를 바꾸리라는 점을 나타내려고
(C) 남자가 강의를 제대로 따라올 준비가 되었는지를 알아보려고
(D) 과제에 좀 더 주의를 기울이라고 권하려고

해설 수업을 따라가기 위해서는 책을 읽어오는 과제를 할 필요가 있음을 강조하기 위해서 학생이 과제를 하고 있는지 확인하고 있다.

4 교수는 어떤 의미로 다음과 같은 말을 했는가?

P You should have seen my notes as a freshman!

(A) 자신의 메모 기술이 대학교 재학시절 항상 좋았던 것은 아니었다.
(B) 교수는 남자에게 대학시절 자신의 메모를 보여줄 것이다.
(C) 자신의 메모하는 기술은 대학교 1학년부터 훌륭했다.
(D) 교수는 학생에게 자신의 메모를 보여주고 싶어 하지 않을 것이다.

해설 교수 또한 일 학년 때 그다지 능숙하게 메모하지 못했다.

5 다음 각 구절이 교수의 제안을 나타내는지 알맞은 것에 체크하시오.

	예	아니오
교재를 읽고 수업준비를 하라.	✓	
급우와 함께 공부를 하라.	✓	
강의 내용을 녹음하고 수업이 끝난 후에 메모하라.		✓
파트너와의 연습을 통해서 메모하는 기술을 향상시키라.		✓
질문을 함으로써 수업에 참여하라.	✓	

해설 학생의 문제점에 대한 교수의 제안은, 과제로 내준 분량을 읽어서 철저하게 수업준비를 할 것, 파트너를 구해서 노트를 교환하고 함께 공부할 것, 수업내용을 녹음할 것, 속기를 배울 것, 수업 시간에 질문을 해서 몰랐던 내용을 명확하게 알고 시간을 벌 것 등이다.

6 남학생은 어떤 뜻으로 다음과 같이 말하는가?

S Huu.... asking questions...

(A) 그는 그것이 좋은 생각인지 확신이 서질 않았다.
(B) 그는 질문하는 것이 좋은지 의아해한다.
(C) 그는 단호한 마음가짐으로 수업시간에 좀 더 참여를 하겠다고 다짐한다.
(D) 그는 수업시간에 질문하는 것이 마음 편하지 않다.

해설 수업시간에 질문을 할 수 있을지 자신이 없다.

MEMO

MEMO

NEXUS makes your next day
www.nexusEDU.kr | 책에 대해 궁금한 사항은 넥서스에듀 홈페이지 1:1 고객상담 게시판을 이용하세요.

NEXUS TOEFL® *i*BT Listening Series의 특징

1 단계별 기본 학습 훈련 장치 강조
2 다양한 테마의 강의와 대화 체계적 분석
3 체계적인 학습 스킬과 전략 구성
4 어휘력 확장
5 *i*BT 실전에 맞춘 단계별 연습 문제

NEXUS TOEFL® *i*BT Series의 구성

Reading	Starter	Level 1	Level 2	Level 3
Listening	Starter	Level 1	Level 2	Level 3
Writing		Starter	Level 1	Level 2
Speaking		Starter	Level 1	Level 2

Listening

www.nexusEDU.kr
넥서스 초·중·고등 사이트

www.nexusON.com
넥서스 온라인 사이트

NEXUS makes your next day

www.nexusEDU.kr
t.02-330-5500 f.02-330-5555
NEXUS Edu

논리적 사고를 위한
넥서스 리딩 시리즈!

- **차별화된 독해 지문과 문제** : 다양한 분야의 참신한 지문을 논리정연하게 구성하고 이에 대한 이해를 심화시키는 문제 제공
- **글의 요지 파악 및 정리 능력** : 효과적으로 독해 능력을 향상시키기 위해 글의 요지를 정확하게 파악하는 훈련 장치 제공
- **속독 훈련** : 제한된 Reading Time과 학습자의 속도를 비교함으로써 효과적 속독 훈련 및 향상도 측정 가능
- **어휘 확장** : Vocabulary Preview와 Review는 물론 수업 자료로 활용 가능한 어휘 테스트를 부록으로 제공

- MP3 파일
- 해석 파일
무료 다운로드
www.nexusEDU.kr

The best preparation for **Reading** 시리즈 Level 1 / Level 2 / Level 3
The Reading Level 1: Nexus Contents Development Team, Quentin Fincaryk 지음 | 값 9,000원
The Reading Level 2: Nexus Contents Development Team, Jennielee Yoon, Kerry Williamson 지음 | 값 9,000원
The Reading Level 3: Nexus Contents Development Team, The Junior Herald 지음 | 값 10,000원

NEXUS makes your next day

www.nexusEDU.kr
t.02-330-5500 f.02-330-5555
NEXUS Edu

필요한 문법만!
정확하게! 확실하게!
눈으로 귀로 익히는 오디오 문법

- **Concise and core grammar**
  불필요한 설명을 최대한 배제하고 핵심 문법의 예문 중심으로 간결하게 구성
- **A variety of question types**
  규칙 확인 → 응용문제 → 종합 확인 → 영작 → 챕터별 누적 테스트 등의 단계별 내용 학습 확인 장치
- **Preparation for school tests**
  내신대비 다양한 문제풀이 형식 및 서술형 문제 제공
- **Grammar summary: Pouch information**
  학습 내용을 차트 및 표로 정리하여 한눈에 볼 수 있도록 구성
- **Sound-based recognition of language structures**
  눈으로 보며 이해하고 익혔던 문법 예문을 음성으로 복습할 수 있도록 MP3 파일 무료 다운로드 제공

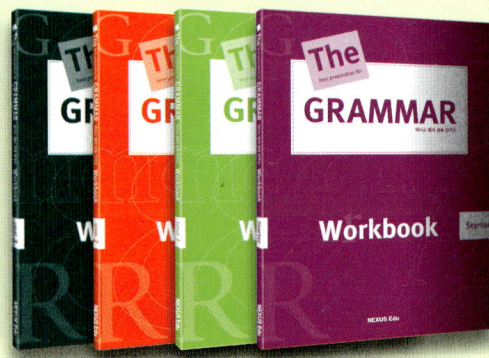

The best preparation for
GRAMMAR

MP3 파일 무료 다운로드 제공 - www.nexusEDU.kr

The best preparation for **GRAMMAR** 시리즈
The Grammar Starter I 값 9,500원 The Grammar Level 1, 2 I 각 권 10,000원
The Grammar Level 3 I 값 11,000원
Workbook Starter, Level 1, 2 I 각 권 5,000원